# 주한미군지위협정(SOFA)

# 서명 및 발효 1

# 주한미군지위협정(SOFA)

# 서명 및 발효 1

## | 머리말

미국은 오래전부터 우리나라 외교에 있어서 가장 긴밀하고 실질적인 우호 · 협력관계를 맺어온 나라다. 6 · 25전쟁 정전 협정이 체결된 후 북한의 재침을 막기 위한 대책으로서 1953년 11월 한미 상호방위조약이 체결되었다. 이는 미군이 한국에 주둔하는 법적 근거였고, 그렇게 주둔하게 된 미군의 시설, 구역, 사업, 용역, 출입국, 통관과 관세, 재판권 등 포괄적인 법적 지위를 규정하는 것이 바로 주한미군지위협정(SOFA)이다. 그러나 이와 관련한 협상은 계속된 난항을 겪으며 한미 상호방위조약이 체결로부터 10년이 훌쩍 넘은 1967년이 돼서야 정식 발효에 이를 수 있었다. 그럼에도 당시 미군 범죄에 대한 한국의 재판권은 심한 제약을 받았으며, 1980년대 후반 민주화 운동과 함께 미군 범죄 문제가 사회적 이슈로 떠오르자 협정을 개정해야 한다는 목소리가 커지게 되었다. 이에 1991년 2월 주한미군지위협정 1차 개정이 진행되었고, 이후에도 여러 사건이 발생하며 2001년 4월 2차 개정이 진행되어 현재에 이르고 있다.

본 총서는 외교부에서 작성하여 최근 공개한 주한미군지위협정(SOFA) 관련 자료를 담고 있다. 1953년 한미 상호방위조약 체결 이후부터 1967년 발효가 이뤄지기까지의 자료와 더불어, 이후 한미 합동위원회을 비롯해 민 · 형사재판권, 시설, 노무, 교통 등 각 분과위원회의 회의록과 운영 자료, 한국인 고용인 문제와 관련한 자료, 기타 관련 분쟁 자료 등을 포함해 총 42권으로 구성되었다. 전체 분량은 약 2만 2천여 쪽에 이른다.

2024년 3월

한국학술정보(주)

## | 일러두기

· 본 총서에 실린 자료는 2022년 4월과 2023년 4월에 각각 공개한 외교문서 4,827권, 76만 여 쪽 가운데 일부를 발췌한 것이다.

· 각 권의 제목과 순서는 공개된 원본을 최대한 반영하였으나, 주제에 따라 일부는 적절히 변경하였다.

· 원본 자료는 A4 판형에 맞게 축소하거나 원본 비율을 유지한 채 A4 페이지 안에 삽입하였다. 또한 현재 시점에선 공개되지 않아 '공란'이란 표기만 있는 페이지 역시 그대로 실었다.

· 외교부가 공개한 문서 각 권의 첫 페이지에는 '정리 보존 문서 목록'이란 이름으로 기록물 종류, 일자, 명칭, 간단한 내용 등의 정보가 수록되어 있으며, 이를 기준으로 0001번부터 번호가 매겨져 있다. 이는 삭제하지 않고 총서에 그대로 수록하였다.

· 보고서 내용에 관한 더 자세한 정보가 필요하다면, 외교부가 온라인상에 제공하는 『대한민국 외교사료요약집』 1991년과 1992년 자료를 참조할 수 있다.

## | 차례

## 정/리/보/존/문/서/목/록

| 기록물종류 | 문서-일반공문서철 | 등록번호 | 448<br>9572 | 등록일자 | 2006-07-27 |
|---|---|---|---|---|---|
| 분류번호 | 741.12 | 국가코드 | US | 주제 | |
| 문서철명 | 한.미국 간의 상호방위조약 제4조에 의한 시설과 구역 및 한국에서의 미국군대의 지위에 관한 협정 (SOFA) 전59권. 1966.7.9 서울에서 서명 : 1967.2.9 발효 (조약 232호) *원본 | | | | |
| 생산과 | 미주과/조약과 | 생산년도 | 1952 - 1967 | 보존기간 | 영구 |
| 담당과(그룹) | 조약 | 조약 | 서가번호 | -- | |
| 참조분류 | | | | | |
| 권차명 | V.1 한.미국 행정협정 체결 관련 각 부처 자료 제출, 1953-54 | | | | |
| 내용목차 | * 일지 :<br>1953.8.7 이승만 대통령-Dulles 미국 국무장관 공동성명<br>- 상호방위조약 발효 후 군대지위협정 교섭 약속<br>1954.12.2 정부, 주한 UN군의 관세업무협정 체결 제의<br>1955.1월, 5월 미국, 제의 거절<br>1955.4.28 정부, 군대지위협정 제의 (한국측 초안 제시)<br>1957.9.10 Hurter 미국 국무차관 방한 시 각서 수교 (한국측 제의 수락 요구)<br>1957.11.13, 26 정부, 개별 협정의 단계적 체결 제의<br>1958.9.18 Dawling 주한미국대사, 형사재판관할권 협정 제외 조건으로 행정협정 체결 의사 전달<br>1960.3.10 정부, 토지, 시설협정의 우선적 체결 강력 요구<br>1961.4.10 장면 국무총리-McConaughy 주한미국대사 공동성명으로 교섭 개시 합의<br>1961.4.15, 4.25 제1, 2차 한.미국 교섭회의 (서울)<br>1962.3.12 정부, 교섭 재개 촉구 공한 송부<br>1962.5.14 Burger 주한미국대사, 최규하 장관 면담 시 형사재판관할권 문제 제기 않는 조건으로 교섭 재개 통고<br>1962.9.6 한.미국 간 공동성명 발표 (9월 중 교섭 재개 합의)<br>1962.9.20~ 1965.6.7 제1-81차 실무 교섭회의 (서울)<br>1966.7.8 제82차 실무 교섭회의 (서울)<br>1966.7.9 서명<br>1967.2.9 발효 (조약 232호) | | | | |

### 마/이/크/로/필/름/사/항

| 촬영연도 | *롤 번호 | 화일 번호 | 후레임 번호 | 보관함 번호 |
|---|---|---|---|---|
| 2006-11-21 | I-06-0066 | 09 | 1-304 | |

0001

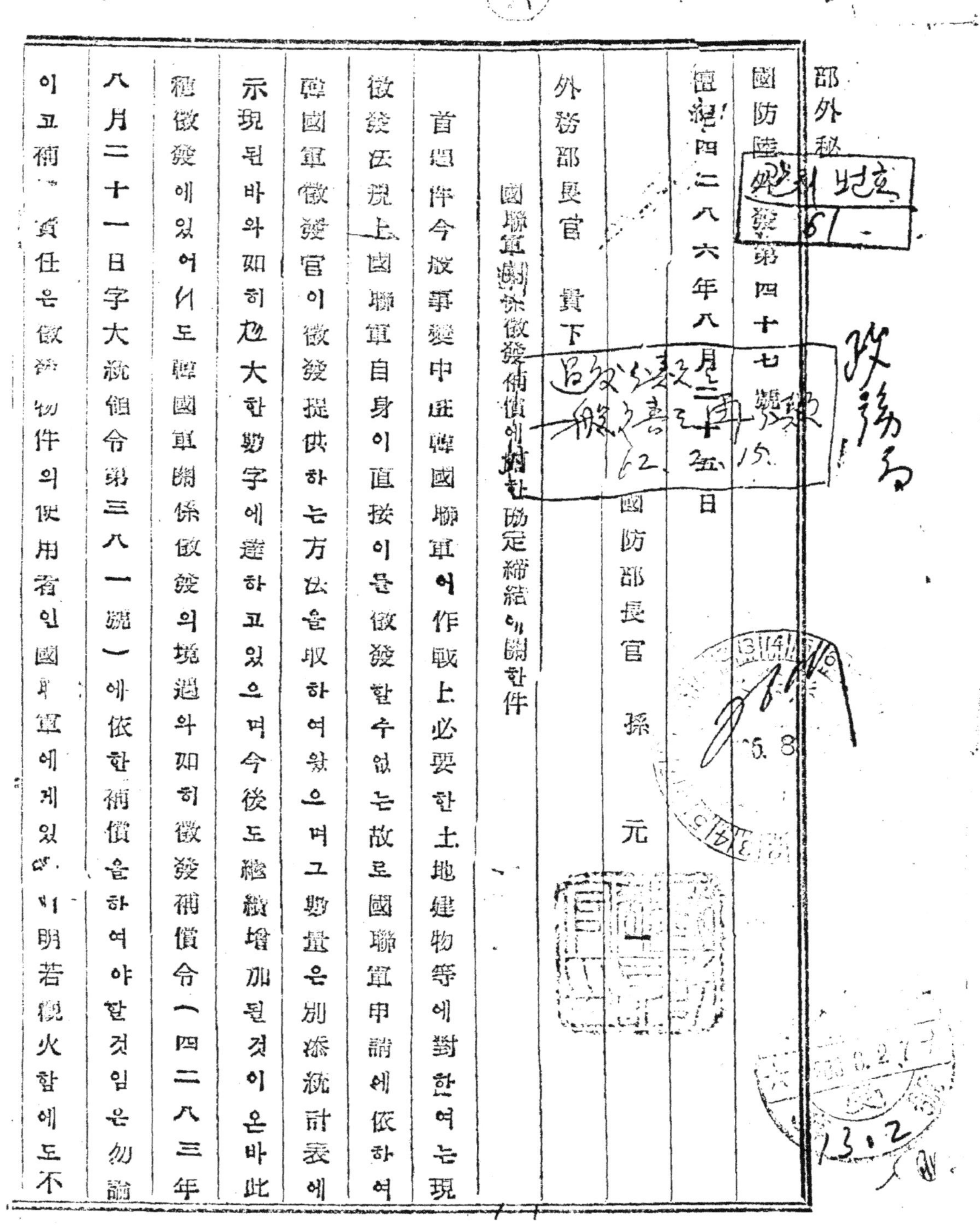
部外秘

國防陸諮發第四十七號

檀紀四二八六年八月二十五日

國防部長官 孫 元 一

外務部長官 貴下

國聯軍關係徵發補償에對한協定締結에關한件

首題件今般事變中在韓國聯軍이作戰上必要한土地建物等에對하여는現徵發法規上國聯軍自身이直接이를徵發할수없는故로國聯軍申請에依하여韓國軍徵發官이徵發提供하는方法을取하여왔으며그數量은別添統計表에示現된바와如히尨大한數字에達하고있으며今後도繼續增加될것이온바此種徵發에있어서도韓國軍關係徵發의境遇와如히徵發補償令(四二八三年八月二十一日字大統領令第三八一號)에依한補償을하여야할것임은勿論이고補償責任은徵發物件의使用者인國聯軍에게있음이明若觀火함에도不

0002

拘하고 尙今 大韓民國과 國聯軍間에 있어서 國聯軍關係徵發補償에 關한 明文
協定이 없는 關係로 責任의 所任조차 確然치 못하여 被徵發者側의 不安과 苦痛
이 莫甚한 現狀인바 이는 財産權保障에 關한 憲法規定에 對하여 重大한 違反일뿐
더러 巨額에 達하는 此種補償問題를 如斯長期間 浮動狀態에 放置하여 둠은 再
建上 重大한 支障을 招來할 것임으로 早速히 國聯軍關係徵發에 對하여는 國聯
軍側에서 補償責任을 負擔하는 內容의 「國聯軍關係徵發補償에 關한 協定」
을 締結하여 주심을 務望함

追而 探聞한바에 依하면 國聯軍側에서는 本件補償에 關하여 一九五二年
五月二十四日 締結된 「大韓民國과 統一司令部間의 經濟調整에 關한 協定」
第三條十三項 「韓國國民을 除外한 統一司令部의 個人 또는 機關에 對하여 前
記國際聯合의 諸決議에 依하여 賦與되었거나 또는 玆後 双方 또는 双方의 關係
機構에 依하여 公式 또는 非公式으로 協約될 特權免除便益을 附與한다」의 規

0003

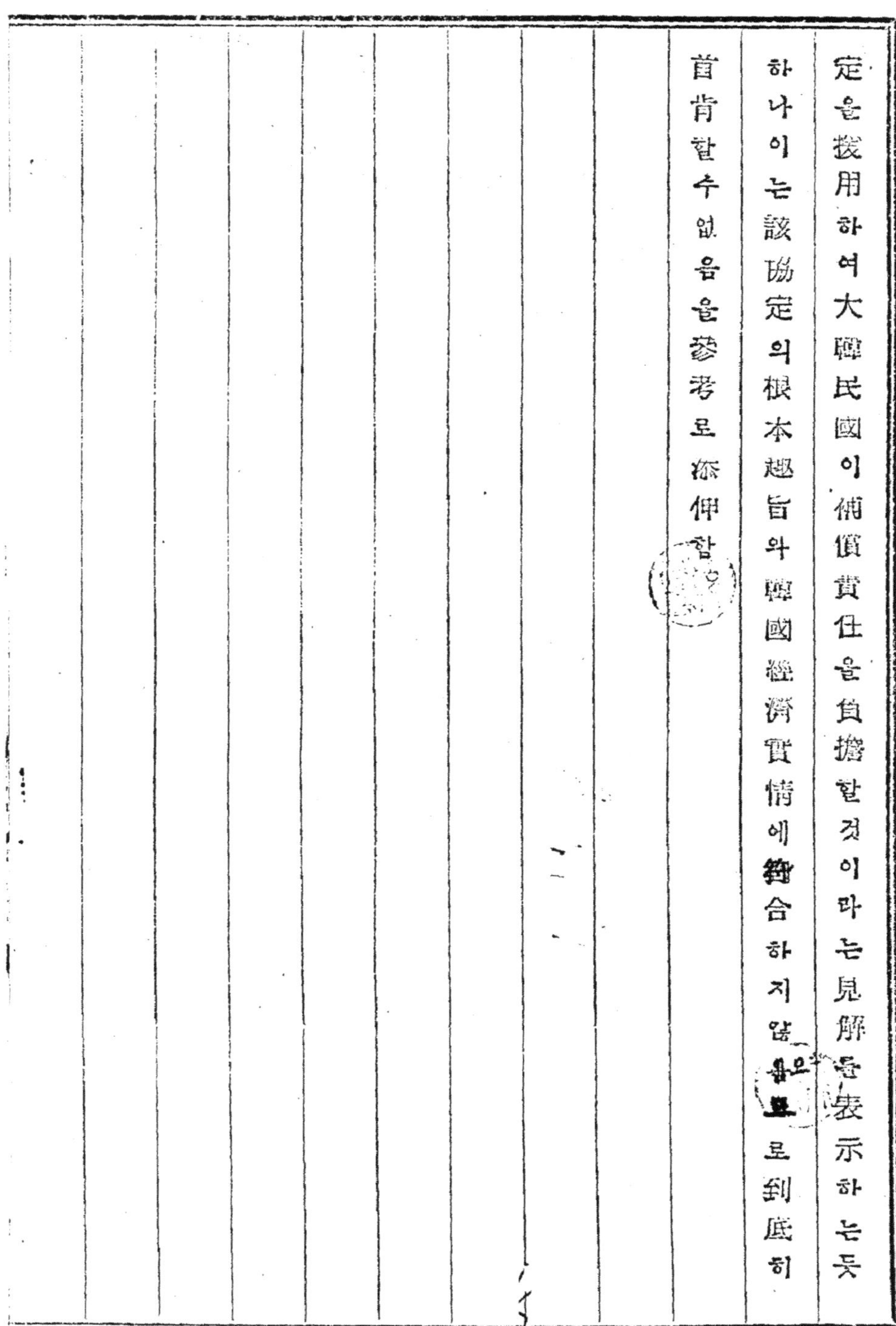

定을援用하여大韓民國이補償責任을負擔할것이라는見解를表示하는듯하나이는該協定의根本趣旨와韓國經濟實情에符合하지않음으로到底히首肯할수없음을參考로添附함.

0004

徵発分 　聯合軍[illegible]用不動産徵発統計表(建物) 　4286.6.30 現在

| 所有別 | 構造 | 棟数 | 建坪 | 評定価格 | 備考 |
|---|---|---|---|---|---|
| 國有 | 瓦葺 | 209 | 38.154 | | 評定価格算出에對하여는 |
| | 도단葺 | 40 | 1.704 | | 目下調査中 |
| | 煉瓦建 | 845 | 174.208 | | |
| | 草家 | 17 | | | |
| | 小計 | 1111 | 212.066 | | |
| 敵産 | 瓦葺 | 202 | 17.454 | | |
| | 도단葺 | 19 | 1.070 | | |
| | 煉瓦建 | 118 | 41.468 | | |
| | 草家 | | | | |
| | 小計 | 339 | 59.992 | | |
| 公有 | 瓦葺 | 168 | 48.972 | | |
| | 도단葺 | 10 | 1.744 | | |
| | 煉瓦建 | 177 | 21.995 | | |
| | 草家 | 1 | 100 | | |
| | 小計 | 356 | 62.811 | | |
| 民有 | 瓦葺 | 202 | 11.658 | | |
| | 도단葺 | 29 | 270 | | |
| | 煉瓦建 | 216 | 18.056 | | |
| | 草家 | 204 | 2.713 | | |
| | 小計 | 651 | 32.697 | | |

但 國防部取扱分은 建坪不記載.

0005

徵發分 聯合軍使用不動産徵發額統計表 (建物) 4286.6.30 現在

| 所有別 | 構造 | 棟數 | 建坪 | 推定價格 | 備考 |
|---|---|---|---|---|---|
| 合計 | 瓦葺 | 781 | 116,238 | | |
| | 도단葺 | 98 | 4,788 | | |
| | 煉瓦建 | 1,356 | 255,729 | | |
| | 草家 | 222 | 2,813 | | |
| | 總計 | 2,457 | 379,566 | | |

但 國防部取扱分은 建坪不記載

0006

(解除分) 聯合軍使用未解除 財産統計表 (建物) 4286. 6. 30 現在

| 所屬別 | 構造 | 棟數 | 建坪 | | 評定價格 | 備考 |
|---|---|---|---|---|---|---|
| 國有 | 瓦葺 | 17 | 22044 | | | |
| | 도단葺 | 13 | | | | |
| | 煉瓦建 | 19 | 6155 | | | |
| | 草家 | | | | | |
| | 小計 | 39 | 8359 | | | |
| 敵屬 | 瓦葺 | 30 | 1463 | | | |
| | 도단葺 | 1 | 100 | | | |
| | 煉瓦建 | 8 | 3012 | | | |
| | 草家 | | | | | |
| | 小計 | 39 | 4575 | | | |
| 公有 | 瓦葺 | 106 | 30573 | | | |
| | 도단葺 | | | | | |

0007

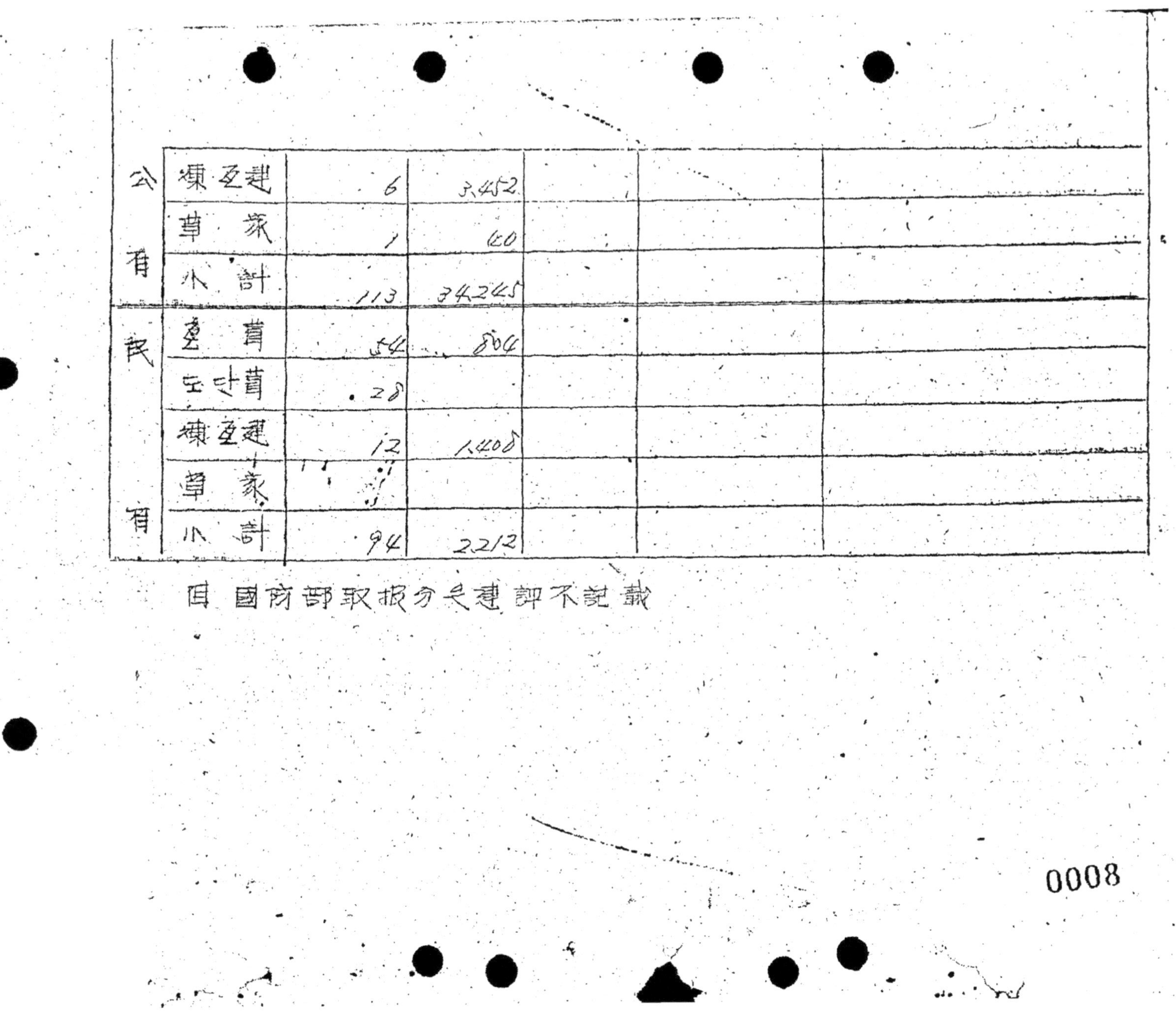

| | | | | | | |
|---|---|---|---|---|---|---|
| 公有 | 煉瓦建 | 6 | 3,452 | | | |
| | 草家 | 1 | 60 | | | |
| | 小計 | 113 | 34,245 | | | |
| 民有 | 土幕 | 54 | 804 | | | |
| | 半土幕 | 28 | | | | |
| | 煉瓦建 | 12 | 1,408 | | | |
| | 草家 | | | | | |
| | 小計 | 94 | 2,212 | | | |

但 國防部取扱分은 建設部不記載

0008

(解除分) 聯合軍使用不動產擬接收總括統計表 (建物) 4286. 6. 30 現在

| 所有別 | 構造 | 棟數 | 建坪 | 評定價格 | 備考 |
|---|---|---|---|---|---|
| 合計 | 瓦葺 | 207 | 35,044 | | |
| | 도단葺 | 32 | 100 | | |
| | 煉瓦葺 | 45 | 14,027 | | |
| | 草家 | 1 | 40 | | |
| | 總計 | 285 | 49,211 | | |

但 國防部取扱分은 建坪不記載

0009

徵発分　聯合軍使用不動產徵発統計表(土地)

4286. 6. 30.現在

| 所有別 | 坪数 評定価格 | 田 | 畓 | 垈地 | 林野 | 墓地 | 雜地 | 合計 |
|---|---|---|---|---|---|---|---|---|
| 國有 | 坪数 | 65.224 | 331.932 | 1,4051,153 | 3441.966 | | 4781.424 | 100,256,613 |
| | 評定価格 | | | | | | | |
| 敵屬 | 坪数 | 156.301 | 20.354 | 170.213 | 83.366 | | | 430.234 |
| | 評定価格 | | | | | | | |
| 公有 | 坪数 | 1.062 | 1.073 | 2560.431 | | | | 2562.566 |
| | 評定価格 | | | | | | | |
| 民有 | 坪数 | 157.570.347 | 98.830.274 | 1.634 668 | [illegible]24 | 1.115 | 640.118.220 | 898.971.148 |
| | 評定価格 | | | | | | | |
| 合計 | 坪数 | 157.792.934 | 99.183.633 | 10.770.427.3 | 4343.856 | 1.115 | 644.897.644 | 916.989.609 |
| | 評定価格 | | | | | | | |

0010

(解除分) 聯合軍使用不動産徵発總括統計表 (建物) 4288. 6. 30現在

| 種別 | 構造 | 棟數 | 建坪 | 評定価格 | 備考 |
|---|---|---|---|---|---|
| 合計 | 木造 | 207 | 35,044 | | |
| | 土石造 | 32 | 100 | | |
| | 煉瓦造 | 45 | 14,027 | | |
| | 韓家 | 1 | 40 | | |
| | 總計 | 285 | 49,211 | | |

但 國防部取扱分은 建坪不記載

0011

(解除分) 聯合軍使用不動産徵発統計表(土地) 4286. 6. 30現在

| 所有別 | 坪数 / 評定価格 | 田 | 畓 | 垈地 | 林野 | 墓地 | 雑地 | 合計 |
|---|---|---|---|---|---|---|---|---|
| 國有 | 坪数 | 7,104 | 2,209 | 24,254 | | | 56,711 | [illegible]78 |
| | 評定価格 | | | | | | | |
| 敵産 | 坪数 | 38,903 | 30,397 | 2,339 | 29,400 | | | 101,[illegible] |
| | 評定価格 | | | | | | | |
| 公有 | 坪数 | | | 326,588 | 2,266 | | | 3[illegible]54 |
| | 評定価格 | | | | | | | |
| 民有 | 坪数 | 163,707 | 98,113 | 50,819 | 92,754 | | 433,127 | 838,520 |
| | 評定価格 | | | | | | | |
| 合計 | 坪数 | 209,714 | 130,719 | 404,[illegible] | [illegible]4,500 | | 489,838 | 1,358,771 |
| | 評定価格 | | | | | | | |

0012

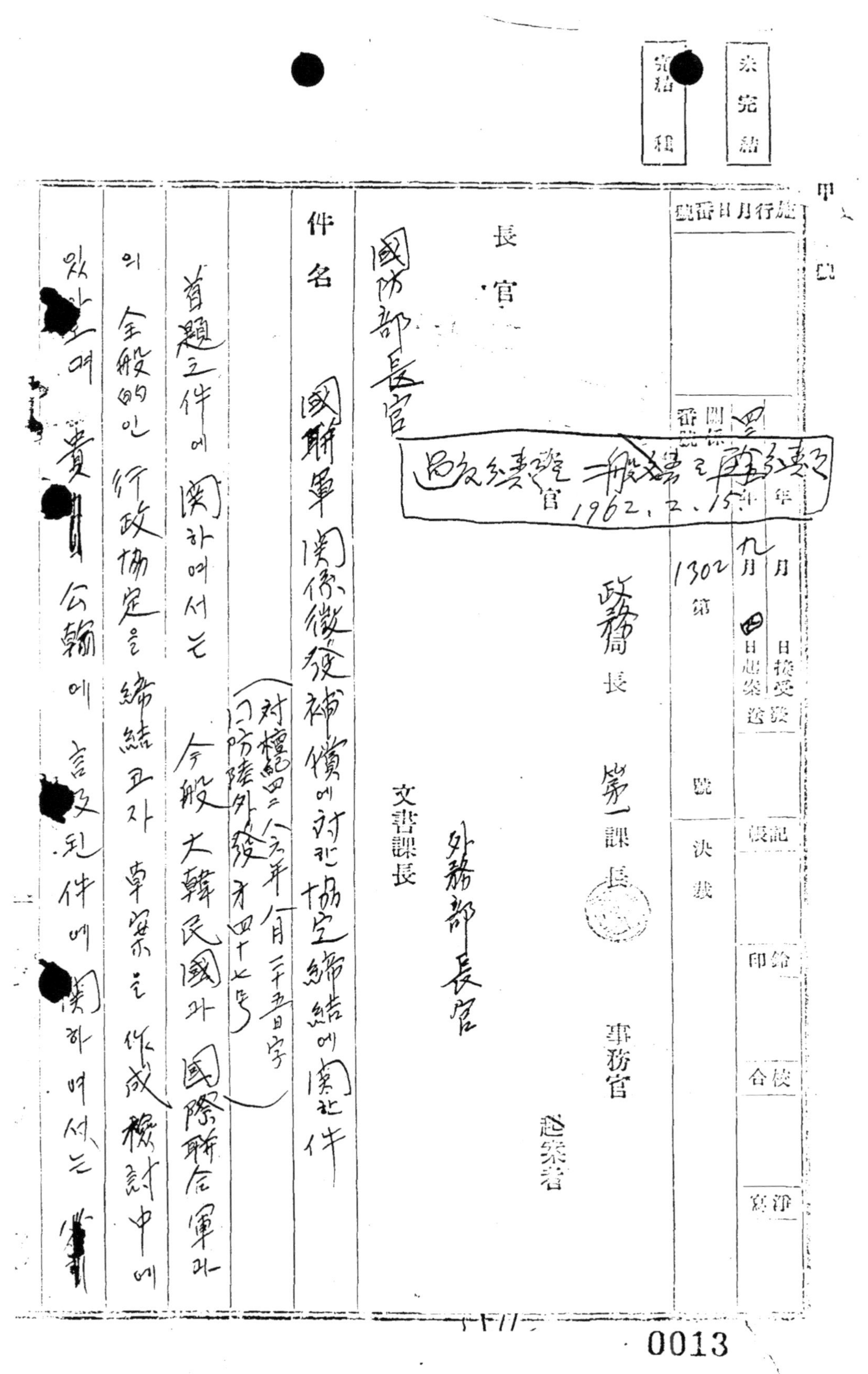

完結 綴 / 未完結 綴

施行日月番號

關係番號 四二八六年 九月 四日 第1302號

외교문서 일반문서로 재분류 [illegible]

政務局長 第一課長 事務官 起案者

外務部長官

文書課長

長官 國防部長官

件名 國聯軍關係徵發補償에對한協定締結에關한件

首題之件에 關하여서는 (対檀紀四二八六年八月二十五日字 國防陸外發 第四十七号) 今般 大韓民國과 國際聯合軍과의 全般的인 行政協定을 締結코자 草案을 作成檢討中에 있사오며 貴部 公翰에 言及된 件에 關하여서는 ...

0013

必히 其中에 包含되도록
特히 留意하여 하겠아오니 諒知하시와라며 次後에도 此件에 關한
資料를 繼續 提供하여 주심을 務望
하나이다.

0014

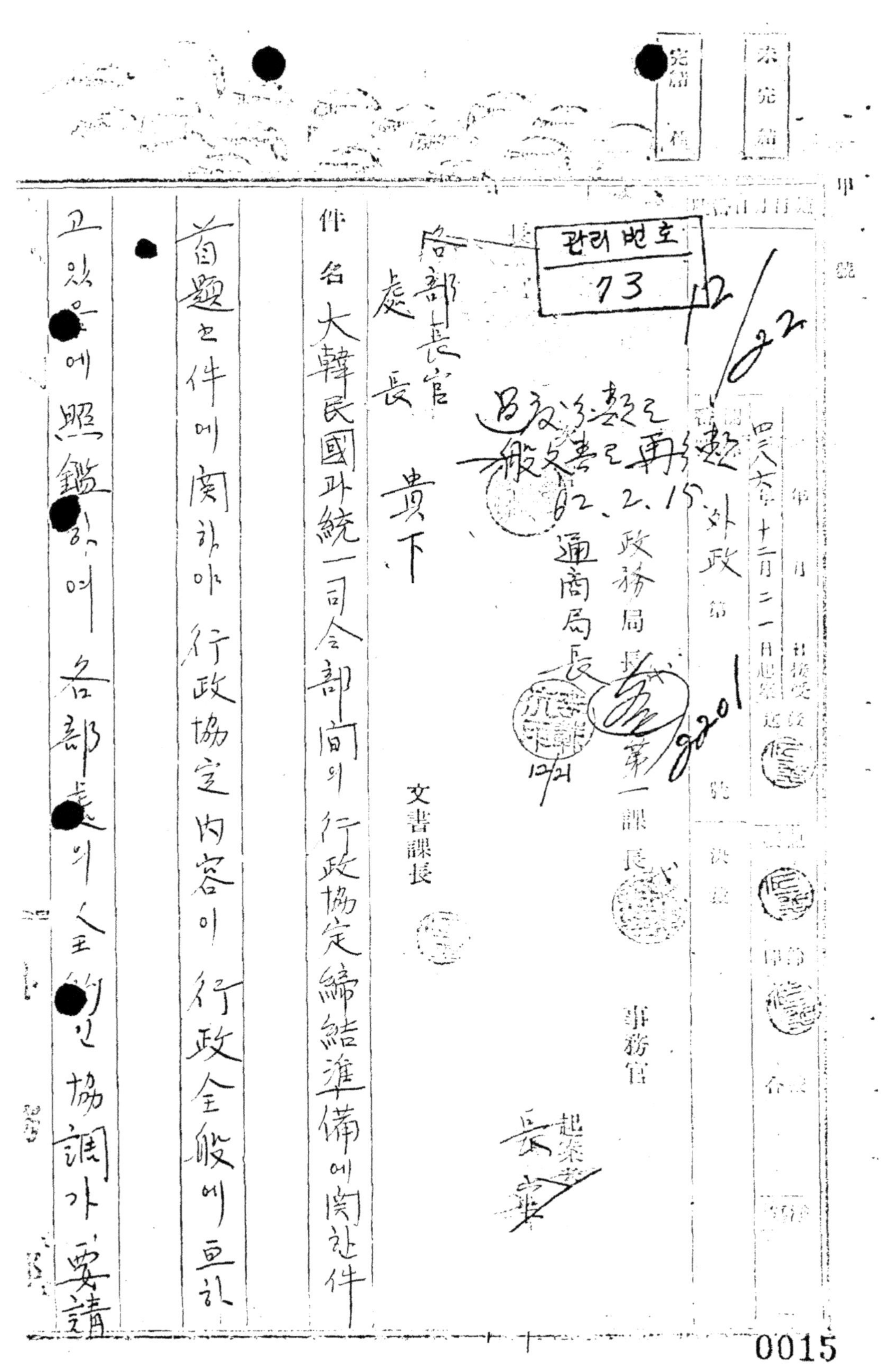

관리번호 73

件名 大韓民國과統一司令部間의行政協定締結準備에関한件

各部長官 貴下
處長

文書課長

首題의件에関하야 行政協定内容이 行政全般에亘하고있음에照鑑하야 各部長의全的인協調가要請

政務局長
通商局長
第一課長
事務官

0015

되옵기 于先 參考로 行政協定締結의 經緯와 對處問題 件 美比·美日 行政協定 概要를

添送하오니 貴部處 該當 事項에 關하여 銳意檢

討하시와 左記 各部處 連席會議에 無漏

參席하여 주심을 務望하나이다

記

一. 時日 檀紀四二八六年 十二月 二十九日(火) 上午九時半

0016

一. 場所 外務部次官室

一. 參席者 関係局課長

外務部

0017

行政協定締結의 對象問題

行政協定의 対象者가 國際聯合軍임으로 國際聯合軍總司令部를 締結相対者로 擇하자는 意見에 対하야 統一司令部로 하여야 한다는 理論

國際聯合은 一九五〇年 六月二十七日字 安全保障理事會의 決議에 依하여 國際聯合會員國家가 大韓

0018

民國領域內에서 軍事侵略을 擊退하며 國際平和와
安全을 回復함에 所要되는 援助를 大韓民國에 供與
할것을 建議하였으며
國際聯合은 一九五〇年七月七日字 安全保障理事會의
決議에 依하며 大韓民國에 軍事兵力과 其他援助
를 供與하는 會員國家가 如斯한 兵力과 援助를 美合衆國當

0019

理下의 統一司令部에 提供할것을 建議한바 있고
國際聯合은 一九五〇年七月三十一日字 安全保障理事會의
決議에 依하야 統一司令部에게 韓國國民의 救護와
援助에 關한 必要를 決定하며 如斯한 救護와 援助를
供與함에 關한 現地節次를 樹立할 責任을 履行할것
을 要請한바 있으므로

0020

一九五○年七月七日字 國際聯合安全保障理事會의 決議에
依據하여 統一司令部는 韓國에 있어서 統一司令部의
責任을 履行하기 爲하여 國際聯合軍總司令官을 指
名하였으며
國際聯合軍總司令部는 大韓民國領域內에서 侵略
에 對抗하여 共同行動을 取하였고 現在도 取하고

0021

있으며 大韓民國에게 軍事兵力과 其他援助를 供與하

고 있는바

一九五二年五月二十四日字로 大韓民國과 統一司令部間의 經濟

調整에 關한 協定을 締結하므로서 大韓民國의 主權을 侵害

함이 없이 國際聯合軍總司令部의 軍事兵力의 有效

한 支援을 保障하고 韓國國民의 苦難을 救濟하며

0022

大韓民國의 健全한 經濟를 樹立維持하기 爲한 協定에
署名하고 있으므로
經濟調整問題만을 除外한 國際聯合軍의 大韓民國
領域
內及 그 附近에 있어서의 配備를 規律하는 條件을 決定
하고 國際聯合軍總司令部와 大韓民國政府間의 相互
利益과 敬意의 緊密한 聯繫를 強化하는 實際的인

0023

行政問題를 規整함이 要請되므로.
一九五〇年七月七日字 및 一九五〇年七月三十一日字 國際聯合
安全保障理事會決議에 따라서 權限을 行使하
는 美合衆國의 統一司令部와 行政協定을 締
結하여야 한다

0024

MINISTRY OF FOREIGN AFFAIRS

OFFICE OF THE MINISTER　　　　DATE;

其二

地域施設定義前文

0025

前文

(一) 侵略者를 共同擊退하였고, 人間의 自由

民主韓國의 平和統一을 目的으로 韓國과

UN이 共同으로 鬪爭하고 있는 事實에 鑑하여

(二) 右記目的을 達成하기 爲하여 韓國과 UN軍의 緊密한 協

協力이 必要함에 鑑하여 UN은 UN軍總

司令部를 設置하고 그 밑에 自由를 愛好하는

諸國의 諸國이 參加하고 있음에 鑑하여

(三) 自由國家 歷史上에 빛나는 이 集團防衛와 UN

[illegible] 62. 2. 15.

0026

作戰●●●의 目的을 ●最 有效하게 成就하기 爲하여서는, UN과 韓國과의 緊密한 協助와 [illegible] 理解가 必要함에 鑑하며.

(四) 韓國政府와 UN軍總司令部와 右記한 協助와 理解를 보障을 規定하며 相互間에 發生될지도 모르는 모든 問題를 友好的 精神下에 處理할 것을 保障하며

玆에 韓國政府와 UN軍總司令部는 以下와 如한 條約協定을 締結하는데 同意한다.

第一條

0027

②

第一條 (國聯軍構成員, 軍屬, 家族 및 特殊契約者의 定義)

本協定에

가. 「國聯軍의 構成員」이라함은 大韓民國의 領域內에 있는 國聯軍의 陸軍, 海軍, 海兵隊, 空軍 所屬에 所屬하는 人員으로서 現在 服務中에 있는 사람을 稱한다.

나. 「軍屬」이라함은 各 國聯軍本國의 國籍을 가진 市民으로서 國聯軍에 雇用되어, 此를 同伴하며 勤務하고 있고 此에 隨伴하는 사람을 稱한다. 但 [illegible]

韓國에 在留하는 者는 除外한다. ... 

本協定의 適用上만 韓國 士官 國籍者는 韓國

本 (但)

各 國籍과 國聯軍 本國의 國籍과의 二重國籍者

는 該 國聯軍 本國의 國籍所有者로 看做한다.

c. 雇傭契約者는 手續上은 國聯軍 本國에 居住

한 者 該 本國法에 依하여 組織된 法人 또는 個人의

雇用人으로서 國聯軍을 爲하여 國聯軍과의 契約에 依하여

履行만을 目的으로 韓國에 있는 者를 云稱한다.

0023

③

D. 「家族」 다음은 다음의 者를 稱한다.

(1) 配偶者 및 二十一才未滿의 子女

(2) 父母 및 二十一才以上의 子女 그 生活費의 半額

以上을 同 軍隊構成員, 軍屬 및 特殊契約者

에 依存하고 있는 者

第三條

1. 大韓民國은 同 軍隊에 對하여 作戰上 必要한

韓國內에 있는 施設 및 區域의 使用權을 許與한다.

個々의 施設 및 區域에 關해서는 兩 韓國政府와 同 軍隊當局

간의 合意에 依하여 決定한다. 此 協定의 效力發生日까지

0030

決定 利權能을 合意치 못한 施設과 区域에 関하여는 本協定 第 條에 規定한 合同委員會를 通하여 決定하여야 한다. 如此한 施設과 区域은 当該施設과 区域의 運營에 必要한 現存의 設備, 備品及 定着物을 包含한다.

2. 大韓民国 及 合衆国 当局은 어느 一側 當事者의 要請이 있을 때에는 前記의 決定事項을 再議討할 수 있으며, 前記 施設 및 区域 등의 返還 또는 新施設 及 区

0031

④

地의 提供에 關하여 協議하여 決定은 合意하였다
中 軍이 使用하고 있는 施設及區域은 作戰上 必要치 않을
때 韓國政府에 返還하여야 한다. 使用
軍은 必要없는 施設及區域을 返還할 때에 上記施設
地는 原狀으로 回復하지 않고 回復自身이 韓國에 補償
하는 義務는 없다. 韓國은 合衆國에 上記施設及區域에
對하여 同軍이 加한 改良 增築 等에 因한 要求에
工作物에 對하여 補償할 義務는 없다.

0032

3. 同將軍은 本協定의 期限滿了時에는 別途規定이 없는限 合軍이 使用하고 있는 施設及區域을 全部 韓國에 返還하며 그때에 있는 施設과 區域이 作戰上 必要가 없게 된 境遇에는 卽時 返還하여야 한다.

第四條

1. 同將軍은 施設及區域內에 있어서 그들의 設定, 使用, 運營, 防衛 또는 管理를 爲하여 必要한, 또는 適當한 當該 權利, 權力及權能을 有한다. 가진다. 同將軍은 上記의 明記

의 施設 及 區域에 隣接한 土地·領水 及 空間 또는
前記의 施設 及 區域의 近傍에서 그 維持, 防衛 及
管理를 [illegible] 又는 使用人의 便利를 圖謀하기 爲하여 必要한 權利
權力 及 權能을 有하며, 措置를 取할 수 있다. 本條
未日本國에 許與된 權利, 權力 及 權能을 施設 及
區域外에서 行使할 때에는 必要에 應하여, 合同委員會를
通하여 相互協議하여야 한다.

2. 日本國은 前記의 權利, 權力 及 權能을 韓日의 領

0034

域으로의, 領域 밖의 또는 領域内에 있어서의 航海·航
空, 通信 又는 陸上交通을 妨害하는 方法
으로 行使하여서는 않 된다. 미聯軍이 使用하는 電波
放射의 裝置가 使用하는 周波數·電力 及 此에 類한 (放射의 型式) 關
係 있는 事項에 關한 問題는 韓國 政府 및 미聯軍
關係當局의 合意에 依하여 解決한다. ~~韓國의 使用~~ 原則的으로
[illegible]
하는 미 周波數, 電力, 放射의 型式 等은 韓國政府의
[illegible] 妨害하는 ~~[illegible]~~ (同一) [illegible] 裝置의 作用을 妨害하여서는

0035

(d)

아니었다. 또 同援軍이 使用한 施設及區域內에 있는

의 모든 作業은 公衆의 安全을 害하지 않도록 適

當한 考慮를 하여 行하여야 한다.

第 條

0036

國際司法裁判所規程

第三十六條 (裁判所의 管轄)

1. 裁判所의 管轄은, 當事國이 裁判所에 付託하는 모든 事件及 國際聯合憲章 또는 實施中의 條約에 特히 規定된 모든 事項에 미친다.

2. 이 規定의 參加國인 國家는 다음 事項에 關한 모든 法律的 紛爭에 關하여 裁判所의 管轄을, 同一의 義務를 受諾하는 他國에 對한 關係에 있어서 當然 또한 特別의 合意없이 義務的인 것으로서 認定할 것을 언제든지 宣言할 수 있다.

가. 條約의 解釋

나. 國際法上의 問題

다. 確認되면, 國際義務의 違反이 되는 事實의 存在

라. 國際義務 違反에 對하여 行하여야 할 賠償의 性質 또는 範圍

0037

3. 前項의 宣言은 無條件으로 多數國 또는 特定國과의 相互條件으로 또는 一定期間에 關하여 할 수 있다.

4. 右記의 宣言書는 國際聯合事務總長에게 寄託한다. 事務總長은 그 謄本을 裁判所規程의 參加國 及 裁判所書記에 送付한다.

5. 常設國際司法裁判所規程 第三十六條에 基하여 行하여지고 또한 尙今도 效力을 가지는 宣言은 이 規程의 參加國 間에 있어서는 右記 宣言은 이 今後 存續하는 期間에 關하여 또한 그 條項에 따라서 國際司法裁判所의 義務的 管轄을 受諾한 것으로 看做한다.

6. 裁判所가 管轄權을 가지는 與否에 關하여 爭議가 있을 때는 그 問題는 裁判所의 決定에 依하여 解決한다.

第五十三條 (欠席判決)

1. 當事國의 一方이 出廷하지 않든가 又는 그 事件의 防衛를 하지 않을 境遇에는 他方當事國은 그 請求에 有利한 決定을 行함을 裁判所에 要求할 수 있다.

2. 右의 決定을 行함에 앞서 裁判所는 自己가 第三十六條及第三十七條에 依하여 管轄을 가질뿐만 아니라, 右의 請求가 事實上으로도 法律上으로도 充分히 根據가 있음을 確認하지 않으면 안된다.

第六十五條 (勸告的意見의 要請)

1. 裁判所는 國際聯合憲章에 依하여

0039

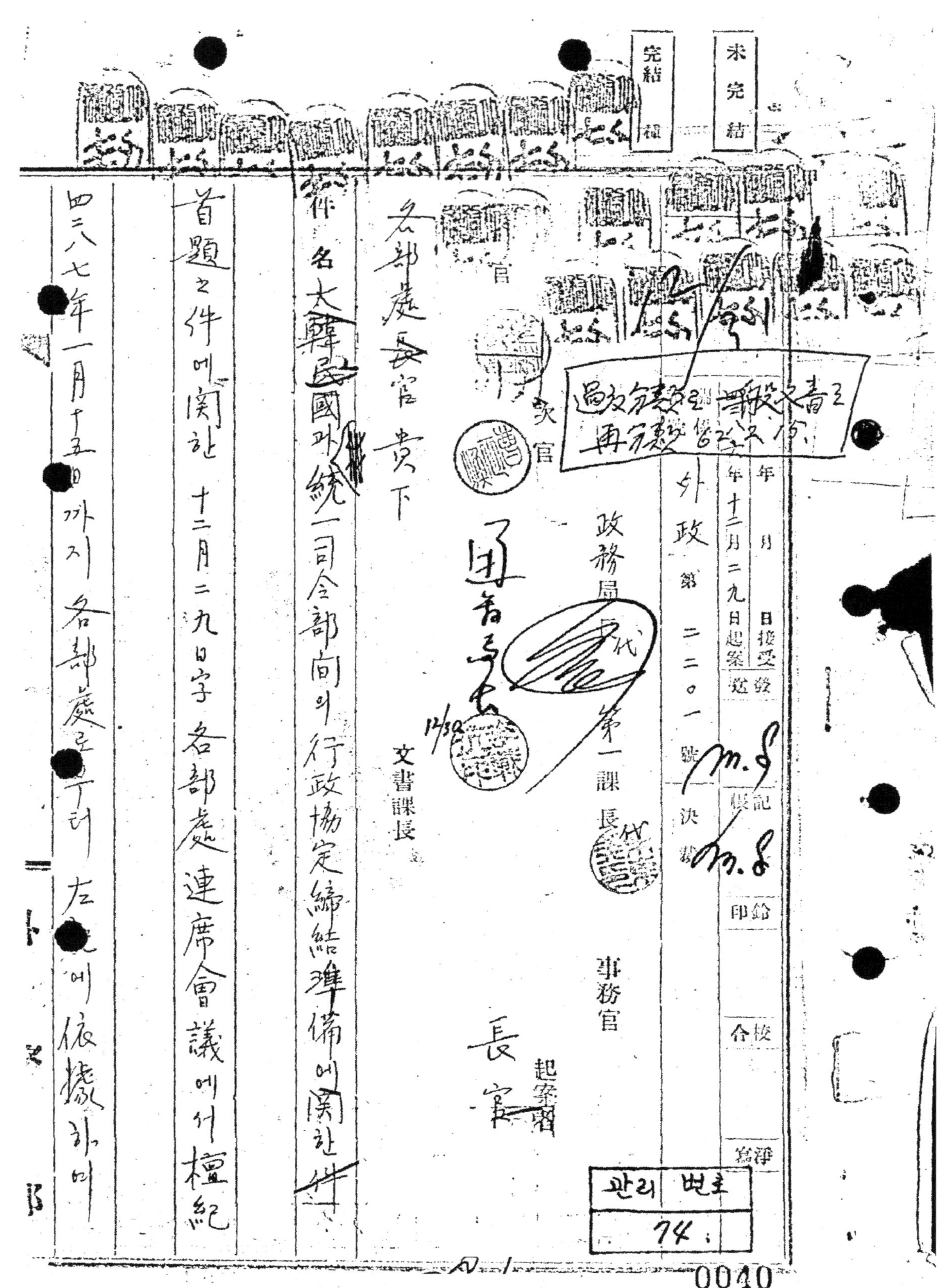

未完結

完結

官

次官

政務局長代

第一課長

事務官

文書課長

長官

起案者

外政第二二〇一號

年月日接受

年十二月二九日起案

過去分첨부의件은 그대로 再分類함

各部處長官 貴下

件名 大韓民國과 統一司令部間의 行政協定締結準備에 關한 件

首題之件에 關한 十二月二九日字 各部處連席會議에서 付擅紀

四二八七年一月十五日까지 各部處로부터 左記에 依據하여

관리 번호 74

0010

當部에 資料를 提出하도록 決定되었압기 參考로 通報

하오니 期必 資料를 提出하여주심을 敬望하나이다

記

各部處가 國內法規에 依據하여 行政的措置를 取함에 있어

서 UN軍으로 말미아마 行政遂行上 隘路를 느끼는 바를 提

示하고 UN軍 및 管下 機関과 各部處가 口頭 또는

0041

文書等으로 契約을 締結한 事項이 있으면 그 寫本 또는
內容을 通報하고, 既而 行政的으로 合意를 본 契約等
이 UN軍에 依하야 侵害를 한 事實이 있으면 具体的인
內容을 明記하고 各部處 該當事項에 關한 是正案 또는
資料 意見等을 提出한다

0042

行政協定締結準備各部處連席會議

十二月二十九日

參席者

法制委員会 幹事長 高在珠 大領

國防部 第二局 企劃課長 李鍾[illegible] 中佐 白慶植 少領

第五局 金秉烈 中佐

第一局 法務課長代理 鄭德均 大尉

內務部 治安局 搜查課長

警務官 邊宗鎬

搜查課 警監 張昌海

方局 金甫炫

043

財務部

會計局 韓相萬

法務部

法務課長 李丙洗

法務局 姜淳宇

商工部

水產局漁撈課長 李和[illegible]

工業局技監 尹弘[illegible]

商政課長 李[illegible]

電政課長 [illegible]

電氣局建設課 李[illegible]

0044

農林部

交通部

監理局長 張德馨

理事官 李星煥

文教部

国立中央観象台長 李源喆

技術教育局長 朴哲在

0045

保健部

社會部

遞信部

郵政局長 崔鳳廷

電務局長 尹台殷

軍事郵便課長 孫永禄

0046

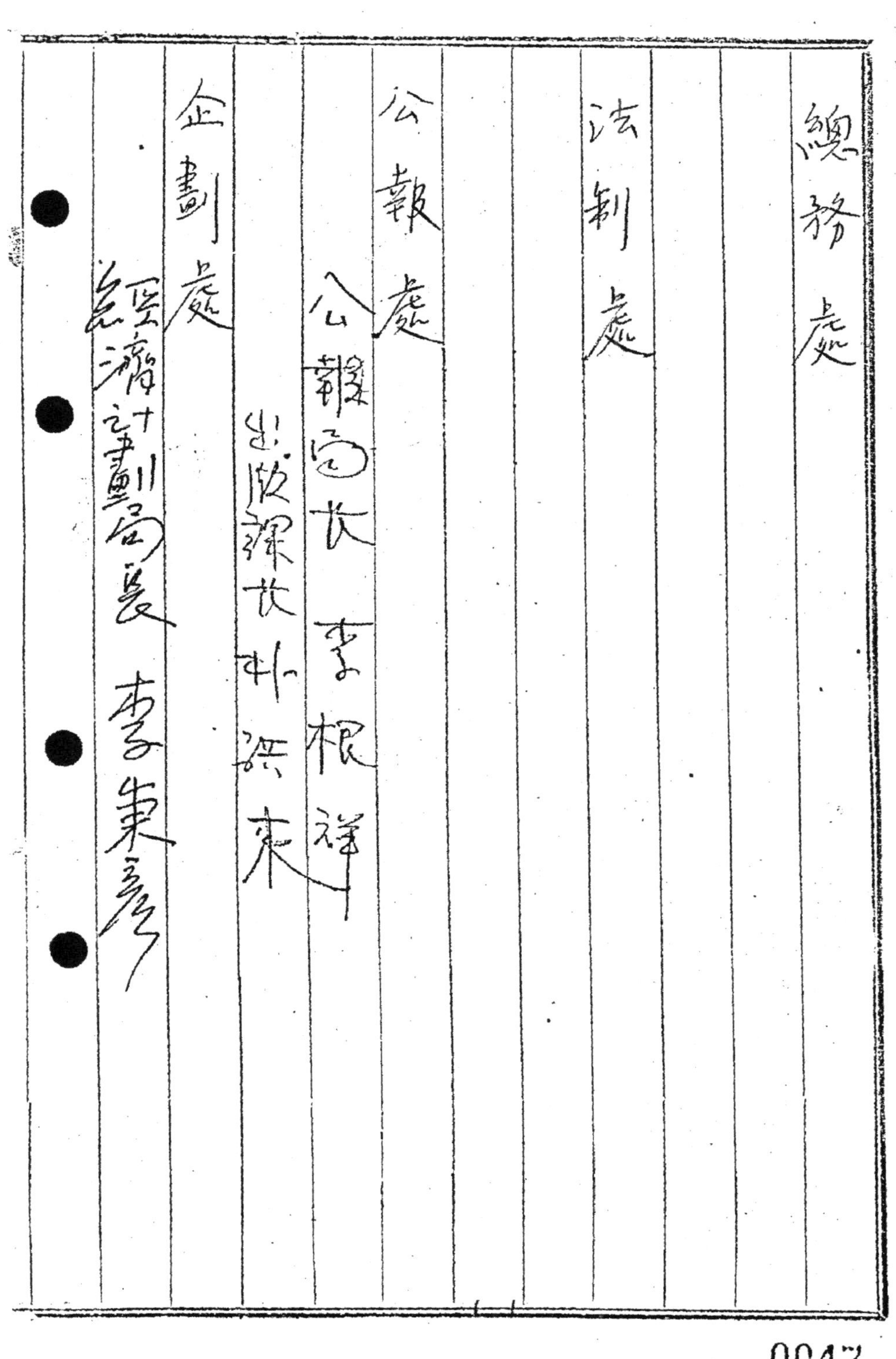

總務處

法制處

公報處

公報局長 李根祥

出版課長 朴洪來

企劃處

經濟計劃局長 李東彦

0047

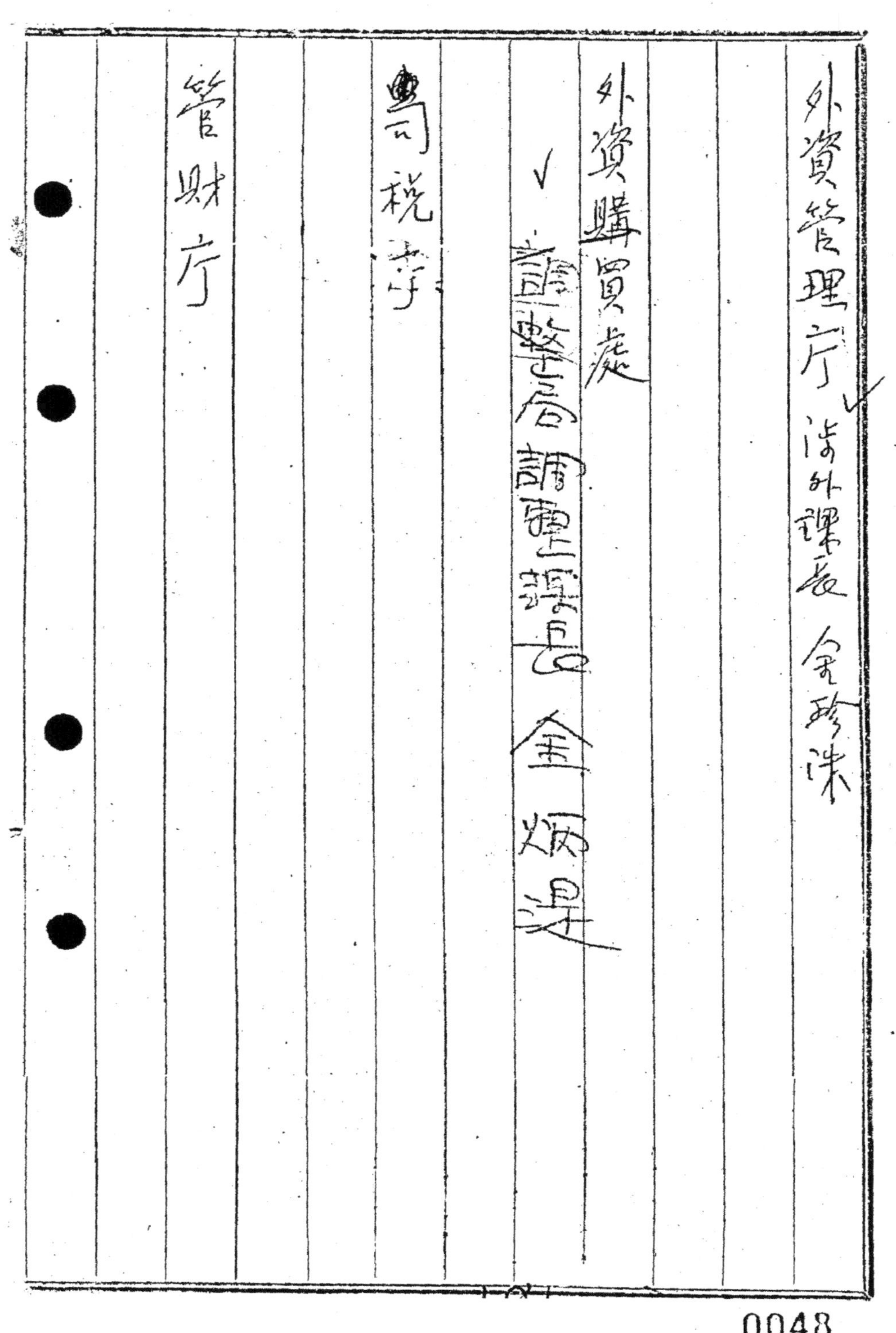

外資管理庁 渉外課長 金珍洙

外資購買處 調整局 調理課長 金炳湜

関稅局

管財庁

0048

外務部次官
通商局長
情報局長
第二課長
第一課 職員二名
計 二十八名
總計 三四名

0049

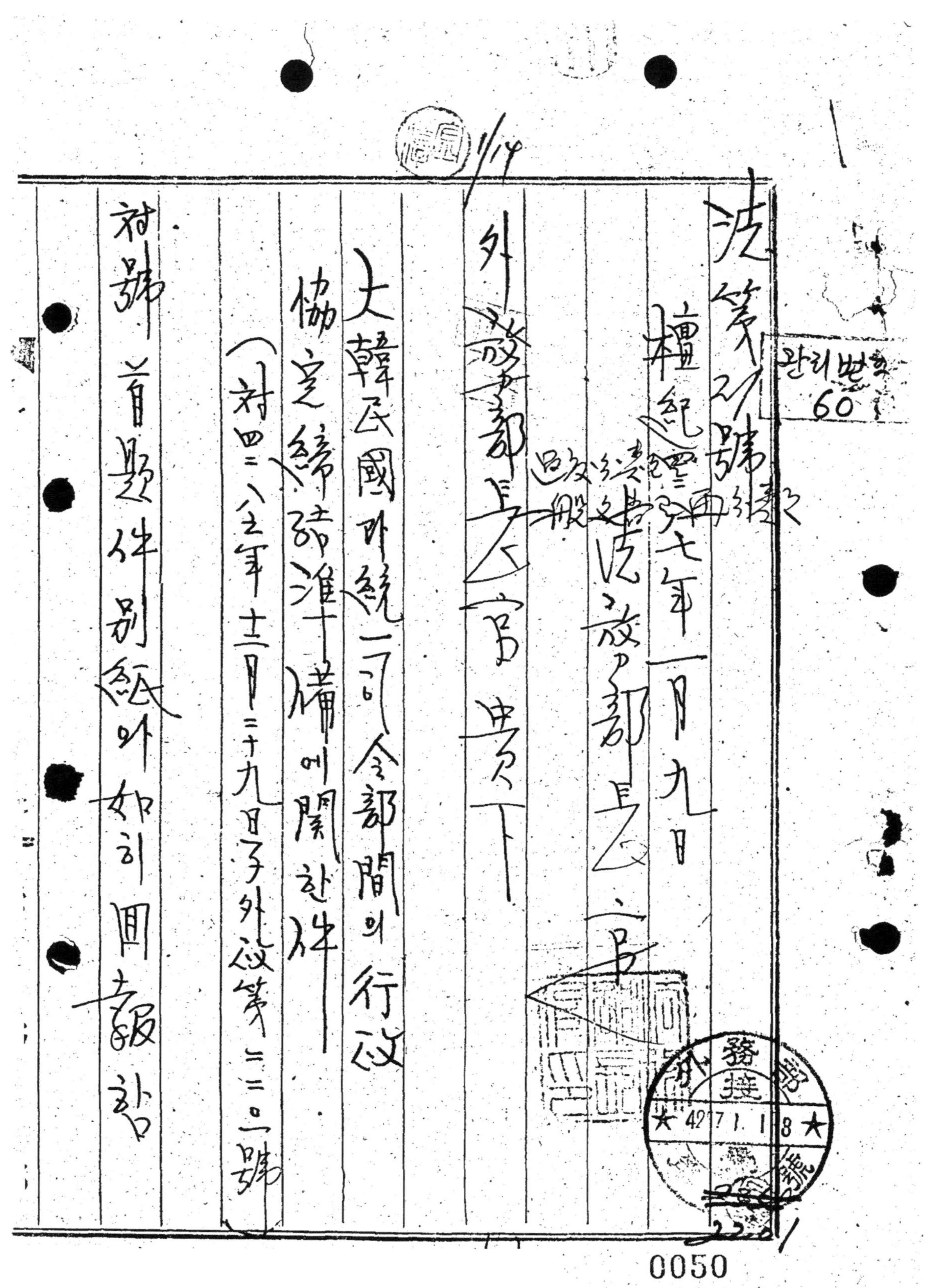

관리번호 60

法第 21號

檀紀四二九七年一月九日

法務部長官

過去公文 一般文書로 再分類

外務部長官 貴下

大韓民國과 統一司令部間의 行政協定締結準備에 關한 件

(對四二八五年十二月二十九日字 外政第二二○號)

對號 首題件 別紙와 如히 回報함

外務部 接受 4297.1.18

0050

大韓民國과 統一司令部間의 行政協定締結準備에 関한 件

韓國動乱으로 UN軍의 作戰上 必要에 依하여 不得已 刑務所 建物 土地 其他施設의 使用이 一方的인 要求에 依하여 行하여졌으며 地方刑務所当局의 協助的인 默示의 承認으로 既而 使用한 것도 許多하거니와 現在 無償으로 使用中인 것이 있어 行政遂行上 隘路를 느끼는 바가 不尠하니

0051

一、事實

1. 永登浦刑務所의 建物 및 垈地의 全部를 美第八軍 第五二六工兵大隊가 現在까지 三年十個月間 使用하여 受刑者 收容에 狹隘와 障害를 招來하고 他刑務所로 하여금 負担을 지게하며 刑政上 困難을 가져왔으며

2. 麻浦, 安東, 金泉 刑務所 農場에 飛行場 敷設 部隊

0052

駐屯地로 使用함으로서 農作物, 果樹等의 撤去(除去)와 함께 農
産物耕作栽培를 不能케하여 刑務所在所者用 蔬菜其他食
料品供給에 支障을 주며 受刑者職業訓練과 國家歲에 影響
을 미치는 바가 甚大하다

二. 要望事項

1) UN軍과의 새로운 契約을 締結함으로서 使用期間의 確定 使

0053

用料의 決定 使用期間中의 保存 修理 等에 関한 諸問題를
決定하여야 할 것이라고 思料함

0054

# 現在UN軍使用中의施設및不動産調

| 施設또는不動産의別 | 使用또는撤去毁損分 | 所在地 | 使用期間 | 推算使用料 | 使用部隊名 | 備考 |
|---|---|---|---|---|---|---|
| 一、永登浦刑務所所有 | | | | | | |
| 建物 | 建坪六、三六一坪 | 서울特別市永登浦區楊坪洞 | 自四二八六年四月十四日 至現在까지 四十五個月間 | 四三、七五八圓 | 美第八軍第五三六工兵隊 | [illegible] |
| 建物 | 工場二棟 建坪二五五坪 | | 仝 | 一、二〇〇、〇〇〇 | 仝 | |
| 建物 | 二層倉庫 一棟一六〇坪 | | 仝 | 三〇〇、〇〇〇 | 仝 | |
| | | | | 一、五四三、七五八 | | |
| 一、麻浦刑務所所有 | | | | | | |
| 土地(田) | 一〇、四九〇坪 | 京畿道楊州郡別内面高山里 | 自四二八六、九 至現在까지 五個月間 | 一五一、三五〇 | 노―스、스타 飛行場 | |
| 土地(田) | 四〇、〇三七坪 | 仝 | 自四二八六、七、一 至四二八七、二現在 七個月間 | 八四〇、七七七圓 | 土耳其軍第一旅團 | |
| 各種果木 | 二九〇株 | 仝 | 四二八六、九 [illegible]株 | 二九〇、〇〇〇 | 노―스스타 飛行場 | 既撤去 |

0055

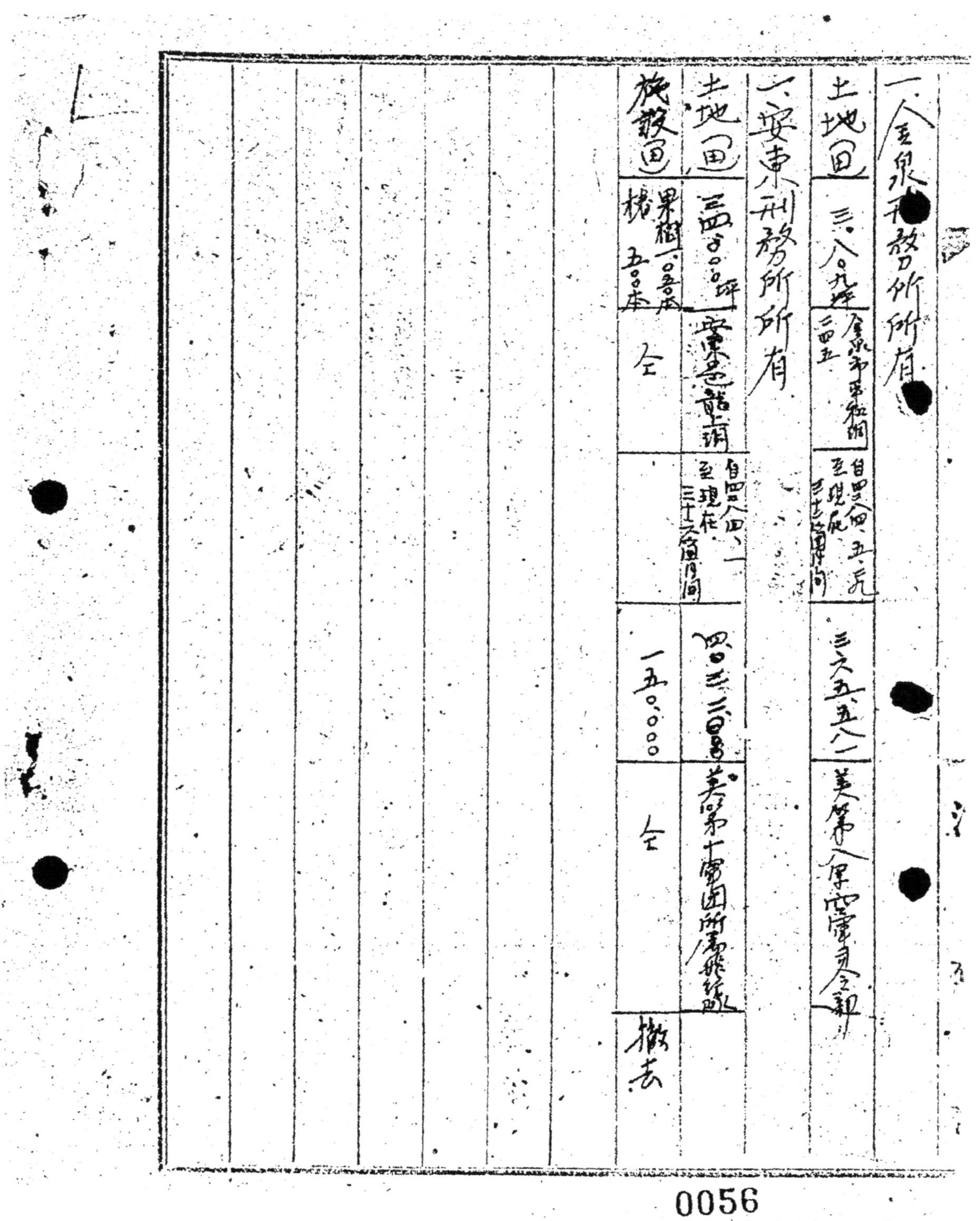

一、金泉刑務所所有

| 土地(田) | 三、八〇九坪 | 金泉市栗和洞 二四五 | 自四八、四、五、至現在 三十五個月間 | 三六五、五八一 | 美第八軍空軍員全部 | |
|---|---|---|---|---|---|---|

一、安東小刑務所所有

| 土地(田) | 三四〇〇坪 | 安東邑龍上洞 | 自四八、四、一 至現在 三十五個月間 | 四三二、〇〇〇 | 美第十軍団所属飛行隊 | |
|---|---|---|---|---|---|---|
| 施設(田) | 果樹一〇〇本 桃五〇本 | 仝 | | 一五〇、〇〇〇 | 仝 | 撤去 |

0056

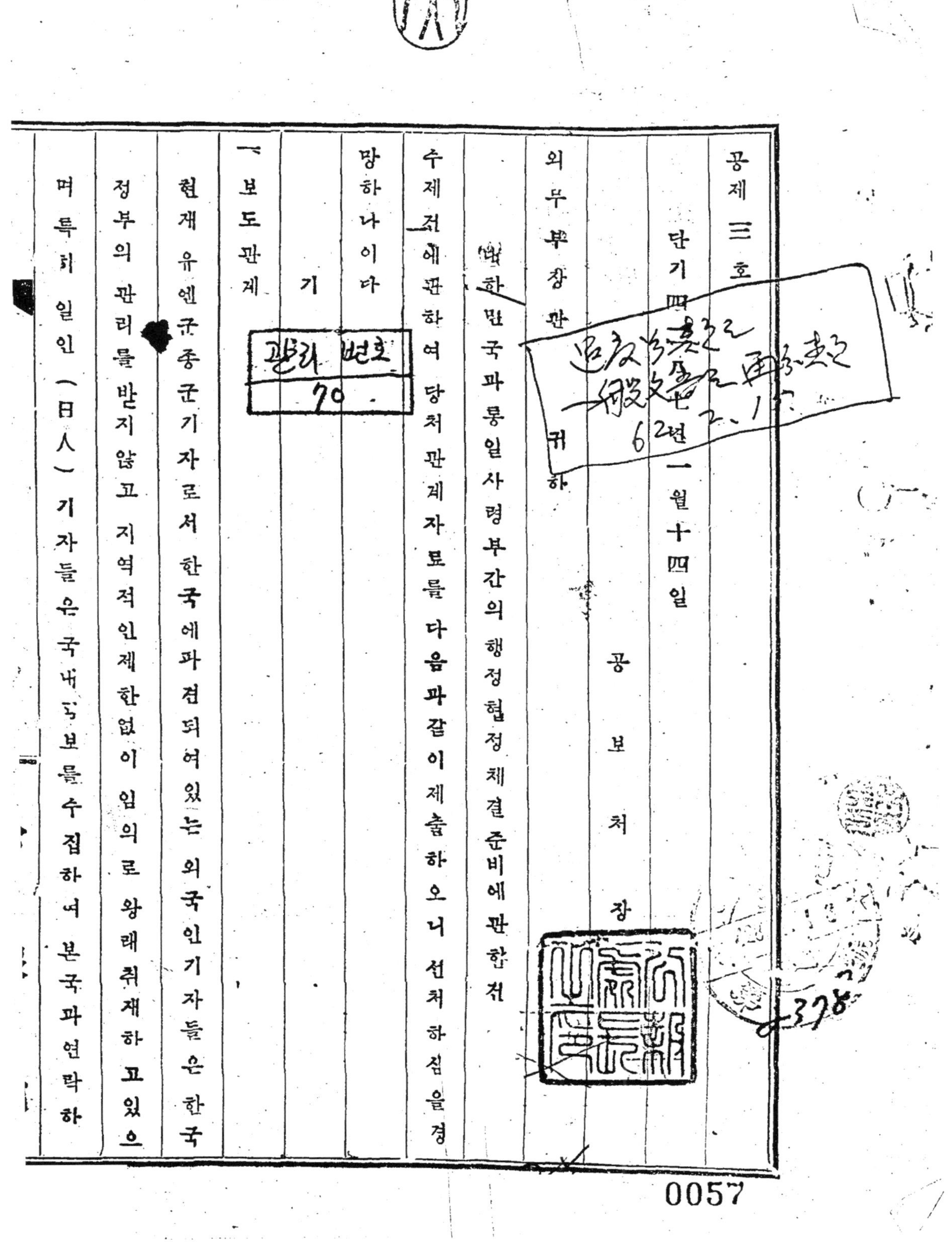

공제 三 호

단기四[illegible]년 一월 十四일

외무부장관 귀하

공보처장

대한민국과 통일사령부간의 행정협정체결준비에 관한 건

수제 건에 관하여 당처 관계자료를 다음과 같이 제출하오니 선처하심을 경망하나이다

기

一 보도관계

현재 유엔군종군기자로서 한국에 파견되여있는 외국인기자들은 한국정부의 관리를 받지않고 지역적인 제한없이 임의로 왕래취재하고있으며 특히 일인(日人) 기자들은 국내정보를 수집하여 본국과 연락하

관리번호 70

0057

므로써 그 폐단이 적지 않은 것이 있음에 따라서

(1) 외국인 기자가 입국할 때에는 그 명목여하를 막론하고 한국정부(외무부)의 허가를 받어야 할 것

(2) 외국인 기자의 국내활동은 한국정부(공보처)의 관리 및 국내법규의 적용을 받을 것

二. 출판관계

외국인이 대한민국 국내에서 자의로 신문 및 출판물을 발간하여 일반공중에 판매배포한다면 대한민국이 규정한 법규가 무시되여 주권국가의 권익이 침해됨으로

(1) 신문 및 출판물이 일반공중에 판매배포될 때는 대한민국법규에 의하여 관리될 것

三. 방송관계

0058

(1) 매일하오十시부터十一시三十분까지의一시간三十분을UN군총
사령부의방송시간으로할당해서실시중에있음
(GHQ심리작전파와의구두협약)

(2) 부산시수영(水營)소재GHQ심리작전파부산파견대의一KW
중파송신 시설을부산방송국에一〇KW을설치할때까지 임시로 부
산방송국이 사용중에있음
GHQ심리작전 파와의 구두협약)

(3) 화재로인하여 소실된 부산지방방송국 청사의재건을원조받기로
되여있음
(부산소재통일사령부소속미후방기지사령부와의협약)

0059

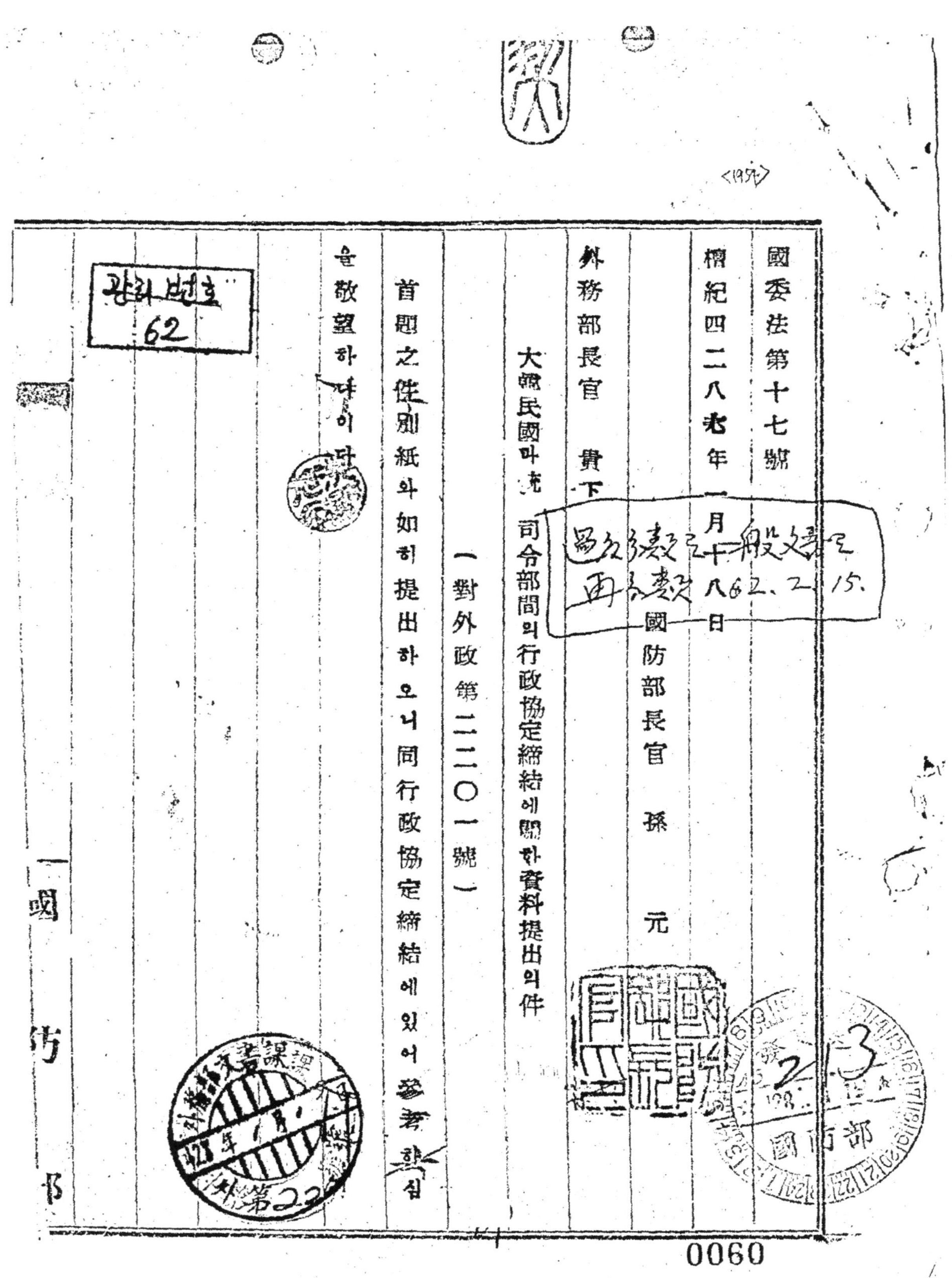
<1959>

國委法第十七號

檀紀四二八九年一月十八日

國防部長官 孫 元

外務部長官 貴下

大韓民國과 美流司令部間의 行政協定締結에 關한 資料提出의 件

(對外政第二二〇一號)

首題之件 別紙와 如히 提出하오니 同行政協定締結에 있어 參考하십을 敬望하나이다

관리번호 62

國防部

0060

一、要望事項

1. 連合統一司令部所屬各部隊에있는韓國人從業員은韓國兵役法및勤務動員法其他法令에依하여徵召集및勤務動員에應하도록措置하다

特히徵召集該當者(滿十九歲滿二十九歲以下의者)를採用또는UN軍에編入케할境遇에는事前에韓美双方의協議가있어야한다

2. 連合統一司令部에서使用하는陸、海、空軍用各地、水面의施設等은一切大韓民國의法令에依하여使用하고그報償은大韓民國法令에依하여이를每年二回式決算할것

3. 一線戰鬪支援勞務者(K、S、C)에對한報酬를戰時勤務動員法에依據하여連合統一司令部가全部負擔하도록措置할것

(註)

0061

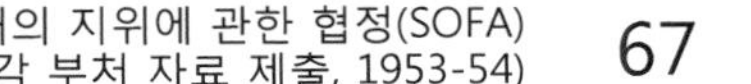

現在美軍은K、S、C勞務者에對하여日當四五圜을支拂할따름임으로大韓民國政府에서五五圜을負擔加算하여日當百圜式支拂하고있는形便임

4. 連合統一司令部管下部隊에勤務타가傷痍、疾病에依하거나不具、廢疾된者와戰傷病者의遺族의援護는大韓民國政府를通하여連合統一司令部에서負擔한다

5. 連合統一司令部에서施設한飛行場、基地其他施設인지라도大韓民國과共同計劃下에實施할것

6. 連合統一司令部에서設置한飛行場基地、其他施設의使用은韓美兩國이使用할것

7. 連合統一司令部가使用하는基地施設及區域은協定의目的을爲한必要가없어질때는大韓民國에返還하여야한다—大韓民國에게補

0062

償發務없이함)

8. 連合統一司令部가使用을許與받은基地、施設及區域을一時的
으로使用하지않을때에는大韓民國이臨時로이것을使用할수있어야
한다

9. 連合統一司令部의電波放射의裝置가使用하는周波數、電力에
關한事項은相互協定에依한다

10. 連合統一司令部와大韓民國은航空機의安全및正確한運航을爲
하여連合統一司令部의通信施設、氣象觀測設備、無線機器及電波
探知機等의施設을利用할수있도록各者便宜를提供한다

11. 連合統一司令部가使用하는基地施設及區域에設置된燈火其他
航空補助施設及航空保安施設은大韓民國에서使用하는樣式에合致
되어야한다

0063

國防部

12. 連合統一司令部가航空射擊및爆擊演習地選擇을함에있어서는大韓民國의合意下에實施할것이며該演習으로因하여韓人의生命財産에被害가有할時는統一司令部가補償할責任이있다

(註)

從前에 斯種爆擊演習으로漁場其他를荒廢케한實例가有함

13. 連合統一司令部는使用을許與받은飛行場、基地施設및區域을第三國에게使用을許與할수없다

14. 連合統一司令部軍事警察은其施設區域外에서韓國人을逮捕할수없다

15. 軍戰鬪力과密接한聯關性있는陸運施設과航空및港灣施設을韓國에서自主的으로管理할수있도록措置한다

二、參考事項

0004

1. 江華地區召集및八二四〇部隊韓人中召集을解除한特典에關한
協約을是正한다

(註)

檀紀四二八六年七月二十三日字極東司令部駐韓連絡派遣隊公函에依하면

ㄱ. 公務團體 徵召集執行官도包含) 出入은八二四〇部隊司令部의事前承認을얻을것

ㄴ. 極東司令部駐韓連絡派遣隊(八二四〇部隊)關係人은同司令部의協議없이動員할수없도록되여있음

2. 모든非軍用및軍用航空、交通管理及通信의關係는相互緊密히協調하여發達을圖謀할것이며또한集團安全保障의利益을達成하기爲하여必要한程度로調整해야한다

0065

66

3. 聯合統一司令部는北緯三八度線以北收復地區의行政權을移讓하여야한다

三 UN軍및管下機關과口頭또는文書로協定된事項없음

0066

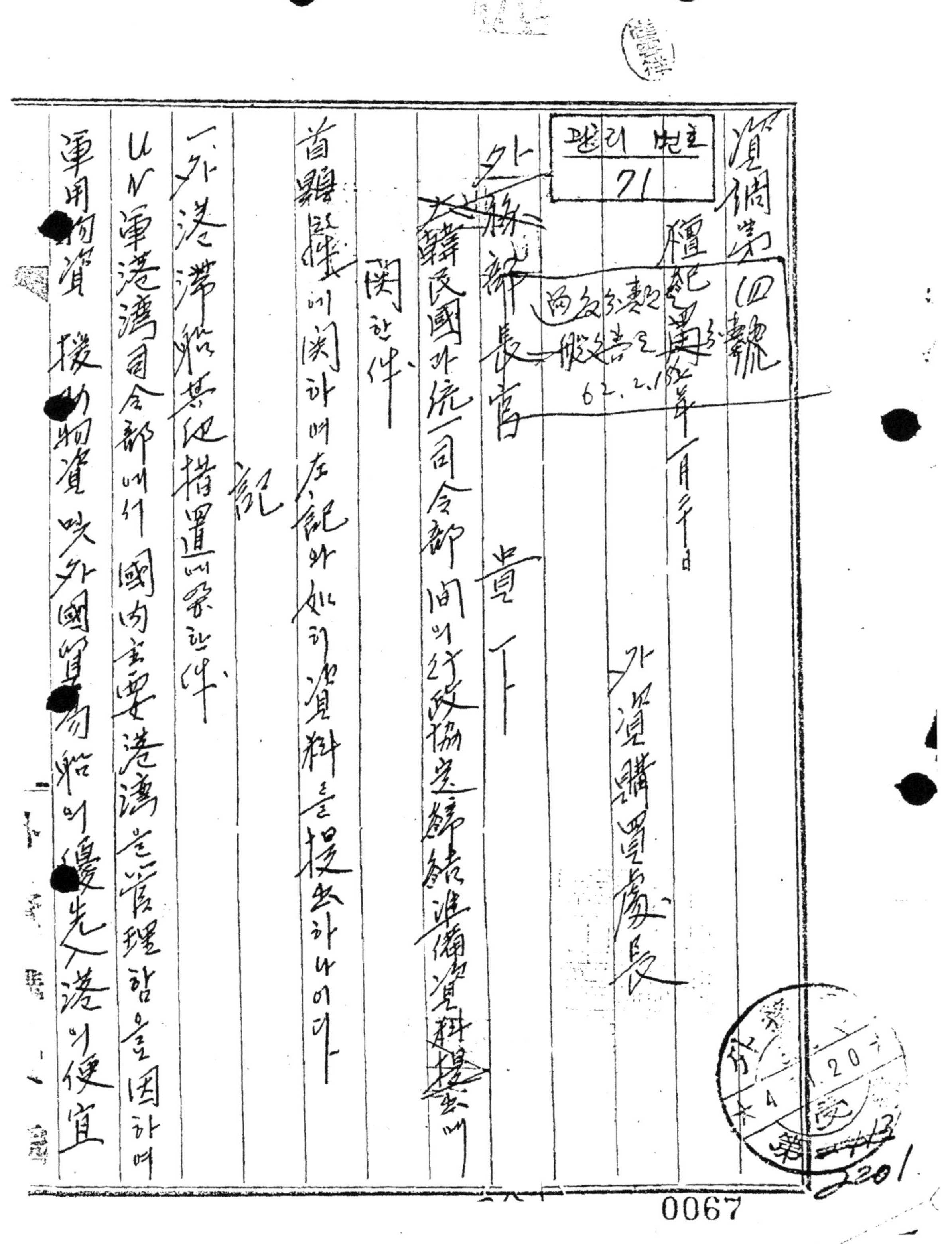

관리 번호 71

일반문서로 재분류 62.2.15

資調第 四 號

檀紀 [illegible]年 一月 二十日

外資購買處長

外務部長官 貴下

大韓民國과 統一司令部 間의 行政協定締結 準備資料 提出에 関한 件

首題 件에 関하여 左記와 如히 資料를 提出하나이다

記

一. 外港 滯船 其他 措置에 関한 件

UN軍 港灣司令部에서 國內 主要港灣을 管理함을 因하여

軍用物資 援助物資 및 外國貿易船의 優先入港의 便宜

0067

을 閣議하고 있음으로 政府保有弗로 當處에서 導入하는 物資를 積載한 船舶이 內港에 入港치 못하며 着港直時 作業을 實施치 못하고 外港에서 長時日을 待期케 되는 例가 不少하며 滯船料 支拂을 不免케 되며 貴重한 政府保有美貨를 外人船舶會社에 支拂케 되는바 去年 一年間에 支拂한 滯船料만 하여도 二十萬弗이라는 莫大한 金額에 達하고 있는 實情이온 今般 統合司令部와의 行政協定을 締結함에 있어서 國內主要港口의 外港滯船에 對하여 全的으로 其責任을 UN軍側에 歸屬토록 措置를 取하여 주심을 要望하나이다

一 不然이면 當處에서 導入한 物資積載船舶에 對하여는 優先內港入港을 容認하도록 措置하여 주시옵기 仰望하나이다

0068

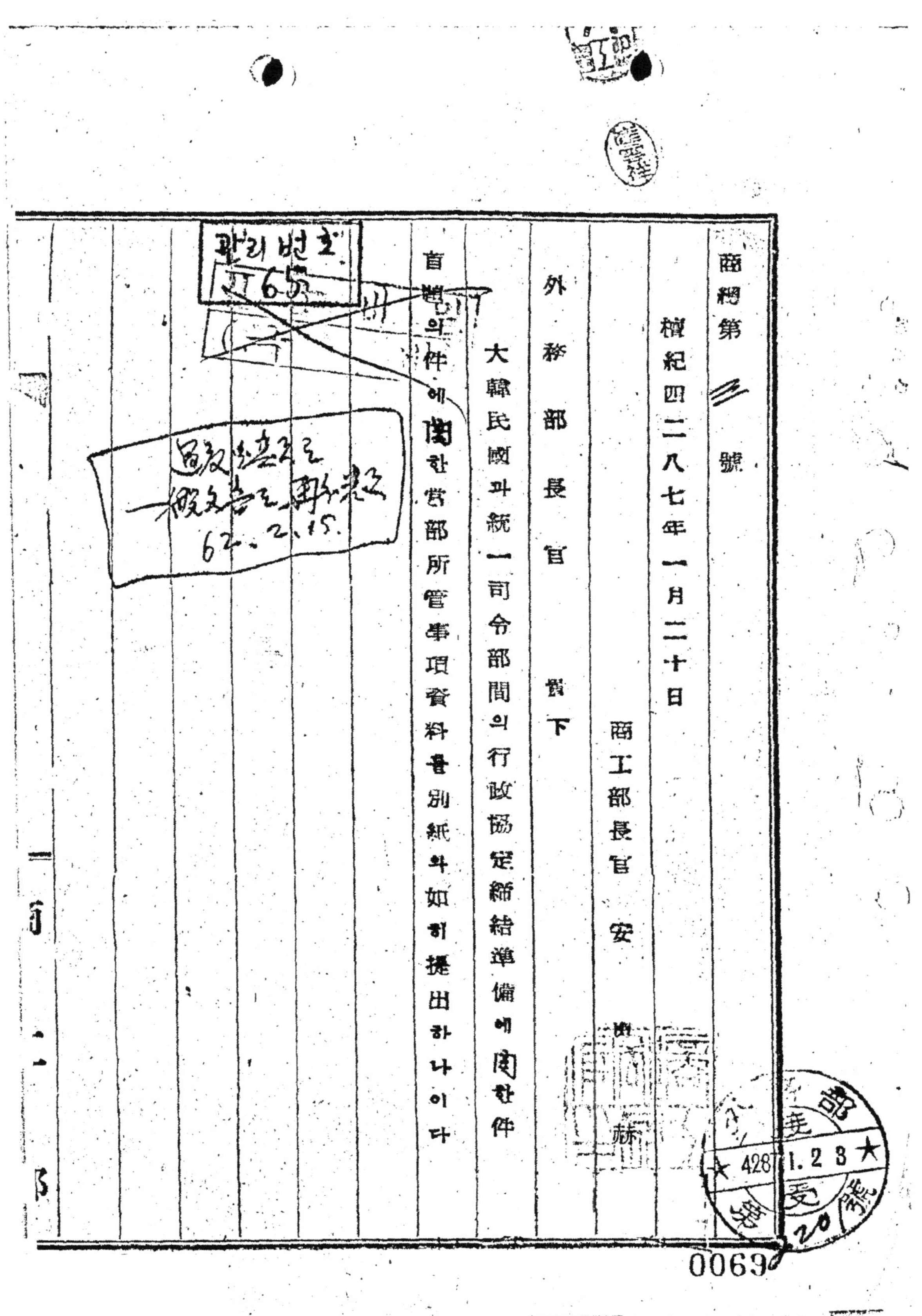

商貿第 號

檀紀四二八七年一月二十日

商工部長官 安 赫

外務部長官 貴下

大韓民國과統一司令部間의行政協定締結準備에関한件

首題의件에関한當部所管事項資料를別紙와如히提出하나이다

관리번호 II65

0069

六、새로이協定을要하는事項

1 輸入에關한事項

(가) UN軍의構成員및軍屬또는그들의家族又는UN軍의厚生機
關(UN軍에從事하고있는韓國軍은本對象에서除外한다)에
있어國外로부터物品을輸入하는境遇에는原則的으로我國의貿
易規程에依하여야할것

(나) 但左의境遇에는此限에不在한다

A UN軍司令部에서公認하여事前에我國政府에通告된調達機關
이UN軍의構成員및軍屬等에所要되는公用또는厚生物品을輸
入할境遇

B 最終的으로UN軍隊가使用하는資材備品施設및其他需用品이
하고UN軍司令部에서證明한物品의輸入이境遇

0070

C) UN軍의構成員및軍屬또는그들의家族이物品을輸入함에當하여我國이商行爲가않이라고認定하는範圍內에서의日常生活必需品으로輸入할境遇

2 國內生産施設또는區域의使用管理에關한事項

(가) 生産施設또는區域의使用管理를UN軍隊에許可함에當하여는使用目的、使用期間을明示할것

(나) 前項에依한使用目的이解消되였을時는使用許可期間內라도目的物을返還바을수있는規定을設置할것

(다) 國防上또는國民生活上緊要한生産施設또는區域의使用或은管理許可에對한特別制限規定을設置할것

(라) UN軍隊가그의使用에屬하는生産施設또는區域을一時的으로使用치않고있을境遇에는當該施設또는區域의正常的인UN

0071

軍隊의 使用目的에 妨害되지 않는다고 認定되는 範圍內에서 大韓民國政府 또는 國民에게 臨時使用을 許與할 수 있는 規定을 設置할 것

마) UN軍隊가 使用許可를 받은 生産施設 또는 區域에서 作業을 할 때의 諸般條件 및 使用完了로 因한 返還時의 條件을 規定토록 할 것

바) UN軍隊가 生産施設 또는 區域을 使用 或은 管理함에 있어 使用 或은 管理하는 生産施設 또는 區域에 相當한 補償에 關한 規定을 設置할 것

자) 個人의 生産施設 또는 區域에 關한 具体的인 協定에 對하여는 兩政府間의 合意를 要하도록 할 것

아) UN軍隊에 生産資材의 使用 또는 管理를 許可할 境遇에는 最少限度로 制限하는 規定을 設置하고 使用 또는 管理 條件을 確立토록

0072

것

二、參考事項

1、交通部運輸用炭에關한事項

六、二五事變前에는交通部鐵道運轉用炭으로每月平均二〇、〇〇〇屯의國產 마세크 를供給하고其余는約五〇、〇〇〇屯의有煙炭을直接輸入하여使用하고있는實情이온바現在國內煙炭工場生產能力은每月二〇、〇〇〇屯以上의마세크를供給할수있도록復舊되고있으며今後는UNKRA計劃에依하여國內煙炭工場이增設될것이오니國產마세크를鐵道運轉用으로使用하고不足量만을輸入有煙炭으로使用토록措置함이緊要함

0073

國聯軍電氣料金淸算의件

六、二五事變勃發以后駐韓國聯軍各機關에對하여京電、南電兩配電會社에서供給한電氣料金은昨年十一月末現在一、二八七百万余圓에達하고있으나現在까지全然徵收치못하고있어此料金未收는發配電両電氣事業体는勿論이고韓國産業全体에對하여深刻한障害가되므로當部로서는本件의早速한解決을爲하여其間國聯軍當局과公式非公式으로屢次交捗한結果國聯軍이支拂할電氣料金中에서國聯軍發電繼運營經費를韓國側이負擔하고此를控除하여淸算하는原則的問題는合意를보았으나細部的인問題에있어左記와如히双方間에見解의差異點이有함으로此를縮少하여解決에到達하고저繼續非公式으로折衷中에있음

(本件非公式으로交換한双方見解別添寫本과如함)

0074

(一) 當局로서는國聯軍發電艦經費를朝鮮電業會社가負擔하되其最高限度額은發電艦으로부터受電한電力量에對한販賣電力料額以內로하고其中OEC援助物資로發電艦에供給된油類代金은控除하여韓國政府에積立케할것을主張하였으나相對方側에서는油類代金의對充資金積立을認定할수없다고主張하고結局은CEB에서石油類는無償으로供給한다는決定을할것을提案하고있음

(二) 發電艦經費中에서電業會社의電力操作費로八%를控除償還할것을主張하였으나相對方側은此를認定치않음으로妥協點을發見키爲하여過去(去年六月末까지)取扱量에對한操作費는其要求를承諾할것이나發電會社는此電力操作에不少한經費가所要됨으로將來(去年七月一日以后)의取扱量에對하여는操作費를認定할것을主張하고있음

0075

(三) 國聯軍使用電氣料金에對하여도電氣까스稅法의規定된바에依하여稅金을賦課決定한데對하여相對方側은發電艦의發電量一部를軍事用에使用하는것이고軍需品의自家消費와同一性格임으로此稅金은認定할수없고主張하고있으나當部로서는現行稅法上賦課를主張안할수없음

0076

國聯軍電力料金明細表 (四二八六年十一月末現在)

一、國聯軍未收電力料金

| 配電會社別 | 販賣電力量 | 電力料金 | 工事費 | 稅金 | 計 | 備考 |
|---|---|---|---|---|---|---|
| 京電 | 八、六四九、八〇〇 KWH | 四三、八六八、一七六 圓 一七 | 一〇四、七〇九 九八 | 二、七六六、〇一八 一一 | 四六、七三九、六〇四 | |
| 南電 | 一七、九五九、七四八一 | 七六、六七二、七一二 五四 | 五二七、五〇八 九四 | 五、九五九、四一〇 〇四 | 八四、六五六、六六四 八 | |
| 計 | 二六、六〇九、五四八一 | 一二〇、五四〇、八八八 七一 | [illegible] 九二 | 七、六六一、九四七 一八 | 一二八、七四四、〇六 九四 | |

二、發電所受電電力料金

| 受電量 | 電力代金 | 備考 |
|---|---|---|
| 五二、〇八〇、二七五 KWH | 七四五、一九五、五六八 〇 圓 | 자코나號外五發電所分 |

0077

(別紙一)

Suggestion by the Ministry of Commerce and Industry.

20 Nov. 1953

1) The UN Forces in Korea shall pay the Korean power distributing companies (Seoul Electric Co. and South Korea Electric Co.) for electric services rendered (power distribution and construction), according to the duly established rate schedule, rules and regulations of these electric companies, as well as taxes in accordance with the ROK law.

2) The Korea Electric Power Co. shall pay the UN Forces in Korea for power delievered by the power barges under control of the UN Forces, at the wholesale rate duly prescribed by the ROK Government, deducting eight percent hadling expenses. Costs for materials, supplies or equipment, if any, financed with other dunds than the UN Army funds, such as CRIK supply, furnished to the power barges, shall be deducted from the amount payable by the KEPCO.

3) The KEPCO shall pay the UN Forces for coal furnished to the Korean thermal plants by the UN Forces, at the coal sale price of the Korea Coal Corporatiob duly prescribed by the ROK Government.

4) The balance between the amount payable by the UN Forces to the Korean power distributing companies and the amount payable by the KEPCO to the UN Forces shall be paid by the UN Forces to a Korean Committee consisted of representatives of the Ministry of Commerce and Industry, KEPCO, SECO and SKECO. In case that the amount due from KEPCO exceeds that from the UN Forces, the KEPCO shall pay the balance to the UN Forces.

5) Old accounts shall be paid in suspence in a lump according to the amount and data submitted with guaranty by the UN Forces, KEPCO, SECO and SKECO; the final settlement shall be made after audit and adjustment, if necessary, by parties concerned during next three years.

6) New accounts shall be settled on the monthly pay basis in accordance with contracts to be entered into by the Ministry of Commerce and Industry, KEPCO, SECO and/or SKECO on the one hand and the UN Forces on the other.

0078

(別紙2)

3 December 1953

Reference the informal electric power proposal, dated 20 November 1953, received from the Ministry of Commerce and Industry. Informal comments are listed categorically with reference to the 6 suggestions contained therein.

1. Reference is made to proposed electric power contractual drafts previously furnished at Seoul conferences on 31 August 1953, and 12 November 1953, and to letter, Commanding General, Korean Communications Zone, 15 September 1953, to Minister of Commerce and Industry, Republic of Korea. The two references state that the United States Army is to pay for electric services in accordance with the existing published rate schedules, rules, and regulations. Electric power contractual instruments state that Korean tax or duty is to be excluded from electric bills presented to the United States Army and is to be deducted if included in electric bills through error or otherwise.

2. The United States Army is interested in recovering only its out-of-pocket and plant rental costs for the power barges and its actual Tangin-Ri coal costs, as outlined in the references mentioned in the previous paragraph. The United States Army desires to use actual costs, not a prescribed wholesale rate. The United States Army does not propose to charge or to be charged any handling expenses. CRIK and similar type supplies are provided free to the Republic of Korea. Neither the United States Army nor the Republic of Korea is to charge or to be charged for any CRIK or similar type aid supplies.

3. The United States Army desires to recover only its actual out-of-pocket coal costs, not to use a prescribed wholesale rate.

4., 5., and 6. The methods for the payments of balances, between the Korean electric bills and the United States Army bills for electric power barges and Tagin-Ri coal costs, for both past and future bills were contained in the proposed contractual drafts presented on 12 November 1953, in Seoul. There is no objection to the Minister of Commerce and Industry being designated as the duly authorized representative of the Republic of Korea to sign the electric power contractual instruments.

0079

(別紙三)

18 December 1953

Reference is made to informal comments on power account proposals dated 3 December 1953 and received via C. M. George 9 December 1953. Comments below correspond with similarly numbered paragraphs to referenced communication, and are forwarded with the approval of the Minister of Commerce and Industry.

1. Paragraph 1.

a. Third Sentence: The distributing companies are obliged by law to collect the Electricity and Gas Tax (15%). The opinion of the Ministry of Finance heretofore has been that the Electricity and Gas Tax is applicable to charges for the service of electric power to the U.N. Forces (U.S. Army). This Ministry desires that electric power furnished to the U.N. Forces(U.S. Army) should not be taxed. It is currently conferring with the Ministry of Finance and recommending that the tax be held not applicable.

2. Paragraph 2.

a. First Sentence:

(1) Must the U.S. Army recover its "out-of-pocket and plant rental costs for the power barges and its actual Tangin-ri coal costs" in U.S. Dollars or ROK Hwan?

(2) If recovery by the U.S. Army is to be in ROK Hwan, conversion at what exchange rate is contemplated?

b. Second Sentence: The necessity for the U.S. Army to recover actual costs rather than a prescribed wholesale rate is recognized and understood. This Ministry (KEPCO), on the other hand, cannot undertake to obligate the ROK Government for the unlimited reimbursement of U.S. Army-incurred power generation expenses over which this Ministry (KEPCO) can exercise no effective control.

-1-

0080

c. Third Sentence:

(1) This Ministry (KEPCO) is required to credit to the foreign aid counterpart fund at the full prescribed wholesale rate (currently HW 1.56 per KWH) for all power received from the power barges. From this fund it was anticipated that KEPCO would be permitted to recover legitimate handling costs after deposits were made to the counterpart fund.

(2) With respect to power generated from domestic plants, the wholesale rate includes elements covering KEPCO's actual handling costs. All receipts and accounts payable from the sale to the distribution companies of power generated by the barges, however, is required to be deposited into, or earmarked for the foreign aid counterpart fund. KEPCO, thus, is prevented from recovering its costs of handling barge-gerated power unless it can recover its handling costs from the foreign aid counterpart fund in accordance with the principle governing the distribution of other aid commodities by ROK agencies.

(3) If the U.S. Army cannot consider the problem of the KEPCO handling charge for barge-generated power, and instead desires to supplant the counterpart fund formula with a direct contractual relationship to furnish supplemental electric power to the ROK at cost, it would appear equitable that this Ministry (KEPCO) should be relieved of further obligation to any foreign aid counterpart fund with respect to the proceeds from the sale of barge-generated power, and should be permitted to revise the wholesale rate to cover the pooled costs of all power generated, including both domestic and barge sources.

0081

d. Fourth Sentence : This sentence is understood to apply only with respect to the relationship between the U.S. Army and this Ministry (KEPCO) in the calculation of costs and offsetting credits.

3. Paragraph 3. The same general position applies as is indicated in par. 2 b above. This paragraph presents a further complication in that the Dae Han Coal Corporation is the sole official agency for the production, exportation, importation and distribution of all coal and coal products in Korea. Currently the Dae Han Coal Corporation has been authorized by the National Assembly action to furnish imported bituminous coal to domestic electric power generation plants at a price of HW 1800 per metric ton. This price, therefore, is required to be used in calculating the wholesale rate. This Ministry (KEPCO) is not authorized to purchase coal from any other source at any other price for this or any other purpose.

4. Paragraphs 4,5, and 6. No questions.

0082

(別紙 II)

21 December 1953

Basis upon which Ministry of Commerce and Industry would like to resume discussion of power accounts:

Past Account:

1. KEPCO recognizes offset of approximately H₩ 604 million for Army expenses of power barges, less any amount which may be due to "proceeds from sale of aid goods" account (thru ROK Office of Supply) for CHIK-supplied POL, (unless it is determined (as by CEB action) that KEPCO is not liable to any counterpart fund).

2. KEPCO will pay for Army-supplied coal to Tangin-ri from a separately existing account, at the official ROK wholesale rate for electric power generation, of H₩ 1100 per metric ton. This account amounts to approximately H₩ 45 million.

3. Less actual costs to KEPCO of handling this power.

Future Account:

1. Offset principle accepted with limitation that total of such costs to KEPCO shall not exceed total income to KEPCO from such operations.

0083

外資調一般第 參號

檀紀四二八七年一月二十六日

臨時外資管理廳長

外務部長官 閣下

大韓民國과 統一司令部間의 行政協定締結準備 에 関한 件

(対檀紀四二八六年十二月二九日字外政第三〇二号)

首題之件에 関하여서는 對UN軍間에 民事, 刑事関係事項이 主要々件으로 되리라고 思料되오나, 六.二五動乱以后의 客觀的情勢에 随伴하야 当庁外資運営取扱에 있어 行政遂行上 UN軍側과의 隘路가 있음에 照鑑하여 隨時此를 打開하고저 累次KCAC

外資管理廳

0084

又는 関係要路와 交涉한 結果 一九五二年五月二十四日에 韓米
協定이 締結되였다 하드라도 其運営에 関한 細則이
없어 이렇다 할 結果를 얻지 못하고 있는 実情이오바
多幸히 本邦과 統一司令部間에 行政協定이 締結
되는 此機会에 当方案을 左記와 如히 送付하오니 査
收하시와 打開策을 講究케 하심을 敬望하나이다.

記

一、援助物資取扱經費支拂証憑書事前監査制度
는 此를 廃止한다.

理由

現在 救護物資 国内操作에 対한 支拂證憑書를
K.C.A.C 会計検査課 또는 地方局에서 事前監査를

0085

実施하고 있는바 此는 救護物資賣上金을 操作費에

充当使用한 関係上 援助友邦에 協助하는 意味에서

如斯한 監査에 同意하여 왔아오나 去年 十二月 十四日字

로 韓美間에 締結된 「経済再建및 財政安定計劃

에 関한 合同経済委員会協約」 本文 및 附録 第二 第

二項과 第三項에 依하면 無償配給物資를 除外하고는

購入[illegible]資는 元價를 一対一로 換算한 額에 国内操作費

를 加[illegible]하여 販賣하는 同時 購入元本額은 援助物資

徴收計定에 設置하고 残余額은 当庁이 国内操作費

로 直接使用케 됨으로 本監査制度는 自然廃止되여야

한다.

二. KCAC에 対한 国内操作経費支拂에 関한 諸般報

外資管理庁

0086

告는此를廢止한다.

理由

現在當庁은首題經費支拂狀況을每月末日現在로支拂出證憑書每件마다內容을明記한一覽表를KCAC会計検査課에報告키로되여있는바本件은支拂証憑書를英文으로再作成하는結果가되고있는実情임으로前記一과如한理由로서当然히廢止되여야한다.

三 援助物資에対한港湾荷役作業, 保管輸送其他一切操作은大韓民国政府가이를担当한다.

前項의操作에必要한操作費料等은大韓民国政府에서決定한다.

理由

0087

戰爭勃発以來軍事作戰上必要로釜山、仁川及群山의三港은美軍管理로됨에따라援助物資의港灣荷役까지도美軍에게契約하고, 實施管理하고, 埠頭에서奧地까지의輸送하는過程에있어도KCAC에서貨車配車의取扱其他實地操作을指示하야援助物資를操作하고있으나戰爭의樣相도變更되고韓美間의「經濟再建및財政安定計劃에関한合同經濟委員会協約」도締結된今日에있어서는우리나라에導入되는一切援助物資의操作은当然히우리政府에서担当하여야할것이고이에附隨된諸般操作料率의決定도우리政府에서自主的으로制定하여야할것입니다.

外資管理廳

0088

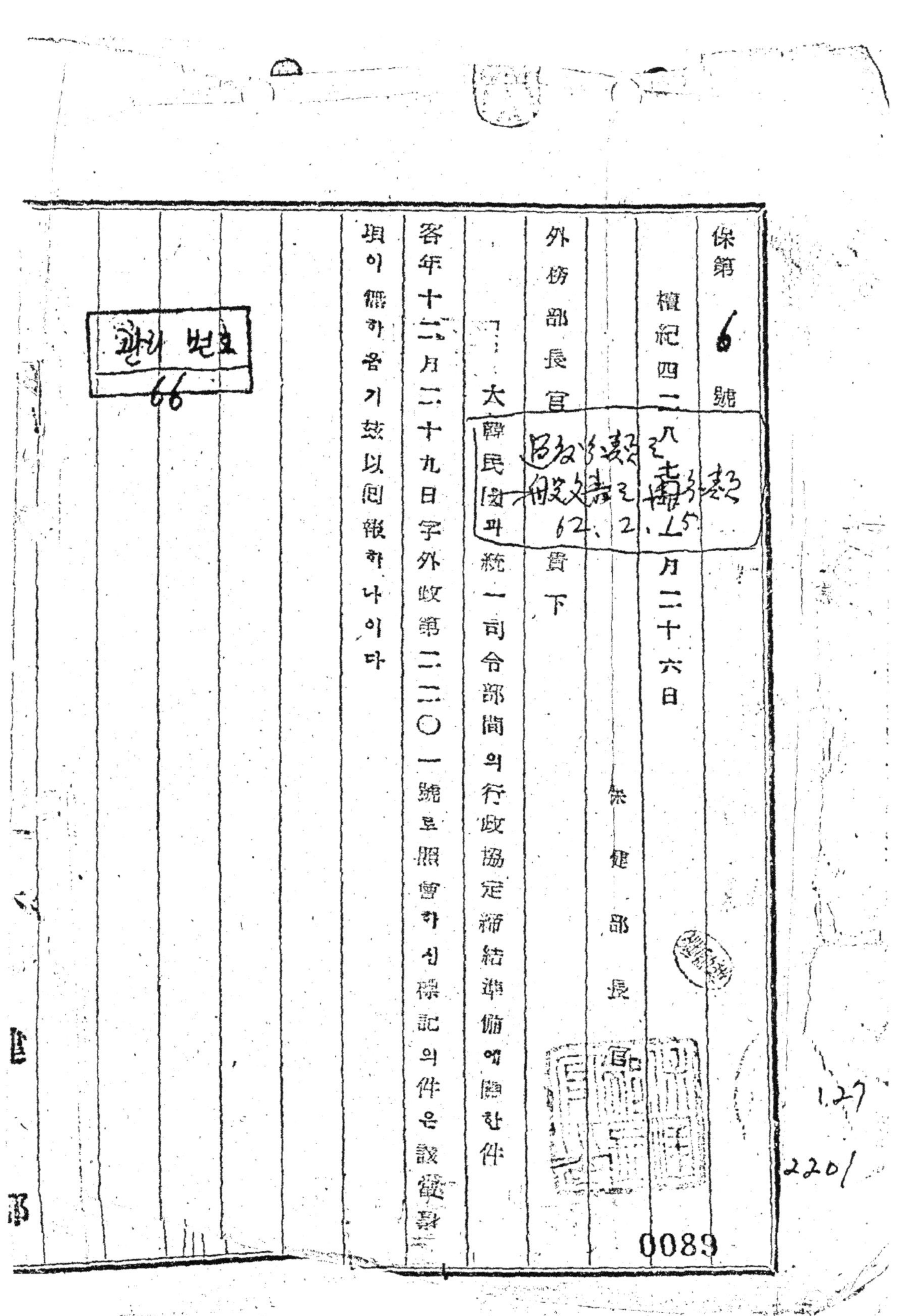

保第 6 號

檀紀四二八八年一月二十六日

保健部長官

外務部長官 貴下

大韓民國과 統一司令部間의 行政協定締結準備에 關한 件

客年十二月二十九日字外政第二二〇一號로 照會하신 標記의 件은 該當事項이 無하옵기 玆以回報하나이다

관리 번호 66

0089

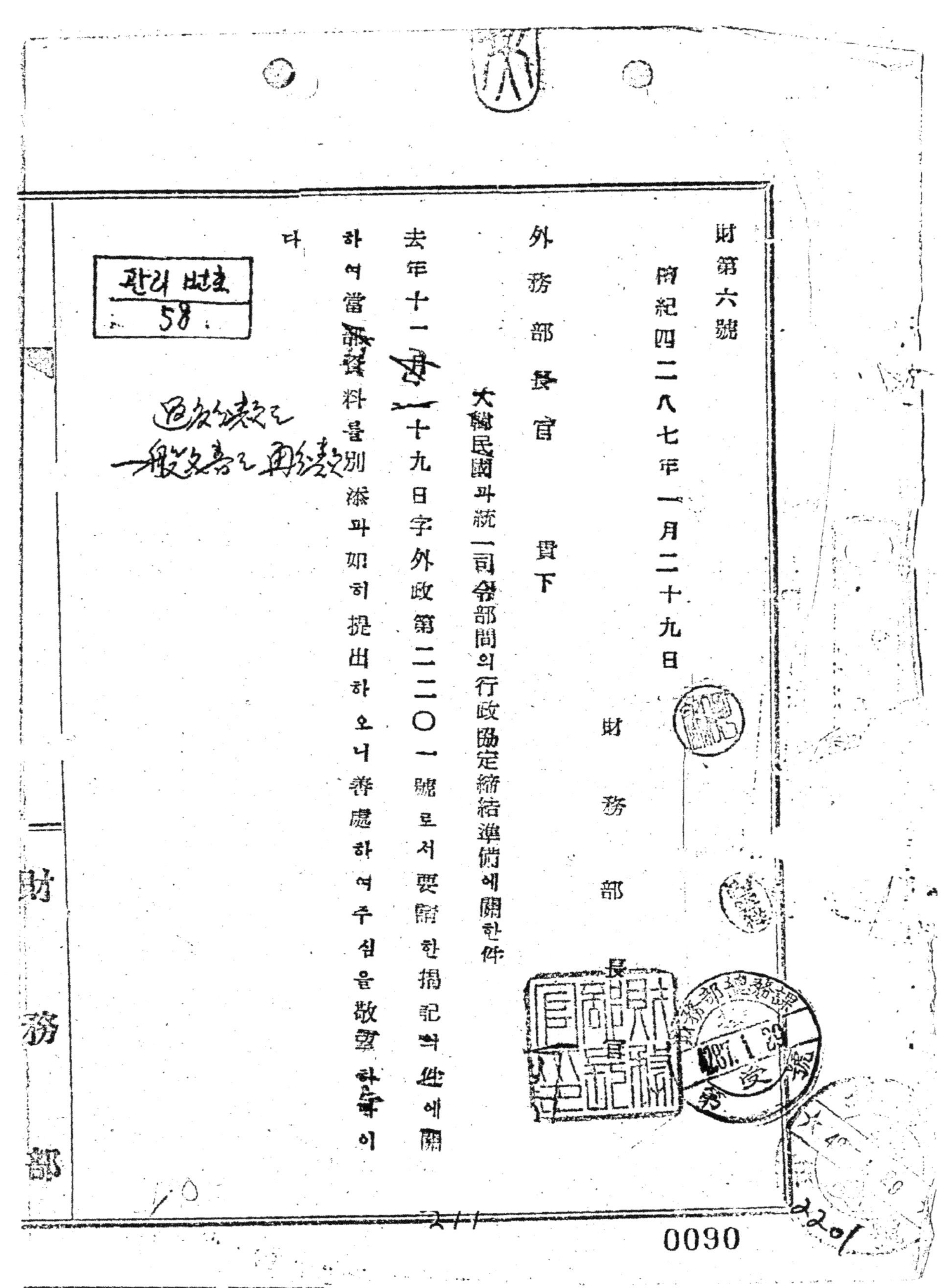

財第六號

檀紀四二八七年一月二十九日

財務部長官

外務部長官 貴下

大韓民國과統一司令部間의行政協定締結準備에關한件

去年十一月十九日字外政第二二〇一號로서要請한揭記의件에關하여當部資料를別添과如히提出하오니善處하여주심을敬望하옵나이다

관리번호 58

0090

# 行政協定資料

稅關局

**第一條** 本協定中에特別한規定이있는것을除外하고國際聯合軍및軍屬은大韓民國의稅關當局에依하여執行되는諸法令에順從하여야한다

**第二條** 國際聯合軍이그軍隊에專用하는軍需品(軍의資金을經理되는것)이軍에서管理하는輸送機關에依하여輸入되였을때는所定手續節次를省略하고通關이許與되며關稅및內國稅를賦課하지않는다

前項의軍需品이民間輸送機關에依하여輸入되였을때에는所屬部隊長의證明書를所管稅關長에게提示하여確認을받은것에限하여關稅및內國稅를免稅通關한다

**第三條** 國際聯合軍當局에서公認管理하는食堂PX、劇場、新聞社等歲出外資金에依한諸機關에서輸入하는公用品은責任經理將校의證明書를所管稅關長에게提示하여確認을받은

0091

것에限하여關稅및內國稅를免稅通關한다

前項의機關에서輸入하는國聯軍人또는軍屬의自用品은大韓民國과國聯軍當局에合意된品目別數量의範圍內에서前項에準하여關稅및內國稅를免稅通關한다

第四條 國際聯合軍및軍屬이輸入하는相當量의自用品에對하여서는輸入許可없이通關하되關稅및內國稅를賦課한다、

但本國에서日常用으로購入되고相當量의衣類및家庭用品을軍事郵便으로輸入되었을때에는關稅및內國稅를免除한다

第五條 左의境遇에는特別한情報가없는限稅關의檢査를免除한다

1. 入國또는歸國하는國際聯合軍의部隊또는軍人
2. 公用의封印있는公文書
3. 軍事郵便物또는軍事貨物

第六條 本協定에依하여免稅한物品은當該物品을免稅輸入할權利

0092

를가지고있지않은者에게處分하여서는않된다

第七條

國際聯合軍은本協定에賦與된特權의濫用을防止하기爲하여必要한措置를取하여야한다

國際聯合軍은그軍人또는軍屬에關聯하여關稅法違反行爲의防止、關稅犯被疑者의搜査、證據의蒐集、犯則物의差押과引渡、稅金과罰金의納付等을確保하기爲하여積極的인援助를提供하여야한다

國際聯合軍은軍補給輸送機關을便乘한密輸를防止하기爲하여軍專用埠頭또는軍用飛行場에稅關監視員을派遣하는데可能한援助를提供하여야한다

外務部

0093

大韓民國과統一司令部間의行政協定草案(司稅局所管內國稅關係)

第一條 統一司令部所屬國의國籍을가진者일지라도、大韓民國內에住所를두거나、一年以上居所를둔者、또는統一司令部所屬國의法律에依하여組織한法人일지라도、大韓民國內에資產또는事業을가진法人은大韓民國의法令에依하여課徵할租稅를納付할義務가있다

第二條 統一司令部軍隊의構成員(統一司令部軍隊의構成員이라함은大韓民國의領域內에滯留하는期間中統一司令部의陸軍、海軍또는空軍에屬하는人員으로서現在服務中에있는者를말한다)또는統一司令部軍隊의公認調達機關(統一司令部의軍當用이公認하고、또는規制하는各販賣所、피ㅣ엑코쓰、食堂、社交子라부劇場、新聞、其他歲出外資金에依한諸機關을말한다)이適當한證明書에依하여公用에依하여調達하는資材、需品、備品및役務에對하여는、大韓民國은다음의租稅를免除한다.

0034

但、本項에依하여免除를받어大韓民國에서購入한物品은當該租稅의免除를받고、當該物品을購入할權利를가지고있지않이한者에對하여大韓民國內에서는處分할수없다.

1. 物品稅
2. 通行稅
3. 遊興飮食稅
4. 電氣가스稅
5. 入場稅

第三條 統一司令部軍隊의公認調達機關에依한商品및役務의販賣에對하여서는大韓民國의租稅를課하지아니한다

但、統一司令部의軍當局이公認하고、規制하는新聞으로서、一般公衆에販賣될境遇에는、當該新聞에限하여도한그頒布에關한限大韓民國의租稅에應할義務가있다

前項의諸機關에依한商品및需品이大韓民國內의大衆에게販賣될

0095

境遇에는大韓民國의租稅에關한義務가있다

第四條 統一司令部軍隊의構成員軍屬(軍屬이라함은統一司令部所屬의國籍을가진文民으로서、大韓民國에滯留하는統一司令部軍隊에雇用되여이에勤務하여또는이에隨伴하는者를말한다)또는이家族(家族이라함은配偶者및二十一歲未滿의子이거나父母및二十一歲以上의子로서그生計費의半額以上을統一司令部軍隊의構成員又는軍屬에依存하는者를말한다)은이러한者가統一司令部軍隊에서의勤務또는統一司令部軍隊或은公認調達機關에依한雇用의結果로서받는所得에對하여、大韓民國의租稅를納付할義務가없다

但、前記의個人이大韓民國의源泉에서發生하는所得에對하여는大韓民國의租稅의納付를免除하는것은않이다

第五條 統一司令部軍隊의構成員軍屬또는그家族이大韓民國內에있어서物品및役務의個人的購入에對하여서는大韓民國의法令에基

40

0096

因하여 課徵하는 租稅를 免除하는것은 않이다

第六條 統一司令部軍隊는 統一司令部軍隊가 大韓民國에서 所有하고 使用하고 또는 移轉할 財產에 對하여 租稅 其他 類似한 公課를 받지 않이 한다

第七條 統一司令部軍隊의 構成員 軍屬 또는 이 家族은 이러한 者가 一時的으로 大韓民國에 滯留한다는 理由로서만 大韓民國에 所在한 有体 又는 無体의 動產의 所有, 使用, 이러한 者의 相互間의 移轉 又는 死亡에 依한 移轉에 對하여 各 大韓民國의 課稅는 免除한다.
但, 이 免除는 投資를 爲하여 또는 事業을 爲하매 大韓民國에서 所有하는 財產 又는 大韓民國에서 登錄한 無体財產權에 對하여는 免除하지 않이 한다

第八條 統一司令部軍隊 軍屬 또는 그 家族이거나 統一司令部軍隊의 公認調達機關은 이에 雇用된 大韓民國國籍을 가진 者이거나 其他國의 國籍을 가진 民間者에 對하여 支拂되는 賃金 및 諸手當에 課하는 勤勞

0097

所得稅의源泉徵收義務와納付義務를진다

第九條 統一司令部가大韓民國內에서契約에依하여、個人이나法人으로부터物品을購入하거나또는이러한者와請負契約을締結할境遇에大韓民國의各稅法에所定된隨時賦課에對한源泉徵收規定에依하여統一司令部는源泉徵收義務와納付義務를진다

第十條 統一司令部軍隊、軍屬또는그家族이거나、統一司令部軍隊의公認調達機關은大韓民國의當局에對하여、大韓民國이稅法에要求하는資料를提供할義務를진다

0098

國有財産에關하여行政協定締結에對한要望(司法局所管國有財産關係)

(說明) 統一軍司令部에依하여過去에徵用되었고또한現在徵用中의韓國領域內基地및施設中에는國有財産도不尠한바今番統一軍司令部와行政協定締結에際하여그使用許與條件을左記原則下에考慮되도록措置함으로서間接的으로財政面效果를圖謀코자함

記

一、統一軍司令部가韓國領域內基地와施設을使用함에는韓國의經濟其他諸般實情을考慮하여有償으로하도록措置할것

一、前號使用料로서既往使用分使用未淸算分에對하여는一定한期限內에이를淸算토록하고爾後使用分에對하여는定期로이를支拂토록措置할것

一、統一軍司令部가韓國領域內의基地및施設을使用中作爲不作爲의非戰鬪行爲로因하여發生한財産上의損害에對하여는統一軍司令部가그損害를報償할것

0099

一 前號損害賠償으로서本協定締結以前分에對하여는一定期限內에이를賠償토록하고締結後發生分에있어서는그때마다調査賠償하도록措置할것

一 前各號에依하여統一軍司令部가支拂하여야할基地및施設使用料와財產損害에對한賠償額은韓國政府와統一軍司令部의共同調査에依하여合意하는條件으로韓國政府를通하여支拂토록措置할것

0100

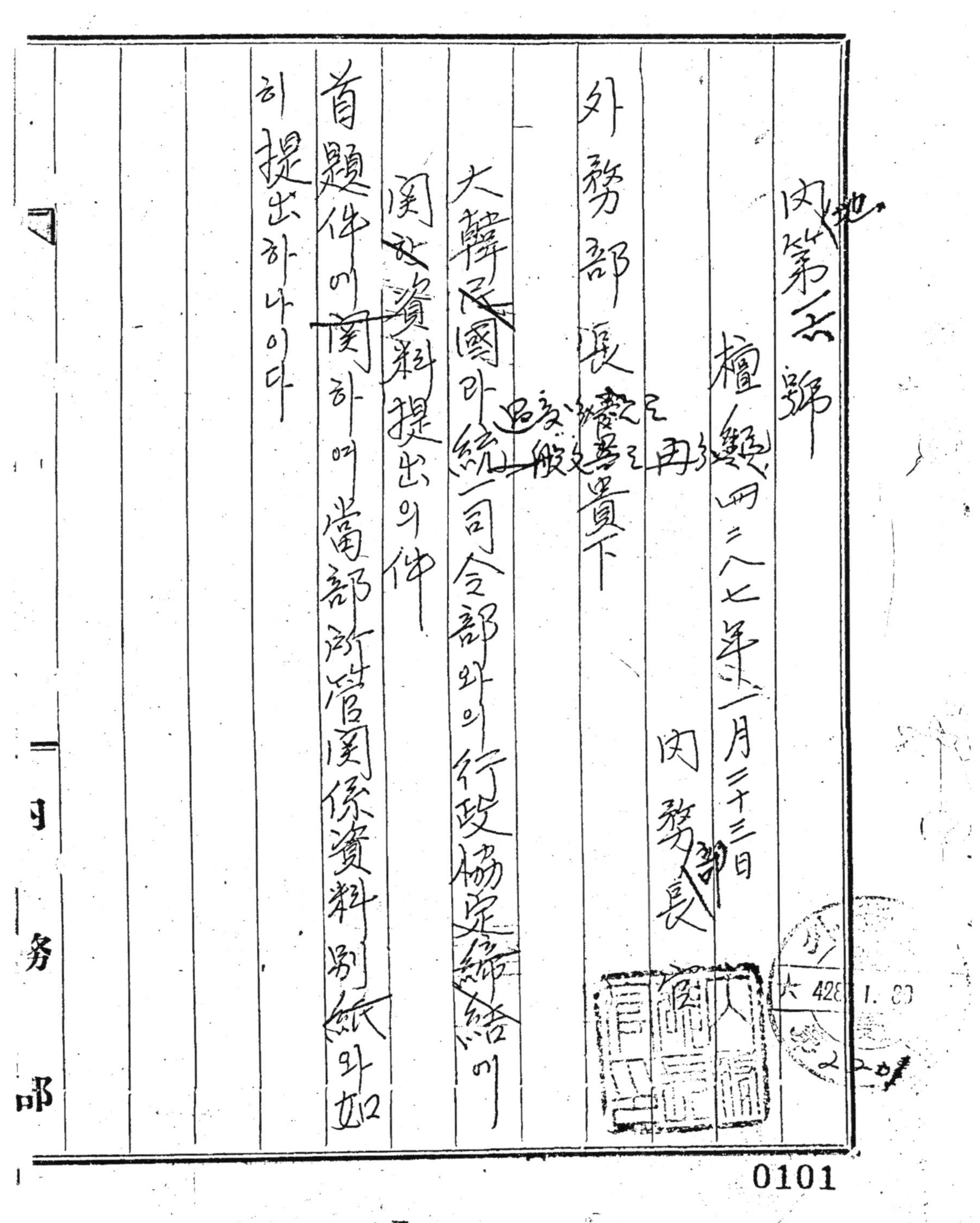

內第六號

檀紀四二八七年一月二十三日

內務部長

外務部長官貴下

大韓民國과 統一司令部와의 行政協定締結에 関한 資料提出의 件

首題件에 関하여 當部所管関係資料別紙와 如히 提出하나이다

0101

# 一、聯合軍水道使用料總括表

自一九五〇、七月
至一九五三、八月分

| 区分 | 使用量 | 使用料金 |
| --- | --- | --- |
| 서울特別市 | 九、一六六、七四〇.七 | 八五、五三二、八〇〇圓 |
| 京畿道 仁川市 | 三、七三六、三三一 | 四九、八四四、六五五 |
| 忠南道 大田市 | 一六二、四二〇 | 一、四九九、八八八 |
| 〃 江景邑 | 六四、九五二 | 九二四、七六〇 |
| 全北道 群山市 | 八八、一五三 | 六〇七、二八三 |
| 慶北道 文邱市 | 一、五四四、八〇六 | 二一、〇〇八、二二四 |
| 〃 浦項市 | 一、九二〇 | 三八、四〇〇 |
| 〃 永川邑 | 七、〇九〇 | 八四、四一〇 |
| 慶南道 釜山市 | 七、一五九、一九〇 | 六〇、五一九、四八〇 |
| 〃 馬山市 | 一五〇、二八 | 九八九、八九二 |

外務部

0102

| | | |
|---|---|---|
| 〃 蔚山邑 | 二、六〇三 | 二九、三八八 |
| 〃 泗川面 | 二、一〇〇 | 八五、九六八 |
| 〃 密陽邑 | 一、八七五 | 六七、八〇〇 |
| | | |
| 計 | 三、二〇三、三九七 | 二一、二二二、九二六 |

二、自動車登錄及運轉免許證에関한件

1. UN軍用車輛에 対하야서는 軍用番號標또는 個別記號를 鮮明히 添記하도록 할것

2. 運轉免許證은 運転試驗또는 手数料를 課하지않고 有効한 것으로 認定取扱할것

3. 私有車輛에 対하여서는 大韓民國의 法的手續을 받어 登錄番號標를 添付한后 運行하도록 할것.

0103

一、防空警報信號에関한件

防空法第一條에依據國土防空上必要한警報를制定発令토록되어있으나 現在各市道美軍基地司令部에서警報信號를任意制定使用할뿐아니라 隨時変更함으로國民이知得키難하며特히各市道의信號가区々함으로旅行者는警報의識別이困難하오니 警報信號制定과吹鳴은防空法에依據大韓民國에서管掌토록할것

一、防空法適用에関한件

陸海空의施設과軍人은軍防空에属할것이나外國軍人으로서営外居住者에対하여는住居地管轄民防空에應하여야할것임에도不拘하고往々燈火管制를爲始한防空實施에不應하는傾向이有하여民防空実施에

內務部

0104

支障을 招來하고 있음

一. 美諜報機關과 韓國警察과의 搜査限界決定에 關한 件

現在 京畿道管下 西海岸地區에는 九.二八 收復以來 至今까지 江華島 喬桐島를 爲始하여 各島嶼에 美極東司令部直屬 美第八二四〇部隊 및 同八二五〇部隊가 駐屯하고 있는바 其人的構成의 實情을 按據컨대 同地區基地司令官을 除外한 各部隊長 以下는 全部 韓國人으로 主로 一.四後退 當時 避難南下한 黃海道地區의 靑年들로 編成되어 있으며 大部分이 徵兵徵用을 忌避하기 爲한 身分保障策으로 入隊한 것으로 認定되오며 渠等은 美軍基地司令官에 阿附하여 特히 韓國軍警의 正當한 職務執行을 妨害 또는 壓力을 加하여 自主國家

0105

의威信을失墜하는事例許多한情況인바其實例로서는

가. 檀紀四二八七年七、八月頃에京畿道兵事區司令部에서江華郡內의徵兵檢査次現地에出張한現役軍人인徵兵檢査官을些少한感情으로韓國人隊員들이美軍基地司令官을使嗾하며不法引致케한事實

나. 同月日不詳頃에當時江華島와喬桐島附近에派遣駐屯中인陸軍CIC部隊及同憲兵隊等을美四四部隊의作戰을妨害한다는口實로서同隊韓國人隊員들이美軍基地司令官을使嗾하며同地區로부터右兩機關을撤收케한事實

다. 四二八八年十二月中旬頃京畿道警察局查察課喬桐分室에서對北工作中인某重大事件을八二四四部隊에

內務部

0106

서 干涉하다가 乃終에는 同事件擔當인 警察官及 工作員을 事前 所屬上官의 承認도 없이 不法引致한 事實

라. 四二八六年 十二月 下旬頃 憲兵總司令部에서 犯罪搜查次 江華島에 憲兵將校를 派遣한바 八二四部隊 韓國人隊員들이 美軍基地司令官을 使嗾 正當한 調査를 妨害한 事實

等々이 有하여 一般의 非難이 藉々할 뿐 아니라 當面緊急한 五列索出 搜查等 國家의 正當한 行政運營上 支障이 莫大하오니 美國機關으로 하여금 韓國機關에서 取扱하는 搜查事件을 干涉치 않도록 限界를 明示하는 協定措置가 必要함

0107

一、國聯搜査機関은國聯軍人및其他外國人의現行犯逮捕또는此에附随한必要한措置를講究하는以外韓國人에対한搜査權을行使할수없다 但我搜査機関에引渡키為한韓國人의現行犯逮捕는此限에不在한다

理由

國聯搜査機関으로서韓國人에対한搜査權을行使할수있다고하면我國主權에対한侵害는勿論이고 이로써國民의基本權을保障하기困難할것임으로國聯搜査機関은國聯軍人및其他外國人의現行犯逮捕또는此에附随한措置를講究하는境遇와我搜査機関에引渡키為한韓國人의現行犯逮捕以外에는韓國人에対한搜査權을行使할수없도록行政協定을締結할必要가有함

內務部

0108

다는 思料함

二、國聯軍各部隊司令官은 內外國人을 莫論하고 現行犯又는 其他重要犯人이 所轄部隊內及艦船에 逃入하였을 時는 韓國官憲의 引渡要求에 應하고 또 協助하여야 한다

理由

現行犯又는 其他重要犯人의 逮捕又는 搜査의 完璧을 期하기 爲하여 此에 行政協定을 締結할 必要가 有하다고 思料됨

三、國聯軍이라 할지라도 部隊行動을 除外한 個人行動에 있어서는 我行政法規를 遵守할 義務가 有하다

理由

0109

國聯軍이 간주하여 部隊에서 外出하여 我行政法規를 無視한 自由行動을 取한다면 一般秩序를 紊亂케 할 것임으로 此에 対한 行政協定을 締結할 必要가 有하다고 思料됨

四. 韓國人이 不法所持한 國聯軍財產回收는 韓國警察官으로 하여금 主動的인 役割을 하도록 한 美憲兵은 補助的인 範圍内에서 此에 協助하도록 할 것이다

理由

韓國人이 不法所持한 國聯軍財產을 美捜査機関에서 押收할 時에 際하여 美捜査機関에서는 韓國警察官을 帶同하는 其捜査를 韓國警察이 主動이되어 執行하는 様形式을 假裝하고 있으나 其実 此와 正反対로 韓國警察은 美捜査機関의 指示에 依하야 被動的으로 補助的

0110

인 役割을 하였을 다름이오 國主權에 依한 搜査權行
使를 하였다고는 認定키 困難할 뿐 不當라 如斯 搜査
權行使의 誤謬로 因한 國民의 被害가 不尠함에 照鑑하
여 從今 韓美合同搜査時에는 美搜査機關은 補助的
인 協助에 끝이도록 行政協定을 締結 爲要

(檀紀四二八五年 七月 二十四日 民事援助處 會議室에서 韓
美關係者 連席 會議時 合議된 事項)

一、六二五動亂으로 因하여 警備通信施設은 八〇%以上이 破
壞되여 收復后 軍用電話線으로서 臨時架設하여 警
備通信運營의 使命을 完遂하고 있는 바 美軍關係通
信線과 同一한 電柱에 竝行架設된 곳이 許多하여 美
軍通信線隊에서 架設又는 撤去及整理에 있어 一方的

0111

을 施工하는 関係上 警察通信網을 一言半句의 諒解와 連
絡도 없이 切斷又는 撤去하는 事例가 有하여 莫大한 支障을
招來하는 實情이오니 美軍과 行政的 相互連絡을 充分히
取하여 警備通信事務運營에 萬全을 期하여주심을
仰望함.

二, 治安本部와 各局間에는 遞信委託線으로서

서울 釜山間 一回線
서울 大田間 一回線
서울 光州間 一回線
大田 釜山間 一回線

以上 四回線의 長距離에 亘하는 警備通信線이 有하였으나
六二五動乱으로 因하여 破壞되었든바 遞信當局에서 復

0112

旧한回線中에서는 美軍이 専用할 있는 関係上 此를 引受
使用치 못하고 있는 現狀이오니 通信資料가 豊富한 美軍
으로서는 別途架設하여 本回線을 警察에 讓渡하심을
要請함

三、現서울市內에는 通信케―블線路에 警備有線通信線
을 依賴使用케되면 都市美觀上에도 相當히 整理할 것을 思
料되나 美軍에서 이를 全的使用하고 있는 関係上 当局에
서 別途로 己의 線으로 架設計劃中에 있으나 財政面에도 莫
大한 經費가 所要될 実情임으로 美軍과 共同使用토록
行政的 相互連絡을 取하여주시요

追伸 一、例擧하면 四二八六年三月二十六日부터 四月十三日 間에
美軍이 서울市內에서만 切断된 警備電話線路는 九○

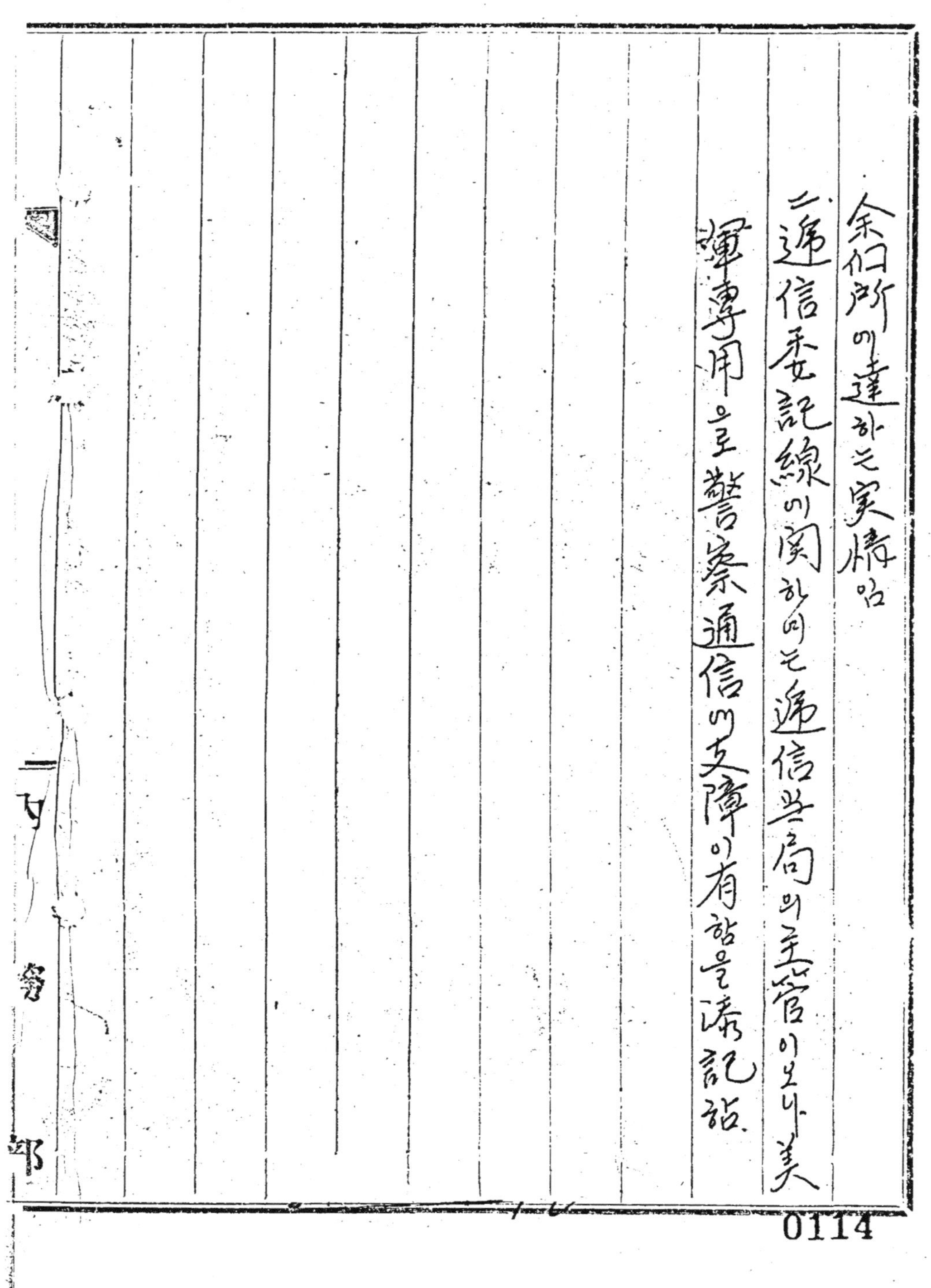
余他所에 達하는 実情임

二. 逓信委託線에 関하여는 逓信当局의 主管이오나 美

軍専用으로 警察通信에 支障이 有함을 添記함.

0114

0115

一、聯合軍水道使用料總括表

自一九五〇、七月
至一九五三、八月分

| 区分 | 使用量 | 使用料金 |
| --- | --- | --- |
| 서울特別市 | 九、一六六、七四〇七 | 八五、五二二、八〇〇圓 |
| 京畿道 仁川市 | 三、七三六、三三一 | 四九、八四四、六五五 |
| 忠南道 大田市 | 一六二、四二〇 | 一、四九、六八八 |
| 〃 江景邑 | 一六四、九五二 | 九二四、七六〇 |
| 全北道 群山市 | 八六、一五三 | 六〇七、二八三 |
| 慶北道 大邱市 | 六五四、八〇六 | 二一、〇〇八、二四四 |
| 〃 浦項市 | 一、九二〇 | 三八、四〇〇 |
| 〃 永川邑 | 七、〇九〇 | 八四、四一〇 |
| 慶南道 釜山市 | 七、一五九、一九〇 | 六〇、五一九、四八〇 |
| 〃 馬山市 | 一五〇、二八 | 九八九、八九二 |

外務部

0116

| | | |
|---|---|---|
| 〃蔚山邑 | 六〇二 | 二九、三八八 |
| 〃泗川面 | 二、一〇〇 | 八五、九六八 |
| 〃密陽邑 | 一、八八五 | 六七、八〇〇 |
| | | |
| 計 | 三、二〇二、三九七 | 二二、二二二、九二六 |

二、自動車登錄及運轉免許證에關한件

1. UN軍用車輛에対하여서는軍用番號標또는個別記號를鮮明히添記하도록할것

2. 運轉免許證은運転試驗또는手數料를課하지않고有効한것으로認定取扱할것

3. 私有車輛에対하여서는大韓民國의法的手續을받어登錄番號標를添付한後運行하도록할것

0117

一、防空警報信號에 関한件

防空法第一條에 依據國土防空上必要한 警報를 制定発令토록되어 있으나 現在各市道美軍基地司令部에서 警報信號를 任意制定使用할 뿐만 아니라 隨時変更함으로 國民이 知得키 難하며 特히 各市道의 信號가 区々함으로 旅行者는 警報의 識別이 困難하오니 警報信號制定과 吹鳴은 防空法에 依據大韓民國에서 管掌토록 할 것

一、防空法適用에 関한件

陸海空의 施設과 軍人은 軍防空에 属할 것이나 外國軍人으로서 営外居住者에 対하여는 住居地管轄民防空에 應하여야 할 것임에도 不拘한 往々燈火管制를 爲始한 防空實施에 不應하는 傾向이 有하며 民防空實施에

0118

支障을 招來하고 있음

一、美諜報機関과 韓國警察과의 搜査限界決定에 関한 件

現在 京기道管下 西海岸地区에는 九、二八 收復以來 至于까지
江華島 喬桐島를 為始하여 各島嶼에 美極東司令
部直属 美第八四○○部隊 및 同八二五○部隊가 駐屯하고 있
는바 其人的構成의 實情을 按察컨데 同地区基地司令
官을 除外한 各部隊長以下는 全部 韓國人으로 什主
로 一、四後退 当時 避難南下한 黃海道地区의 青年으로
編成되어 있으며 大部分이 徵兵徵用을 忌避하기 為
한 身分保障策으로 入隊한 것으로 認定되오며 渠等
은 美軍基地司令官에 阿附하여 特히 韓國軍警의 正
當한 職務執行을 妨害 또는 壓力을 加하여 自主國家

0119

의威信을失墜하는事例許多한情況인바其實例로서는

가. 檀紀四二八八年七八月頃에京畿道兵事区司令部에서
江華郡内의徵兵檢査次現地에出張한現役軍人인
徵兵檢査官등이些少한感情으로韓國人隊員을이美
軍基地司令官을使嗾하여不法引致케한事實

나. 同月日不詳頃에當時江華島와喬桐島内에派遣
駐屯中인陸軍C.I.C部隊及同憲兵隊等을八二四部
隊의作戰을妨害한다는口実로서同隊韓國人隊員들이
美軍基地司令官을使嗾하여同地区로부터右両機関
을撤收케한事實

다. 四二八八年十二月中旬頃京畿道警察局查察課喬桐
分室에서対北工作中인某種重大事件을八二四部隊에

서 干涉하다가 乃終에는 同事件擔當者인 警察官及

工作員을 事前 所屬上官의 承認도 없이 不法引致한 事

實

라. 四二八六年 十二月下旬頃 憲兵總司令部에서 犯罪搜査

次 江華島에 憲兵將校를 派遣한바 八四○部隊韓

國人隊員들이 美軍基地司令官을 使喉 正當한 調査

를 妨害한 事實

等々이 有하야 一般의 非難이 藉々할 뿐아니라 當面緊急

한 五列索出 搜査等 國家의 正當한 行政運營上 支障

이 莫大하오니 美國機關으로 하여금 韓國機關에서 取扱

하는 搜査事件을 干涉치 않도록 限界를 明示하는

協定措置가 必要함

0121

一、國聯搜査機関은 國聯軍人및 其他外國人의 現行犯逮捕
또는 此에 附隨한 必要한 措置를 講究하는 以外 韓國人에
対한 搜査權을 行使할수없다 但 我搜査機関에 引渡키
為한 韓國人의 現行犯逮捕는 此限에 不在한다

理由、

國聯搜査機関으로서 韓國人에 対한 搜査權을 行使할수
있다고 하면 我國主權에 対한 侵害는 勿論이고 이로써 國民
의 基本權을 保障하기 困難할 것임으로 國聯搜査機関
은 國聯軍人및 其他外國人의 現行犯逮捕 또는 此에 附
隨한 措置를 講究하는 境遇와 我搜査機関에 引渡
키 為한 韓國人의 現行犯逮捕 以外에는 韓國人에 対한 搜査
權을 行使할수없도록 行政協定을 締結할 必要가 有하

內務部

0122

다고 思料함

二、國聯軍各部隊司令官은 內外國人을 莫論하고 現行犯又는 其他重要犯人이 所轄部隊內 및 艦船에 逃入하였을 時는 韓國官憲에 引渡要求에 應할 또 協助하여야 한다

理由

現行犯又는 其他重要犯人의 逮捕又는 搜査의 完璧을 期하기 爲하야 此에 行政協定을 締結할 必要가 有하다 思料함

三、國聯軍이라 할지라도 部隊行動을 除外한 個人行動에 있어서는 我行政法規를 遵守할 義務가 有하다

理由

0123

國聯軍이 관하여 部隊에서 外出하여 我行政法規를 無視한 自由行動을 取한다면 一般秩序를 紊亂케 할 것임을 此에 対한 行政協定을 締結할 必要가 有하다고 思料됨

四、韓國人이 不法所持한 國聯軍財産回收는 韓國警察官을 하여금 主動的인 役割을 하도록 할 美憲兵은 補助的인 範圍内에서 此에 協助하여야 할 것이다

理由.

韓國人이 不法所持한 國聯軍財産을 美搜查機関에서 押收함에 際하여 美搜查機関에서는 韓國警察官을 帶同하는 其搜查를 韓國警察이 主動이 되여 執行하는 様形式을 假装하고 있으나 其實此와 正反対로 韓國警察은 美搜查機関의 指示에 依하여 被動的으로 補助的

0124

인役割을 하였을 다름이오 또한 國主權에 依한 搜査權行
使를 하였다고는 認定키 困難할 뿐 不啻라 如斯搜査
權行使의 誤謬로 因한 國民의 被害가 不尠함에 照鑑하
여 從今 韓美合同搜査時에는 美搜査機關은 補助的
인 協助에 끝이도록 行政協定을 締結 爲要

(檀紀四二八五年七月二十四日 民事援助處 會議室에서 韓
美關係者 連席 會議時 合議된 事項)

一、六二五動亂으로 因하여 警備通信施設은 八○%以上이 破
壞되여 收復後 軍用電話線으로서 臨時架設하여 警
備通信運營의 使命을 完遂하고 있는바 美軍關係通
信線과 同一한 電柱에 竝行架設된 곳이 許多하여 美
軍通信線隊에서 架設又는 撤去 및 整理에 있어 一方的

0125

을 施工하는 関係上 警察通信網을 一言半句의 諒解와 連絡도 없이 切断 又는 撤去하는 事例가 有하여 莫大한 支障을 招来하는 実情이오니 美軍과 行政的 相互連絡을 充分히 取하여 警備通信事務運営에 万全을 期하여 주심을 仰望함

二. 治安本部와 各局間에는 遞信委託線으로서

서울 釜山間 一回線

서울 大田間 一回線

서울 光州間 一回線

大田 釜山間 一回線

以上 四回線의 長距離에 亘하는 警備通信線이 有하였으나

나. 六二五動乱을 因하여 破壊되였는바 遞信当局에서 復

內務部

0126

이한 回線中에서는 美軍이 專用하고 있는 關係上 此를 引受

使用치못하고 있는 現狀이오니 通信資料가 豊富한 美軍

으로서는 別途 架設하여 本回線을 警察에 讓渡하심을

要請함

三. 現 서울 市內에는 遞信케-블 線路에 警備有線通信線

을 依賴使用케되면 都市美觀上에도 相當히 整理할 것으로 思

料되나 美軍에서 이를 全的使用하고 있는 關係上 當局에

서 別途 己무線으로 架設計劃中에 있으나 財政面에도 莫

大한 經費가 所要될 實情임으로 美軍과 共同使用토록

行政的 相互連絡을 取하여주시옵

追伸一. 例擧하면 四二八六年 三月二十六日부터 四月十二日間에

美軍이 서울 市內에서만 切斷된 警備電話線路는 九

0127

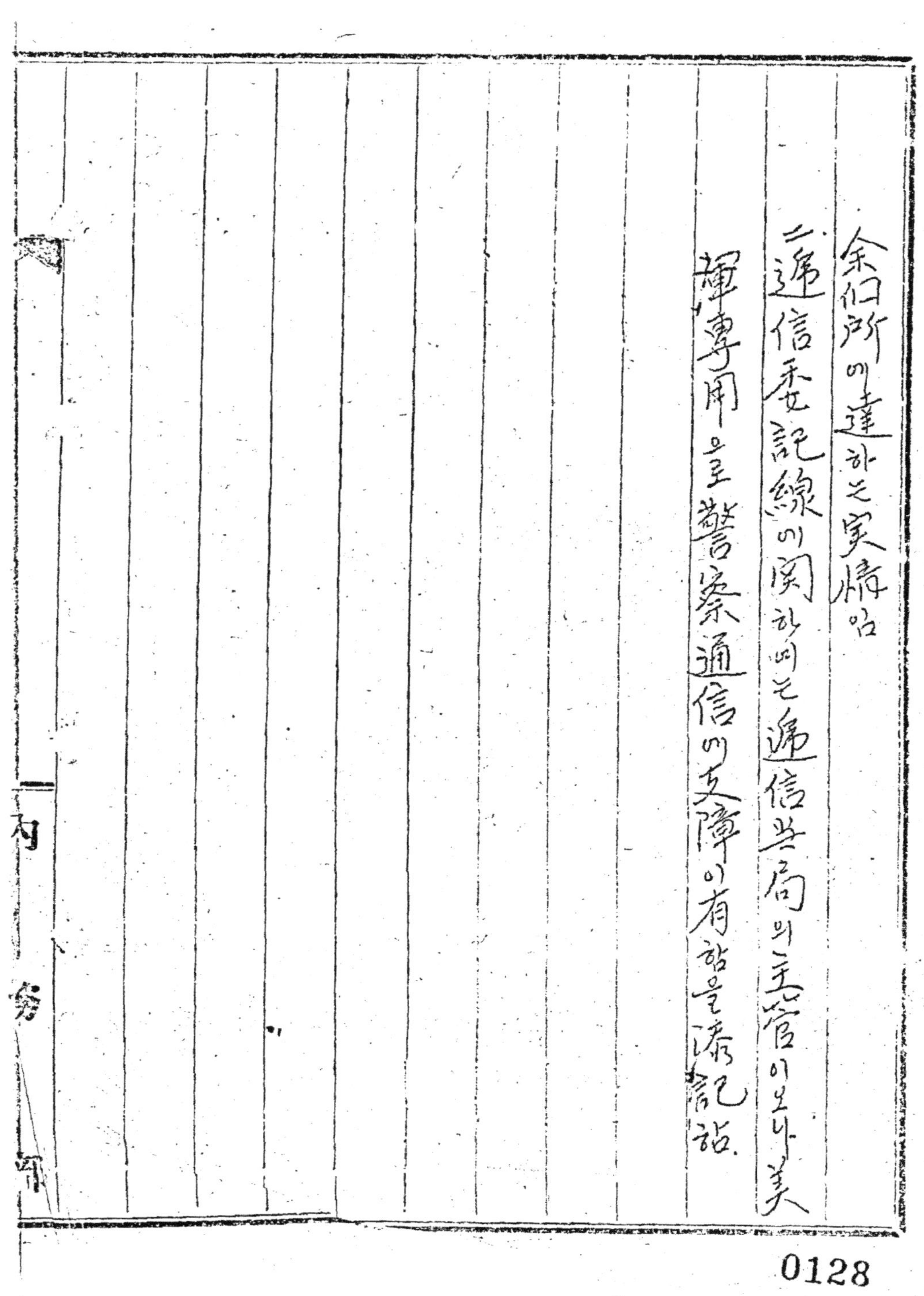

余们所에 達하는 実情임

二. 通信委託線에 関하여는 通信부局의 主管이오나 美軍專用으로 警察通信에 支障이 有함을 添記함.

0128

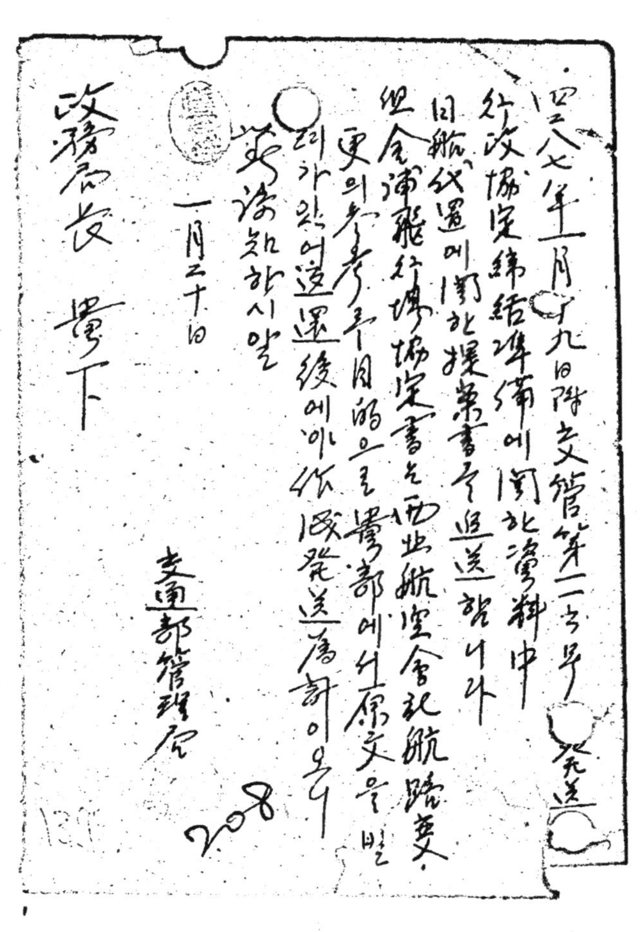

四二八七年一月十九日附交管第一六号

行政協定締結準備에 關한 參考資料中

同船舶位置에 關한 提案書를 返送합니다

但金浦飛行場協定書는 西北航空會社航路變

更의 參考目的으로 貴部에서 原文을 빌

리가 있어 返還後에야 作成發送할 計이오니

照諒知하시압

一月二十日

交通部管理局

政務局長 貴下

208

0129

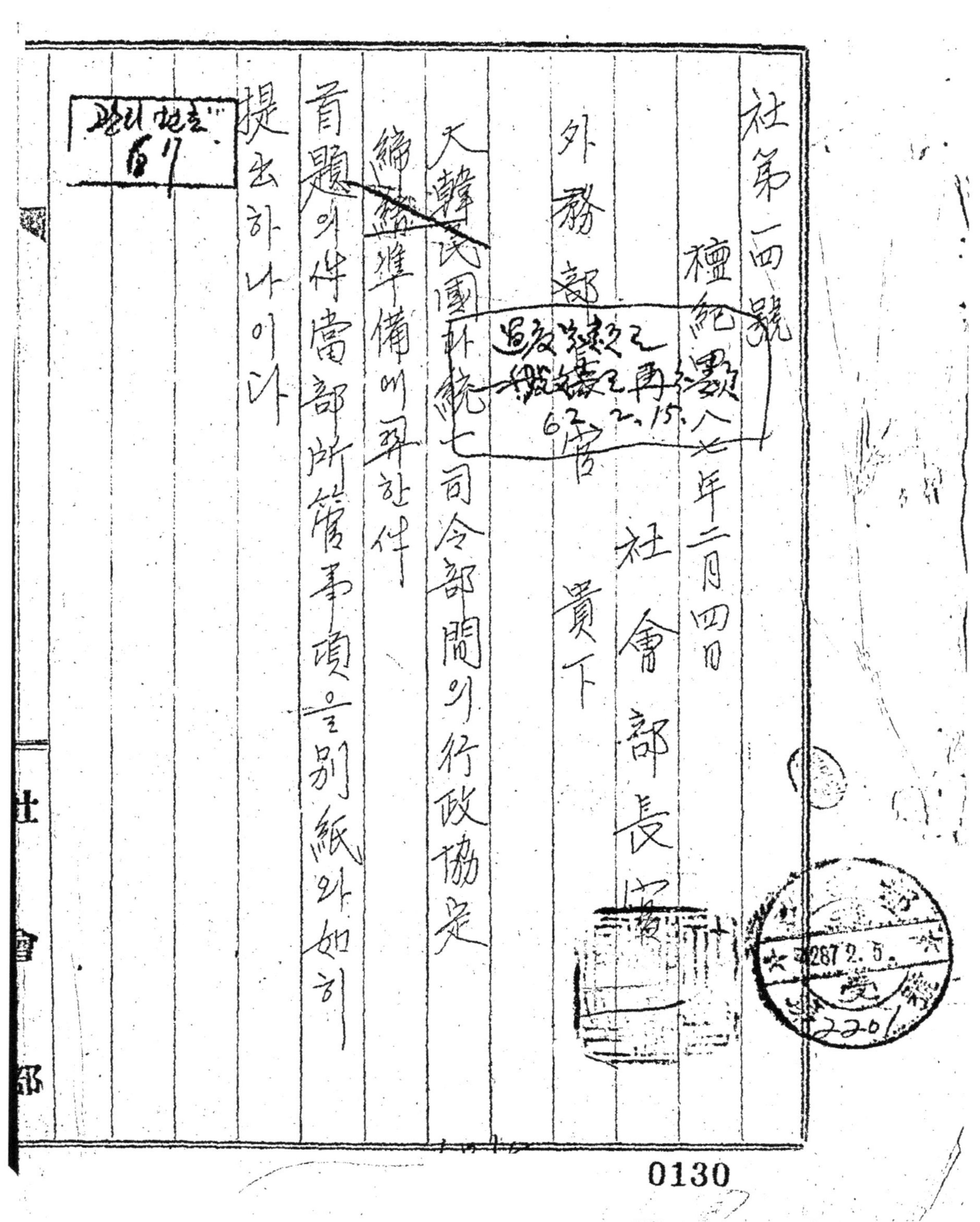

관리번호 61

社第一四號

檀紀四二八七年二月四日

社會部長官

外務部長官 貴下

大韓民國과 統一司令部間의 行政協定

締結準備에 關한 件

首題의 件 當部所管事項을 別紙와 如히

提出하나이다

社會部

0130

大韓民國과 統一司令部 間의 行政協定

締結準備에 關한 件

社會部 社會局 住宅課 所管

一、KCAC 計劃에 依한 各地方學生住宅建設의 件

去年度 學生住宅 一三、一〇〇戶를 各戰災地方에 建設키로 연객으로부터 左記와 如한 資材의 配定을 받었으나 現在까지 各地方에 輸送된 것은 十% 遲延되므로 建設工事 進行이 円滑치 못하니 연객에서 早速輸送하여주기를 要望함

配定된 援助資材 內容

一、割當年月日 四二八六年四月二日字

二、割當書號 自四七 至五二號

0131

(3) 割當資材 木材 一、六六五、〇〇〇 BFT

세멘 四六、〇〇〇 B/G

못 三三三、〇〇〇 LBS

유리 二五五、〇〇〇 S/F

루핑 六、〇〇〇 S/F

二、UNKRA 計劃에 依한 再建住宅建設의 件

去八六年에 UNKRA와의 再建計劃에 依하여 別紙写本과 如한 協定을 締結하고 再建住宅 五五〇〇戶를 建設키로 되엿는바 現在까지 二〇〇戶分에 不過하는 主要資材만을 받엇으므로 協定實行을 累次 UNKRA에 要望하엿으나 于今까지 成果를 보지 못하고 있읍니다

0132

三、當部所管什을 特別市永登浦区楊平洞所在
中央覺心學院(建坪一、五〇〇坪 垈地八、〇〇〇坪)은 檀紀四二八三年
十月二十八日以後 現在에 이르기까지 UN軍에서
使用中에 있는바 此에 對한 行政的措置를 要
望함

社會部 勞動局所管

一、協定事項要旨

人、雇傭과 勤勞條件、勤勞者保護條件과
勤勞者의 權利는 大韓民國法令에 依據한다

二、理由

主로 美軍이 國內에 駐屯하게된 以後 特히
六、二五를 契機로 하여 作戰救護其他物資

0133

輸送等에 있어서 第一線的 後方에 多數의
韓人을 雇傭하고 있는바 이들 韓人労務者
에 対한 勤労條件 其他 労務保護에 있어서
美軍側이 一方的인 決定을 強要할 뿐만 아
니라 労動関係法令이 實施된 現在에 있어
서도 勤労者의 團結權, 團体協約權에
對한 協助가 不足하거나 또는 不応하고 있는
現狀이며 더욱이 現下 가장 重大事項인
駐韓勤労動員法實施에 있어서 八軍側이
本法律에 依據하여 決定한 勤労條件을
履行하지 않은 結果 賃金의 一部 (一日當
一〇〇환中 八軍負担 四五환 政府負担 五五환)

0134

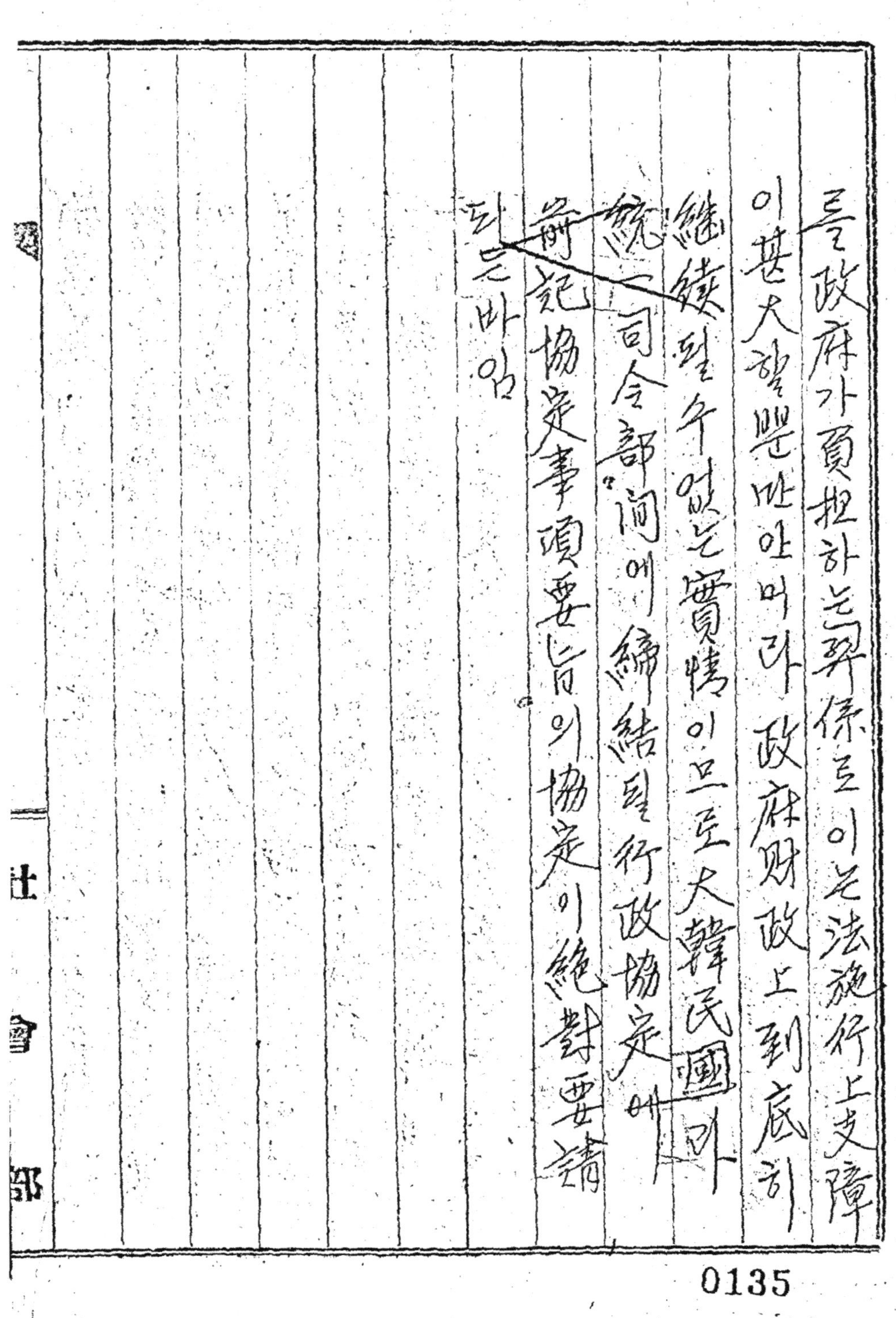

를政府가負担하는關係로이는法施行上支障
이甚大할뿐만아니라 政府財政上到底히
繼續될수없는實情이므로大韓民國과
統一司令部間에締結될行政協定에
前記協定事項要旨의協定이絶對要請
되는바임

社 會 部

0135

六月 日(一九五三年) UNKRA의 書翰

飜譯文(UNKRA側 提案)

住宅計劃

『大韓民國政府』를 政府라 稱하고

『韓國UN再建團』은『UNKRA』라고 稱한다

『UN司令部』는 一九五三年부터 一九 年까지 下記事項을 合意한다

第一款 目的

一九五三年 UNKRA計劃範囲에서 約四四〇〇戶의 住宅을 建築하는데 있어서 合意하는것이 目的입니다

이 建築計劃은 將次每年度의 住宅建築擴張

0136

計劃의最初段階이다、 이目的을爲하여住宅營團이나社會部가管理하는合法的인法人이政府를代行하여運營할것이며合意된條目下에서履行한데있어서政府代行으로서活動할것이다

第二款 住宅

標準都市型및標準農村型은社會部와UNKRA住宅局과의協力으로研究設計하여야한다 이機關들은合意下에諸般建築이 이러한標準型으로서잘進行될것이다

(A) 條項에는住宅建築計劃及資材와價格에亘한諸般內容이表示되여있다

第三款 場所 및 時期

(B) 條項에는 住宅建設時期及場所의 内容이 되였다 此도 亦是 社會部와 UNKRA의 兩側에서 合意하여야 한다

第四款 導入된 資材 및 施設

UNKRA는 政府와 合意下에 外資를 導入할것이며 導入할 時는 韓國港口까지 輸送하여 온다 (B)의 計劃内容대로 建築資材購入과 輸送에 便宜를 供與한다

第五款 受渡

到着한 資材는 適當한 代行機関을 通한 政府는 資材의 補給을 UNKRA로서 計劃된 船舶或은 指定

社會部

0138

場所에서 受領하며 그 荷役 및 保管은 政府가 準備하여야 하며 따라서 建築地에 輸送할 것이다

第六款 建築

一、上記와 같이 導入된 資材를 가지고 政府가 管理하는 住宅營團이나 合法的 法人을 代行으로 한 政府는 國産資材와 勞力을 準備하고 (B)條項에 表示된 것과 같이 計劃된 場所와 時期에 建築할 것이다

二、UNKRA는 政府에게 技術的 援助를 賦與할 것이다

(A) 各種 住宅 担當者와 土木技術者의 努力을 提供하며 指導할 것이다

(B) 建築에 使用된 煉瓦機의 使用法에 있어서도 政府의 特殊한 講習生들을 訓練시킬 것이다

0139

第七款 所有權

一、住宅建設希望者는 其垈地를 提供할 것이며

二、建築物이 竣工되면 政府는 住宅建設希望者에 그住宅의 飛當과 運用金을 十年以內 償還拂로 賣渡하여 그 所有權을 移換한다

三、政府는 住宅所有者로부터 償還義務의 總價格에 該當되는 金額을 受納하며 此의 十年間을 通하여 償還받은 金額은 UNKRA 援助資金計定口座나 或은 復興資金口座나 其外의 와맞안가지 口座에 預金할 것이다. 이 資金은 UNKRA 再建計劃에 導入하기 爲하여 賣買된 資材및 器具의 價格交換率로 換算

0140

하야 UNKRA에 納付할 것이다 ( )

四 UNKRA 再建會計에 入金된 此의 總金額은 將次 韓國住宅建設의 發展을 爲하여 運營基金으로서 社會部가 管理하는 住宅營團이나 合法的機関에 自發的으로 支拂할 것임니다 (政府와 合意하지 않이하면 此限에 不在)

第八款 政府의 協助

一, 政府는 UNKRA에 此計劃의 統計 및 進行狀況을 報告할 것이며 UN總會에 對하여 UNKRA가 義務完遂함에 必要로 할 때 何時를 不問하고 恒常 住宅營團이나 合法的法人으로 하여금 此計劃에 對한 帳簿와 金錢出納會計簿 및

0141

住宅建設地一覧表를備置시켰다가要求에
依하여閱覧할수있게할것이다

二、政府는될수있는限國内資材를利用하되不得
已한事情에있어서外資를必要로할때
NK側는其導入을是認할것이다

第九款 UN司令部의協助

以上와計劃이合意를보게되였을時는 UN司令
部는此計劃推進에있어서必要되는諸般港灣
및鉄道便과이게따르는機関을通하여便宜를
供與할것이다

一九五三年六月 日 釜山에서

大韓民國政府를爲하여

0142

UN韓國再建團을 [illegible]하며

UN司令部를 爲하며

0143

「美第八軍司令官에게보낸書翰文」(一九五三年七月九日字)

敬愛하는테일러將軍閣下

閣下께서는本官이一九五三年七月一日字로閣下께보내드린大韓國法律第二九二號戰時勤勞動員法과同施行令을充分히詳考하셨을줄로믿읍니다

同法은法에依하여大韓民國々民을勞務에動員함에있어서優越하고도最高의權威를갖이는것입니다

이法律은大韓民國領土內에서大韓民國々民을勞務에動員하고저할때에는大韓民國政府는勿論、軍官民을莫論하고如何한使用者라도그適用을받은것이며、따라서이法에依하지아니하고는大韓民國々民을種類와如何를不問하고强制로勞務에從事시킬수없는것입니다

於九

0144

本官●閣下께서 ●管轄하고있는 勞務●師団(K.S.C)에 対한 過去의 勞務者動員成績이 良好하지못하였다는것을 잘알고있으며 또한 至極히 遺憾으로 生覺하는바입니다 이와같이 動員이 如意하지 못하였든 理由로는 動員計劃과 이들勞務者自身과 그家族의 生計를 維持할수있는勞動條件(賃金、被服、給食、其他勞務管理)이 法律에 依하여 保障되지못하였다는 点을 들수있읍니다. 그런까닭에 大韓民國政府와 國會는 過去의 經驗에 비추어 勞務動員에 있어서 不合理한 点을 除去하고 戰爭遂行과 後方建設에 所要되는 勞動力을 円滑하게 供給하기爲하여 前記와같은 戰時勤勞動員法을 制定實施하게되었으며、 一九五三年七月三日부터는 戰時勤勞動員法에 依하여서만 韓國人勞務者를 動員하기로 되었읍니다

그러므로 閣下께서는 閣下께서管轄하고계시는 勞務師団에、 繼續하여

0145

韓國人勞務者를 使用하고저 할때에는 戰時勤勞動員法과 同施行令에 定하는바에 依하여 세로운 節次를 밟어야 할것입니다

即 戰時勤勞動員法第五條의 規定에 依하여 閣下가 勞務師团에 所要되는 人員數, 就業場所, 作業種類, 動員期間, 賃金, 給食, 被服, 傷害補償, 旅費 其他 勤勞條件을 明示하여 大韓民國國防部長官을 經由하여 本官에게 새로히 申請하여야 하며 法第十四條第一項의 規定에 依한 旅費와 第十六條第一項의 規定에 依한 治療費와 慰藉料로 支拂하여야 하며 特히 法第十四條第二項의 規定에 依하여 別途로 定하여지는 賃金의 一個月分에 該当하는 金額을 그 家族에게 先拂하여야 한다

그리고 本官은 法第七條의 規定에 依하여 勞務師团에 韓國人勞務者가 使

0146

用될境遇에 貴下께서는 最少限度左의 勤労條件을 履行하여주시기를要請하는바입니다 그리고 아울러 提示하는 勤労條件은 労務師団에 從事하는 労務者는 一線地区에서 服務하다는 点을 考慮에 넣고 韓國에 있어서의 現行一般労賃을 基準으로 하였다는 것을 参考로 말씀드립니다

一、給食、被服、寝具宿所는 服務期間中 労務를 堪当하고 그 体力을 減少하지 않을 程度의 것을 一切 貴下가 負担할 것

二、賃金(前項의 給食、被服、寝具、宿所外에)은 固定給으로 月二〇〇圓으로 하되 労務時間이 (時間超過時에는 基本賃金에 五割加算의 時間外手当을 支拂할 것

三、時히 就業場所가 着弾距離内인 境遇에는 前項賃金의 五倍를 支拂할 것

四、労務者의 往復旅費는 戰時勤労動員法施行令附表旅費額을 支拂할 것

0147

있는 戰時勤勞動員法을 根據로 한 것입니다 그리고 勞務動員에 關한 權限은 本官이 保有하고 있으며 最大限度 上記한 勤勞條件이 充足되지 않는 限 遺憾되나마 本官은 法에 依하여 動員을 命令할 수 없는 것입니다

그러므로 作戰에 支障이 없도록 勞務動員의 萬全을 期하기 爲하여서는 法에 依據하여 貴下와 本官과의 緊密한 協調가 要請되는 바이오니 貴下께서는 早速한 時日內에 法에 依한 새로운 節次를 밟아주심을 바랍니다

勞務師団에 從事할 韓國人 勞務者의 円滑한 動員을 期하기 爲하여 本社會部의 關係官과 貴側의 關係官 사이에 充分하고도 隔意 없는 協議가 있기를 要請하는 바입니다

社會部長官

朴述音

0148

美八軍司令官

테일러 將軍 閣下

0143

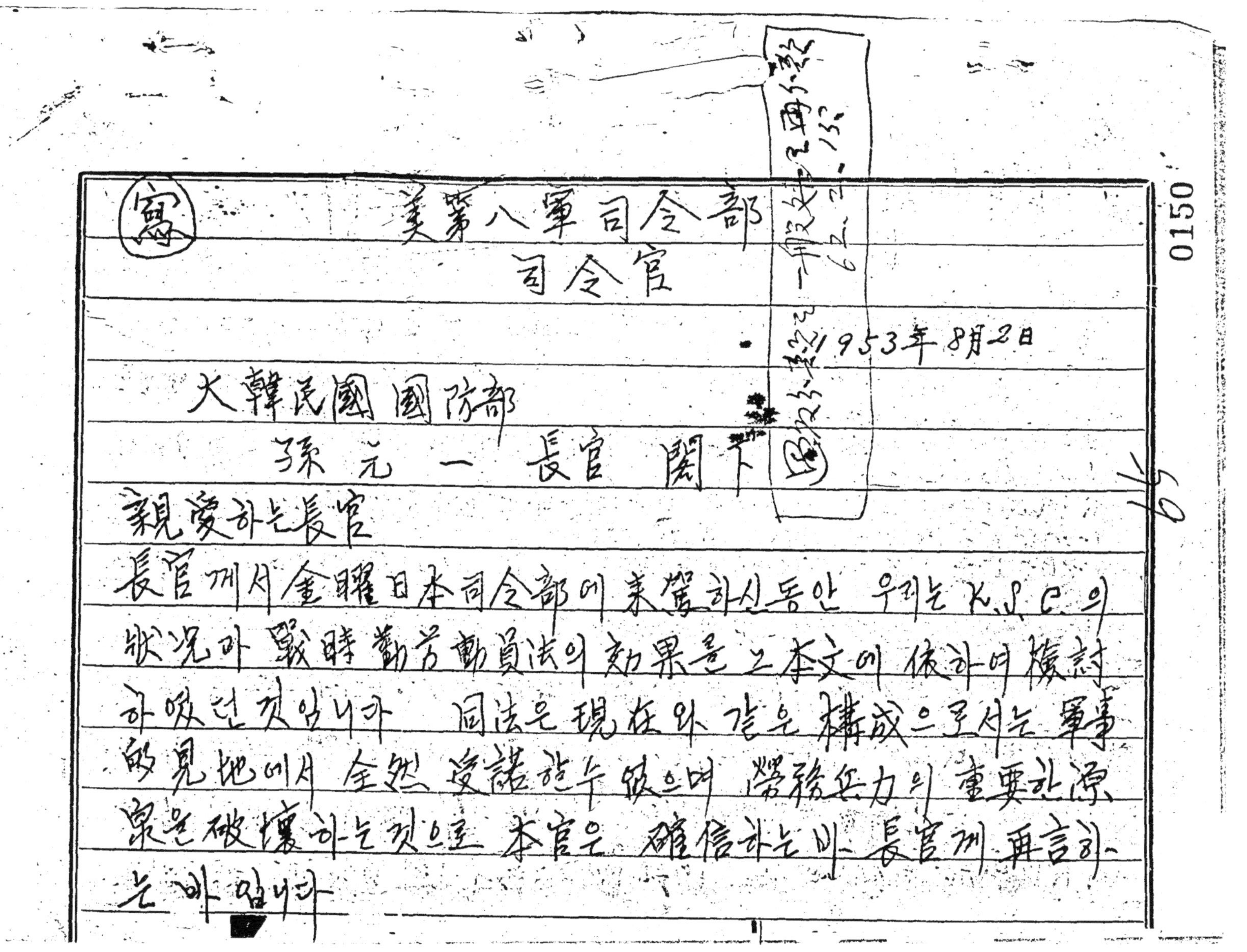

0150

寫

美第八軍司令部

司令官

1953年 8月 2日

大韓民國 國防部

孫元一 長官 閣下

親愛하는 長官

長官께서 金曜日 本司令部에 來訪하신 동안 우리는 K.S.C의 狀況과 戰時勤労動員法의 効果를 그 本文에 依하여 檢討하였던 것입니다. 同法은 現在와 같은 構成으로서는 軍事的 見地에서 全然 受諾할 수 없으며 労務兵力의 重要한 源泉을 破壞하는 것으로 本官은 確信하는 바 長官께 再言하는 바 입니다

K.S.C.의 將來에 關하여 韓國政府는 그 輪廓을 明白히하는
決定을 早速히 지어주도록 本官은 强調하고 싶습니다
戰時勤労動員法이 失効한 日字인 1953年7月3日以後募集이
缺如으므로 因하여 K.S.C.의 實際兵力은 承認된 100,000名
으로부터 90,951名으로 減退하였읍니다 이外에 契約條件인
6箇月의 服務期限이 넘어 即時解雇하여야할 労動者가 現在,
26,699名 있읍니다 本官은 參謀에서 이들의 解雇를 即時実施하
고 6箇月의 服務를 마친 K.S.C. 労務者의 分類를 継續하도록
指示하였읍니다 이 措置는 K.S.C.의 現兵力을 더 減少시킬
것입니다 混乱을 加一層惹起케한 要因은 無責任한 情報
의 流布乃至戰時勤労法에 規定된 3箇月 服務期間에 根據한
命令等의 發布입니다 本官은 長官께서 勤労動員法의 適用이

0151

確定的으로 施行되기 前에 이러한 狀態를 갖고 있어서 6個月
의 服務를 繼續하도록 勸誘하여 주심을 바랍니다.
要約컨대 K.S.C.는 新規의 募集은 없지 그러나 6個月服務
期間이 滿了된 사람은 繼續服務되어 나가므로 말미암아 漸々
消滅 解體될 것입니다
美人軍은 軍의 戰闘力 增進을 위하여 그 最大의 協力을 傾注
하려 할때 그 軍事力의 重大한 附屬隊인 勞務部隊를 이와같
이 消失하여 가고 있읍니다 軍의 勞務提供은 그 軍의 戰斗
를 擁護하려는데 그러나 彼此가 相反된 行動을 取하고
있는 것입니다
K.S.C.의 將來에 關한 大韓民國 政府의 意向을 早速히 알려
주시고 또한 政府의 所信이 [illegible]

0152

敬具

막스웰 D 테일러

司令官

0153

親愛하는 헤일리 將軍閣下 (一九五三、八、一〇)

閣下께서 一九五三年八月二日字로 K.S.C 問題에 關하여 大韓民國國防部長官에게 보내신 書翰을 國防部로부터 勞務社会部에 傳達된 바에 依하여 本官은 同書翰에서 表示된 閣下의 見解를 알게되었읍니다 同書翰에 對하여서는 別途國防部

0154

長官으로부터 閣下에게 回答이 있을 것으로 믿습니다만은 이 機会에 労務動員을 主管하는 本官의 見解를 거듭 披瀝하는 바입니다.

첫째 閣下께서는 同書翰에서 大韓民國法律인 戰時勤労動員法을 受諾할수 없으며 服務期間 六個月이 満了한 者에 限하여 解除한다고 하였

0155

戰時勤勞動員法은 大韓民國의法律이며 K.S.C.에 服務하고 있는 韓人勞務者에게 適用되는 同法에는 服務期間이 三個月로 規定되어있다는 것을 再言하는 바입니다.

万一 閣下께서 K.S.C. 勞務者에게 該當한 法에 依한 報酬를 支拂하지 아니하거나 服務期間 三個月이 滿

0156

了한後 그들의 自由歸還을 制止한다고하였음 閣下께서는 韓國人을 不法으로 抑留하고 自由意思에 反하여 勞動을 强制하였다는 結果를 招來케 할것입니다.

둘째 閣下께서는 戰時勞動者로 因하여 K.S.C의 破綻을 招來한다고 하였는데 이는 戰時勞動者法의 精神에

0157

韓國政府의 方針이라는 全然 相反되는 誤解라는 것을 本官은 明確하게 指摘하고 싶읍니다.

그 理由로는 戰時勤勞動員法은 韓國의 實情에 비추어 勞務動員이 가장 円滑히 達成되기를 目的으로 制定된 法律인바 閣下께서 戰時勤勞動員法과 同法에 依據하여 發布된 命令에

規定된 節次를 가추고 勞務者의 供給을 要

請하신다면 韓國政府는 그 要請에 應할 用意

를 가지고 있는 것입니다. K.S.C.를 包含

한 一切의 勞務動員에 關한 事項은 一九五三年 七

月 三日부터 本官이 管掌하는 바이오니 閣下께서는

K.S.C 問題에 對하여 直接 本官에게 連絡하여

0159

주시기를 바라오며 本官이 閣下에게 보내드린 一九五三年 七月 一日字, 同 七月 九日字附 公書翰을 充分히 研究하시와 K.S.C. 問題의 早速한 解決이 있으시기를 要請하는 바입니다

一九五三年 八月 日

社會部長官 朴述音

0160

社勞第　號

檀紀四二八六年　月八日

(보존문서를 일반문서로 재분류 62. 2. 15.)

社會部長官

國防部長官 貴下

戰時勤勞動員法實施에 關한 件

首題의 件 戰時勤勞動員法實施에 隨伴하여 美第八軍所管勞務部隊에 勤務하고 있는 韓人勞務者에 對한 同法適用에 關하여서는 其間當部와 美第八軍當局間에 動員節次 勤勞條件等問題에 關하여 折衝이 進行되고 있는 中 美第

0161

八軍當局은 一九五三年八月二日字 貴官許 美第八
軍司令官名儀書翰(八月七日貴部로부터 當部
에 傳達된 書翰寫本에 依함)으로서 戰時勤勞
動員法을 受諾할수 없다 고 하였으며 戰時勤勞
動員法과 勞務師團과의 關係에 對하여서는
屢次에 亘한 別添本官의 公函外에 貴部또는
當部 關係官으로부터 屢次에 亘하여 八軍當局
에 說明하였을 뿐아니라 別添 一九五三年 七月十
日字 八軍司令官書翰에 對한 貴官의 一九五三年
七月二十五日字書翰에 依하여 過去國防部와
八軍사이에 締結된 諸種協定으로 戰時勤勞動員法
에 依하여 處理된것이 公式文書로서 明瞭하게

0162

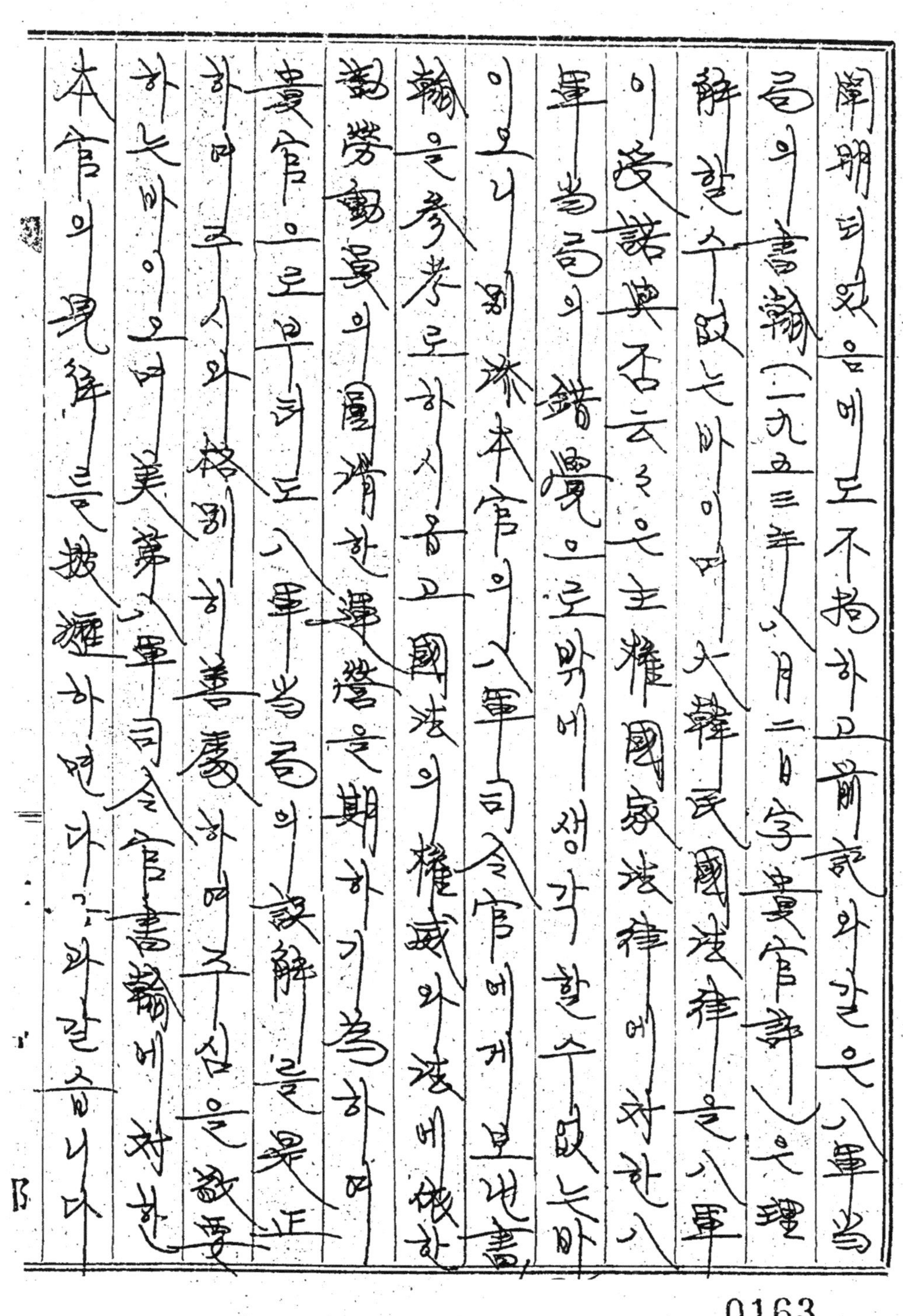

闡明되었음에도 不拘하고 前記와 같은 軍當局의 書翰(一九五三年 八月 二日字 貴官許)은 理解할 수 없는바이며 大韓民國法律을 軍이 受諾與否云云은 主權國家法律에 對한 軍當局의 錯覺으로 밖에 생각할 수 없는바이오니 別添 本官의 軍司令官에게 보낸 書翰을 參考로 하시옵고 國法의 權威와 法에 依한 勤勞動員의 圓滑한 運營을 期하기 爲하여 貴官으로부터도 軍當局의 誤解를 是正하여주시와 格別히 善處하여주심을 敬要하는바이오며 美第八軍司令官書翰에 對한 本官의 見解를 披瀝하면 다음과 같읍니다

0163

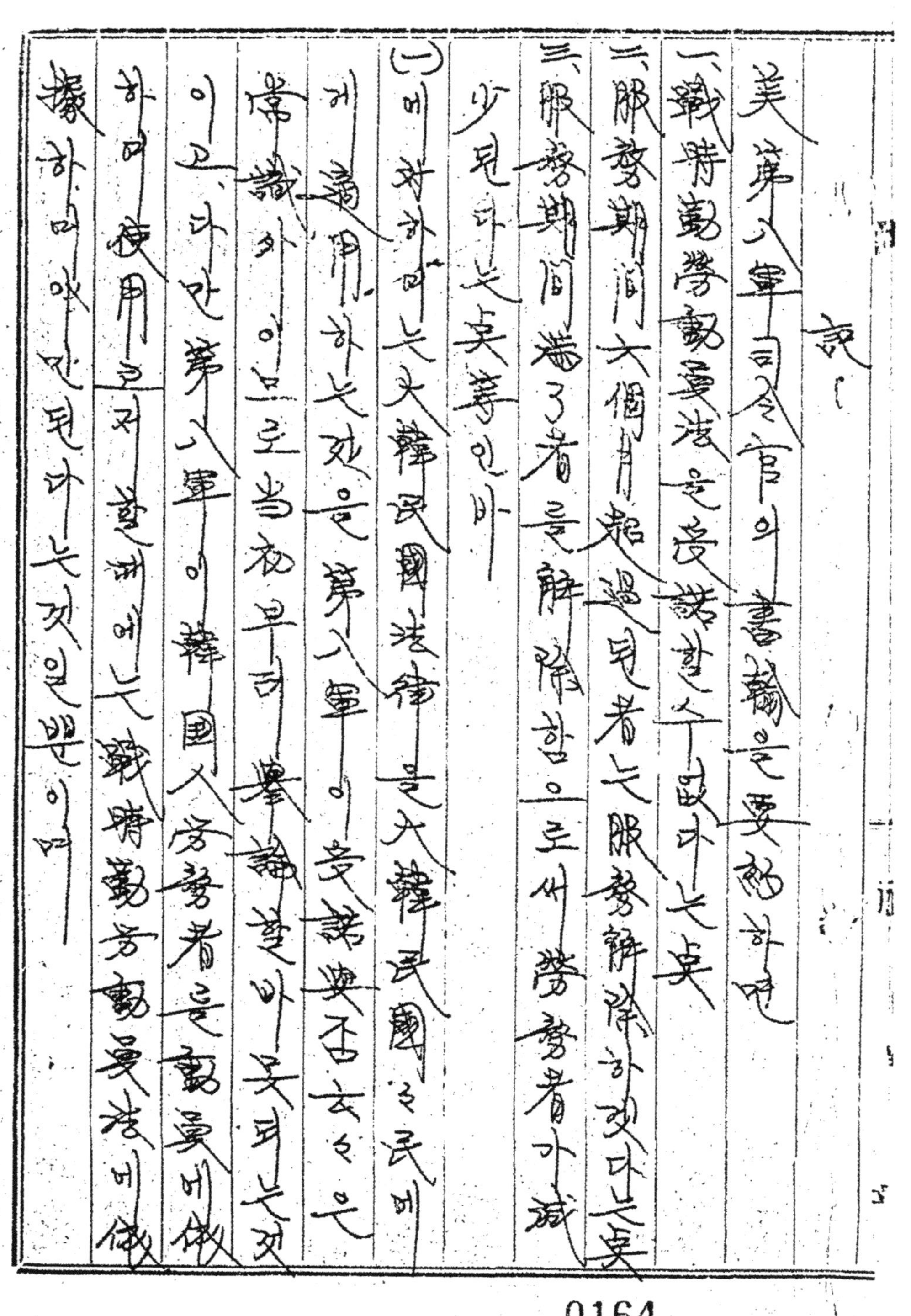

記

美第八軍司令官의 書翰을 要約하면

一、戰時勤勞動員法을 受諾할 수 없다는 点

二、服務期間 六個月 超過된 者는 服務解除하겠다는 点

三、服務期間 滿了者를 解除함으로써 勞務者가 減少된다는 点等인 바

(一) 에 對하여는 大韓民國法律은 大韓民國 及 民에게 適用하는 것은 第八軍이 受諾與否 云々은 常識外이므로 当初부터 議論할 바 못되는 것이고, 다만 第八軍이 韓國人 勞務者를 動員에 依하여 使用코자 할 時에는 戰時勤勞動員法에 依據하여야 된다는 것일 뿐이며

0164

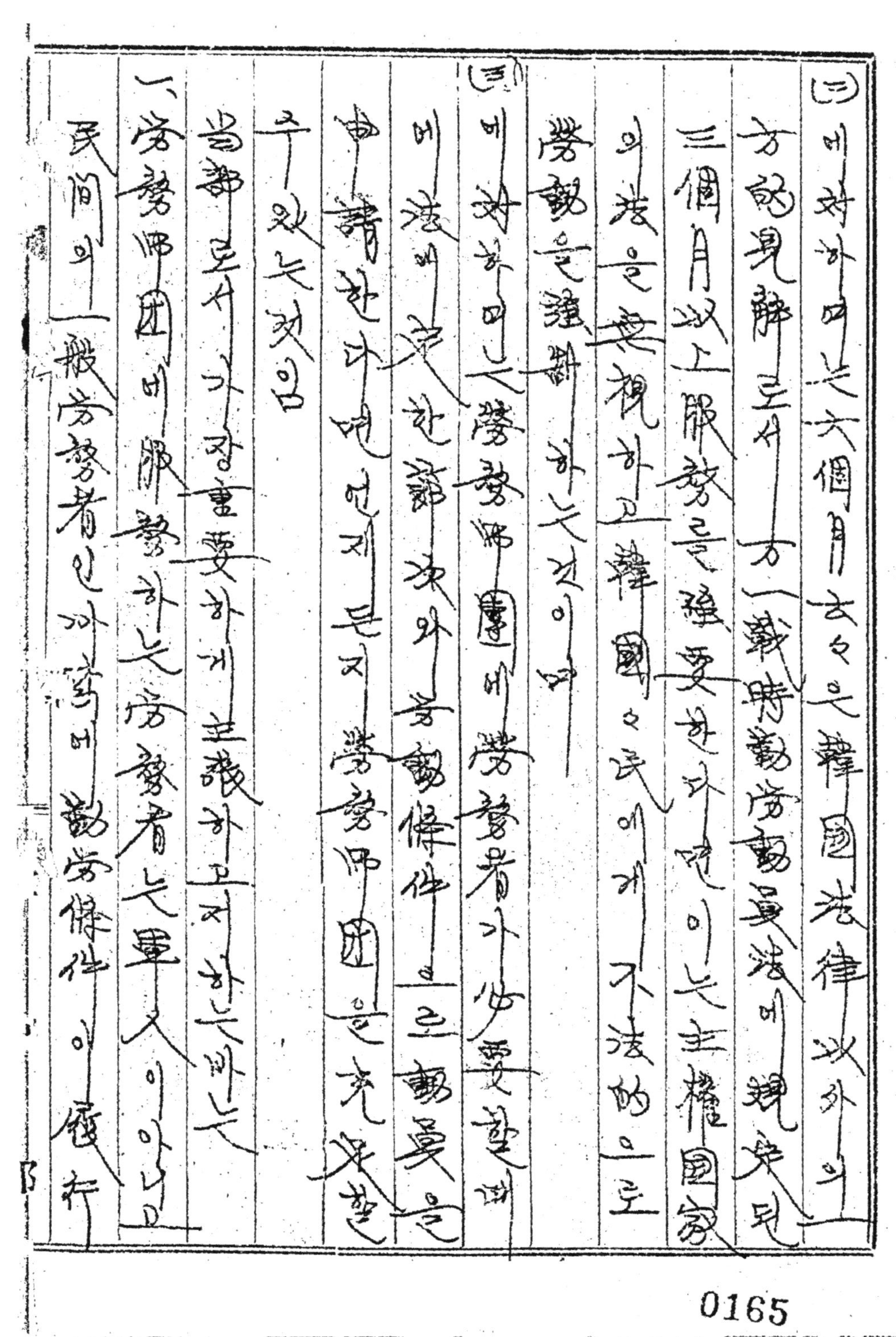

(二) 에 對하여는 六個月 又는 韓國法律 以外의
方式見解로서 一方 戰時勤勞動員法에 規定된
三個月 以上 服務를 強要한다면 이는 主權國家
의 法을 無視하고 韓國々民에게 不法的으로
勞動을 強制하는 것이다
(三) 에 對하여는 勞務團에 勞務者가 必要할 때
에 法에 定한 辭令과 勞動條件으로 動員을
申請한다면 언제든지 勞務團을 充足할
수 있는 것임
當部로서 가장 重要하게 主張하고저 하는 바는
一, 勞務團에 服務하는 勞務者는 軍人이 아니고
民間의 一般勞務者인 까닭에 勤勞條件이 履行

0165

채용하고

六, 그들은 韓國人인 경우에 韓國法律에 依하여

야 動員되고 服務된다는 뜻입니다

以 上

0166

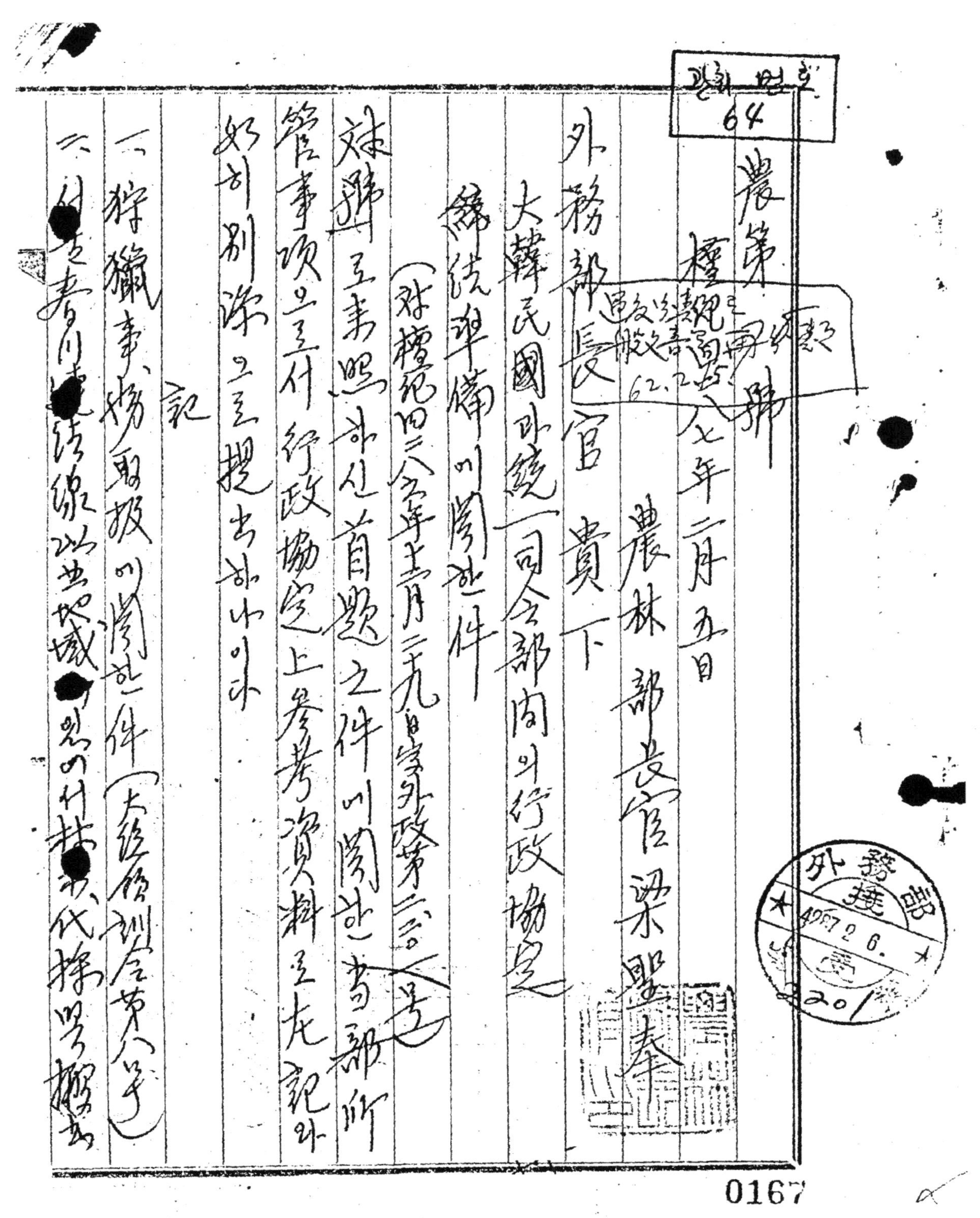

관리번호 64

農第　　號

檀紀四二八七年二月五日

農林部長官 梁聖奉

外務部長官 貴下

大韓民國과 統一司令部間의 行政協定

締結準備에 關한 件

(外 檀紀四二八六年十二月二十九日字 外政第二三〇〇號)

對號로 照會하신 首題之件에 關한 當部所管事項으로서 行政協定上 參考資料로 左記와 如히 別添으로 提出하나이다

記

一、狩獵事務取扱에 關한 件 (大統領訓令第八號)

二、[illegible] 境界線 以北地域[illegible]에 있어서 林産物 代採 [illegible]

0167

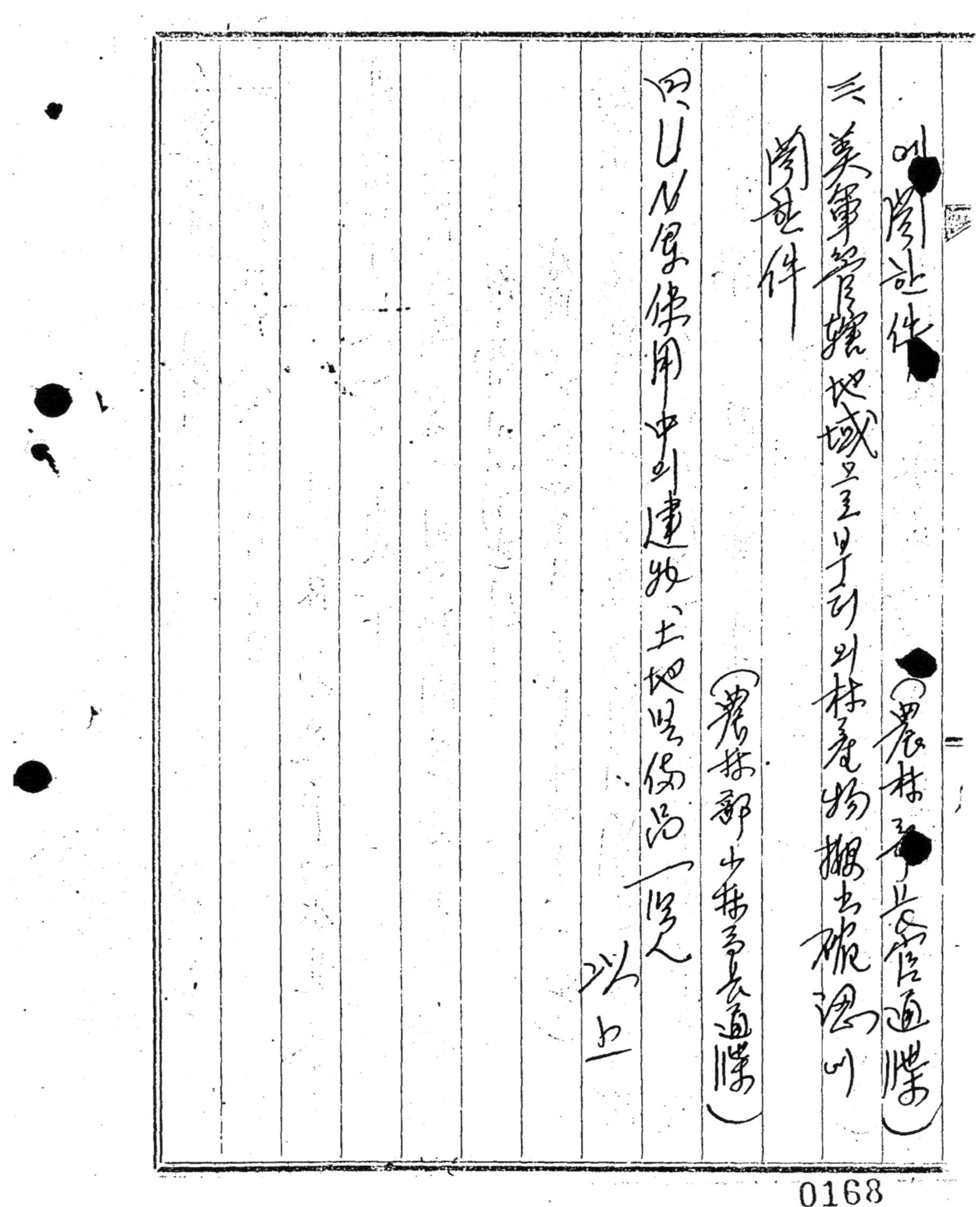

에 關한 件 (農林部長官 通牒)

三、美軍管轄地域으로부터의 林產物 搬出 確認에 關한 件 (農林部 山林局長 通牒)

四、U.N.軍 使用中의 建物、土地 및 備品 一覽表

以上

0168

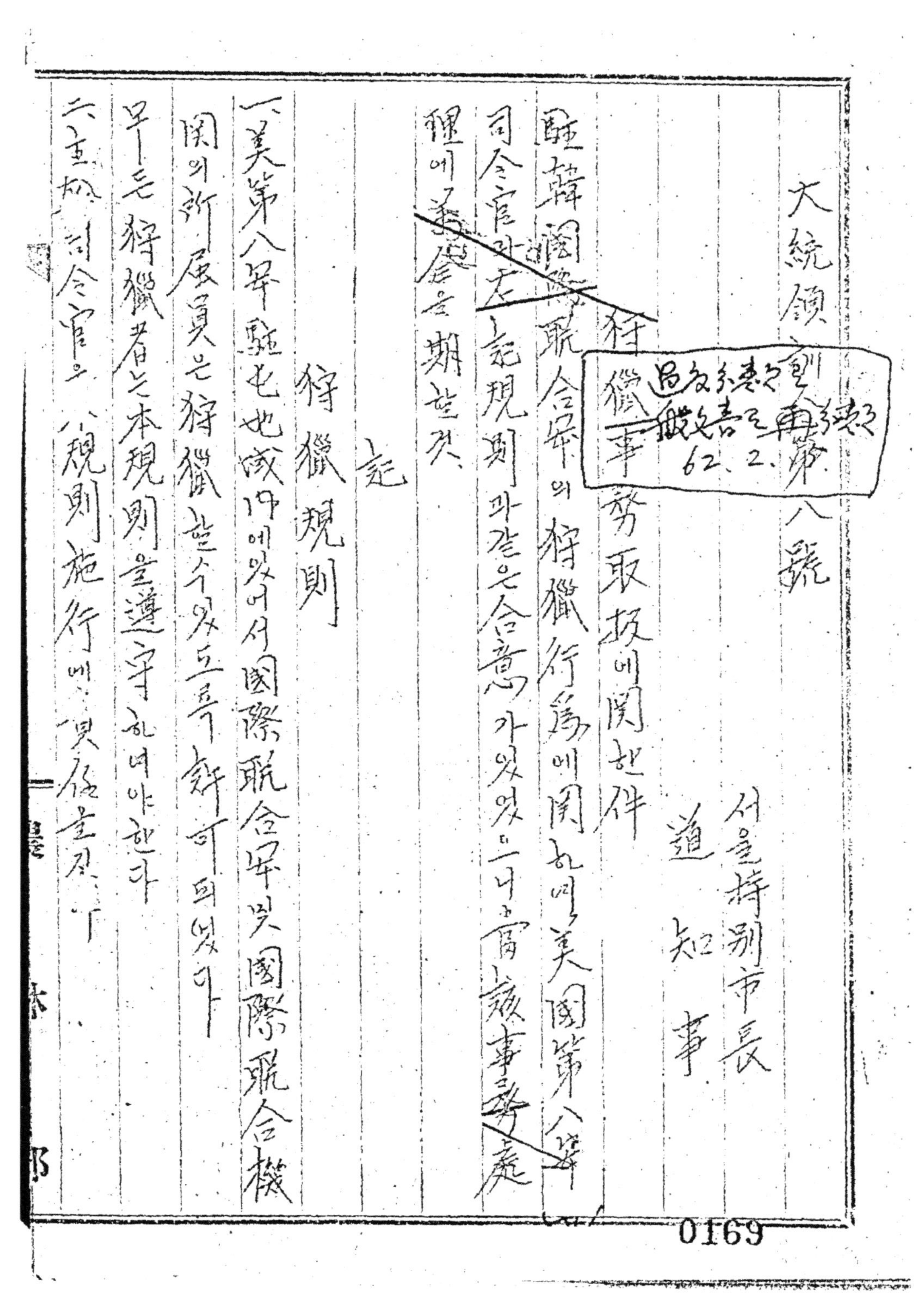

大統領訓令第八號

過去 未表示된
一般文書로 再分類
62. 2.

서울特別市長
道 知 事

狩獵事務取扱에關한件

駐韓國際聯合軍의狩獵行爲에關하여美國第八軍司令官과左記規則과같은合意가있었으니當該事務處理에萬全을期할것

記

狩獵規則

一、美第八軍駐屯地域內에있어서國際聯合軍및國際聯合機關의所屬員은狩獵할수있도록許可되었다
모든狩獵者는本規則을遵守하여야한다

二、主級司令官은、規則施行에、및 [illegible]

0169

二、狩獵은 左記의 季節과 獲物數量에 制限된다

| 獵鳥獸의 種類 | 獲物의 數量 | | 狩獵季節 |
|---|---|---|---|
| A 水鳥類 | | | |
| 오리(鴨) | 四十日 | 六 | 自十一月一日―至翌年二月末日 |
| 鷲 鳥 | 四十日 | 四 | 〃 |
| 황새 | 無制限 | | 〃 |
| 물새(鷸) | 〃 | | 〃 |
| 千 鳥 | 〃 | | 〃 |
| B、陸上鳥類 | | | |
| 鳩 | 四十日 | 五 | 自十一月一日―至翌年二月末日 |
| 멧주라기(鶉) | 〃 | 五 | 〃 |
| C、陸上獸類 | | | |
| 山猪 | 一人十日 | 一 | 自十一月一日―至十二月三十一日 |

0170

野兎 無制限 自十一月一日至翌年二月末日

다람쥐 〃 〃

D、害鳥獸類

까마귀 無制限 自九月十五日至翌年四月三十日

鷹 〃 〃

狐 〃 自九月十五日至翌年二月末日

너구리 〃 〃

독수리 〃 〃

까치 〃 〃

四、다음狩獵은어떠한때에도行하여서는아니된다

鹿、노루、범、곰、꿩、鶴、원앙새(鴛鴦)、갈가마귀(鴨)

黑貂、鶇、鶯、

五、地 [illegible]

0171

A 公園、寺院과 教會域內、王陵、公衆遊園、共同墓地
公路或은 通路、市街、人口稠密한 곳、部落內 또는 벌판에
사람을 두르고 사람과 家畜이 있는 곳에서는 狩獵하여서는 아니된다
B 明確히 사람을 두른 便에 있는 鳥獸이거나 穀物을 심고 있는 場所에
서는 所有主의 許諾없이는 狩獵하여서는 아니된다

六、武器

規格 一호으로부터 四호의 獵銃을 除外하고는 使用할 수 없다
陷穽、爆發藥、毒藥은 禁止된다

七、時間

狩獵은 日中에만 이를 行할 수 있다

八、狩獵免許

A、韓國의 狩獵免許는 國際聯合所屬員에게는 必要하지 아니한다
狩獵許可狀은 國際聯合軍各部隊憲兵司令官이나 그가 指名

0172

한者가 이를 発給한다
二弗의 手数料가 徵收될 것이며 其金額은 美国第八軍司令部
에서 指名하는 韓國慈善機関에 寄贈될 것이다
B、狩猟許可状発給前에 있어서 部隊長 或은 機関長은 許
可를 받을 者가 이 狩猟規則과 使用되는 武器에 熟達되였음을
確認하여야 한다、韓国警察、韓国의 狩猟 또는 山林을 團
束한 官憲의 要求가 있을 때에는 許可状을 提示하여야 한다
九、食用獸禽은 狩猟者가 必要로 하지 아니한 境遇에도 射殺한 場
所에 放置되어서는 아니되며 消費하기 爲하여 地方人에게
引渡하여야 한다、狩猟에 関係된 部隊長은 書面으로 付
狩猟獲物頭数 및 状況을 憲兵司令官 또는 適当한 憲兵將校
에게 報告하여야 한다、
十、狩猟隊의 警備

0173

A、狩獵은 반드시 二人以上으로 할것이며 그中一人은 野獸에 대한 保護手段으로서 카ー빈 或은 M一銃으로 武裝하여야 한다 狩獵銃으로서 鹿彈00을 使用하는 것은 카ー빙이나 小銃의 適當한 代用을 看做할수있다.

B、狩獵隊의 上級者는 使用되는 車輛의 警備에 對하여 責任을 진다.

C、部隊或은 機関長은 모든 狩獵隊에 関한 記錄을 하여야 하며 同記錄은 最少限 左記事項을 包含하여야 한다

1、狩獵隊의 人員數

2、種別車輛數 및 陸軍省番號

3、隊中上級者의 姓名、機関(隊)名、軍番號

4、狩獵地域의 坐標

5、歸還豫定時間

D、隊中上級者는 同隊歸還의 日時를 報告하여야 한다.

0174

E、모ー든 狩獵은 夜陰前에 駐屯地區 構內或은 地域內에 歸還할수 있도록ー끝나야 한다.

F、司令官(部隊長)은 知得하고있는 地雷設置地域을 狩獵隊에ー알리워주어야 한다

狩獵隊는 知得하고있는 地雷設置地域에 드러가서는 아니된다

十一、다음 行爲는 禁止된다.

A、航空機로부터의 又는 遊動的인 狩獵

B、發動(機關)船으로부터의 移棲鳥類의 狩獵

C、車輛으로부터의 発射.

大統領

檀紀四千二百八十六年十二月二十四

國務委員

國務總理

0175

國務委員 內務部長官

國務委員 農林部長官

0176

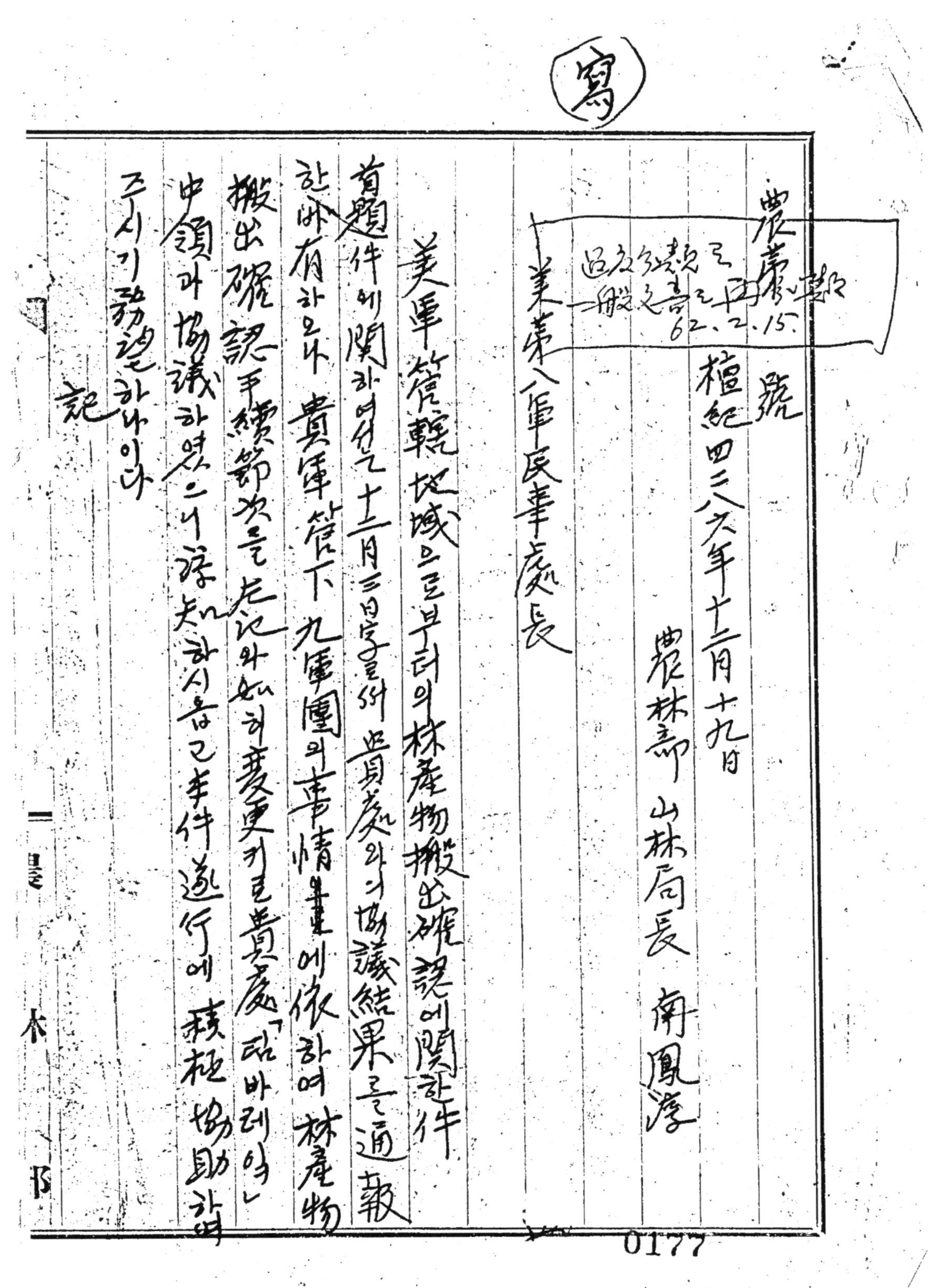

寫

農山 號

[illegible] 一般文書로 再分類 62.2.15

檀紀四二八六年十二月十九日

農林部 山林局長 南鳳濬

美第八軍民事處長

美軍管轄地域으로부터의 林産物搬出確認에關한件

首題件에關하여서는 十二月三日字로써 貴處와의協議結果를通報한바有하오나 貴軍管下 九軍團의事情等에依하여 林産物搬出確認手續節次를 左記와如히 變更키로 貴處「라바레」中領과協議하였으니 諒知하시옵고 本件遂行에 積極協助하여주시기務望하나이다

記

0177

一、英文搬出證은 別紙 寫本樣에 依하여 關係地方長 又는 營林署長이 發行함

二、地方長官 又는 營林署長이 英文搬出證을 發行하였을時는 其二通을 農林部 山林局에 進達함

三、山林局은 此를 伐採許可와 對照 檢討後 證明認印하며 其二通을 入軍民事處에 進達함

四、入軍民事處는 山林局으로부터 提出된 關係報告書와 對照後 正當한 分에 限하여 確認署名하고 此를 山林局에 回送함

五、山林局은 右確認證을 本人에게 交付함과 同時 關係機關에 通報함

0178

農山第　　號

檀紀四二八六年十月十六日

農林部長官 梁聖奉

美第八軍 民事處長 貴下

서울春川連結線以北地域에있어서林木伐採및搬出에關한件

首題件에關하여貴處와의協議에依하여今後左記와如히處理코저하오니積極協助하여주시기務望하나이다

記

一、一線地域에있어서의林木伐採

山林技術官의任意出入이不可能함으로原則的으로許可되지않음 但 軍作戰上必要時에限하여軍司令官의命에依

0179

하야 伐採된 木産物은 現地軍 所用에 限하고 後方搬入을 嚴禁키로 함

二、 서울 春川 連結線 以北 地域의 林木伐採

農林部長官이 該地域內의 林木伐採를 承認하였을 時는 別紙 一號 書式에 依하여 美八軍 民事處長에게 通報함

三、 許可 生産品의 搬出 方法

別紙 二號 書式에 依한 英文 搬出證(所轄 道知事 또는 營林署長이 發行함)과 所定 書式에 依한 國文 搬出 確認證을 所持한 者에 限하여 許容할 것

但 生産地 및 生産者의 姓名 等은 農林部長官의 通報와 對照 檢討토록 할 것

0180

Form No. 1

MINISTRY OF AGRICULTURE AND FORESTRY
BUREAU OF FORESTRY, R.O.K.

Date ____________

Subject: Authorization of timber cutting

To : Chief Civil Affairs Office,
Headquarters 8th United States Army

This is to certify that following forests are authorized to be cut as follows;

| location | species | sorts to be produced | amounts to be cut pieces | cu.m. | producer |
|---|---|---|---|---|---|

Nam Bong Soon
Chief Bureau of Forestry,
Ministry of AgricultureandForestry

0181

Form No. 2

MINISTRY OF AGRICULTURE AND FORESTRY
0000 NATIONAL FOREST STATION

or (00000000000 PROVINCIAL GOVERNMENT)

Date____________

Subject: Transportation permits of forest products

To : Whom it may concern

This is to certify that Mr.______________ is authorized to transport forest products as follows;

LOCATION OF PRODUCTS:

NAME OF PRODUCER :

| SORTS AND AMOUMTS OF PRODUCTS : | | | |
|---|---|---|---|
| | Logs | 0000 cubic meters | 000 trucks |
| | Charcoal | 0000 bags (000 Cu.m.) | 000 trucks |
| | Firewood | 0000 pyongs (000 Cu.m.) | 000 trucks |

DESTINATION :

PERIOD : From date____________ to date____________

Signature
000000(Name)
Chief, 0000 National Forest Station,
Ministry of Agriculture and Forestry

or (0000 Provincial Governor, R.O.K.)

Approved by:
Nam Bong Soon
Chief, Bureau of Forestry
Ministry of Agriculture and Forestry

0182

| 構造 | 建坪 | 建物名 | 建物使用部隊名 | 備考 |
|---|---|---|---|---|
| 煉瓦造三階建 | 五八 | 圖書館 | 土耳其部隊 | |
| 木造平家 | 一二 | 自動車庫 | 〃 | |
| 鐵造鋼葺 | 五〇 | 倉庫 | 〃 | |
| 木造平家建 | 二〇 | 木工室 | 〃 | |
| 瓦葺 | 三 | 消防器具倉庫 | 〃 | |
| | 一二 | 貯藏庫 | 〃 | |
| 〃 | 一五 | 病理室 | 〃 | |
| 〃 | 一三 | 細菌室 | 〃 | |
| 〃 | 八二 | 院長官舍 | 〃 | |
| 〃 | 一六八 | 實驗室 | 〃 | |
| 〃 | [illegible] | 官舍 | 〃 | |

[illegible] 一般文書로 再分類 67.2.15

UN軍[illegible]

中央農業技術院

0183

| | | | | |
|---|---|---|---|---|
| 燻蒸室 | 一二 | 〃 | | |
| 作業室 | 四六 | 〃 | 〃 | |
| 甘藷乾燥場及作業室 | 二三 | 〃 | 〃 | |
| 交配室及暗室 | 八二 | 〃 | 〃 | |
| 甘藷貯藏庫 | 四二 | 〃 | 〃 | |
| 蠶種倉庫 | 三〇 | 〃 | 第九三四航空部隊聯隊 | |
| 蠶種檢査室 | 一三五 | 〃 | 〃 | |
| 便所 | 四五 | 〃 | 〃 | |
| 栽蠶係事務室 | 三〇 | 〃 | 〃 | |
| 蠶種係事務室 | 四四六 | 〃 | 〃 | |
| 栽桑係作業室 | 六 | 〃 | 〃 | [illegible] |
| 消毒室 | 一四五 | 木造平家瓦葺 | 〃 | |
| 蠶種貯藏室 | 一五七 | 〃 | 〃 | |

0184

| | | | |
|---|---|---|---|
| 〃 | 七四、三 | 寄宿舎 | 〃 |
| 〃 | 六 | 廊下 | 〃 |
| 〃 | 一四二、五 | 機械事務室 | 〃 |
| | 一〇七、二 | 揚返室 | 〃 |
| | 五七三 | 選繭及乾繭室 | 〃 |
| | 一〇二、三 | 煮繭室 | 〃 |
| | 三三 | 汽鑵室 | 〃 |
| 木造二階建瓦葺 | 九九 | 繭倉庫 | 〃 |
| 木造平家 瓦葺 | 五〇 | 食堂 | 〃 |
| 〃 | 五六、一 | 倉庫 | 〃 |
| 〃 | 三、二 | 給水室 | 〃 |
| 〃 | 六 | 洗濯室 | 〃 |
| 〃 | 三、二 | 休憩室 | |

0185

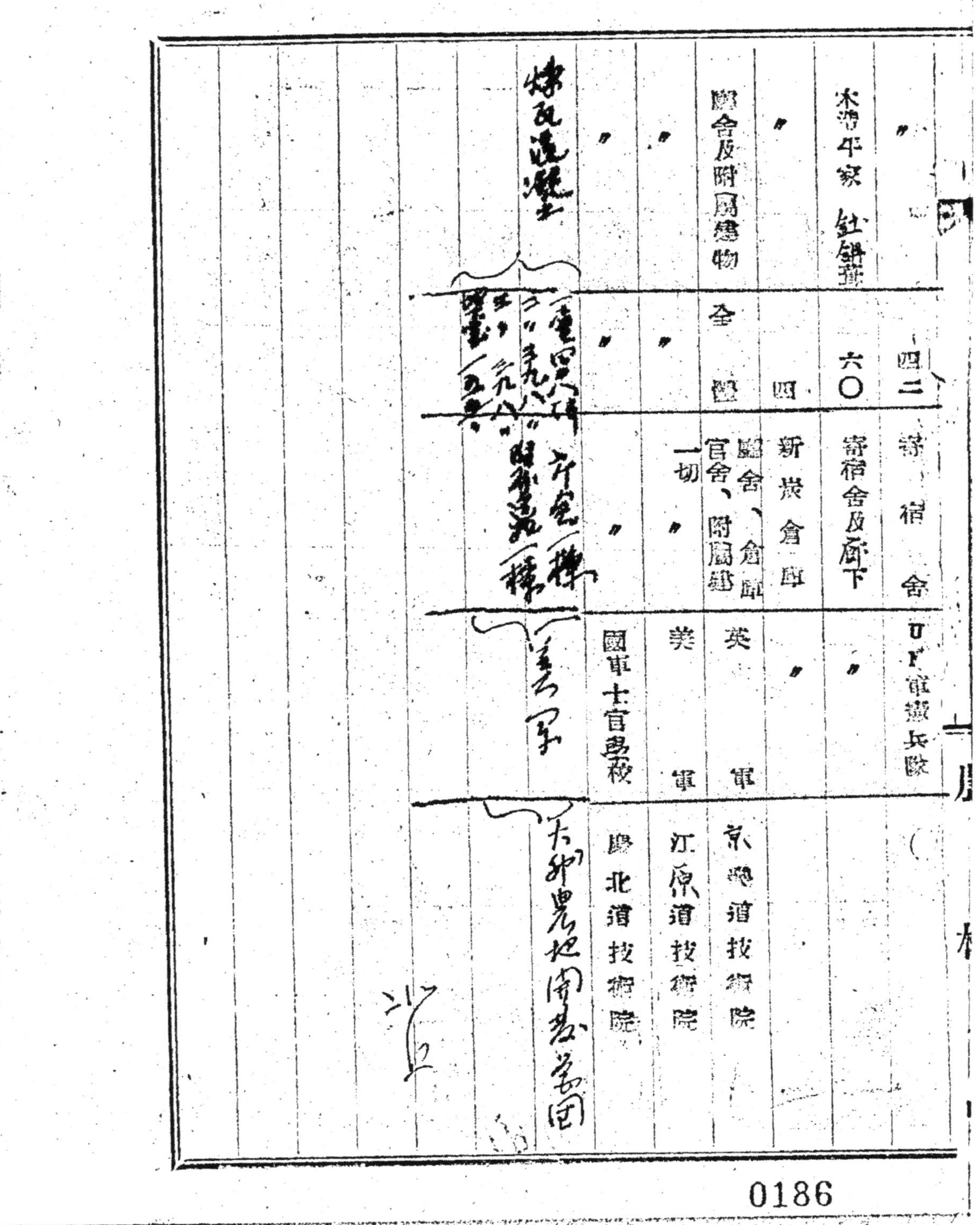

0186

# 韓國馬事會

## 米軍使用施設

| 區分 | 種別 | 所在地 | 使用期間 | 使用坪數 | 備考 |
| --- | --- | --- | --- | --- | --- |
| 釜山競馬場 | 土地 | 釜山市凡一洞 | 四二八三.七月 現在使用中 | 四七,九四七坪 | |
| | 建物 | 〃 | 同時破損 | 二,六七六坪 九五3 | |
| | 備品 | 〃 | | 五三点 | |
| 大邱競馬場 | 土地 | 大邱市院垈洞 | 四二八三.七月 — 四二八五.十二月 | 三三,八五五 | |
| | 建物 | 〃 | 同時破損 | 一,七七〇.二合 | |
| | 備品 | | | 六二点 | |
| 慶州牧場 | 土地 | 慶州郡內東面 晧谷里 | 四二八三.十月 現在使用中 | 五〇,〇〇〇 | |
| | 建物 | 〃 | 〃 | 二八四坪五合 | |
| | 備品 | | 同時破損 | 六二点 | |
| 서울競馬場 | 土地 | 서울市東大門区 新設洞 | 四二八四.四月 現在使用中 | 二,三五五 | |

0187

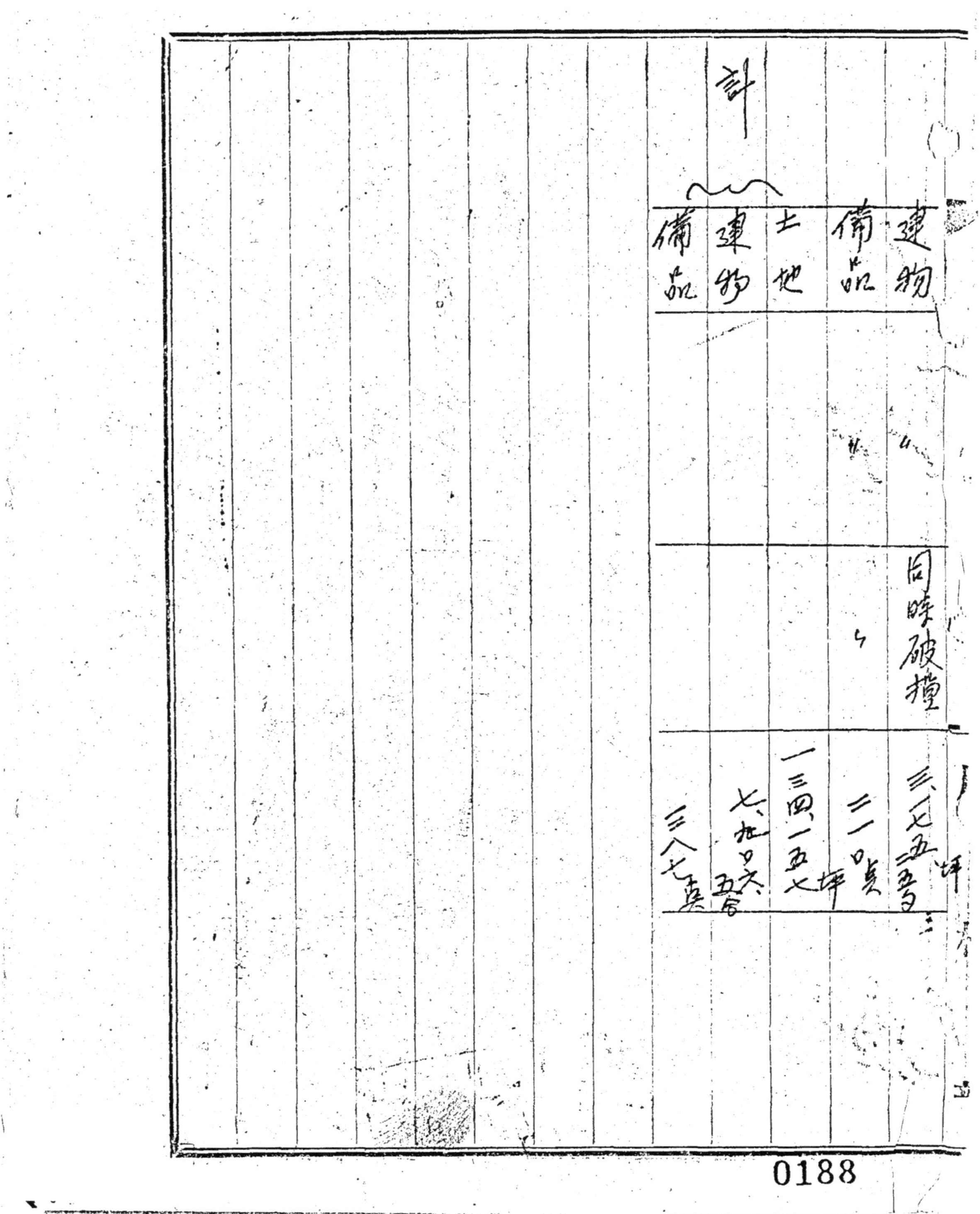

計

| 建物 | 備品 | 土地 | 建物 | 備品 |
|---|---|---|---|---|
| 〃 | 〃 | | | |
| 同時破壞 | 〃 | | | |
| 三、七五三坪 | 二一〇点 | 一三四、一五七坪 | 七、九〇六、五〇 | 三八七点 |

0188

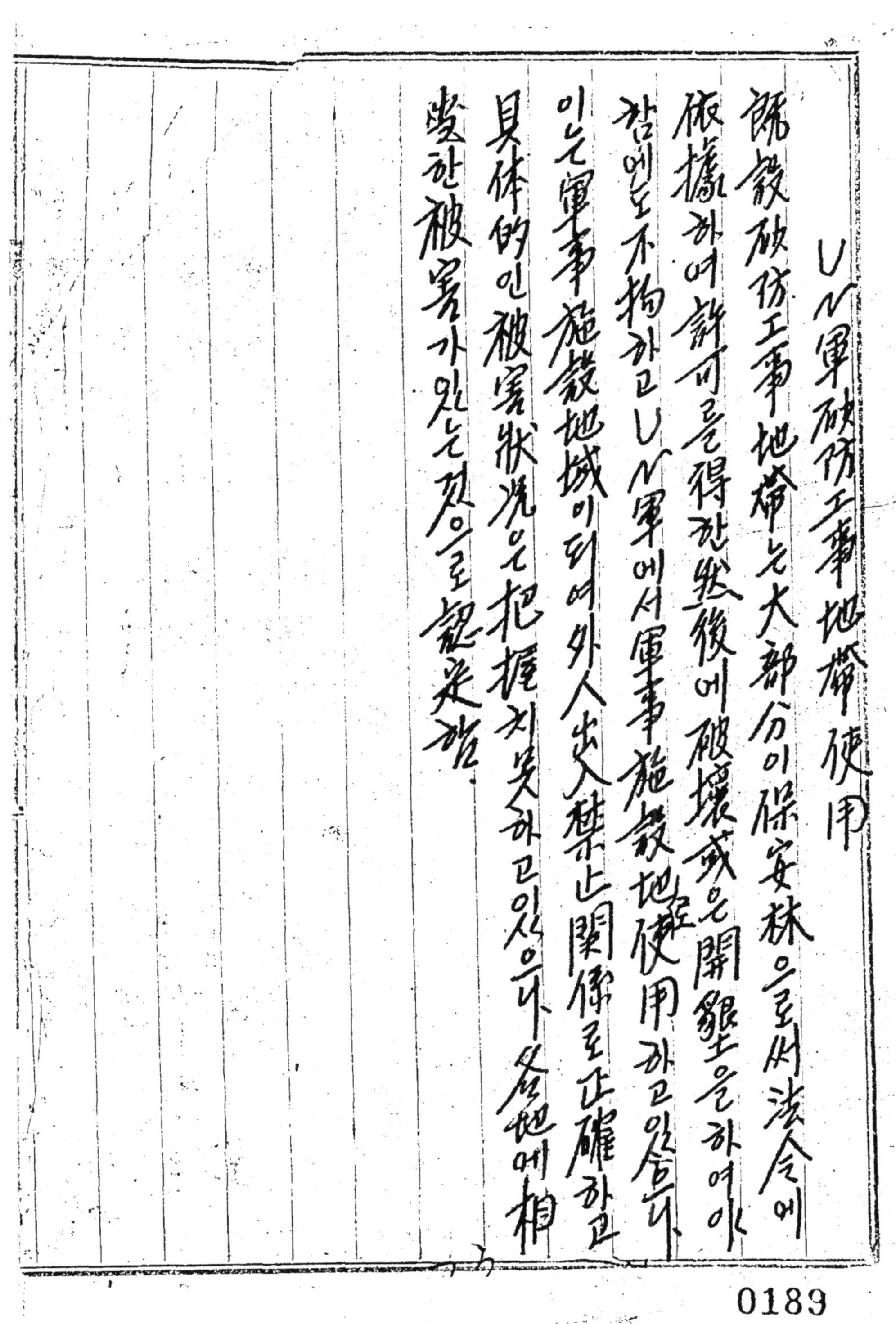

UN軍陣防工事地帶使用

陣設陣防工事地帶는大部分이保安林으로서法令에依據하여許可를得한然後에破壞或은開墾을하여야함에도不拘하고UN軍에서軍事施設地로使用하고있으나, 이는軍事施設地域이되여外人出入禁止關係로正確하고具体的인被害狀況은把握치못하고있으나, 各地에相當한被害가있는것으로認定함.

0189

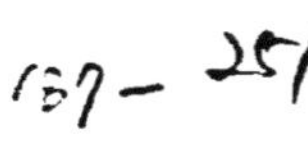

교통부

1954. 2. 8

0130

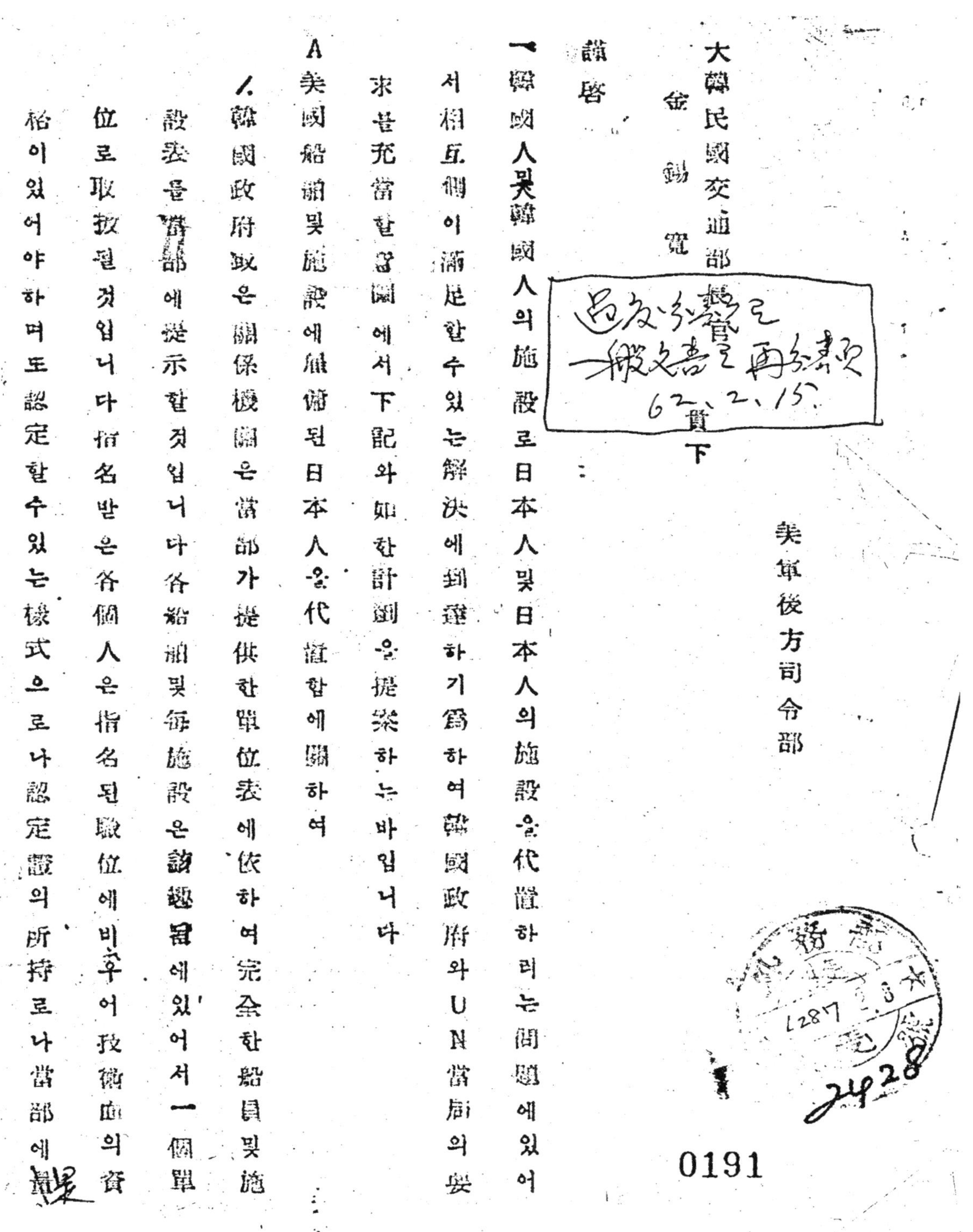

大韓民國交通部

金錫寬 貴下

美軍後方司令部

謹啓:

一 韓國人및韓國人의施設로日本人및日本人의施設을代置하려는問題에있어서相互側이滿足할수있는解決에到達하기爲하여韓國政府와UN當局의要求를充當할意圖에서下記와如한計劃을提案하는바입니다

A 美國船舶및施設에雇備된日本人을代置함에關하여

1. 韓國政府或은關係機關은當部가提供한單位表에依하여完全한船員및施設表를當部에提示할것입니다各船舶및每施設은該趣旨에있어서一個單位로取扱될것입니다指名받은各個人은指名된職位에비추어技術面의資格이있어야하며또認定할수있는様式으로나認定書의所持로나當部에報

0191

認될 수 있는 證據書類로나 免許證이라야 합니다

2. 指名받은 各單位의 成員은 그 資格과 技術의 審査를 當部의 代表가 할 수 있게 措置되여야 할 것입니다 合當한 資格이 缺하는 境遇에는 그 代表들의 任意로 却下될 것이다

3. 當部가 資格을 준 各單位의 船員을 採用한 다음에 그 雇傭主는 KBS의 契約官과 一日單位의 運營(船舶 및 施設)을 爲하여 契約을 相議할 것입니다 雇傭主는 반드시 會社體이거나 또는 契約官이 被契約体라고 認定하는 其他의 合法的團体이어야 합니다 그리고 契約은 契約官이 要求하는 모든 條件에서 作成될 것입니다 또 契約은 韓國의 海上勞動者의 通例賃金에 依據할 것이며 通例的手當金을 考慮하되 厚生費 및 經常費는 二五%를 超過못할 것입니다 또 圓貨支拂을 特記할 것입니다 契約은 下記와 如한 것을 規定할 것입니다 船舶의 運航方法은 契約官의 任意로 決定될 것입니다 船員이 解傭도 되고 懲戒를 받을

0192

것입니다 全雇傭員의 採用은 九十日間이라는 暫定的인 試用을 基本으로 할
것입니다 그리고 이 契約의 規範안에 있는 職員은 美國政府 政은 同政府의 代
行補助機關의 職員일수는 없읍니다 이 規定은 各船舶의 規定 또는 採用規定
의 一部分이 될것입니다 이 契約에 關한 事務行政處理 및 組織如何는 完全
契約官의 任意로 합니다

4. 그 單位의 成員으로 指名하고 審査하고 當部가 承認하고 그리고 契約이 承認
되여 實行될 때에 그 單位의 日人成員은 解雇될것이지만 能率的이 그 支障없
는 適當이라할 至高의 要求를 充當해야 할것입니다

B 日人 및 日人의 所有나 適當의 船舶을 韓國人 및 韓國人의 所有나 適當의 施設로
代値하는데 關하여

1. A項 1. 2 中의 規定을 準用함

0193

2. 韓國政府는 當部가 提供한 船舶表에 提示된 바와 같은 代置計劃中의 船舶들과 型 또는 機能에 있어 同等한 船舶 및 施設의 所在를 明示할 것을 同意할 것이다 따라서 韓國政府는 直接的인 그리고 自發的인 協意를 그 船舶所有者와 할 것이다 但 仲介業者를 除外한다 選出된 船舶은 検査와 適合與否의 試驗을 爲하여 當部에 遂行된 것이며 따라서 船舶의 認定은 當部의 單獨任意로 할 것이다

3. 一個船舶單位와 職員이 當部에 資格審査에 依하여 採用된 다음에 그 單位船舶과 船員에 雇傭主는 民間個傭船에 依據하여 當部契約官과 契約할 것입니다 그 雇傭主는 반드시 會社일것이며 또는 契約對象으로 契約官이 認定한 其他法的個体이여야할 것입니다 契約은 民間個傭船을 爲主하되 契約官의 要求하는 全條件을 지킬 것이요 契約은 韓國에서 現金如斯한 作業과 船舶에 支

採하는通例的比率에依據하여그比率의最適의人件費와[illegible]

하시있는經常費에두어야할것입니다契約은圜貨支拂을特記할것입니다

다 契約은다음과같은것을規定합니다契約에規範안에있는雇員은何人을與論코美國政府및同政府代行및補助機關의職員일수없읍니다契約에關한事務處理및行政그리고繼續與否은契約官의單獨的인任意로합니다

4 宿名된成員을當部가審査하고是認하고그리고契約의是認을얻어雇傭되는때에그單位의日人成員은解雇될것이지만能率的이고支障없는運用이라는至高한要請에依據하여야할것입니다

O 陸地에서의補助的海事作業에關한日本人技術者에對하여韓國人技術者로代置하는것

0195

1. 當部는 所要技術의 一體表各技術에 要하는 人員數運營單位에 配置될 未熟技術者의 人員數를 韓國政府에 提供할 것입니다

2. 韓國政府는 技術者 및 準技術者 或은 所要技術을 習得할 有資格者를 指名할 것입니다 韓國政府 또는 同政府의 關係當局은 叙上 指名者를 調査하여 書類證明을 할 것이며 그 適應性을 審査할 것입니다 指名된 者의 資格이며 技術에 對한 審査는 當部의 代表들이 하도록 하여 줄 것입니다

3. 指名된 者가 技術者로 或은 有資格의 技術習得者로 認定받은 後에 그 사람은 傭船期間 傭船 또는 船舶修繕 같은 契約作業의 傭員으로 될 것입니다

作業契約은 다음과 같은 것을 規定합니다

全技術者와 技術習得者는 (技術訓練을 補佐하는 當部代表者의 指導밑에 九十日間의 試用이라는 條件으로 採用됩니다 技術者와 技術習得者에 對

0196

한 韓國■國에서의美軍勞務者等別파同一하게할것입니다船舶의規約이
며採用의規約은다시말하면技術者와技術習得者는누구를莫論하고美國
政府및同政府의代行或은補助機關의職員이될수없다는것입니다

二 此計劃의承認에附隨하여成果를關心한다는意味에서韓國政府는그制限
的態度를緩和하여日人을最後的으로代置하기까지는日本人에게所要한
陸地作業을實施하게할것입니다

三 韓國政府에協力및關與는此計劃의成果에있어不可缺이라고思料됩니다
韓國政府및그代行機關의建議와協助를努力의相互性에빛우어要望하는
바입니다

四 貴下가署名하신다면그것은此計劃을承認하신다는것이될것입니다

陸軍准將 라스타이오

0197

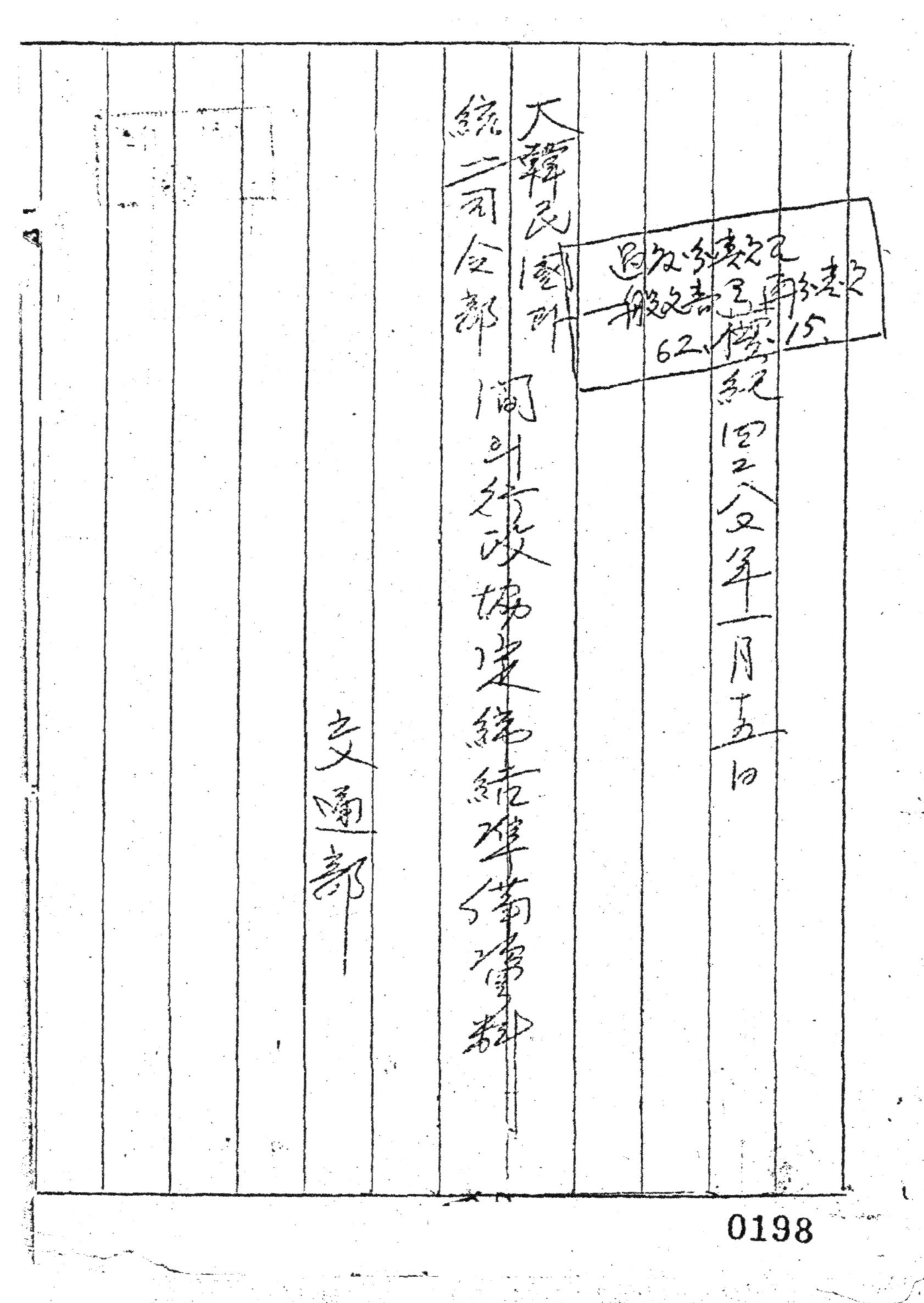

檀紀四二九五年一月十五日

大韓民國 統一司令部 間의 行政協定締結準備書類

交通部

一般文書로 再分類
62. 1. 15.

0198

# 目次

一、KCOMZ、KCAC 및 交通部間의 協定書

二、自動車에 關한 運營協定書

三、鐵道輸送契約書

四、鐵道工事契約書

五、UN軍이 使用하는 通信回線施設에 關한 口頭約束

六、要望事項

甲、鐵道車輛修繕關係

乙、車輛入廠手續 等의 件

丙、現場作業進行指示의 件

丁、保線資材補修及交換等의 件

七、海運關係

0199

1. 港灣(埠頭施設等含)地帶管理에 關한 件

2. 外國船舶의 UN軍需物資沿岸輸送業務從事排除의 件

3. UN軍에 依한 不法船舶徵發排除의 件

4. 港灣修築, 灯台建設時의 事前에 關係當局과 協議要請의 件

5. 釜山港 外港에 美港灣司令部에 設置한 標灯浮標의 件

(明細表別添)

0200

KOOMZ、KOAO및交通部間의協定書

一、目的

大韓民國交通部下에手續設定은一般積荷人에게貨車配當을하기爲하여責任이負課된다

二、範圍

全般人의積荷貨物輸送에適用될此手續은特別承認을받은輸送과共히計劃된다

三、管理

KOOMZ의輸送監은韓國內의貨車配當에對한責任을진다 全体的遂行을爲하여、KOOMZ輸送監은救護物輸送에對하여KOAO에貨車를多量配當을하여亦是救護物資以外의民貨輸送을爲하여交通部에配當한다

0201

救護物資輸送은KOAO에서責任지、그以外의民需貨物輸送은KOAO의援助와管理下交通部長官이責任을진다

四、計劃貨物

同一場所發、同一貨物主에依하十五日期間內로完輸送하며十五輛或은그以上의貨物車를申請한民需物資輸送은計劃되어야한다

交通部長官은每月初一日、十五日에七日前으로此申請에對하여整理하여KOOMZ輸送監에게提出하여야한다

此申請은鐵道貨物計劃을包含하고그期間內로輸送키爲하여申請된貨車는日平均隨落될것이며또交通部長官에게配當된곳에서控除되여야한다

五、臨時貨物(一般貨物)

全一般民需物資輸送에包含치않으며KOOMZ輸送監이發行한特別

0202

承認輸送은交通部配當總量中에包含된다

其다음此貨車는控除된計劃貨物輸送에申請된다 特別承認을얻을

節次는左記와如하다

1 荷主는課長、局長또는長官에게申請書를提出함

2 課長은申請書를整理하여同時에局에提出함

3 各局에서는申請書를整理하는同時運輸局長에게提出하다

4 交通部長官은全申請書를評價하고優先輸送에對한設定을하여KCO

MZ輸送監에게提出하다

임이是認된申請書는殘留配當數를超過치않이하다

寫本은KCAC에發送함

KCOMZ輸送監 Frod고린

AOKCAC代表 Fonay 앞슨

0203

通部次官

金 錫 明

0204

# 自動車에關한運營協定書

UNKRA 計劃 6.5(432-A)

一九五三年 月 日大韓民國政府(以下政府라고稱함)國際聯合再建團(以下UNKRA라고稱함)과國際聯合司令部(以下UNC라고稱함)間에左記와如한協定을作成締結한다

一 目的

救護와復興을爲하여大韓民國間에現存한輸送機關을補充하고저 트럭과其他自動車를取得함을目的으로한다

二 取得

UNKRA는韓國交通部에서編成하고本協定書에署名한其外部署에서承認한目標에記載된數量과種類의 "추럭" 과自動車를自動車를自己經費로韓國以外地域에서取得하여此等施設의便宜한韓國內港口에

0205

輸送한다、同目錄은「附屬書A」로 玆에添付하여本協定의一部가
된다

三 檢收及保管

1 政府는自己가選擇한代行機關을通하여韓國內港口에入港한母船에 積載한車輛을檢收하고同品의檢收日부터下記와如한最終處分日까지에荷役、保管과安全保守를擔當한다

2 政府는各車輛을檢收直後 車輛檢收時間及場所車輛의名稱及種類 車台及番號와車輛에附隨된全附屬品과工具一切을記入한檢收證을 UNKRA에手渡한다

四 配定

1 韓國內에서一般販賣와最終需要者에對한本車輛의配定計劃書는交通部에서作成하고本協定書에署名한其外部署에서承認한다

0206

同計劃書는「附屬書B」로서茲에添付하여本協定書의一部로한다

2 本協定書에依한車輛이各々船積하여入荷되는卽時로交通部에서設定한優先順位에依하여配定計劃된最終需要者에게交通部의代行機關을通하여遲滯없이販賣한다

3 車輛은現金販賣로서만最終需要者의所持에歸하고最終需要者는仕入價格과取扱手數料(第六條參照)를支拂하고車輛을所得함으로서同車輛의所有와權利를獲得한다

4 配定된車輛을二年間以內에는政府의許可없이轉賣 貸與 又는車輛이나同部分品의處分을하지못한다 此를違反하는境遇에는第十條第二項에制定한車輛販賣價格의三倍에該當한金額의罰金을政府에納付할것을誓約한者以外의最終需要者에게는販賣하지못한다

但 自己의過失이아니고不得已한 故로車輛이完全히使用不能에

0207

關한境遇에는此限에不在하다

五 財定措置

1 最終需要者에게負擔될輸入原價는韓國에있어서UNKRA計劃係

과類似한取扱을받을것같이美弗交換率의計算과同等價인韓國引渡

價格、UNKRA價格을代表한다

2 政府는UNKRA에依하여徵收된販賣正價를韓國銀行援助資上金計

算書에供託한다

그러치않으면再建費計算書는再建計算書에依하여徵收된日字에서

十五日을除外한時부터設定한다

六 取扱料와國內輸送費

政府又는代行機關은荷役、國內輸送、車輛의維持及販賣에關한費用

을支拂하고此等費用은車輛의最終需要者에게서徵收한는車輛代金에

0208

加算하다

七 取扱部分品

1. 「附屬書」A에依한車輛의取得과同樣으로UNKRA는本協定書의一部로서添付한「附屬書」C에依한取扱部分의取得을爲한庶事를行하다

此部分品은交通部에서認定하는作業狀態와優先順位에依하여、車輛의指定又는販賣를받은最終需要者에게修理及維持를遂行하고저交通部와契約한有資格한修理及維持機關에게車輛의取扱과同樣으로販賣하다

八 UNKRA의保留權利

1. UNKRA는韓國再建計劃에利用하기爲하여「附屬書A」에記載된車輛에對하여入荷當時에UNKRA使節團長이決定하는數量만

0209

을保留하는權利를가진다 그러나單位의總數量二〇%및壹噸半積

載量級以下의單位에서七五%超過量이아니다

九 保證

UNKRA는本協定書에依한車輛과部分品에關하여如何한保證도附

與하지않는다

車輛이나部分品의製造者나元賣捌者가保證하는部分品에缺陷이보이

거나生하는境遇에는最終需要者의利益을爲하여如斯한保證에對한權

利를保護하는必要한全手續을取하여준다

十 政府의協助

ㄱ 政府는大韓民國에入荷하는本協定書의車輛과部分品에對하여韓國

에輸入하는物資에正常的으로規定된關稅其他課稅의免除를認許하

고政府代行機關에는最終需要者에販賣할제取扱費用을包含한價格

0210

總計에對한一〇%以上의利潤을不許한다

2.各者는終需要者에게서徵收하는總販賣價格은左記를構成한다

a 購入原價(第五條에依하算出方法으로)

b 取扱料(第六條에依함)

c a와b의合算額의一〇%

3.政府는UNKRA又는UNO의正式代表로하여금車輛及代行機關의代業을監理調査하는것을許容하고同代表는何時든지適當한時間에帳係記錄書類를調査할수있게하며本計劃遂行에關한詳細한進行報告를四半期로UNKRA에提出한다

4.政府는第四條第四項에依한最終需要者의誓約을嚴重하게監督하며實行시킨다

一一UN司令部의協助

UNO는 本協定을 履行하기 爲하여 港灣及荷役施設을 通하여 軍需品

取扱에 支障없는 諸般優先權을 供與함으로서 UNKRA와 政府의 作

業을 便利케 하다

大韓民國政府

國際聯合再建團

國際聯合司令部

0212

輸送契約 （陸軍省）

契約者名及住所 大韓民國交通部 釜山

契約額 一五〇万弗 （概算）

地域 民國各地

支拂 美陸軍省第九支出課支出官이行한다本契約書에依하여取得되는資材및輸送은下記項目에依하여承認되며別記目的에爲한것이며下記項目에依하여支拂된다

二一一二四〇九、九一-二〇八、P四六一-〇七 S九九-九九

九 資金使用에關한財務官의說明은必要하지않다

本契約은下記法律에依하여承認되며協定된다一九四七年制定陸軍勞務調達法第二條 （法律四一三-八〇號）

0213

輸送契約

一九五〇年十月一日附로本契約을執行하는契約將校에依하여代表되는北米合衆國(以下政府라고稱함)과大韓民國法令에依하여創設되고存在되는機關인交通部(以下契約者라고稱함)間에締結된本契約書는當事者雙方이下記와如히協定하였음을證明한다

第一條 輸送의性質과範圍

A 契約者는別紙明細書甲號에指定되고있는條件期限等에一致되도록貨物及旅客輸送을下記契約條項을考慮하면서實行하여야한다

明細書甲號의條件期限等은本契約의一部로된다

B 交通部가某從事員을繼續勤務시키는것이美國政府의利益에反한다고契約將校가認定할적에는그從事員을卽時異動시켜야한다

第二條 契約變更

0214

契約將校는 何時든지 輸送 또는 그 事業 增加或은 縮減시키는데 書面命令으로서 本契約을 變更시킬 수 있다 그러한 變更으로 因하여 本契約에 要求되고 있는 輸送 또는 工事를 增加 또는 縮減시키게 될 境遇에는 適當한 調整을 하여 本契約을 更新하여야 한다 上記 調整에 對하여 訴請이 있을 적에는 契約變更이 發表된 日字부터 三〇日 以內에 文書로서 提出하여야 한다 契約將校는 그러한 訴請이 事實이 正當化시키고 있다고 確認할 적에는 美極東司令官 或은 그 代表者의 承認下에 契約變更이 確定的으로 決定되기 前에 提出되는 此 訴請을 接受하여 考慮하여야 한다 万一 契約當事者間에 契約變更調整案에 合意치 못하면 第六條(紛爭)에 依하여 處理된다 然히나 本 第二條는 契約者에게 變更된 輸送及工事를 繼續實行할 것을 免除시키는 것은 않이다

第三條 輸送期間

0215

契約者는本契約成立日부터輸送業務를始作하여六箇月以內에完遂하여야한다然하나美國政府는期限滿了十五日以前에契約期間을延期(六箇月以上超過치못함)시킬選擇權을가지고있다

第四條 契約者에對한報酬

本契約에依하여要求되는輸送業務를滿足할만큼完遂한데對한金錢報酬를別添甲號明細書에依하여支拂한다

第五條 支拂方法

A 契約者가契約將校의要求에一致하도록正當히證明된請求書와證憑書의提出에對하여支拂한다

B 契約將校는契約者에게運賃支拂前에正當히證明된俸給表及其他報告書提出을要求할수있다

C 契約將校는最終支拂前에契約者가本契約에依하여生긴美國政府

交通部

0216

에 關한 訴請權 一切을 拋棄할 것을 要求할 수 있다

第六條 紛糾

本契約에 別途規定이 없는 限 本契約에 依하여 惹起된 事態에 關한 모든 紛糾로서 協議에 依하여 解決되지 않으면 契約將校가 決定한다 契約將校는 그의 決定案을 書面으로서 契約者에게 郵送하거나 寫本一通을 送付하여야 한다 契約者 上記決定案을 接受한 지 三〇日 以內에 美極東司令官 許로 된 訴請書를 契約將校에게 提出할 수 있다 美極東司令官이 그러한 訴請書를 聽取한 後 내리는 處決案은 契約將校와 契約者間 紛糾된 金額이 五万弗未滿이면 決定的 效果를 가지게 된다 万一 契約者가 三〇日 以內에 上記訴請을 提出하지 않으면 契約將校의 決定이 有效로 된다

紛糾된 金額이 五万弗以上이면 極東司令官의 決定은 契約者가 極東司令官의 決定案을 接受한 지 二十日 以內에 美陸軍長官에게 訴請書를 提出하

0217

聽取한後내리는決定案은最終的解決이다万一契約者가美極東司令官의決定을接受한지三十日以內에訴請書를提出하지않으면美極東司令官의決定이有效로된다本條項下에進行되는訴請에關하여契約者는質問을받고訴請한據物을提出할機會를얻을수있다紛議가最終的解決에到達할때까지는契約者는契約將校의決定에依하여契約을忠實히實行하여야한다

第廿條 契約將校의決定

契約者가實行하여야할輸送及工事의限度性質等에關하여는契約將校의監督指令承認下에實行하여야하며契約者는契約將校에게報告其他의責任을지게된다契約者가實行할業務의限度性質에關하여紛議가생겼을적에 契約將校의決定이支配하는것이지만契約者는第

0218

六條에記載된바와如히訴訟權을가지고있다

第八條 法律及規定遵守

契約者는大韓民國法律을遵守할것을約束한다

第九條 政府에對한勞動紛議報告

契約者는本契約의正常的實行을遲延시키는或은遲延시키可能性이있는實際的或은潛在的勞動紛料가發生할적에는直時適切한報告를契約將校에게提出하여야한다

第 條 輸送業務의制限과廢止

A 契約者의輸送業務의或은一部를終結시키는것이美國政府에利益이된다고契約將校가決定할적에는契約者에게通知함으로서終決된다契約將校는契約者에게現在까지實行한輸送에對한支拂外에는아무런責任도없게된다契約者는別途指示가없는限通知書에要求된대로終結日字에輸送의全部或은一部를終止시켜야한다

0219

B 契約者의怠慢或은不正當한輸送遲延이있을적에는何時든지輸送業務의全部或은一部를移結시킬수있다 然히나 契約實行에있어서契約者의實衆이人力으로抑制못할事由或은神의行爲暴動火災洪水傳染病罷業或은政府指令等이事由로서生길적에는契約者의怠慢不正當한輸送遲延으로因定하지않는다

契約將校가어떤鐵道從事員을異動能免시키는것이美國政府에利益이된다고生覺할적에는契約者는契約將校의指令要求에依하여行動을取하여야한다 그러한指令이契約者의從事員의不法行爲怠慢不能力等에因할적에는契約將校는그決定을書面으로作成하여契約書寫本에添付하여야한다

第十一條 調整

契約者에게輸送을要求한日字에契約者의從事員이下記와如한理由로

0220

서實行하지못하였을적에는契約者에게支拂할金額을差引하는데對한
契約將校의決定에準據하여美國政府는金額調整을할수있다

1 自發的怠慢

2 從事員의非行怠慢無資格으로因한無能力

3 從事員의無能力은않이나契約期間인六個月中七日以上要求한檢診을
못할境遇

4 第十條에依하여能免當한故로檢診을못할境遇

上

上記調整에依하여契約者가異議가있을적에는第六條에依하여訴請할
수있다

第十二條 本契約에對한複契約은認定하지않는다

第十三條 訴請權의不讓渡性

0221

本契約下에發生되는契約者의金錢에關한或은其他의訴請權은讓渡할수없다

第十四條 雇傭契約

契約將校에依하여要求되는輸送業務를實行하는데必要한從事員을雇傭할적에締結한契約書或은承認書의寫本을契約將校에게提供하여契約將校의使用을도옵게하여야한다

第十五條 美國政府의財産이될資料

本契約에依하여契約者가提供하는通信計劃表圖案覺書其他技術的資料는美國政府의財産이된다美國政府는契約者에게何等에附加的金錢을支拂하지않고契約者가所有하고있는上記資料를契約將校의要請에依하여何時든지使用할權利가있다

第十六條 從事員에對한保險金

0222

契約者는会從事員에必要한保險金을準備確保하고있어야한다또다만
女子保險金에만限할것이아니라不測의死亡事故疾病에對한損害賠償金
도包含시켜서準備하여야한다

第十七條 臨時費契約

契約者는今日까지正當한從事員及事業을持續시키는데必要한正當한
代理店以外는本契約에手數料仲立料或은臨時費에對한承認을挿入시
켜날라고願하는從事員도없고代理店도없었다고確言한다万一契約者가
가此確言을違反하는일이있으면美國政府는任意로本契約을取消할수
있고그러한手數料仲立料臨時費를契約額에서差引할수있다

第十八條 利益을取得하지못할官吏

如何한國會議員國內諸委員도本契約에參加할수없으며本契約에依하
여生기는利益에도參與할수없다然히나本條項은万一本契約이一般大

0223

求의利益을圖謀하는法人團体와締結될적에도適用된다고解決하면않된
다

第十九條 - 再協議

A 本契約은一九四八年制定의協議法을適用받는다

B 契約者는本契約書에署名된寫本을接受한지三十日以內에住所姓名
을明示하여再協議案을陸軍省軍事再協議檢討委員會에通知할것을
合議한다万一契約者가以前에再協議法에基準되는契約書或은往文
書를軍事再協議檢討委員會에發送한일이있드라도그러한再協議委
은必要가없는것이다

第二十條 檢査

美國政府는本契約下에實行되는輸送業務와費用等에關하여適當한時
期에契約者의作業現場을檢査하며文書其他記錄을審査할權限을가지

0224

고있다

第二十一條 飜譯上錯誤

万一本契約書英文과國文間에錯誤或은曖昧한点이있으면英文이支配
한다

第二十二條 定義

本契約을通하여使用된下記用語는이러한意味을가지고있다

가 長官 次官 次官補
長官을爲하여行動할權限을가진사람或은委員會(契約將校는除外)

나 極東司令官
極東司令官을爲하여行動할權限을가진사람或은委員會(契約將校는
除外)

다 美國政府를爲하여本契約을執行하는사람및正當히契約將校로부터

0225

指命된모든將校와軍屬을意味한다此用語는또本契約에別途로定한外
에는契約將校가認定한代理로서그의權限內에서行動하는모든사람을
包含한다

第二十三條 明細書

甲號明細는別添되여있으며本契約의一部다

第二十四條 承認

本契約書는極東司令官의決裁에基礎를둔다決裁가나기前에는效力이
없다

第二十五條 規定外報酬

本契約에別途로定한外에는契約者가書面으로認定하지않은規定外業
務및報酬는一切此를支拂하지않은다

第二十六條 檢査

0226

檢査計劃의 檢査는 滿足히 檢査을 實行하며 終結되여 있는가를 司令官의 代表者가 行한다

第二十七條 變更

下記와 如한 變更은 契約當事者가 署名하기 前에 實行되였다 (變更이 無함)

本契約의 當事者 双方이 前記한 年月日에 本契約을 締結하였음을 玆에 證明함

美國代表 (휘셔ㅣ大尉)　韓國代表 (朱昌燁)　立會者 (오하란少領) (마ㅣ런中領)

本官이 觀察하고 問議한 바에 依하여 確信되는 것은 交通部를 代表하여 署名한 朱昌燁氏는 以上과 如히 締結할 權限을 가졌으며 또한 一般과의 類似契約에 있어서 交通部를 代表하여 署名하는 사람에 相違無함을 證明한다

휘셔ㅣ大尉　極東司令官의 名義下에 承認함　머라ㅣ大領

0227

DA:九二:○八四:FEO:二五一號契約에對한甲號明細書

本甲號明細書는上記契約에一部다契約者는本明細書의規定과條件에

依하여下記事項을實行할事

A UN車鐵道輸送은積載貨車一輛이一將定行에對하여弗三二○、○○

씩 車隊積載客車는一輛이將定行에對하여弗七五○、○○씩計算한다

B 病院車모ㅣ타카는旅客車로서看한다故로運賃도旅客運賃에準한다

C 支線料滯留置料는支拂치않은다

D 旅客貨物車의客車廻送料는支拂하지않은다

E 契約者는勞動力과材料를利用하여線路建物橋梁機關車車輛等을優秀하

한狀態로維持할것

F 列車는契約將校또는그代理人의要求대로運轉할것

G 契約──는契約將校또는그의正當히認定한代理人이別途로輸送의優先

0228

順位를定한外에는民間輸送에優先하야軍隊輸送에應한다

H 契約者는積載車輛에對한運轉報告를作成한다契約者와契約將校또는美國軍省이任命한將校가輸送의完遂를證明한證明書는請求書支拂承認에對한根據가된다

I 契約者는契約將校에게二種의月報를提出한다各報告書는一通의正本과五通의寫本으로되여每月느저도十五日以前에提出하여야한다月報의一種은日別取扱積載貨車의總數와總走行粁의該月分合計를記載하여야한다다르一種의月報는各車에對한同樣의資料를記載한다

J 美國政府는將次各政府間에合意될때에調整할것을條件으로UN會員國을代表하여旅客및貨物輸送에對하여上記한料金을支拂한다

K 本契約에關聯되는諸請求書와其他諸書類에本契約書의同一性과必要한資料를表示하여야한다

0229

L 本契約條項에依하여契約者는美軍鐵道器具를使用할것이許容된다

本甲號明細書에明示되여있는諸料率은美軍및交通部器具를다使用하여旅客貨物을輸送하든지한쪽만使用하여輸送하든지間에適用되는것이다

0230

輸送契約更新經過

1. 一九五〇年一〇月一日에交通部와美國政府間에UN軍軍事輸送協定을一九五一年三月三十一日期限으로契約番號DA-九二-〇八四FEC-二五一號로締結하였음、

2. 一九五一年四月一日에輸送契約期間을一九五一年九月三十日까지延長하고運賃率을貨車一KM走行에六六〇圓、客車一KM走行에一、六〇〇圓으로引上하였음、(第一次契約修正)

3. 一九五一年一〇月一日에契約期限을一九五二年三月三十一日까지延長하고契約番號를DA-九二-〇八四FEC五八七號로變更하고運賃率을貨車一KM走行에七六八圓客車一KM走行에一、八六〇⊗圓으로引上하였음(契約再協定)

4. 一九五一年一〇月二八日에契約條項中、誤字訂正、不要條文削除

0231

或은更正하였음、（第一次契約條修正）

5. 一九五二年三月一九日에契約期限을一九五二年五月三一日까지延長하였음（第二次修正）

6. 一九五二年五月五日에契約期限을一九五二年六月三十日까지延長하였음（第三次修正）

7. 一九五二年六月十四日에契約期限을一九五二年七月三十一日까지延長하였음（第四次修正）

8. 一九五二年六月三十日에契約番號를DA－九二－〇九三FEC－三三號로變更하고還貸支出項目을二一三二〇二〇－九一－一〇五二P一一〇－〇七 S九二－〇九三 L－二〇八로變更하였음（第五次修正）

9. 一九五二年七月十九日에契約期限을一九五二年九月三十日까지延長하였음（第六次修正）

0232

10. 一九五二年九月十二日에契約期限을一九五二年十月三十一日까지延長하였음 (第七次修正)

11. 一九五二年一〇月에契約期限을一九五二年十一月三十日까지延長하였음 (第八次修正)

12. 一九五二年一一月五日에契約期限을一九五二年十二月三十一日까지延長하였음 (第九次修正)

13. 一九五二年十一月五日에運賃支出項目을二一三二〇二〇 九一·一〇七七P二一一〇·〇七 S九二·一二二 L·二〇八로變更하였음 (第十次修正)

14. 一九五二年十二月十五日에運賃支出項目中 P番號를二一三〇으로變更하였음 (第十一次修正)

15. 一九五二年十二月十七日에契約期限을一九五三年一月三十一日까지

0233

延長하였음 (第十二次修正)

16. 一九五三年一月二十日에契約期間을一九五三年二月二八日까지延長하였음 (第十三次修正)

17. 一九五三年二月十七日에幣貨改革에順應하여運任率及請求書도圓貨로表示하기로하였음 (第十四次修正)

18. 一九五三年二月二十三日에契約期限을一九五三年三月三十一日까지延長하였음 (第十五次修正)

19. 一九五三年三月一五日에契約期限을一九五三年四月三十日까지延長하였음 (第十六次修正)

20. 一九五三年四月一五日에契約期限을一九五三年五月三十一日까지延長하였음 (第十七次修正)

20. 一九五三年五月十二日에契約期限을一九五三年六月三十日까지延長

0234

히였음 (第十八次修正)

22 一九五三年六月一〇日에契約期限을一九五三年七月三十一日까지延長하였음 (第十九次修正)

23 一九五三年九月十二日에美人個人이韓國鐵道客車를使用할時의運賃計算法을協定하였음、卽客車一輛을二五名定員으로看做하여每一人員이協定行KM를二五로除한것이客車一輛이走行한것을計算하기로協定하였음

0235

工事

鐵道契約（陸軍省）

契約者 交通部

住所 釜山

金額 六〇万弗（槪算）

地域 釜山及其附近

支拂 APO五九 美陸軍省第九支出課支出官이行한다

本契約에依하여取得되는資材및工事는下記項目에依하여承認되며別記目的에關한것이며下記項目에依하여支拂된다此項目에支出할수있는額은工事費充當에充分한것이다

二一一二四〇九 九一－二〇八 四六一－〇七 S九九－九九九

本契約은下記法律에依하여承認되며協定된다

一九四七年制定軍陸軍務務調達法第二條〇六（法律四一三－八〇號）

0236

資金使用에關한財務官의證明은必要하지않다

0237

工事契約

前文...輸送契約參照

第一條 工事의 性質과 範圍

契約者는 以下明記된 것을 考慮하면서 契約將校가 要求하는 韓國鐵道의 建設再建 및 復舊를 本契約의 一部로 되어있는 一九五〇年九月二十一日附 KNR-CRE-一號의 韓國鐵道建設再建 및 復舊明細書의 內訳에 嚴格히 服依하여 實行하여야 한다

第二條-第二十七條...輸送契約參照

DA-九二-〇八四 FEC-二五二號契約에 對한 甲號明細書

1. 契約者는 契約將校或은 그가 正當히 任命한 代理人이 要求하는 바에 依하여 鐵道建設再建 및 復舊를 遂行하여야 한다

2. 契約者는 契約將校 또는 그가 正當히 任命한 代理人이 要求한 바에 依하

0238

여鐵道建設、再建및復舊에對하여優先的取扱을한다

3. 鐵道建設再建및復舊에對한標準은契約將校또는그의正當히任命한代理人이指示하는바에依할것이며또그의承認을얻어야한다

4. 契約者는契約將校또는그의正當히任命한代理人이要求한鐵道建設再建및復舊에對한勞賃을支拂하고同工事의勞賃에對하여同額의辨濟를美國政府에請求한다

5. 契約者는本甲號明細書의附表를提出한다此附表는辨濟額請求의基礎가될種目別適用勞賃率을表示한다本賃率은事前申請과契約者의引上要求에對한詳細한理由書가添附된當事者双方의更正協定書가作成되지않으면此를變更할수없다前記附表는本契約書의一部가된다

6. 契約者는各工事의竣工後十五日以內에下記三項目으로分類된詳細한竣工報告六通을契約將校또는그의正當히任命한代理人에게提出하

0239

여야한다

第一項

A 竣工된工事의仔細한明細를記錄하여完全한工事件名及性質

B 着工日

C 竣工日

D 備考

第二項

契約者가使用한勞務者에支拂하는勞賃은鐵道建設工事에共出되는勞務者種類別各種勞務者의資格當實動延日數、各種勞務者의全体人員에對한延日數、各種勞務者의勞賃單價合計及總勞賃別로區分하여야한다

第三項

交通部

0240

契約者는鐵道建設工事에共通되는物件을種目別區分하여使用한物品의一覽表를提出하여야한다本一覽表의寫本은契約將校또는그가正當히任命한代理人을通하여駐韓ECA長官에게送付된다

7.手數料事務費等追加費用은그러한名目으로는一切支拂하지않으며모―든經費는本勞賃附表의單價및金價率에包含되여있다

8.契約者가支拂을받기爲하여提出하는모―든請求書는美陸軍省이任命한將校에依하여工事完全히竣工되고支拂金은本契約條項에一致되고勞務는公共事業에必要하였다고證明하여야한다

9.本契約에關聯되는諸請求書及諸書類에는本契約의同一性과日字를表示하여야한다

丁. 轉契約更新經過

1. 一九五〇年十月一日에 交通部와 美國政府間에 UN丁轉協定을 一九五一年三月二十一日期限으로 契約番號 DA:九二:〇八四FEC:二五二號로 하였음

2. 一九五一年四月 日에 丁轉契約期限을 一九五一年九月三〇日까지 延長하였음 (第 次契約修正)

3. 一九五一年十月 日에 契約期限을 一九五一年十一月三十日까지 延長하고 契約番號를 DA:九二:〇八四FEC:七二六號로 變更하였음

(契約再協定)

4. 一九五一年十二月一日에 契約期限을 一九五二年五月三十一日까지 하고 契約番號를 DA:九二:〇八四FEC:七二七號로 變更하고 勞賃單價를 引上하였음 (第一次契約修正)

交通部

0242

5. 一九五二年五月五日에契約期限을一九五二年十一月三十日까지延長하였음 （第二次契約修正）

6. 一九五二年六月三十日에契約番號를DA:九二:○九三FEC:四二號로變更하고工事代金支出項目을二一三二○二○ 九一-一○五二 P二一一○:○七 S九二:○九三 L二○八로變更하였음

7. 一九五二年九月二十六日에工事代金支出項目中P二一一○-○七으로變更하였음 （第四次契約修正）

8. 一九五二年十一月一日에契約期限을一九五二年十二月三十一日까지延長하였음 （第五次契約修正）

9. 一九五二年十一月五日에工事代金支出項目을二一三二○二○ 九一:一○七七P二一一○-○七 S九二-一二二 L二○八로變更하였음 （第六次契約修正）

0243

10. 一九五二年十二月八日에工事代金支出項目中P二一三〇으로變更하였음 (第七次契約修正)

11. 一九五一年十二月三〇日에契約期限을一九五三年六月三〇日까지延長하였음 (第八次契約修正)

12. 一九五三年二月十七日에通貨改革에關聯하여賃率及請求書도圜貨로表示하기로하였음 (第九次契約修正)

13. 一九五三年四月二十八日에支出項目을二一三二〇 九一一〇七〇
P二九一一一〇七 S九二一一二二 L:二〇八로變更하였음
(第十次契約修正)

14. 一九五三年五月二十日에契約期限을又一九五三年十二月三十一日까지延長하였음 (第十一次契約修正)

0244

甲號明細書의附表

交通部가支拂하는勞務者및監督에對한賃金基準(八時間勞働制에基準)

基準賃金表

| 部類 | 種目 | 基本賃金(八時間制) |
|---|---|---|
| 1 | 牛車 | 六、〇〇〇圓 |
| 2 | 機械運轉手 | 二、四〇〇圓 |
| 〃 | 瓦工 | 二、四〇〇圓 |
| 〃 | 石工 | 二、四〇〇圓 |
| 3 | 鎔接工 | 二、三〇〇圓 |
| 〃 | 仕上工 | 二、三〇〇圓 |
| 4 | 마이平工 | 二、二〇〇圓 |
| 〃 | 木手 | 二、二〇〇圓 |

交通部

0245

| | 職種 | 金額 |
|---|---|---|
| | 配電線工 | 二、二〇〇圓 |
| 〃 | 미싱工 | 二、二〇〇圓 |
| 〃 | 뎍기工 | 二、二〇〇圓 |
| 5 | 重量物運搬人 | 二、〇〇〇圓 |
| 〃 | 톤넬파는人夫 | 二、〇〇〇圓 |
| 〃 | 鐵筋工 | 二、〇〇〇圓 |
| 〃 | 煉瓦工 | 二、〇〇〇圓 |
| | 塗裝工 | 二、〇〇〇圓 |
| 〃 | 鐵力工 | 二、〇〇〇圓 |
| 6 | 勞務者監督 | 一、八〇〇圓 |
| 7 | 特殊勞務者 | 一、四〇〇圓 |
| 8 | 一般勞務者 | 一、二〇〇圓 |

0246

備考

1. 上記各部類勞務者中自己居住地에서떠러진場所又는一定한場所에서
作業을하는境遇에는生活費로서上記料金外에六〇〇圓을받는다

2. 上記部類勞務者가緊急工事에從事할때는日當二食分三〇〇圓을받는
다

3. 上記賃率은一日八時間勞働에基準한것인데万一八時間을超過한時는
每超過時間當日當賃金의一二、五%를追加하여받는다

交通部

0247

UN軍이使用하는通信回線([illegible])에關한口頭約束

一九五四年六月 TMRS Communication Section ~~Communication Section~~ Col. Suit[illegible]와

R.O.T 通信監長과의 協議로 什年間을 二分하여 KCOMZ로부터

로 Pagoda 計劃에 依한 通信線路保修材料의 一部를 繼續供給받

기로 口頭約束됨

龍山 — [illegible] 三回線

龍山 — 清凉里 四 〃

清凉里 — 春川 二回線

龍山 — 大田 四 〃

大田 — 大邱 三 〃

大邱 — 釜山 四 〃

大田 — 裡里 二 〃

0248

交通部

| | |
|---|---|
| 裡里 — 群山 | 二個線 |
| 慶州 — 安東 | 二〃 |
| 安東 — 永川 | 二〃 |
| 永川 — 登山 | 一〃 |
| 永川 — 大邱 | 二〃 |

0249

要望事項

二、海運關係

1. 港灣(埠頭施設等包含)地帶管理에 關한件

六、二五事変當時 韓美間에 締結된 協定締結與否는 不知이나 (閣議)에 依하면 UN軍總司令官과 我國交通部當局間에 協定되었다 함

仁川、釜山、群山、墨湖等 五個港의 主要部分은 UN軍管理下에 두워 我國行政機關의 權限이 미치지 못하는 狀態로 今日에 이르고 있음으로 旣히 締結된 協定이 없을 時는 此際에 明文化하여 當部에 港灣管理運營에 支障이 없도록 하여야 함

參考 本件에 對하여서 休戰后 我國一般民間貿易量 港灣荷役能率增進으로 關議키 爲하여 軍 管理의

交通部

0250

一部解除案을 國務會議에 上程코자 去年 八月

總務處長에게 依賴한 바 있음

2、外國船舶의 UN軍需物資沿岸輸送業務從事排除의 件

四二八五年度以後 各年間의 UN軍需物資의 沿岸輸送은

外國(日本)船舶(含外國船員)이 擔當케 되여 此는 獨立國의

主權을 侵害하고 海運業能力을 我國에서 獲得될 몫을

하게 됨으로 韓國政府로 本件是正을 UN軍側에 折衝하여

왔고 其結果現在 其一部分은 我國船舶(含船員)으로

代替되고 있으나 完全히 代替를 보고 있는 現狀인데 最近 報

告에 依하면 日人船員 代身 我國船員이 數百名 代替되였다

하므로 本件 善處하도록 外務部長官에 通報하는 一方 UN軍

側에는 照會하고 있는바 將次 沿岸輸送에 外國船舶從事

作業檢查에서 個別船舶調査를 積極的으로 拒否排除토록
하여야 하겠음
參考 日船代用으로 方今船舶購買計劃이 二00 万弗 (政府保有弗)
로서 購買事業을 推進中에 있음
3. UN軍에 依한 不法船舶徵發排除의 件
UN軍側에서 民間船舶徵發이 必要한 時에는 海軍總參謀長
을 通하여 一定手續에 依하여 徵發토록 要請할 것
4. 港灣防備 灯台接收을 事前에 關係部와 協議要望의 件
首題의 件 事前協議가 없어서 我國의 港灣灯台의 建設
保守計劃과의 相馳 等의 錯誤를 招來하고 있으니 UN軍側
에서 何種의 施設을 하였을 時는 迅速 通知되어 前後 計劃에
參考가 될 것임

0252

5. 今次 北岸外 港灣 美港灣司令部에 保管 又는 設置한 燈浮標의

件(明細表 別添)

別添 燈台 浮標等은 美港灣司令部에서 保管하는 程

元港口 出入時에 航行安全을 確保하고 있는데 同港이

美軍司令部의 管理에서 解除된 時의 一般商船의 航海

安全上 該燈浮標等 施設의 移管을 要請함

美港灣當局에서 ~~釜山外港에~~ 設置한 標燈浮標는 아래와 같다

| 標識名 | 位置 | 燈質 | 構造 | 記事 |
|---|---|---|---|---|
| 釜山外港標燈浮標 No.1 | N. 35° 05' 01"<br>E. 129° 06' 39" | Fl.G ev 5sec | 黑櫓形 鋼造 | 流失 |
| 〃 No.3 | 〃 35 05 07<br>〃 129 06 22 | 〃 | 〃 | 〃 |
| 〃 No.5 | 〃 35 04 58<br>〃 129 06 10 | 〃 | 〃 | 消灯中 |
| 〃 No.7 | 〃 35 04 52<br>〃 129 05 38 | 〃 | 〃 | 〃 |
| 〃 No.9 | 〃 35 06 02<br>〃 129 04 16 | 〃 | 〃 | 〃 |
| 〃 內港 〃 No.11 | 〃 35 06 13<br>〃 129 03 59 | 〃 | 〃 | 〃 |
| 〃 外港 〃 No.2 | 〃 35 05 22<br>〃 129 06 50 | Fl.R ev 5sec | 紅櫓形 鋼造 | 〃 |
| 〃 No.4 | 〃 35 05 25<br>〃 129 06 [illegible] | | 〃 | 〃 |
| 〃 No.6 | 〃 35 [illegible] 17<br>〃 129 05 59 | | 〃 | 〃 |
| 〃 No.8 | 〃 35 [illegible] 11<br>〃 129 05 48 | | 〃 | 〃 |

0254

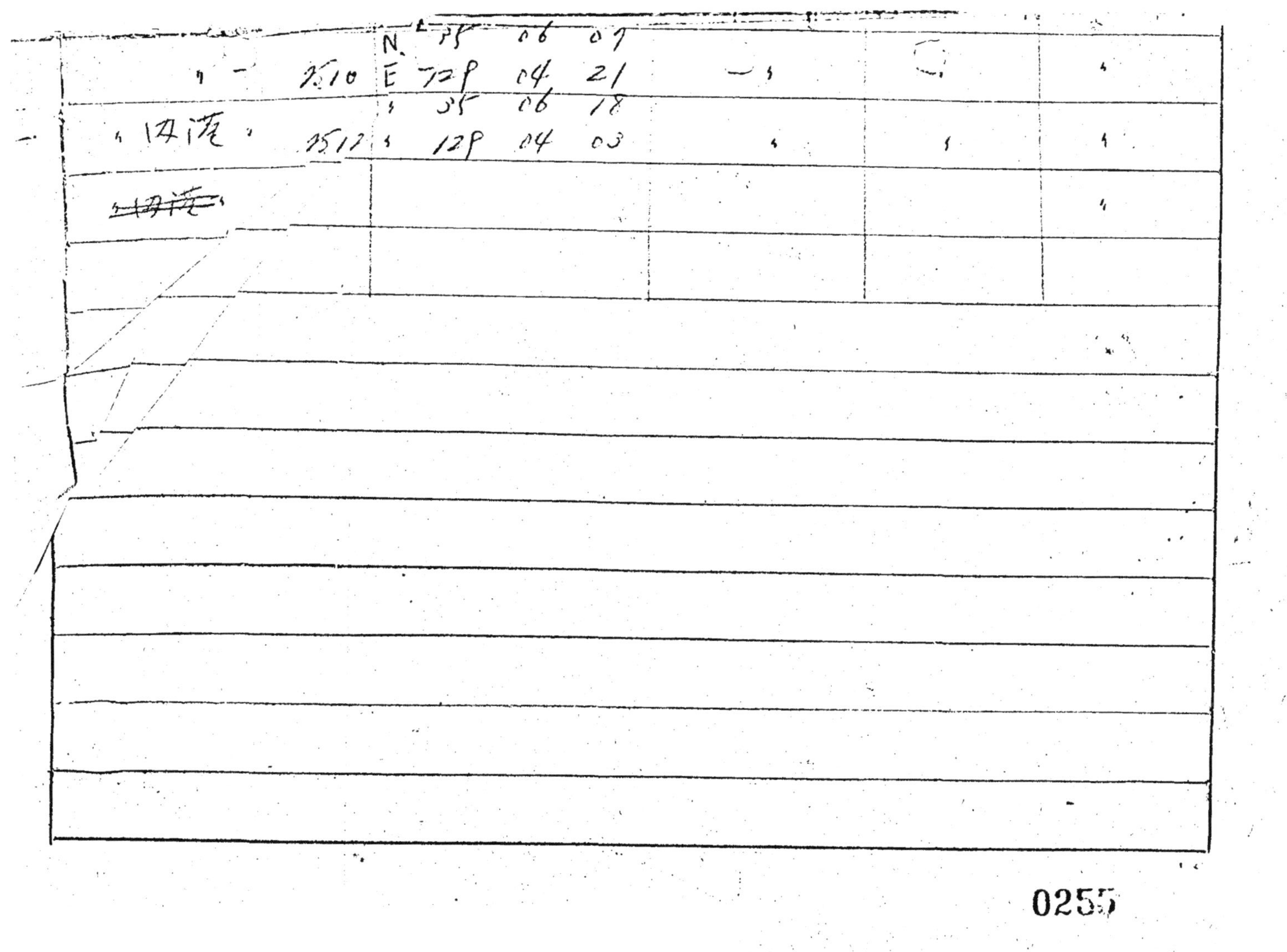

| | | | | | |
|---|---|---|---|---|---|
| 〃 〃 | 2510 | N. 35 06 07<br>E 128 04 21 | — 〃 | ◯ | 〃 |
| 〃 [illegible] 〃 | 2512 〃 | 〃 35 06 18<br>〃 128 04 03 | 〃 | 〃 | 〃 |
| ~~[illegible]~~ | | | | | 〃 |

0255

12 January 1954

SUBJECT: Preparation for the administrative agreement conclusion

FROM : Director of Marine Bureau

TO : Minister of Transportation

1. Management of theports & the port facilities;

It is unknown whether a written agreement about the management of theports and theport facilities was concluded after the outbreak of Korean war, but there is an uncertain report that theagreement has been concluded between commanding officer of UN forces and ROK Government.

To tell the truth, five ports-Inchon, Pusan, Masan, Kunsan, and Chaiju - and there facilities are under the management of UN forces and outside of our government control. Therefore, if not concluded the above agreement, its conclusion in written is much desirous to exclude some inconvenience in managing and operating of the facilities of our government.

In this connection, we have requested officer of general affairs to submit the release program of some part of UN forces managing part facilities to the cabinet council with the purpose to increase the efficiency of the port stevedoring business and private forign trade.

2. Elimination of forign vessel using in Korean coastwise Transportation for UN forces service;

After the Korean war, forign (Japanese) vessels and forign seamen operating their vessels are engaging in coastwise transportation of UN forces military service, which means to violate sovereignty of our nation, and can't gain the valuable dollars of the charterals and wages.

Whole nation opposed against this and resulted in accomplishment of some replacement of those forign seamen and vessels with that of Koreans thorough our negotiations, but still we can't accomplish the whole replacement.

According to the recent information that some hundreds of philipine seamen instead of Korean seamen. In future, it should be eliminated firmly that forign vessels engage in Korean coastwise transportation.

For reference, the purchasing group of vessels to replace with forign vessels is carrying on their duty with $2,000,000,00 authorized to buy them.

3. Elimination of irregal commandeering of private vessels by UN forces;

We should request that UN forces must take the regular steps thorough chief of ROK Navy general staff when UN forces needs a private vessel.

4. Previous consultation with the concerning organization pertaing to the repair of port facilities and the building of light house;

According to the previous consultation, we can draw a comparison whether it my run counter to our program pertaining to the repair of port facilities and the building of light house, and for reference we can recognize what kind of facilities UN forces built.

0256

5. Lighting buoys established outside and inside of Pusan Port;

The lighting buoys showned by the attached sheet have been established by US port commanding and serving in convenience of vessels entering or ~~leaving Pusan Port.~~ In release of the management of US port commanding, it is requested that he should transfer the mangement authority of the above equipments to our government for safe voyage of general merchat vessels.

0257

Lights buoys are as the following

| Name of lighting buoy | Position | Characteristic of buoy | Construction of buoy | Remark |
|---|---|---|---|---|
| No.1 Lighting buoy of Pusan Port outside | N 35' 05' 01"<br>E 129' 06' 39" | FI. Ger. 5 sec | Made iron black tower type | Swept away |
| No 3 | N 35 05 07<br>E 129 06 10 | " | " | " |
| No 5 | N 35 04 58<br>E 129 06 10 | " | " | Working |
| No 7 | N 35 04 52<br>E 129 05 38 | " | " | " |
| No 9 | N 35 06 02<br>E 129 04 16 | " | " | " |
| No 11. Lighting buoy of Pusan post inside | N 35 06 13<br>E 129 03 59 | "<br>" | "<br>" | "<br>" |
| No 2 Lighting buoy of Pusan port outside | N 35 05 22<br>E 129 06 50 | FIR. pr 5sec | Made in iron red tower type | " |
| No 4 | N 35 05 25<br>E 129 06 16 | | | " |
| No 6 | N 35 05 17<br>E 129 05 59 | | | " |
| No 8 | N 35 05 11<br>E 129 05 48 | | | " |
| No 10 | N 35 06 07<br>E 129 04 21 | | | " |
| No 12 | N 35 06 07<br>E 129 04 03 | | | " |

0258

23 April 1953

AGREEMENT BETWEEN TO, KCOMZ, KCAC REPRESENTATIVE AND MINISTER OF TRANSPORTATION

Purpose: To establish a procedure under which the Minister of Transportation, Republic of Korea will assume responsibility for the allotment of rail cars to civilian shippers.

Scope: This procedure to apply to the movement of all civilian shipments, both programmed and those moving under special releases.

Control: The Transportation Officer, KComZ, is responsible for the allocation of rail cars in Korea. Within overall commitments, the Transportation Officer, KComZ will make a bulk allocation of rail cars to KCAC for the movement of relief supplies, and also an allocation to the Minister of Transportation for the shipment of civilian supplies other than relief. The movement of relief supplies will be the responsibility of KCAC. The movement of all other civilian supplies will be the responsibility of the Minister of Transportation, with the assistance and under the supervision of KCAC.

Programmed Freight: Civilian shipments by the same consignor originating at one point, and which require 15 or more rail cars to accomplish movement within a 15 day period, will be programmed. The Minister of Transportation will consolidate and submit such request to the Transportation Officer, KComZ seven days prior to the 1st and 15th of each month. These requests will then be included in the Rail Movement Program and the rail cars required for movement within the period will be broken down to a daily average and deducted from the overall allocation to the Minister of Transportation.

Non-Programmed Freight: All other civilian shipments not included in the Rail Movement Program will move on Special Releases issued by the Transportation Officdr, KComZ, within the overall allocation to the Minister of Transportation, after those cars required to move the programmed shipments have been deducted. Procedure in obtaining Special Releases is as follows:

1. Consignor will make application to KNR Station Master, Regional Officer or to the Minister of Transportation.

2. KNR Station Master will consolidate requests and submit same to Regional Office.

3. Each Regional Office will consolidate requests and submit same to the Director of Land Transportation, Minister of Transportation.

4. The Minister of Transportation will then evaluate all requests, establish priorities for movement, and submit to the Transportation Officer, KComZ, those requests which have been approved not to exceed the remaining overall allocation. Copies to be forwarded to KCAC.

/s/ Fred Greene, TO KComZ

/s/ Tony Jepson, Rep. KCAC

/s/ S.M. Kim
Vice-Minister of Transportation

OPERATIONAL AGREEMENT
ROK TRANSPORT VEHICLES
UNKRA PROJECT 6.5 (432-A)

The following agreement was made and entered into this 3rd day of June 1953, BETWEEN:

The Government of the Republic of Korea, hereinafter referred to as the Government,

The United Nations Korean Reconstruction Agency, hereinafter referred to as UNKRA; and

The United Nations Command, hereinafter referred to as UNC.

## ARTICLE 1 OBJECTIVE

It is the objective of this agreement to procure trucks and other motor vehicles to supplement the existing transportation facilities in the Republic of Korea available for purposes of relief and rehabilitation.

## ARTICLE 11 PROCUREMENT

UNKRA will, at its own expense procure from outside Korea and transport to one or more Korean ports according to availability of port facilities, trucks and motor vehicles in numbers and types as set forth in a list compiled by the Korean Ministry of Transportation and approved by the other parties to this agreement which list has been attached hereto and made a part hereof as Annex "A".

## ARTICLE 111 RECEIPT AND STORAGE

1. The Government shall through suitable agents or agencies of its own choice, receive the motor vehicles on board ships in Korean ports, and provide for their unloading, storage and safe-keeping from the date of receipt until final disposal as described below.

2. Upon receipt of each vehicle the Government will hand over to UNKRA a receipt, containing time and place of receipt of the vehicle, make and type of the vehicle, chassis and engine Numbers and a complete list of all accessories and tools received with the vehicle.

## ARTICLE 1V. DISTRIBUTION

1. A plan of allocation of these vehicles by sale to public and private end-users in Korea has been developed by the Ministry of Transportation, approved by the other parties to this agreement, and is attached hereto and made a part hereof as Annex "B".

2. Upon arrival of the individual shipments of the vehicles listed, the Government through its agents shall provide for immediate sale to the end-users listed, according to priorities established by the Ministry of Transportation.

3. Vehicles shall be transferred into the possession of end-users against cash payment only, and the end-users upon payment of purchase price and handling charges (see Article VI) and upon taking possession of the vehicles, shall acquire title and ownership of same.

0260

4. No vehicle shall be sold to an end-user, unless an undertaking is executed by him to the effect that without permission ofhte Government he will not sell, lease, or otherwise dispose of the vehicle or prts thereof for a period of two years, except when, through no fault of his, the vehicle has been rendered completely unserviceable by accident, and that should be violate this undertaking, he will pay a stipulated penalty to the Government upon demand.

ARTICLE V. FINANCIAL PROVISIONS

1. The net prices to be charged to end-users shall represent cost to UNKRA, c.i.f.. Korean port, equivalent to the amount of U.S. Dollars at the rate of exchange as shall be applicable to similar transactions under UNKRA program in Korea.

2. The Government shall deposit the net sales prices collected in the UNKRA Aids Proceeds Account with the Bank of Korea, or, if the Reconstruction Account should be established by such time, in the Reconstruction Account, without 15 days from the date of collection.

ARTICLE VI. HANDLING CHARGES AND INLAND TRANSPORTATION

The Government or its appointed agents shall defray the charges for unloading, inland transportation, initial maintenance and sale, and such charges shall be added to the purchase price collected from the end-users of the vehicles.

ARTICLES VII. SPARE PARTS

1. Coincident with the procurement of the vehicles listed in Annex "A" UNKRA will take action for the procurement of spare parts as described in a list attached hereto and made a part hereof Annex "A".

These spare parts shall be similarly sold to one or more qualified automotive parts supply agencies who shall be under contract with the Ministry of Transportation to provide spare part service to the end-users to whom the vehicles have been allocated and sold, under conditions of service and priorities as specified by the Ministry of Transportation.

2. The provisions of Articles III through VI shall also apply with respect to these spare parts.

ARTICLE VIII. UNKRA RESERVE POOL

1. UNKRA reserves the ritht to retain as many of thevehicles including appropriate spare parts listed in Annex "A" for utilization in its Korea reconstruction program, as shall at the time of their arrival be determined by UNKRA, not, however in excess of 20% of the total number of units and of 75% of units of less than 1½ ton capacity.

ARTICLE IX. WARRANTIES

UNKRA makes no warranty whatever in respect to the vehicles and spare parts that are subject of this agreement. Should however any of the vehicles or parts show or develop any defects for which a warranty was made by the manufacturers or suppliers, UNKRA sahll on the end-users behalf take all steps necessary to protect their rights from such warranty.

0261

ARTICLE X. GOVERNMENT SUPPORT

1. The Government will admit the vehicles and spare parts into the Republic of Korea free of customs, excise, or any other levies normally exacted upon the impotation of goods into the country, and shall not allow its agencies in performing the sales to end-users a margin of profit in excess of 10% of the total of the sales price including handling expenses.

2. The total sales price collected from individual end-users will, therefore consist of

(a) the net price (computed as described in Article V)

(b) the handling charges (as described in Article VI)

(c) 10% of the total of the sums computed as per((a) and (b) above.

3. The Government will permit and enable authorized representatives of UNKRA and/or the United Nations Command, to observe and inspect the activities of its agents in respect to the handling, transportation, maintenance and sale of the vehicles and spare parts, made available to suchrepresentatives at any reasonable time, all pertinent records, and shall submit to UNKRA quarterly detailed progress reports on the execution of this project.

4. The Government shall closely supervise and enforce the end-users undertakings as described above under IV, 4.

ARTICLE XI. UNITED NATIONS COMMAND SUPPORT

The UNC undertakes to make available to UNKRA all port, rail and other facilities under its control as may be necessary in the implementation of this agreement and compatible with military requirements.

DONE at Pusan on the day first hereinabove written.

For the Government of the Republic of Korea:

Sgd. SUNG SOON YOON

For the United Nations Korean Reconstruction Agnecy:

Sgn. JAMES V McCULLOUGH

For the United Nations Command:

Sgn. CHARIES E. SHEPHERD

0262

PROJECT 6.5 (432-A) TRUCKS

ANNEX "A" and ANNEX "B"

The Government has name the ROK Office of Supply as its agent to receive and collect payment for the trucks, spare parts, accessories, tires and tubes, and distribute the trucks.

The ROK Office of Supply will deliver the spare parts, accessories, tires and tubes to the Auto Supply Company, a Government agency, which shall act as the distributing agency for these items.

The nomenclature and number of 574 trucks to be allocated are as follows:

| Number of Vehicles | Nomenclature |
|---|---|
| 10 | AUSTIN 2-TON L.W.B. CHASSIS CAB FITTED WITH ALL-STEEL PICK-UP BODY II'6 "x6'7"x1'6" |
| 10 | AUSTIN 1-TON 4x4 TRUCK ASSENBLED TO STANDARD SPECIFICATIONS. |
| 10 | AUSTIN FORWARD CONTROL COACH CHASSIS, STANDARD SPECIFICATIONS. |
| 10 | SUTIN 5-TON S.W.B. CHASSIS CAB FITTED WITH TASKER SEA "KING PIN" COUPLING SERVO BRAKE CONVERSION TO ENABLE UNIT TO BE COUPLED TO AUSTIN 8/10-TON SEMI-TRAILER (ITEM 5) |
| 12 | AUSTIN HARDWOOD FLOORED SEMI-TRAILER TO CARRY 8/10-TON LOAD FITTED WITH SEA COUPLING TASKER LEG GEAR WITH RAISED SIDE RAVES, THE FLOOR CARRYING STEEL RUNNERS |
| 410 | AUSTIN 2-TON L.W.B. CHASSIS CAB FITTED WITH MULLINER ALL STEEL PLATFORM BODY WITH STAKE SIDES |
| 10 | AUSTIN 2-TON L.W.B. CHASSIS CAB FITTED WITH HOPPER BODY OF 4 CUBIC YARD CAPACITY |
| 2 | AUSTIN 5-TON S.W.B. CHASSIS CAB FITTED WITH MANN EGERTON BREAKDOWN BODY AND EQUIPMENT, TYPE "S" BODY AND BUE 5 EQUIPMENT. |
| 50 | AUSTIN 2-TON L.W.B. CHASSIS CAB FITTED WITH MULLINERS BODY AND STAKE SIDES FOR ITEM 6, AND TARPAULIN |
| 50 | AUSTIN 5-TON S.W.B CHASSIS CAB FITTED WITH ANTHONY HOIST NO.17 GEAR OF 4 CUBIC YARD CAPACITY DROPSIDE STEEL BODY |

0263

The general plan of allocation ismade in the order of priority as listed below:

1. Industry:

| | |
|---|---|
| Irrigation | Machine |
| Ship-building | Power Ind. |
| Marine | Technical |
| Textile | Fertilizer |
| Fishery | Chemical |
| Mining | Paper |
| Coal | |

11. Commercial Use:

General commercial transport, Grain and Economic Aid Supply Transport.- ROK Office of Supply

111. Government Use:

| | |
|---|---|
| Quarantine | Sanitary Disposal |
| Hospital | School |
| Sanatorium | Speical Use (trailer) |

1V. UNKRA Use:

V. Other Uses:

| | |
|---|---|
| Forestry | Salt and carrot farming |
| Peat | Others |
| Port stevedoring | |
| Tobacco farming. | |

The specific allocation of trucks within the above general plan will be made by the Ministry of Transportation subject to approval by the parties concerned.

0264

Contract No.DA-92-084FEC-251
(Negotiated)

Dated 1 October 1950

CONTRACT FOR SERVICES

DEPARTMENT OF THE ARMY

CONTRACT & ADDRESS: Korean National Railways
Pusan, Korea

AMOUNT: (Estimated) $1,500,000,00

LOCATION: Korea (Whoever required)

PAYMENT:

To be made by: The Disbursing Officer, 9th Finance Disbursing Section, Department of Army of United States, APO 59.

The supplies and services to be obtained by this instrument are authorized by, are for the purpose set forth in, and are changeable to the following allotment.

2112409 91-208 P 461-07 899-999

Certificate of the Fiscal Officer as to availability of funds is not required.

This contract is authorized by and negotiated under the following laws;

Section 2c (6) of the Armed services Procurement Act of 1947 (Public Law 413-80th Congress).

0265

Contract No. DA-92-084 FEC-251

CONTRACT FOR SERVICES

This contract, entered into as of the 1st day of October, 1950, by and between the United States of America (hereinafter called the "Government"), represented by the Contracting Officer executing thi cotract, and theKorean National Railways, a corporation organized and existing under the laws of the Republic of Korea, having its principal office and place of business at Pusan, Korea, (hereinafter referred to as the "Contractor"), witnesseth that the parties hereto do mutually agree as follows:

ARTICLE 1. Character and Extent of Services: a. The contractor shall furnish and deliver for the consideration herinafter specified, Railway service as required, including transportation of both Freight and Passenger traffic as specified, in strict accordance with conditions, specifications, and terms, which are designated and set forthin Schedul "A" attached hereto and all of which are made a part hereof.

b. Should the continued employment under this contract of any person in the contractor's organisation be deemed by the Contracting Officer to be prejudicial to the interest of the Government, that person shall be immediately removed from the work.

ARTICLE 2. Changes: The Contracting Officer may at time, by a written order make any changes in this contract which may either increase or decrease the work and services hereunder. If such changes cause an increase in the work and services required under this contract, or in the time required for performance, an equitable adjustment shall be made and the contract shall be modified in writing accordingly. Any claim for adjustment under this Article must be assented in writing within 30days from the date the change is ordered. Provided, however, that the Contracting Officer, if he determines that the facts justify such action,may receive and consider, and with the approval of the Commander-in-Chief, Far East, or his duly authorized representative, adjust any such claim asserted at any time prior to the date of final settlement of the contract. If the parites fail to agree upon the adjustment to be made, the dispute shall be determined as provided in Article 6.(Disputes), but nothing in this article shall excuse the contractor from proceeding with the prosecution of the work and services so changed.

ARTICLE 3. Period of Services: The contractor shall commence all work and services under this contract as of the effective date hereof and shall complete all work and services within six(6) months after the effective date hereof, provided, however, that prior to expiration of the above period the Government shall have the option to extend the Contract upon the same terms for an additional period of not more than six(6) months, upon fifteen (15) days written notice from the Contracting Officer, or his authorized representative, in advance of the time it would otherwise expire.

-2-

0266

ARTICLE 4. Compensation to the Contractor: As sole and entire monetary consideration for the satisfactory performance of the services required to be performed by and under this contract; except as otherwise expressly provided herein, the Government will pay the Contractor as stated in attached Schedule A.

ARTICLE 5. Method of Payment: a. Payments will be made to the Contractor upon presentation of properly ceritfied payment vouchers and such other supporting documents as may be required by the Contracting Officer or his authorized representative.

b. The Contractor may be required to furnish the Contracting Officer with properly authenticated payrolls and/or other reports prior to the effecting of payment above provided.

c. Prior to final payment, the contractor may be required by the Contracting Officer to furnish to Government with a release of all claims against the Government arising out of and by virtue of this contract.

ARTICLE 6. Disputes: Except as otherwise provided in this contract, any dispute concerning a question of fact arising under this contract which is not disposed of by agreement shall be decided by the Contracting Officer, who shall reduce his decision to writing and mail or otherwise furnish a copy thereof to the Contractor. Within 30 days from the date of receipt of such copy, the Contractor may appeal by mailing or otherwise furnishing to the Contracting Officer a written appeal addressed to the Commander-in-Chief, Far East, and the decision of the Commander-in-Chief, Far East, or that of his duly authorized representative (other than the Contracting Officer under this contract) for the hearing of such appeals, upon personal approval by the Commander-in-Chief, Far East, or his desingnated deputy, shall be final and conclusive upon the parties hereto when the amount involved in the appeal is $50,000 or less; provided that, if no appeal is taken, within the said 30 days, the decision of the Contracting Officer shall be final and conclusive. When the amount involved is more than $50,000 the decision of the Commander-in-Chief, Far East, shall be subject to written appeal within 30 days after the receipt thereof by the Contractor to the Secretary of the Army and the decision of the Secretary or his duly authorized representative for the hearing of such appeals shall be final and conclusive; provided that, if no such further appeal is taken, within the said 30 days, the decision of the Commander-in-Chief, Far East, shall be final and conslusive. In connection with any appeal proceeding under this clause. the Contractor shall be afforded an opportunity to be heard and to offer evidence in support of its appeal. Pending final decision of a dispute hereunder, the Contractor shall proceed dilignetly with the performance of the contract and in accordance with the Contracting Officer's decision.

ARTICLE 7. Contracting Officer's Decisions: The extent and character of the work and services to be performed by the contractor shall be subject to the general supervision, direction, control and approval of the Contracting Officer to whom the Contractor shall report and be resoponsible. In the event that there shall be any dispute with regard to the extent and character of the work to be done the decision of the Contracting Officer shall govern, bug the Contractor shall have the right of appeal as provided in Article 6, (Disputes).

ARTICLE 8. Compliance with Laws and Regulations: The Contractor undertakes that he will comply with all Republic of Korea national and local laws.

ARTICLE 9. Notice to the Government of Labor Disputes: Whenever the Contractor has knowledge that an actual or potential labor dispute is delaying or threatans to delay the timely performance of this contract, the Contractor shall immediately give notice thereof, including all relenvent information with respect thereto, to the Contracting Officer.

ARTIBLE 10, Termination and Cancellation: a. The services of the Contractor, or any part thereof, may be terminated for the convenience of the Government at any time, upon notice to the contractor or its representatives, without liability other than for services already performed, whenever the Contracting Officer may determine that such action is for the best interest of the Government. At the specified date of termination, unless the notice otherwise directs, the Contractor shall discontinue all work and services or the specified part thereof, as required in the notice.

b. The services of the contractor also may be terminated at any time in whole or part upon the default or unjustifiable delay of the Contractor, However, any failure to perform the contract or part thereof arising out of causes beyond the control and without the fault or negligence of the Contractor such as, but not limited to, acts of God, public enemy, fire, floods, epidemics, strikes, and acts of the Government shall not constitute default or unreasonable delay by the Contractor.

c. The Contractor shall be guided by and shall act in accordance with directions and requests of the Contracting Officer whenever the transfer, dismissal, or replacement of any employee shall be deemed by the Contracting Officer to be necessary or advisable in the interests of the Government. In case such directions or request of the Contracting Officer is based upon a determination by him of misconduct, negligence, or inefficiency on the part of the Contractor's emplyee, he shall state such determination in writing and the grounds thereof shall be documented in the contract file.

ARTICLE 11. Adjustments: a. The Government shall be entitled to an adjustment as determined by the Contracting Officer in reduction of Payments to the contractor, on account of any day when services hereunder are required, upon which any employee of the Contractor does not perform.

-4-

0268

services by reason of : (1) voluntary idleness; (2) disability resulting from his own misconduct, neglignece, or inefficiency; (3) disability which does not result from the emplyee, th the extent that it exceeds seven (7) days during a six (6) months' period of the contract; and (4) having been discharged from employment by the Contractor in connection with this contract under Article 10c above, or having ceased employment for any other reason. Any dispute concerning adjustment hereunder shall be deemed to involve a question of fact and shall be subject to appeal under Article 6, (Disputes) hereunder.

ARTICLE 12. No Sub-Contracts: No sub-contracts are authorized under this contract.

ARTICLE 13. Non-assignability of Claims: Claims by the contractor for any sums due or to become due and/or any other claims under this contract shall not be assignable.

ARTICLE 14. Employee Contracts: The Contractor shall make available to the Contracting Officer such copies of emplyment contract or agreements entered into with any employees of the contractor engaged in performing services to be rendered under this contract as may be required by the Contracting Officer.

ARTICLE 15. Data to Become Property of Government. All notes, designs, drawings, memoranda, and other technical data, etc., any, furnished by the Contractor pursuant to or developed in connection with the provisions of this contract shall become and remain the property of the Government and it shall have the rights to use them for any purpose without any additional compensation to the contractor and any such data, etc., in the possession of the contractor shall be delivered to the Government whenever requested by the Contracting Officer.

ARTICLE 16. Employee Insurance: The Contractor will provide and maintatin for his employees all required insurance, including but not limited to workmen's Compensation Insurance, providing compensation for disability, death, accident or illness.

ARTICLE 17. Convenant Against Contingent Fees: The Contractor warrents that no person or selling agency has been employed or retained to solicit or secure this contract upon an agreement or understanding for a commission, percentage, brokerage, or contingent fee, excepting boan fide employees or bona fide established commercial or selling agencies maintained by the Contractor for the purpose of escuring business. For breach or violation of this warranty, the Government shall have the right to annul this contract without liability or, in its discretion, to deduct from the contract price or consideration the full amount of such commission percentage, brokerage, or contingent fee.

ARTICLE 18. Officials Not to Benefit: No member of or delegate to Congress, or resident commissioner, shall be admitted to any share or part of this contract or to any benefit that may arise therefrom; but this provision shall not be construed to extend to this contract if made with a corporation for its general benefit.

ARTICLE 19. Renegotiation: a. This contract is subject to the Renegotiation Act of 1948.

b. The Contractor (which term as used in this clause means the party contracting to furnish the articles or perform the work required by this contract) agrees, within thirty (30) days after receipt of its signed copy of this contract, to notify the Military Renegotiation Policy and Review Board, Office of the Secretary of Defens, Washington 25, D.C. of such contract, indicating its own name and address: Provided that, if the Contractor has previously reported to the Military Renegotiation Policy and Review Board any contract or purchase order subject to the Renegotiation Act of 1948, such notification shall not be necessary.

ARTICLE 20. Audits: The Government at any reasonable time shall have the right inspect theworking premises and to audit the books and records of the Contractor, so far as relates to the Performance and costs under this contract.

ARTICLE 21. Confliction in Translation: In cases of any conflict or ambiguity between the English text of this contract or any translation thereof, the English shall prevail.

ARTICLE 22. Definitions: As used throughout this contract, the following terms shall have the meanings set forth below:
a. The term "Secretary" means the Secretary, the Under Secretary, or any Assistant Secretary of the Department; and the term "his duly authorized representative" means any person or persons or board (other than the Contracting Officer) authorized to act for the Secretary.

b. The term "Commanding General" means the Commander-in-Chief, Far East; and the term "his duly authorized representative" means any person or persons or board (other than the Contracting Officer) authorized to act for the Commanding General.

c. The term "Contracting Officer" means the person executing this contract on behalf of the Government, and any other officer or civilian employee who is a properly designated Contracting Officer; and the term shall include, except as otherwise provided in this contract, the authorized representative of the Contracting Officer acting within the limits of his authority.

ARTICLE 23. Schedule: Schedule A is hereto attached and is made a part hereof.

ARTICLE 24. Approval: This contract shall be subject to the written approval of the Commander-in-Chief, Far East, or his duly authorized representative and shall not be binding until so approved.

-6-

0270

ARTICLE: Extras: Except as otherwise provided in this contract, no payments for extras shall be made unless such extras and theprice therefor have been authorized in writing by the Contracting Officer.

ARTICLE 26. Inspection: Inspection of work projects will be by representatives of the Commanding General to assure satisfactory performance and completion.

ARTICLE: 27. Altherations: The following changes were made in this contract before it was signed by theparties hereto . None.



0271

IN WITNESS WHEREOF, the parties hereto have executed this contract as ofthe day and year first above written.

TWO WITNESSES: THE UNITED STATES OF AMERICA:

BY: ______

HOWARD W. MARTENS
Lt Col
714th Trans Railway Opr Bn
APO 59
( Address )

WILLIAM O FISCHER
Capt QM
Purchasing & Contracting Officer
(Official Title)

KOREAN NATIONAL RAILWAYS:

BY: ______

PAUL F. O'HARAN
Major TC
714th Trans Railsay Opr Bn
APO 59
( Address )

Director of Finance Bureau
Ministry of Transportation
Republic of Korea
Pusan, Korea
(Business Address)

I hereby certify that, to the best of my knowledge and belief, based upon observation and inquiry ______, who signed this contract for the Korean National Railways, Pusan, Korea, had authority to execute same, and is the individual who signs similar contracts on behalf of this corporation with the Public generally.

______
( Signature of Contracting Officer)

APPROVED FOR, AND IN THE NAME OF
THE COMMANDER-IN-CHIEF, FAR EAST

BY ______
H.T.MILLER,
Colonel,TC
Transportation Officer,
GHQ, FEC.

-8-

0272

SCHEDULE "A" TO CONTRACT NO. DA-92-084-FEC-251

This Schedule A is attached to and made a part of the above numbered contract. In accordance with the terms and conditions thereof the Contractor will furnish the following:

Railway services for themilitary forces of the member countries of the United Nations, including transportation of both passenger traffic and freight traffic at (a) Three Hundred Twenty Korean Won, per loaded freight car, per kilometer of haulage; (b) Seven Hundred Seventy Five Korean Won, per loaded passenger car occupied by Armed Forces personnel, per kilometer of transportation.

Hospital cars and self-propelled moter coaches are classed as passenger cares under this agreement and charges will be accordingly.

No charges will be assessed to the United States Government for any movement(s) of empty freight or empty passenger equipment.

The Contractor will maintain its tracks, structures, bridges, locomotives, and rolling stock to the highest standard consistent with availability oflabor and materials.

The trains will be operated as requested by the Contracting Officer orhis duly authorized representative.

The Contractor will furnish a list ofmovements ofloaded cars. A certification by the Contractor and Commissioned Officer of the Department of Army of theUnited States, that such services were performed, will be supporting basis for approval of appropriate invoices for payment.

The Contractor will submit two separate monthly reports to the Contracting Officer. Each report will be made up of original and five duplicate copies, certified corredt, and will be submitted no later than the fifteenth day of each month. One report will list by days, the total number ofloaded freight cars handled and total kilometers of haulage, together with a grand total of each for the month. The second report will list the same information for loaded passenger cars.

The United States Government will make payment of such charges as aforeindicated for both passenger and freight traffic for member countries ofUnited Nations, with provision for future adjustment as when so agreed between Goverments.

Contract indentification and data will appear on all bills and any other documentation ofcorrespondence pertinent to this contract.

Use of United States Army railroad equipment by the Contractor is allowable under this Contract. All rates contained in this Schedule "A" are for movements of passengers and/or freight in either or both United States of Korean National Railways equipment.

0273

The Modification Process of theContract for Railway Service

1. The Contract for military Railway Service of UN Foreces (Contract No. DA-92-084 FEC-251), ofwhich duration was from 1st October 1950 to 31st March 1951, was entered into by the United States of America and Korean National Railways on 1st October 1950.

2. The Contract duration was extended to 30th September 1951, and freight car rate per kilometer was increased to W600.00 and passenger car rate per Kilometer to W1,600,00 on 1st April 1951.
.......... 1st Modification..........

3. The Contract duration was extended to 31st March 1952, the Contract No. was changed to DA-92-084 FEC-587, and freight car rate per kilometer was increased to W 768,00 and passenger car rate per Kilometer to W 1,860,00 on 1st October 1951.
.......... Negotiated ..........

4. Some articles of the Contract were amended or excluded on 28th October 1951.
..........1st Modification .......

5. The Contract duration was extended to 31st May 1952 on 19th March 1952.
.........2nd Modification.........

6. The Contract duration was extended to 30th June 1952 on 5th May 1952.
.........3rd Modification...........

7. The Contract duration was extended to 31st July 1952 on 14th June 1952.
.........4th Modification...........

8. The Contract No. was changed to DA-92-093 FEC-33, and the appropriation symbole was changed to 21320 91-1052 P110-07 892-093 L-208.
........5th Modification.............

9. The Contract duration was extended to 30th September 1952 on 19th July 1952.
.........6th Modification..........

10. The Contract duration was extended to 31st October 1952 on 12th September 1952.
.........7th Modification.........

11. The Contract duration was extended to 30th November 1952 in October 1952.
..........8th Modification...........

12. The Contract duration was extended to 31st December 1952 on 9th Nov. 1952.
..........9th Modification..........

13. The appropriation symbole was changed to 2132020 91-1077 P2110-07 892-122 L-208 on 5th November 1952.
....... .10th Modification..............

14. The Project No. P2110 was changed to P2130 on 15th December 1952.
........11th Modification.............

15. The Contract duration was extended to 31st January 1953 on 17th December 1952.
........12th Modification..........

16. The Contract duration was extended to 28th February 1953 on 20th Jan. 1953.
........13th Modification.......... 0274

17. In accordance with the currency reform dated 17th February 1953, old Won rates and prices were amended to read Hwan at 1/100th of Won rates and prices.
...........14th Modification.......

18. The Contract duration was extended to 31st March 1953 on 23rd Feb. 1953.
...........15th Modification .......

19. The Contract duration was extended to 30th April 1953 on 15th Mar. 1953.
...........16th Modification.........

20. The Contract duration was extended to 31st May 1953 on 15th April 1953.
..........17th Modification..........

21. The Contract duration was extended to 30th June 1953 on 12th May 1953.
..........18th Modification.........

22. The Contract duration was extended to 31st July 1953 on 10th June 1953.
..........19th Modification........

23. Compasation for individual travel on KNR passenger car was agreeded on 12th September 1953, namely, the number of passengers per "whole car" should be considered 25 passengers.

0275

Contract No DA-92-084 EEC-252

(Negotiated)

CONTRACT FOR CONSTRUCTION SERVICE

DEPARTMENT OF THE ARMY

CONTRACTOR: KOREAN NATIONAL RAILWAYS

ADDRESS: Pusan, Korea

AMOUNT: (Estimated) $600,00,00

LOCATION: Pusan, Korea, and Vicinity

PAYMENT: To be made by the Disbursing Officer, 9th Finance Disbursing Section. Department of Army of United States, APO 59

The supplies and services to be obtained by this instrument are authorized by are for the purposes set forth in, and are chargeable to the following allotment, the available balance of which is sufficient to cover the cost of the same:

2112409 91-208 461-07 899-999

This Contract is authorized by and negotiated under the follwing laws:

Section 2c(6) of the Armed Services procurement Act of 1947 (Public Law 413-80the Congress).

Certificate of the Fiscal Officer as to availability of funds is not required.

0276

CONTRACT FOR CONSTRUCTION SERVICE

DEPARTMENT OF THE ARMY

THIS CONTRACT. entered into as of 1st day of October 1950. by the UNITED STATES OF AMERICA, (hereinafter called the Government), repesented by the Contracting Officer executing this Contract, and the Korean National Railways, a cerperation organized and existing under the laws of the Republic of Korea, having its principal office and place of business at Pusan, Korea, (hereinafter referred to as the "Contractor"), withnesseth that the parties hereto do mutually agree as follows:

ARTICLE 1. Character and Extent of Services: The Contractor shall for consideration hereinafter specified, perform such construction, reconstruction, and/or rehabilitation of the Korean National Railways, as requested by the Contratting Officer, as required and specified, in strict accordance with the specifications entitled "Spercifications for Construction, Reconstruction, and/or Rehabilitation of the Korean National Railways, code No. KNR-CRE-1, dated 21 September 1950", which are made a part hereof.

ARTICLE 2. Changes: The Contracting Officer may at time, by a written order, make any changes in this contract which may either increase or decrease the work and services hereunder. If such changes cause an increase or decrease in the work and services required under this Contract, or in the time required for perfermance, and equitable adjustment shall be made and the Contract shall be modified in writing accordingly. Any claim for adjustment under this Article must be asserted in writing within 30 days from the date the change is ordered. Provided, however, that the Contracting Officer, if he determines that the facts justify such action may receive and consider, and with the approval of the Commander-in Chief, Far East, or his duly authorized representative , adjust any such claim asserted at any time prier to the date of final settlement of the Contract. If the parties fail to agrees upon the adjustment to be made, the dispute shall be determined as provided in Article 6. (Disputes), but nothing in this article shall excuse the Contractor from proceeding with the presecution of the work and services so changed.

ARTICLE 3. Period of Services: The Contractor shall commence all work and services under this Contract as of the effective date hereof and shall complete all work and services within six(6) months after the above period the Government shall have the option to extend the Contract upon the same terms for an additional period of not more than six (6) months, upon fifteen (15) days written notice from the Contracting Officer, or his authorized representative, in advance of the time it would otherwise expire.

ARTICLE 4. Compensation to the Contractor: As sole and entire monetary consideration for the satisfactory performance of the services required to be performed by an under this Contract, except as otherwise expressly provided herein, the Government will pay the contractor as stated in attached Schedule "A".

ARTICLE 5. Method of Payment: a. Payments will be made to the Contractor upon presentation of properly certified payment vouchers and such other supporting documents as may be required by the Contracting Officer or his authorized representative.

b. The Contractor may be required to furnish the Contracting Officer with properly authenticated payrolls and/or other records prior to the effecting of payment above provided.

c. Prior to final payment, the contractor may be required by the Contracting Officer to furnish the Government with a release of all claims against the Government arising out of any by virtue of this contract.

ARTICLE 6. Disputes: Except as otherwise provided in this Contract, any dispute concerning a question offact arising under this Contract which is not disposed of by agreement shall be decided by the Contracting Officer, who shall reduce his decision to writing and mail or otherwise furnish a copy thereof to the Contractor. Within 30 days from the date of receipt of such copy, the Contractor may appeal by mailing or otherwise furnish to the Contracting Officer a written appeal addressed to the Commander-in- Chief, Far East, and the decision of the Commander-in-Chief, Far East, or that of his duly authorized representative (other than the Contracting Officer under this Contract) for the hearing of such appeals, upon personal approval of the Commander-in-Chief, Far East, or his designated deputy, shall be final and conclusive upon the parties hereto when the amount involved in the appeal is $50,000 or less; provided that, if no appeal is taken within the said 30days, the decision of the Contracting Officer shall be final and conclusive. When the amount involved is more than $50,000 the decision of the Commander-in-Chief, Far East, shall be subject to written appeal within30 days after the receipt thereof by the Contractor to the Secretary of the Army and the decision of the Secretary or his duly authorized representative for the hearing of such appeals shall be final and conclusive; provided that, if no further appeal is taken, within the said 30 days, the decision of the Commander-in-Chief, Far East, shall be final and conclusive. In connectionwith any appeal proceeding under this clause, the Contractor shall be afforded an opportunity to be heard and to offer evidence in support of its appeal. Pending final dispute hereunder, the Contractor shall proceed diligently with the performance of the Contract and in accordance with the Contracting Officer's deicision.

3

0278

ARTICLE 7. Contracting Officer's Decisions: The extent and charactor of the work and services to be performed by the Contractor shall be subject to the general supervision,,direction, control and approval of the Contracting Officer to whom the Contractor shall report and be responsible. In the event that there shall be any dispute with regard to the extent and character of the work to be done, the decision of the Contracting Officer shall govern, but the Contractor shall have the right of appeal as provided in Article 6, (Disputes).

ARTICLE 8. Compliance with Laws and Regulations: The Contractor undertakes that he will comply with all Republic ofKorea National and Local Laws.

ARTICLE 9. Notice to the Government of Labor Disputes: Whenever the Contractor has knowledge that an actual or petential labor dispute is delaying or theatens to delay the timely performance of this Contract, the Contractor shall immediately give notice thereof, including all relevant information with respect thereto, to the Contracting Officer.

ARTICLE 10. Termination and Cancellation: a. The services of the Contractor, or any part thereof, may be terminated for the convenience of the Government at any time., upon notice of the Contractor or his representative, witout liability other than for payments for services already performed, whenever the Contracting Officer may determine that such action if for the best interest of the Government. At the specified date of termination, unless the notice otherwise directs, the Contractor shall discontinue all work and services or the specified part thereof, as required in the notice.

b. The services of the Contractor also may be terminated at any time in whole or part upon the default or unjustifiable delay of the Contractor. However, any failure to perform the Contract or part thereof arising out of clauses beyond the control and without the fault or negligence of the Contractor such as, but not limited to, acts of God, public enemy, fire, floods, epidemics, strickes, and acts, of the Government shall not constitute default or unreasonable delay by the Contractor.

c. The Contractor shall be guided by and shall act in accordance with directions and requests of the Contracting Officer whenever the transfer, dismissal, or replacement of any emplyee shall be deemed by the Contracting Officer to be necessary or advisable in the interests of the Government. In case such directions or request of the Contracting Officer is based upon a determination by him of miscenduct, negligence or inefficiency on the part of the Contractor's employee, he shall state such determination in writing and the grounds thereof shall be docemented in the Contract file.

ARTICLE 11. Adjustments: The Government shall be entitled to an adjustment as tetermined by the Contracting Officer in reduction of payments to the Contractor, on account of any day when services hereunder are required, upon which any employee of the Contractor does not performservices by reason of: (1) voluntary idleness; (2) disability resulting from his own misconduct, negligence, or inefficiency; (3) disability which does not result from the employee, to the extent that it exceeds seven (7) days during a six (6) months' period of the Contract; and (4) having been discharged from employment by the Contractor in connection with this Contract under Article 10c above, or having ceased employment for any other reason. Any dispute concerning adjustment hereunder shall be deemed to involve a question of fact and shall be subject to appeal under Article 6, (Disputes) hereunder.

ARTICLE 12. No Sub-Contracts: No sub-contracts are authorized under this Contract.

ARTICLE 13. Nonassignability of Claims: Claims by the Contractor for any sums due or to become due and/or any other claims under this Contract shall not be assignable.

ARTICLE 14. Employee Contracts: The Contractor shall make available to the Contracting Officer such copies of employment Contracts or agreements entered into with any employees of the Contractor engaged in performaing services to be rendered under this Contract as may be required by the Contracting Officer.

ARTICLE 15. Data to Become Property of Government: All notes, designs, drawings, memoranda, and other technical data, etc., if any furnished by the Contractor pursuant to or developed in connection with the provisions of this Contract shall become and remain in the property of the Government and it shall have the right to use them for any public purpose without any additional compensation to the Contractor and any such data, etc., in the possession of the Contractor shall be delivered to the Government whenever requested by the Contracting Officer.

ARTICLE 16. Employee Insurance: The Contractor will provide and maintain for his employees all required insurance, including but not limitted to Workmen's Compensation Insurance, providing compensation for disability, death, accident or illness.

ARTICLE 17. Covenant Against Contingent Fees: The Contractor warrants that no person or selling agancy has been employed or retained to solicit or secure this Contract upon an agreement or understanding for any commision, percentage, brokerage, or contingent fee, excepting bona fide employees established commercial or selling agencies maintained by the Contractor for the purpose of securing business. For Branch of violantion of this warranty, the Government shall have the right to annul this Contract without liability or, in its discretion, to deduct from the Contract price or consideration the full amount of such commision, percentage, brokerage, or contingent fee.

5

0280

ARTICLE 18. Officials Not to Benefit: No member of or delegate to Congress, or resident commissioner, shall be admitted to any share or part of this Contract or to any benefit that may arise therefrom; but this provision shall not be construed to extend to this Contract if made with a corporation for its general benefit.

ARTICLE 19. Renegotiation: a. This Contract is subject to the Renegotiation Act of 1948.

b. The Contractor (which term as used in this clause means the party contracting to furnish the articles or perform the work required by this Contract) agrees, within thirty (30) days after receipt of its signed copy of this Contract, to notify the Military Renegotiation pooicy and Review Beard, Office of the Secretary of Defense, Washington 25, D.C., of such Contract, indicating its own name and address: Previded that, if the Contractor has previeusly reported to the Military Renegotiation Policy and Review Board any Contract or purchase order subject to the Renegotiation Act of 1948, such notification shall not be necessary.

ARTICLE 20. Audits: The Government at any reasonable time shall have the right to inspect the working premises and to audit the books and records of the Contractor, so far as relates to the performance and cost under this Contract.

ARTICLE 21. Conflict in Translation: In cases of any conflict or ambiguity between the English text of this contract or any translation thereof, the English shall prevail.

ARTICLE 22. Definitions: As used throughout this Contract, the following terms shall have the meanings set forth below: a. The term "Secretary" means the Secretary, the Under Secretary, or any Assistant Secretary of the Department; and the term "his duly authorized representative" means any person or persons or beard (other than the Contracting Officer) authorized to act for the Secretary.

b. The term "Commander-in-Chief" means the Commander-in-Chief, Far East; and the term "his duly authorized representative" means any person or person or beard (other than the Contracting Officer) authorized to act for the Commander-in-Chief.

c. The term "Contracting Officer" means the person executing this Contract in behalf of the Government, and any other officer or civilian employee who is a properly designated Contracting Officer, and the term shall include, except as otherwise provided in this Contract, the authorized representative of a Contracting Officer acting within the limits of his authority.

ARTICLE 23. Schedule: Schedule "A" is hereto attached and is made a part hereof.

ARTICLE 24. Alterations: The following changes were made in this Contract before it was signed by the perties hereto. None.

ARTICLE 25. Extras: Except as otherwise provided in this Contract, no payment for extras shall be made unless such extras and the pricew therefor have been authorized in writing by the Contracting Officer.

ARTICLE 26. Inspection: inspection of work projects will be by representatives of the Contracting Officer to assure satisfactory performance and completion

ARTICLE 27. Approval: This Contract shall be subject to the written approval of the Commader-in-Chief, Far EAst, or his duly authorized representative and shall not be binding until so approved. None.

7

0282

IN WITNESS WHEREFOR, the parties hereto have executed this contract as of the day and year first above written.

TWO WITNESSES:

THE UNITED STATES OF AMERICA:

BY: WILLIAM C. FISCHER
Capt
Purchasing & Contracting Officer
(Official Title)

HOWARD W. MARTENS
Lt Col
714th Trans Railway Bn
APO 59
(Address)

KOREAN NATIONAL RAILWAYS:

BY: Director of Finance Bureau
Ministry of Transportation
Republic of Korea
Pusan, Korea
(Business Address)

PAUL F. O'HARAN
Maj TC
714th Trans Railway Bn
APO 59
(Address)

I hereby certify that, to the best of my knowledge and belief, based upon observation and inquiry ______________________, who signed this contract for the Korean National Railways, Pusan, Korean, has authority to execute same, and is the individual who signs similar contracts on behalf of this corporation with the public generally.

(Signature of Contracting Officer)

APPROVED FOR, AND IN THE NAME OF
THE COMMANDER-IN-CHIEF, FAR EAST

BY: H.T. MILLER
Colonel, TC
Transportation Officer,
GHQ,FEC.

0283

SCHEDULE "A" TO CONTRACT NUMBER DA-92-084 FEC-252

The Contractor will perform such railway construction, reconstruction, and/or rehabilitation, as requested by the Contracting Officer, or his duly authorized representative.

The Contractor will adhere to established priorities for railway construction, reconstruction, and or rehabilitation, as requested by the Contracting Officer, or his duly authorized representative.

Standards for railway construction, reconstruction, and/or rehabilitation, will be as prescribed by and be subject to approval of the Contracting Officer, or his duly authorized representative.

The Contractor will pay all labor costs for railway construction, reconstruction, and/or rehabilitation, requested by the Contracting Officer or his duly authorized representative, and will in turn bill the United States Government for equivalent reimbursement, specifically identifying project or projects covered by identical labor billed.

The Contractor will submit an Appendix to the Schedule "A", which will show all applicable employee category rates upon which reimbursement requests will be based. No changes in rates specified will be made or accepted without prior petition and mutual written agreement for such changes by both parties to this contract, supported by written justifications in detail by the Contractor of any increases requested. The Append: will be made a part of this Contract.

The Contractor will, within fifteen calendar days after completion of each project, submit in six (6) copies, a detailed report of completion to the Contracting Officer, or his duly authorized representat -ive, such report to be in three sections as follows:

Section 1. (a) Complete descriptive title and nature of project, including a full detailed list of work and services performed.

(b) Date Project commenced.

(c) Date Project completed.

(d) Remarks.

Section 11. Charges for labor supplied will be submitted by Contractor, itemized by categories of employees common to all railway construction projects, man days of service per employee of each category, total man days for such category of employees and unit rates and total labor charges per category and grand total.

Section 111. Contractor will furnish a list of all materials used, which will itemized under various headings common to all railway construction projects. A copy of such list will also be furnished for forwarding through the Contracting Officer or his duly authorized representative to Chief, EOA Korea.

0284

No extra charges such as commissions, administrative overhead, etc., will be payable as such, and all costs will be included in unit and total rates to be contained in Appendix hereto of labor rates.

All invoices, submitted by Contractor for payment, will be subject to certification by a Commissioned Officer of Department of Army of the United States, that services have been rendered and were satisfactory, that prices charged are in accordance with the terms of the Contract and that labor was necessary to the public service.

Contract identification and date will appear on all bills and on any other documentation or correspondence pertinent to this Contract.

0285

APPENDIX ONE TO SCHEDULE "A# OF CONTRACT NUMBER DA-92-084 FEC-252

Standard wages for laborers and Labor Foremen paid by the Korean National Railways (Based on 8 hours per day).

STANDARD WAGES

| CATEGORY | KIND OF LABORERS | UNIT WAGE (8 HRS) |
|---|---|---|
| 1 | Ox-cart | ₩ 6,000 |
| 11 | Machine driver | 2,400 |
| " | Roofing tile man | 2,400 |
| " | Masonry worker | 2,400 |
| 111 | Welding man | 2,300 |
| " | Finishing man | 2,300 |
| 1V | Piping Driver | 2,200 |
| " | Carpenter | 2,200 |
| " | Wire man | 2,200 |
| " | Sawing man | 2,200 |
| " | Plasterer | 2,200 |
| V | Heasingodrayer | 2,200 |
| " | Heading driver | 2,200 |
| " | Steel Bar driver | 2,200 |
| " | Brick man | 2,200 |
| " | Painter | 2,200 |
| " | Tin smith | 2,200 |
| V1 | Laborer manager | 1,800 |
| V11 | Special Laborer | 1,400 |
| V111 | Common Laborer | 1,200 |

REMARKS:

1. When an employee in any of these categories is used for work at a place distant from his home or regular place of work, he is allowed 600 Won above standard wages for living cost.

2. When employees in above categories are engaged in emergency construction work, they are allowed two meals (300 Won) per day.

3. The above wages are based on 8 hours of labor per day, if over 8 hours are worked, add 12.5% of the daily wages per hour of overtime.

0286

List of grades and salaries of employees (Official) of the Korean National Railways.

MONTHLY RATES

| | Salary | 2ns Class | Grade Salary | 3rd Class | Grade Salary | 4th Class | Grade Salary |
|---|---|---|---|---|---|---|---|
| Minister | 30,000 | 1 | 17,900 | 1 | 14,700 | 1 | 11,100 |
| Vice-Minister | 24,000 | 2 | 17,100 | 2 | 14,300 | 2 | 10,900 |
| | | 3 | 16,300 | 3 | 13,900 | 3 | 10,700 |
| | | 4 | 15,500 | 4 | 13,500 | 4 | 10,500 |
| | | 5 | 14,700 | 5 | 13,100 | 5 | 10,300 |
| | | 6 | 13,900 | 6 | 12,700 | 6 | 10,100 |
| | | | | 7 | 12,300 | 7 | 9,900 |
| | | | | 8 | 11,900 | 8 | 9,700 |
| | | | | 9 | 11,500 | 9 | 9,500 |
| | | | | 10 | 11,100 | 10 | 9,300 |
| | | | | 11 | 10,700 | 11 | 9,100 |
| | | | | 12 | 10,300 | 12 | 8,900 |
| | | | | 13 | | 13 | 8,700 |
| | | | | | | 14 | 8,500 |
| | | | | | | 15 | 8,300 |
| | | | | | | 16 | 8,100 |
| | | | | | | 17 | 7,900 |
| | | | | | | 18 | 7,700 |

| 5th Class | Grade Salary |
|---|---|
| 1 | 8,500 |
| 2 | 8,400 |
| 3 | 8,300 |
| 4 | 8,200 |
| 5 | 8,100 |
| 6 | 8,000 |
| 7 | 7,900 |
| 8 | 7,800 |
| 9 | 7,700 |
| 10 | 7,600 |
| 11 | 7,500 |
| 12 | 7,400 |
| 13 | 7,300 |
| 14 | 7,200 |
| 15 | 7,100 |
| 16 | 7,000 |
| 17 | 6,900 |
| 18 | 6,800 |
| 19 | 6,700 |
| 20 | 6,600 |
| 21 | 6,500 |
| 22 | 6,400 |
| 23 | 6,300 |
| 24 | 6,200 |
| 25 | 6.100 |
| 26 | 6,000 |

REMARKS:

1. A temporary (wartime) allowance of 10,000 Won per Month per man was authorized effective 1 July 1950.

0287

The Modification Process of the Contract for Construction Service of Korean National Railways.

1. The Contract for construction serice of Korean National Railways ( Contract No. DA-92-084 FEC-252), of which duration was from 1st October 1950 to 31st March 1951, was entered into by the United States of America and Korean National Railways on 1st October 1950.

2. The Contract duration was extended to 30th September 1951 on 1st April 1951.
....... 1st Modifcation ......

3. The Contract duration was extended to 30th November 1951 and Contract No. was changed to DA-92-084 FEC-726 on 1st October 1951.
...... Negotiated ..........

4. The Contract duration was extended to 31st May 1952, Contract No. was changed to DA-92-084 FEC-727, and standard wages were char changed on 1st December 1951.
.......1st Modification .......

5. The Contract duration was extended to 30th Nomember 1952 on 15th May 1952.
....... 2nd Modification......

6. The Contract No. was changed to DA-92-093 FEC-42, and the appropriation symbole was changed to 2132020 91-1052 P2110-07 892-093 L 208 on 30th June 1952.
....... 3rd Modification ......

7. The Project No. P2110-07 was changed to P2911-07 on 26th September 1952.
....... 4th Modification ......

8. The Contract duration was extended to 31st December 1952 on 1st November 1952.
....... 5th Modification .......

9. The Appropriation symbole was changed to 2132020 91-1077 P2210-07 892-122 L-208 on 5th November 1952.
....... 6th Modification ......

10. The Project No. P2110 was changed to P2130 on 8th December 1952.
........7th Modification .......

11. The Contract drration was extended to 30th June 1953 on 30th December 1952.
.......8th Modification ........

12. In accordance with the currency reform dated 17th February 1953, old Won rates and prices were amended to read Hwan at 1/100th of Won rates and prices.
........9th Modification .......

13. The appropriation symbole was changed to 21320 91-1070 P2911-07 892-122 L208 on 28th April 1953.
..........10th Modification ......

14. The Contract duration eas extended to 31st December 1953.
.......11th Modification ......

0288

The Table of hending Communication circuit

| | | | | To UN force |
|---|---|---|---|---|
| From | Yongsan | To | Inchon | 3 circuit |
| From | Yongsan | To | Chung Ryang ~~Ri~~ | 4 circuit |
| From | Chung Ryang Ri | To | Choonche on | 2 circuit |
| From | Yongsan | To | Teijon | 4 circuit |
| From | Teijon | To | Teiku | 3 circuit |
| From | Teiku | To | Pusan | 4 circuit |
| From | Teijon | To | Iri | 2 circuit |
| From | Iri | To | Koonsan | 2 circuit |
| From | Yongsan | To | Andong | 2 circuit |
| From | Andong | To | Yungcheon | 2 circuit |
| From | Yungcheon | To | Pusan | 1 circuit |
| From | Yungcheon | To | Teiku | 2 circuit |

1954. January TMRS Communication Section Col. Smith consult with M.O.T. Chief Communication Section about supplying cordiniously one part of Communication protecting material which is supplied by KCOMZ, depending on 73 project during about 6 month and make a promise it in word.

0289

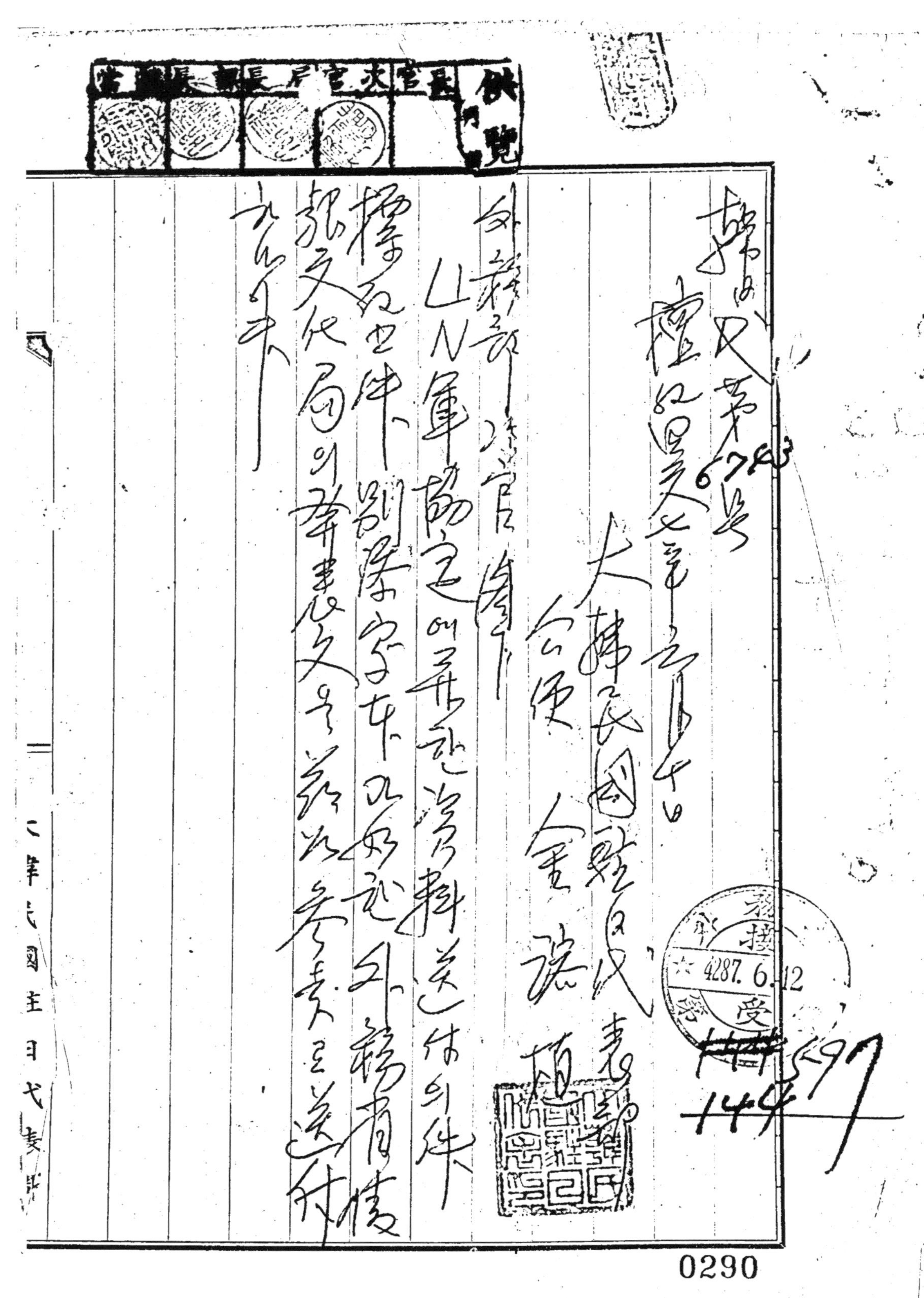

供覽 | 長官 | 次官 | 局長 | 課長 | 擔當

韓日代 第678號

檀紀四二八七年六月八日

大韓民國駐日代表部

公使 金溶植

外務部次官 貴下

UN軍協定에 關한 資料送付의 件

標記의 件, 別添寫本 및 外務省情報文化局의 發表文을 參考로 送付하나이다

外務部 接受 4287. 6. 12

144 597

0290

PRESS RELEASE

Public Information and Cultural Affairs Bureau
Ministry of Foreign Affairs
Tokyo

Vol. 111. No 43 June 1, 1954

JAPAN ACCEPTS U.N. FORCES AGREEMENT

The Japanese Government today formally accepted the Agreement regarding the Status of United Nations Forces in Japan and the Protocal on Claims Arising from Joint Acts or Ommissions of the United States Armed Forces and United Nations Forces in Japan.

At the same time, the Govenments of Canada and New Zealand, which also signed the Agreement and the Potocol "subject to acceptance", deposited their instruments of acceptance with the Japanese Government.

The Agreement and the Protocal, which the Japanese Government signed "subject to acceptance" on February 19 this year in Tokyo, were approved by the Diet on May 17 and necessary domestic legel arrangements were subsequently completed.

Therefore, in accordance with its provisions, the Agreement will come into force on June 11 for the Japanese Government and the Governments of Canada and New Zealand as well as of the United States Acting as the Unified Command, the United Kingdom, Australia, the Philippines, France and Italy, which previously deposited their instruments of acceptance or unconditionally signed the agreement.

Although the South African Government is reported to have completed domestic prodedures necessary for acceptance of the Agreement, her instrument of acceptance has not yet arrived. The coming into force of the Agreement with respect to the Union of South Africa will, therefore, be delayed pending deposit of its instrument of acceptance.

In view of the fact that the United States Governement signed the Protocal "subject to acceptance", the coming into force of the Protocal still must, in accordance with its fifth article, await such acceptance.

2月19日調印
5月17日議会通過
6月11日効力発生

0291

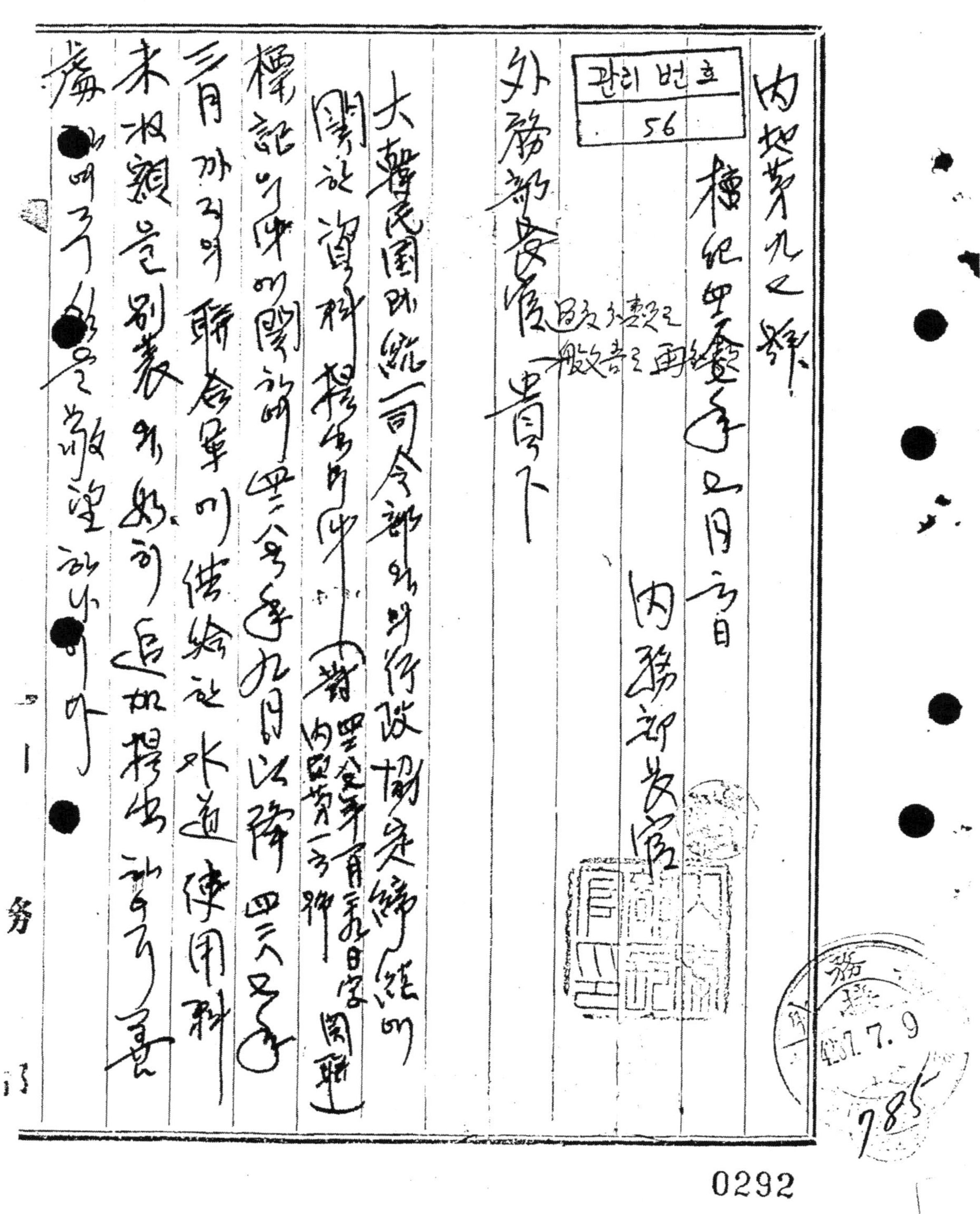

內地第九〇號

檀紀四二九〇年七月六日

內務部長官

外務部長官 貴下 [illegible] 一般文書로 再分類

大韓民國과 統一司令部와의 行政協定締結에 關한 資料提出의 件 (對 四二九〇年 六月 五日字 內[illegible]第一六[illegible]號 關聯)

標記의 件에 關하여 四二八六年 九月 以降 四二八八年 三月까지의 聯合軍에 供給한 水道使用料 未收額을 別表와 如히 追加提出하오니 善處하여 주시기 敬望하나이다.

관리번호 56

4290. 7. 9

785

0292

# 聯合軍水道使用料未收額

| 市道別 | 市郡別 | 自八八年九月 至九〇年三月末 水道使用量 | 使用料金 | 累計 自八八年九月至九〇年三月末 使用量 | 使用料金 |
|---|---|---|---|---|---|
| 서울 | | 二,五六五,五八 | 三[illegible] | 二一五,三三九八 | 一一六,三[illegible] |
| 京畿 | 仁川市 | 一四,四二四八 | 二,三八〇,五二〇 | 五六一,六〇,八九 | 五一,一六三[illegible] |
| 忠北 | 淸州市 | 一〇〇,〇〇〇 | 一四〇,〇〇〇 | 一〇〇,〇〇〇 | 一四〇,〇〇〇 |
| 忠南 | 大田市 | 二一,三六四 | 三八〇,六四〇 | 一九三,七八四 | 一,八七〇,五二八 |
| | 瑞山郡 | 三,五五〇 | 四五,二四〇 | 三,五五〇 | 四五,二四〇 |
| | 江景邑 | 四六,三八 | 三三,一九〇 | 三三,一九〇 | 一,一五五,九六〇 |
| 全北 | 全州市 | 九,九〇 | 七,九七〇 | 九,九〇 | 七,九七〇 |
| | 群山郡 | 八,八八九 | 九五,二〇〇 | 九七,〇二二 | 七〇二,四八三 |
| 全南 | 光州市 | 一四,六二八 | 五六,六六〇 | 一四,六二八 | 五六,六[illegible] |
| 慶北 | 大邱市 | 三八六,五〇〇 | 七九四六,九[illegible] | 六九三,一五[illegible] | 一八九五,一九八 |

0293

| 道別 | 市郡別 | 自一九四八年至一九五二年十二月末 使用地 | 使用料 | 自一九五三年 使用地 | 使用料 |
|---|---|---|---|---|---|
| 京畿 | 議政府 | . | . | 一,九二〇 | 三八四,〇〇〇 |
| | 永川郡 | 一,四〇 | 一六〇,〇〇〇 | 五,一七〇 | 一五一,四二〇 |
| 慶南 | 釜山市 | 一,五九,五四〇 | 三五,三五四,九五 | 八七,五四 | 八七,〇四三,八五 |
| | 馬山市 | 二八,九〇五 | 六三,三〇〇 | 二〇,九一九四 | 一,三五,八九九 |
| | 鎮海邑 | 三二 | 二,八〇〇 | 一,九〇〇 | 三〇,九〇〇 |
| | 蔚山郡 | 九五八 | 一三,五〇〇 | 四,〇〇〇 | 四,八八六 |
| | 四川郡 | 三〇八 | 五,二九二 | 二,二〇八 | 九一,二六 |
| 計 | | 二一一,九五五 | 八九四,〇〇〇四 | 八六三,三〇二,三 | 三〇〇,三五六,九三〇 |

0294

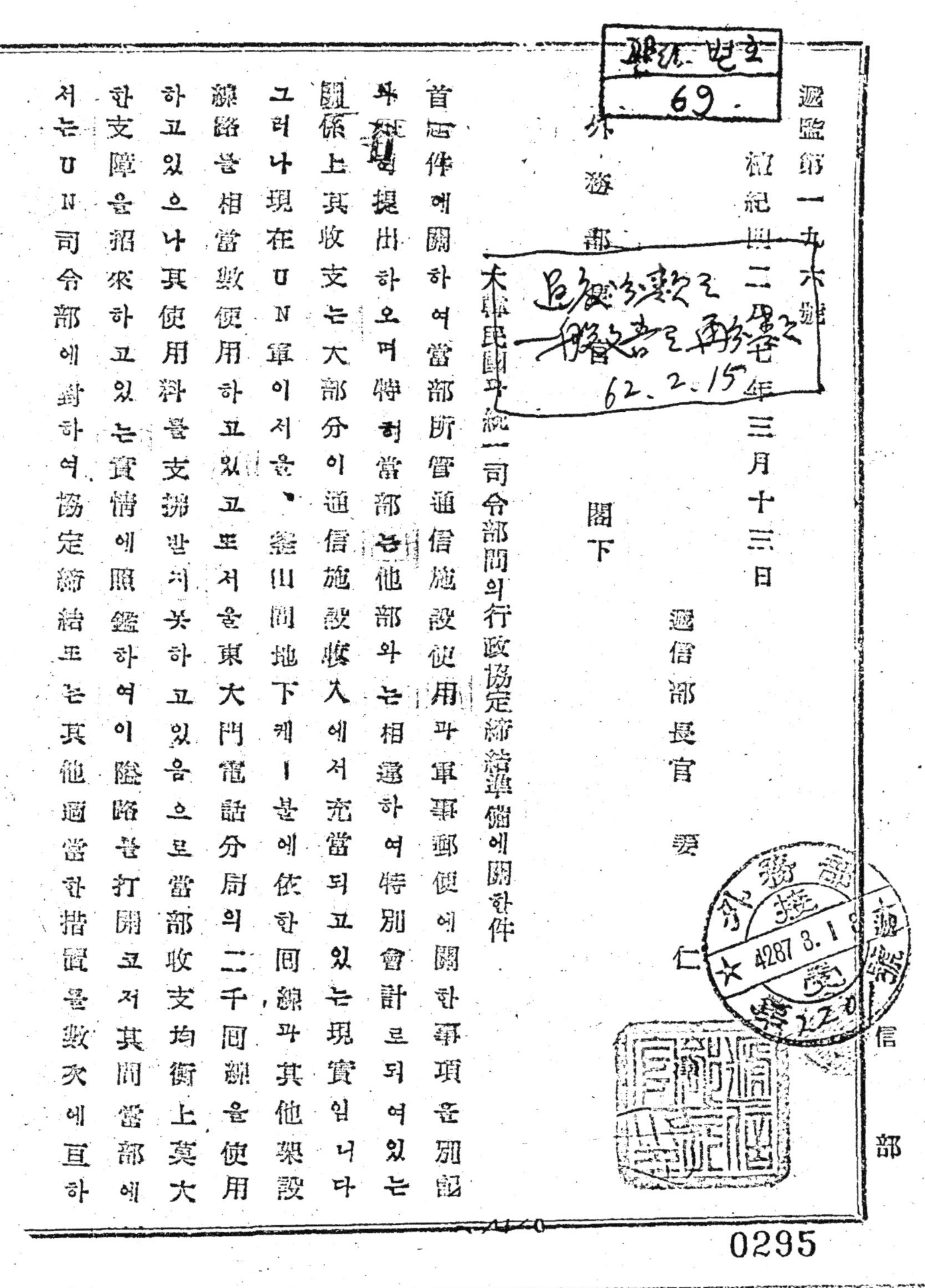

관리 번호 69

遞監第一九六號

檀紀四二八七年三月十三日

遞信部長官 晏 仁

外務部 閣下

大韓民國과 統一司令部間의 行政協定締結準備에 關한 件

首題件에 關하여 當部所管通信施設使用과 軍事郵便에 關한 事項을 別記와 如히 提出하오며 特히 當部는 他部와는 相違하여 特別會計로 되여 있는 關係上 其收支는 大部分이 通信施設收入에서 充當되고 있는 現實입니다

그러나 現在 UN軍이 서울、釜山間 地下케－불에 依한 同線과 其他架設線路를 相當數使用하고 있고 또 서울東大門電話分局의 二千回線을 使用하고 있으나 其使用料를 支拂받지 못하고 있음으로 當部收支均衡上 莫大한 支障을 招來하고 있는 實情에 照鑑하여 이 隘路를 打開코저 其間 當部에서는 UN司令部에 對하여 協定締結 또는 其他適當한 措置를 數次에 亘하

62. 2. 15

0295

여 提議( )衛하여온 ( )인바 玆에 其協定의 草案 및 推( )過程의 寫本을 參考로 添附하나이다

記

一. 通信施設

1. 統一司令部와 作戰期間中 作戰上 必要에 依하여 大韓民國遞信部所有의 通信施設을 使用할때에는 所管機關과 事前協議를 要하며 또한 規定된 使用料를 支拂하여야 한다.

2. 統一司令部는 作戰期間中 作戰上의 必要에 依하여 電波를 發射할때에는 關係各機關과 相互妨害되지 않도록 할것이며 또한 國際通信條約을 遵守하여야 한다

3. 統一司令部는 六、二五事變后 本協定締結發効時까지 (自一九五○年六月二十五日 至一九五四年)의 間에 大韓民國遞信部通信施設使用에 對한 使用料를 支拂하여야 한다

4. 駐韓UN軍이 UN 또는 其他援助資金과 資材로서 施設한 諸般通信設備는 大韓民國遞信部所有로 하며 此施設의 代價는 回線使用料에

(타이푸라이타-用紙全面)

0296

서 相殺되지 않는다

5. 駐韓UN軍이 通信施設을 撤去, 變更또는 新設코저 할 때에는 事前에 大韓民國遞信部와 協議하여야 한다

二 軍事郵便

1. 大韓民國地域에 在한 統一司令部管理下의 軍人또는 軍機關을 爲한 軍事郵遞局을 設置하고 維持管理하는 權利를 賦與하며 統一司令部管理下의 軍事郵遞局은 大韓民國通信機關과의 下記各條項을 履行, 합에 同하여 新하여야 한다

2. 軍事郵便機關을 使用할 수 있는 範圍

가. 駐韓統一司令部管理下의 個人과 機關

나. 統一司令部總司令官에 依하여 任命된 駐韓報導通信員과 同司令部에서 兵站援助를 받고 韓國作戰支援을 爲하여 韓國에 派遣된 個人과 機關

다. 大韓民國國軍의 軍機關과 個人

라. 統一司令部에 配置所屬된 韓國軍部隊또는 個人

마. 韓國軍에 依하여 信任된 赤十字社또는 그와 類似한 機關(駐韓統

遞信部

0297

(司令部에 協助하는 韓國民間雇傭員을 包含함)

3. 郵便物取扱種類의 制限

가. 大韓民國通信機關에서 統一司令部管理下의 軍事郵遞局에 發送되는 郵便이나 統一司令部管理下의 軍事郵遞局에서 大韓民國通信機關에 到着되는 郵便은 普通通常郵便物中 第一種、第二種에 限하여서만 取扱한다

4. 郵便料金

가. 韓國에 있는 軍人이 統一司令部軍事郵遞局管轄內에 있는 韓國人에게 發送하는 郵便物은 無料로 取扱한다

나. 韓國에서 第二號에 限定되어 있는 以外의 民間人이 統一司令部管轄內의 軍事郵遞局을 通하여 韓國民間人에게 發送하는 私書翰은 發送되는 軍事郵遞局의 所屬國에서 要求되는 國內郵便料金을 添附하여야 한다

5. 郵便物遞送方法

가. 統一司令部管轄內의 軍事郵遞局에서 接受한 郵便物이나 韓國通

(다이쭈라이다-用紙全面)

0298

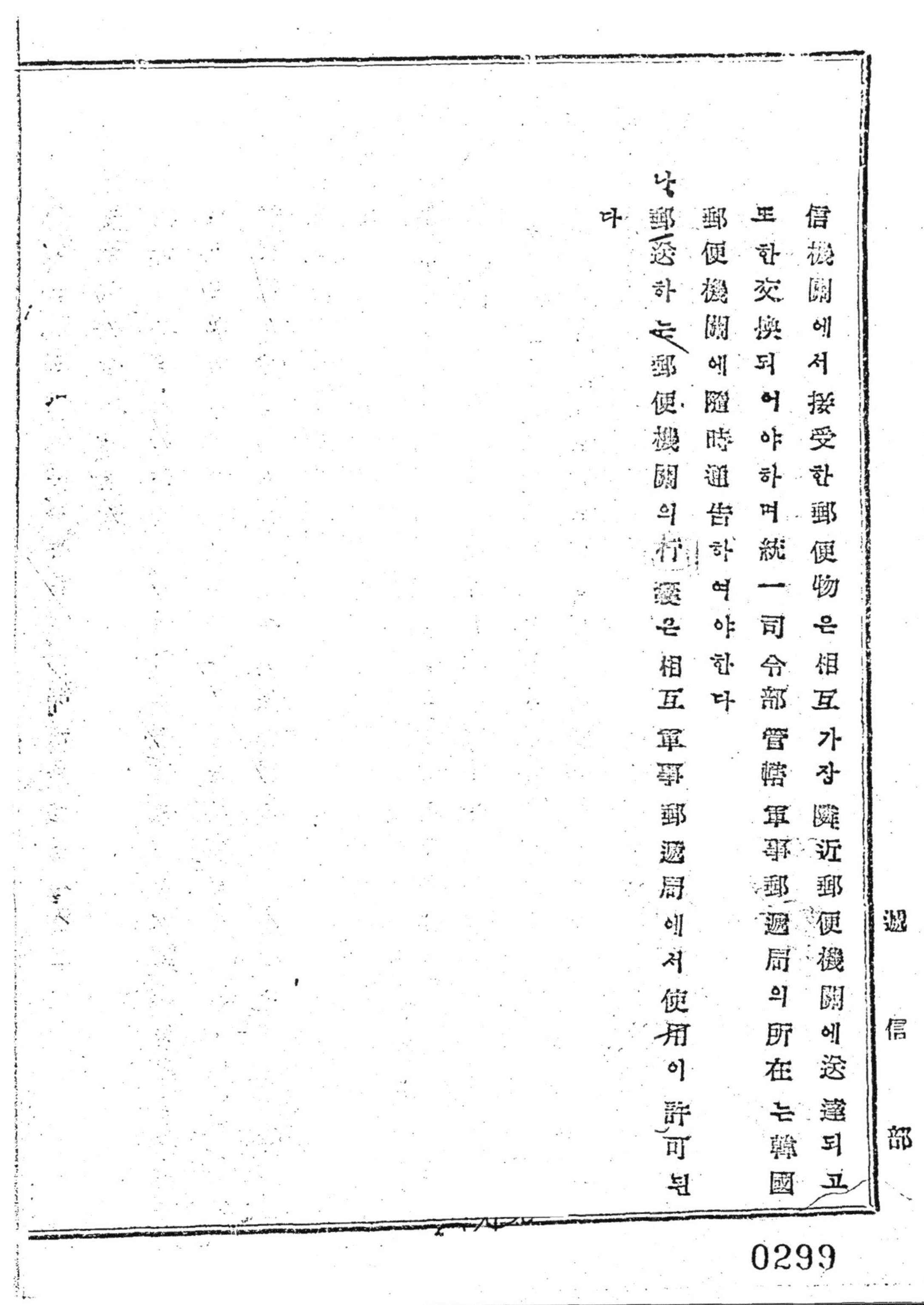

信機關에서 接受한 郵便物은 相互 가장 隣近 郵便機關에 送達되고 또한 交換되어야하며 統一司令部 管轄 軍事郵遞局의 所在는 韓國 郵便機關에 隨時通告하여야 한다

낙 郵送하는 郵便機關의 行囊은 相互 軍事郵遞局에서 使用이 許可된다

遞信部

0299

遞信部

一九五三年九月二二日

美第八軍司令官
通信監室

遞信部長 貴下

서울에있는IX軍CTR(東大門)電話局에關한協定提案에關하야
草案과함게基本的附議를要請한一九五三年九月一六日附貴下의書
翰을받았음니다
美第八軍에는그와같은協定이나契約附議權利를갖지않고있으며그
政策에關한決定을하기爲하야서는合同經濟委員會와相議하지옵기
를말씀을넘니다
저의好意로받으시옵소서

餘不備

후랑 찌트루 大領

0300

韓國通信本部

金次官에게

本部는韓國에있어서聯合軍使用한通信施設에對한使用料를要求한195
3年9月17日附 A L Ham len (함부렌) 代將에게보낸貴翰을받았
읍니다

아시는바와같이聯合軍으로依하여使用되고또供給된施設의調停에關하야
當分間研究(檢討)中이오며그研究를完遂코저繼續努力中에있읍니다
貴政府와聯合軍側에對하야滿足할만한協議를얻고저研究가끝나는即時로
貴政府에通告할것을確約합니다

本件에關한貴下의忍耐를깊이感하나이다

敬具

S. 로一돈

美陸軍少將

0301

四二八六年六月一八日

遞信部經理局長

Brigadier General
A.L. Hamblen 准將 貴下

本料金徵收問題에關하여貴下의理解있는協助를바라마지않읍니다
歷次말씀한바와如히大韓民國遞信事業은其運營財源을獨立採算原則으로하고있는關係로施設体에서收得치않고는財源求得의方途없는바이와같이UN軍이多數의幹線路를專用하고있으므로말미암마生하는財源逼迫은遞信事業全体에미치는影響이莫大한實情입니다

그런故로本專用料徵收에對하여서는如何한難關이있을지라도結實은매저야할것입니다.그리하여本回線專用에附隨되는諸般條件을明示한貴我間의書面協定이于先必要할것으로生覺됨으로別紙通信回

遞信部

0302

線專用과 서울中央電話局東大門分局間市話交[illegible]施設中二千回線을貴側에서專用하는데對한協定書草案을添送하오니檢討하시와貴見을一報하여주시옵기를바랍니다

그리고

一九五三年一月一日부터

一九五三年三月三十一日까지의

同線專用料로

一〇二、八八八、〇〇〇圜이 調定되였읍니다

別表에 其內譯을 通知하오니 諒知하시고 此로서

一九五三年三月三十一日까지의

總料額은

四〇三、八八六、五六〇圜이 됩니다

0303

(다이쿠라이다ー用紙全面)

서울中央電話局東大門分局
自働式電話交換機施設使用協定書

大韓民國遞信部
駐韓美第八軍司令部

大韓民國遞信部所管서울中央電話局東大門分局自動式電話機施設을美第八軍에서使用함에對하여兩側間에左와如히協定한다

第一條 駐韓美第八軍은韓國戰亂遂行期間中作戰上必要할時는大韓民國遞信部所管서울中央電話局東大門分局自動式電話交換機施設中二千回線以內에限하여貸與받어使用할수있다

第二條 前條의施設使用은作戰中이를無償으로하되韓國戰爭終熄後에도繼續使用할때는所定의使用料를支拂하여야한다
但共電式市外電話交換機使用에對한料金은別途協定키로한다

第三條 第一條에使用指定된施設의保守維持는大韓民國遞信部가

遞信部

0304

擔當하되 ㅗ에所要되는資材一切는駐韓美第八軍이提供한다

第四條 本協定에서韓國戰亂遂行期間이라함은實際戰鬪期間을말하는것으로서戰鬪行爲없이單只駐屯하는期間또는休戰條約이締結된以後駐屯하는期間은이에包含되지아니한다

第五條 本協定은檀紀四二八 年 月 日부터有効로한다

以上協定한認證으로서左記와如히署名한다

大韓民國遞信部長官 [illegible] 仁 澤

駐韓美第八軍司令官 맑스웰 데일러

(다이꾸라이다ー用紙全面)

0305

別紙

# 有線通信線 UN軍使用協定書

大韓民國遞信部

駐韓UN軍司令部

大韓民國遞信部所管有線通信線을 UN軍이 使用하는데 對하여 兩者間에 如左히 協定한다

第一條 駐韓UN軍은 作戰上必要로 할時는 大韓民國遞信部所管有線通信線(以下通信線이라 한다)을 使用할 수 있다

第二條 駐韓UN軍은 通信線을 使用할 時는 以下第三條 및 第四條에서 定하는 바에 依하여 回線使用料를 支拂한다

第三條 駐韓UN軍이 使用하는 回線料의 算定은 該專用區間의 通話料를 基準으로 하여 一日一通話에 對한 普通通話料의 二百倍로 計算한 額에 對하여 每月分을 翌月二十日까지 納付하여야 한다

第四條 駐韓UN軍은 回線料金 調定의 基本이 되는 回線數와 使用區

遞信部

0306

間및期間( )을每月一定한期( )內에大韓( )國遞信部에報告하여야한다

第五條 駐韓UN軍은通信線의既設된施設및其附帶施設을撤去變更增設또는新設코저할때는事前에大韓民國遞信部의承認을얻어야한다

第六條 駐韓UN軍이CAC援助資金또는資材로서通信線에施設한諸設設備는大韓民國遞信部所有로하되施設에代價는同線使用料에서相殺되지않는다

第七條 大韓民國遞信部는駐韓UN軍이支拂하는同線使用의對象이되어있는모ー든同線에對하여保守維持의義務가있다

附則

第一條 本協定은檀紀四二八六年 月 日부터有効로한다

第二條 駐韓UN軍은本協定締結前에專用한同線使用料에對하여는遞信部의要求에依하여納付할義務가있다

(다이푸라이다ー用紙조面)

0307

遞信部

檀紀四二八六年　月　日

大韓民國遞信部長官

駐韓UN軍總司令官

0308

| 정/리/보/존/문/서/목/록 | | | | | |
|---|---|---|---|---|---|
| 기록물종류 | 문서-일반공문서철 | 등록번호 | 902<br>9575 | 등록일자 | 2006-07-27 |
| 분류번호 | 741.12 | 국가코드 | US | 주제 | |
| 문서철명 | 한.미국 간의 상호방위조약 제4조에 의한 시설과 구역 및 한국에서의 미국군대의 지위에 관한 협정 (SOFA) 전59권. 1966.7.9 서울에서 서명 : 1967.2.9 발효 (조약 232호) *원본 | | | | |
| 생산과 | 미주과/조약과 | 생산년도 | 1952 - 1967 | 보존기간 | 영구 |
| 담당과(그룹) | 조약 | 조약 | | 서가번호 | -- |
| 참조분류 | | | | | |
| 권차명 | V.4 체결 교섭, 1956-58 | | | | |
| 내용목차 | * 일지 :<br>1953.8.7 이승만 대통령-Dulles 미국 국무장관 공동성명<br>- 상호방위조약 발효 후 군대지위협정 교섭 약속<br>1954.12.2 정부, 주한 UN군의 관세업무협정 체결 제의<br>1955.1월, 5월 미국, 제의 거절<br>1955.4.28 정부, 군대지위협정 제의 (한국측 초안 제시)<br>1957.9.10 Hurter 미국 국무차관 방한 시 각서 수교 (한국측 제의 수락 요구)<br>1957.11.13, 26 정부, 개별 협정의 단계적 체결 제의<br>1958.9.18 Dawling 주한미국대사, 형사재판관할권 협정 제외 조건으로 행정협정 체결 의사 전달<br>1960.3.10 정부, 토지, 시설협정의 우선적 체결 강력 요구<br>1961.4.10 장면 국무총리-McConaughy 주한미국대사 공동성명으로 교섭 개시 합의<br>1961.4.15, 4.25 제1, 2차 한.미국 교섭회의 (서울)<br>1962.3.12 정부, 교섭 재개 촉구 공한 송부<br>1962.5.14 Burger 주한미국대사, 최규하 장관 면담 시 형사재판관할권 문제 제기 않는 조건으로 교섭 재개 통고<br>1962.9.6 한.미국 간 공동성명 발표 (9월 중 교섭 재개 합의)<br>1962.9.20~ 1965.6.7 제1-81차 실무 교섭회의 (서울)<br>1966.7.8 제82차 실무 교섭회의 (서울)<br>1966.7.9 서명<br>1967.2.9 발효 (조약 232호) | | | | |

| 마/이/크/로/필/름/사/항 | | | | |
|---|---|---|---|---|
| 촬영연도 | *롤 번호 | 화일 번호 | 후레임 번호 | 보관함 번호 |
| 2006-11-21 | I-06-0066 | 12 | 1-193 | |

0001

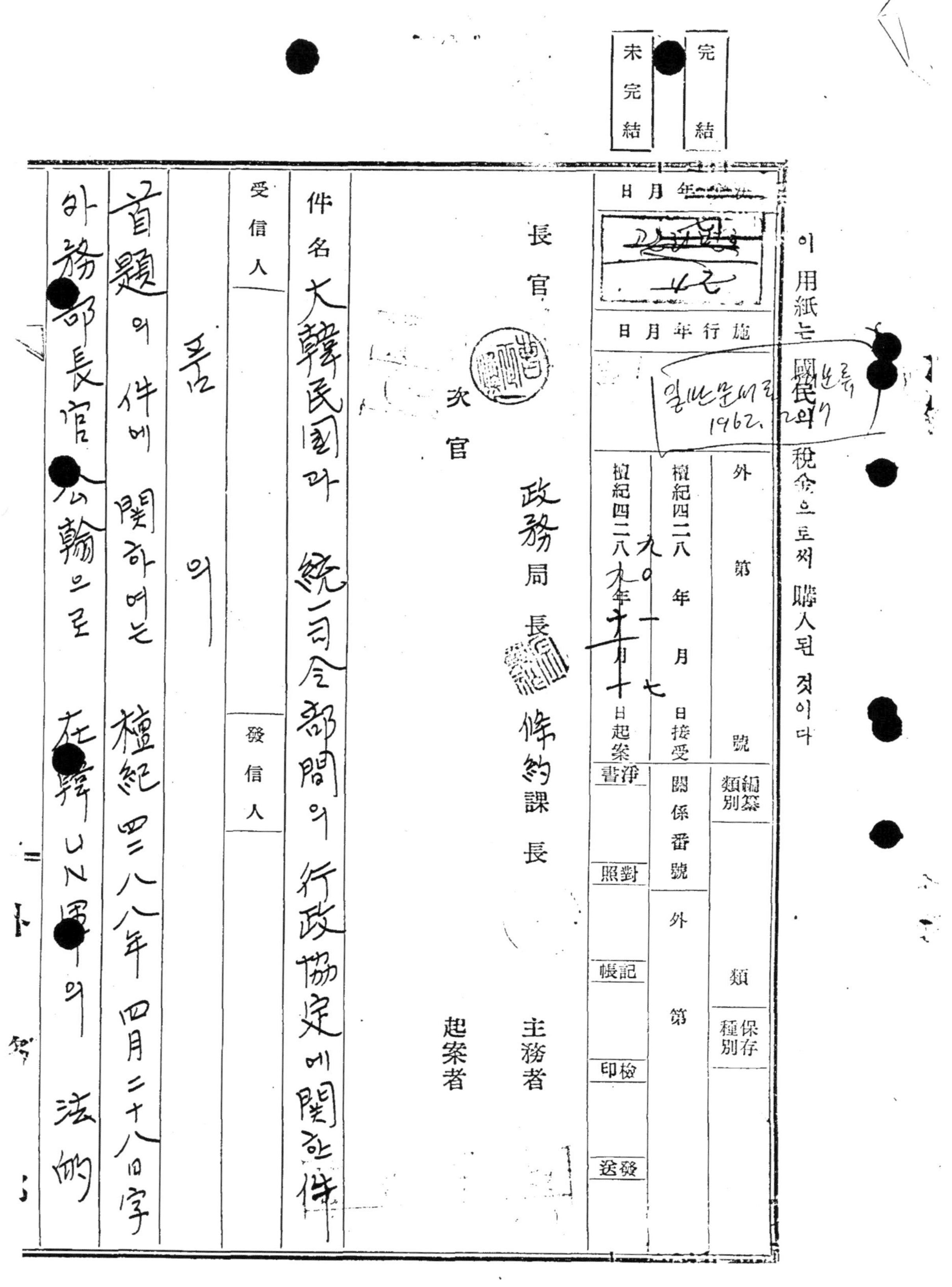

未完結 完結

長官 次官

政務局 長

條約課 長

主務者 起案者

檀紀四二八六年 九月 十一日 起案

檀紀四二八年 月 日 接受

外 第 號

件名 大韓民國과 統一司令部間의 行政協定에 關한 件

受信人

發信人

首題의 件에 關하여는 檀紀四二八八年 四月二十八日字 外務部長官 公翰으로 在韓UN軍의 法的

일반문서로 재분류 1962. 12.31

이 用紙는 國民의 稅金으로써 購入된 것이다

0002

地位를 規定하기 爲하 韓國과 UN軍
統一司令部間의 行政協定을 締結할것은
提案한바있었으나 美國政府로부터 이에
対한 同意回答은 받지못하고 있던중 今般
十月二十五日字 大統領閣下의 吩咐에 依하여
此問題를 促進코저 한바 四二八八年 七月 二十六日字
래므니쩌 將軍의 公翰을 想起시키는 同時에
同書翰에서 本件協定의 締結을 爲한

0003

[illegible]이 困難하다는 理由로서 指摘한
두가지 点은 現在로서는 별서 問題가 되지
않는다는 것을 指摘하여 別添草案과
如히 本件協定의 締結을 再次 提案코자
茲에 高裁를 仰請하는 바입니다.

別添草案





0004

COPY

D R A F T

# ADMINISTRATIVE AGREEMENT BETWEEN THE REPUBLIC OF KOREA AND THE UNIFIED COMMAND REGARDING THE STATUS OF THE UNITED NATIONS FORCES IN KOREA

Bureau of Political Affairs
Ministry of Foreign Affairs

<1957>

55

0005

0006

C O N T E N T S.



56

0007

0008

5-11-62

# ADMINISTRATIVE AGREEMENT BETWEEN THE REPUBLIC OF KOREA AND THE UNIFIED COMMAND REGARDING THE STATUS OF THE UNITED NATIONS FORCES IN KOREA

## PREAMBLE

Mindful that the United Nations Forces under the Unified Command are disposed in and about the territory of the Republic of Korea pursuant to the resolutions of the United Nations Security Council of June 25, 1950, June 27,1950, and July 7,1950;

Considering that active hostilities in Korea have ceased with the conclusion of Armistice Agreement signed on July 27,1953, alleviating the emergent conditions incident to military operations, and that the United Nations Forces will remain in and about the territory of the Republic of Korea until the objectives of the United Nations in Korea will have been achieved;

Believing that the conditions that shall govern the disposition of the United Nations Forces in and about the territory of the Republic of Korea should be determined by mutual agreement between the Republic of Korea and the Unified Command;

And regarding it necessary that the Republic of Korea and the Unified Command conclude practical administrative arrangements which will help minimize misunderstanding and maximize cooperativeness between Korean people and United Nations Forces personnel in Korea

0010

hereunder specified;

Therefore, the Governments of the Republic of Korea and of the United States of America acting as the Unified Command have entered into this Agreement in terms as set forth below:

ARTICLE I

In this Agreement the expression:

(a) "members of the United Nations Forces" means the personnel on active duty belonging to the land, sea or air armed services under the Unified Command when in the territory of the Republic of Korea (hereinafter referred to as Korea) in connection with their official duties.

(b) "civilian component" means the civilian personnel of the nationality of any state sending forces under the Unified Command accompanying the United Nations forces who are in the employ of such forces in Korea. For the purpose of this Agreement only, dual nationals, Korean and of any state sending forces under the Unified Command who are brought to Korea by the United Nations forces shall be deemed as nationals of such state.

(c) "dependents" means

(i) spouse, and children under 21;

(ii) parents, and children over 21, if dependent for over half their support upon a member of the United Nations forces or civilian compnent.

0012

54-11-60

ARTICLE I I

1. Members of the United Nations forces shall be exempt from Korean passport and visa laws and regulations. Members of the United Nations forces, the civilian component, and their dependents shall be exempt from Korean laws and regulations on the registration and control of aliens, but shall not be considered as acquiring any right to permanent residence or domicile in the territories of Korea.

2. Members of the United Nations forces shall be in possession of the following documents upon entry into or departure from Korea:

(a) personal identity card issued by the United Nations forces authorities showing names, date of birth, rank and number, service and photograph;

(b) individual or collective movement order issued by the United Nations forces authorities and certifying to the status of the individual or group as a menber or members of the United Nations forces and to the movement ordered.

For the purpose of identification while in Korea, members of the United Nations forces shall be in possession of the foregoing personal identity card.

59 0013

0014

3. Members of the civilian component, their dependents, and the dependents of the members of the United Nations forces shall be in possession of passports with their status described therein, upon their entry into or departure from Korea, and while in Korea.

4. If a member of the United Nations forces or of the civilian components or his dependent is, by reason of alteration in his status, no longer entitled to the privileges provided for in the foregoing paragraphs, the United Nations forces authorities shall notify the Korean authorities and shall, if such person be requirc by the Korean authorities to leave Korea, assure that transportation from Korea will be provided within a reasonable time at no cost to the Korean Government.

ARTICLE III

I. (a) (i) Korea agrees to grant to the Unified Command the use of the facilities and areas necessary to carry out the missio: and purposes of the United Nations forces in Korea.

(ii) Agreements as to facilities and areas to be used by the United Nations forces in accordance with this Agreement shall be concluded by the two Parties through the Joint Committee provided for in Article XVII of this Agreement.

0016

54-11-58

(iii) Until such agreements are concluded between the two Parties the United Nations forces shall continue to use such facilities and areas as are being used at the time this Agreement becomes effective.

(b) At the request of either Party, Korea and the Unified Command shall review such arrangements and may agree that such facilities and areas shall be returned to Korea or that additional facilities and areas may be provided.

(c) The facilities and areas used by the United Nations forces shall be returned to Korea whenever they are no longer needed for purposes of this Agreement, and the Unified Command agrees to keep the needs for facilities and areas under continual observation with a view toward such return.

(d) When facilities and areas such as target ranges and maneuver grounds are temporarily not being used by the United Nations forces, interim use may be made by Korean authorities and nationals in accordance with the decision made by the Joint Committee provided for in Article XVII of this Agreement.

2. (a) The Unified Command shall have the rights, power and authority within the facilities and

0017

61

0018

5K-11-57

areas which are necessary or appropriate for their establishment, use, operation or defense. The Unified Command shall also have such rights, power and authority over land, territorial waters and airspace adjacent to, or in the vicinities of such facilities and areas, as are necessary to provide access to such facilities and areas, for their support and defense. In the exercise outside the facilities and areas of the rights, power and authority granted in this Article there should be, as the occasion requires, consultation between the two Parties through the Joint Committee.

(b) The Unified Command agrees that the above mentioned rights, power and authority will not be exercised in such a manner as to interfere unnecessarily with navigation, aviation, communication, or land travel to of from or within the territories of Korea. All questions relating to frequencies, power and like matters used by apparatus employed by the United Nations forces designed to emit electric radiation shall be settled by mutual arrangement. Pending such arrangement, the United Nations forces shall be entitled to use, without radiation interference from Korean sources, electronic devices of such power, design, type of emission, and frequencies as are reserved for such forces at the time this Agreement becomes effective.

62.
0019

0020

54-11-56

(c) Operations in the facilities and areas in use by the United Nations forces shall be carried on with due regard for the public safety.

3. (a) The Unified Command is not obliged, when it returns facilities and areas to Korea on the expiration of this Agreement or at an earlier date, to restore the facilities and areas to the condition in which they were at the time they become available to the United Nations forces, or to compensate Korea in lieu of such restoration. In case of private property demolished by such use, the Unified Command shall pay sympathetic consideration to its restoration.

(b) Korea is not obliged to make any compensation to the Unified Command for any improvements made in the facilities and areas or for buildings or structures left thereon the expiration of this Agreement or the earlier return of the facilities and areas.

4. (a) Vessels and aircraft operated by, for, or unde the control of the United Nations forces for official purposes shall be accorded access to any port or airport of Korea free from toll or landing charges.

When cargo or passengers not accorded the exemption of this Agreement are carried on such vessels and aircraft, notification shall be given to the appropriate Korean authorities, and such cargo or passengers shall be entered in accordance with the laws and regulations of Korea.

63

0021

0022

54-11-55

(b) When the vessels mentioned in paragraph 4 (a) enter Korean ports, appropriate notification shall, under normal conditions, be made to the proper Korean authorities. Such vessels shall have freedom from compulsory pilotage, but if a pilot is taken pilotage shall be paid for at appropriate rates.

5.(a) All civil and military air traffic control and communications systems shall be coordinated in accordance with the decision made by Joint Committee.

(b) Lights and other aids to navigation of vessels and aircraft placed or established in the facilities and areas in use by the United Nations forces and in territorial waters adjacent thereto or in the vicinity thereof shall conform to the system in use in Korea. The Korean and the United Nations forces authorities which have established such navigation aids shall notify each other of their positions and characteristics and shall give advance notification before making any changes in them or establishing additional navigation aids.

6. The United Nations forces may use all public utilities and services belonging to the Government of Korea under conditions no less favorable than those applicable to the armed forces of Korea.

7. Korea and the United Nations forces shall cooperate in meteorological services through exchange of meteorological observations, climatological information and seismographic data.

0024

54-11-54

ARTICLE IV

1. Subject to the provisions of this Article,

(a) the United Nations forces authorities shall have the right to exercise within Korea all criminal and disciplinary jurisdiction conferred on them by the law of the United Nations forces over all persons subject to the military law of the United Nations forces.

(b) the authorities of Korea shall have jurisdiction over the members of the United Nations forces or civilian component and their dependents with respect to offences committed within the territory of Korea and punishable by the law of Korea.

2. (a) The United Nations forces authorities shall have the right to exercise exclusive jurisdiction over persons subject to the military law of the United Nations forces with respect to offences, including offences relaing to its security, punishable by the law of the United Nations forces, but not by the law of Korea.

(b) The authorities of Korea shall have the right to exercise exclusive jurisdiction over members of the United Nations forces or civilian compnent and their dependents with respect to offences, including offences relating to the security of Korea, punishable by its law but not by the law of the United Nations forces.

(c) For the purposes of this paragraph and of

0026

54-11-53

paragraph 3 of this Article a security offence against a State shall include,

(i) treason against the State;

(ii) sabotage, espionage or violation of any law relating to official secrets of that State, or secrets relating to the national defense of that State.

3. In case where the right to exercise jurisdiction is concurrent the following rules shall apply:

(a) The United Nations forces authorities shall have the primary right to exercise jurisdiction over a member of the United Nations forces or of a civilian component in relation to

(i) offences soley against the property or security of the United Nations forces or their states, or offences solely against the person or property of another member of the United Nations forces or civilian component or of a dependent ;

(ii) offences arising out of any act or omission done in the execution of official duty.

(b) In the case of any other offence the authorities of Korea shall have the primary right to exercise jurisdiction.

(c) If the Party having the primary right decide

66 0027

0028

54-11-52

not to exercise jurisdiction, it shall notify the authorities of the other Party as soon as practicable. The authorities of the Party having the primary right shall give sympathetic consideration to a request from the authorities of the other Party for a waiver of its right in cases where that other Party considers such waiver to be of particular importance.

4. The foregoing provisions of this Article shall not imply any right for the United Nations forces authorities to exercise jurisdiction over persons who are nationals of ordinarily resident in Korea, unless they are members of the United Nations forces.

5. (a) The authorities of Korea and the United Nations forces authorities shall assist each other in the arrest of members of the United Nations forces or civilian component or their dependents in the territory of Korea and in handing them over to the authority which is to exercise jurisdiction in accordance with the above provisions.

(b) The authorities of Korea shall notify promptly the United Nations forces authorities of the arrest of any member of the United Nations forces or civilian component or a dependent.

(c) The custody of an accused member of the United Nations forces or civilian component over whom Korea is to exercise jurisdiction shall, if he is in the hands

67 0029

0030

of the United Nations forces remain with the United Nations forces until he is charged by Korea.

6. (a) The authorities of Korea and the United Nations forces authorities shall assist each other in the carrying out of all necessary investigations into offences, and in the collection and production of evidence, including seizure and, in proper cases, the handing over of objects connected with an offense. The handing over of such objects may,however, be made subject to their return within the time specified by the authorities delivering them.

(b) The authorities of Korea and the United Nations forces shall notify each other of the disposition of all cases in which there are concurrent rights to exercise jurisdiction.

7. (a) A death sentense shall not be carried out in Korea by the United Nations forces authorities if the legislation of Korea does not provide for such punishment in a similar case.

(b) The authorities of Korea shall have sympathetic consideration to a request from the United Nations forces authorities for assistance in carrying out a sentense of imprinsonment pronounced by the United Nations forces authorities under the provisions of this Article within the territory of Korea.

0032

54-11-50

8. Where an accused has been tried in accordance with provisions of this Article either by the authorities of Korea or the United Nations forces authorities and has been acquitted, or has been convicted and is serving or has served, or his sentence has been pardoned, he may not be tried again for the same offence within the territory by the authorities of the other Party. However, nothing in this paragraph shall prevent the United Nations forces authorities from trying a member of its armed **forces** for any violation of rules of discipline arising from an act or omission which constituted an offence for which he was tried by the authorities of Korea.

9. Whenever a member of the United Nations forces or civilian compnent or a dependent is prosecuted under the jurisdiction of Korea he shall be entitled:

(a) to a prompt and speedy trial;

(b) to be informed, in advance of trial, of specific charge made against him;

(c) to be confronted with the witnesses against him;

(d) to have compulsory process for obtaning witnesses in his favor, if they are within the jurisdiction of Korea;

(e) to have legal representation of his own choice for his defnese or to

0034

54-11-4P

free or assisted legal representation under the conditions prevailing for the time being in Korea;

(f) if he considers it necessary, to have the services of a competent interpreter; and

(g) to communicate with a representative of the United Nations forces and, when the rules of the court permit, to have such a representative present at his trial.

10. (a) Regularly constituted military units or formations of the United Nations forces shall have the right to police any facilities or areas which they use under Article III of this Agreement. The military police of such forces may take all appropriate measures to ensure the maintenance of order and security within such facilities and areas.

(b) Outside these facilities and areas, such military police shall be employed only subject to arrangements with the authorities of Korea and in liaison with those authorities, and in so far as such employment is necessary to maintain discipline and order among the members of the United Nations forces.

ARTICLE V

1. Each Party waives all its claims against the other Party for damage to any property in Korea owned by

707

0035

0036

54-11-48

it and used by its land, sea or air armed services, if such damage

(i) was caused by a member or an employee of the armed services of the other Party, in the execution of his official duties; or

(ii) arose from the use of any vehicle, vessel or aircraft owned by the other Party and used by its amred services, provided either that the vehicle, vessel or aircraft causing the damage was being used in the execution of its official duty or that the damage was caused to property being so used.

Claims for maritime salvage by one Party against the other Party shall be waived, provided that the vessel or cargo salved was owned by the former, and being used by its armed services in the execution of their official duties.

2. (a) In the case of damage caused or arising as stated in paragraph 1 to other property in Korea owned by either Party the issue of the liability of the other Party shall be determined and the amount of damage shall be assessed, unless the two Parties agree otherwise, by the Joint Committee to be established under Article XVII of this Agreement.

(b) Payment of the amount of any compensation

0038

54-11-417

decided by the Joint Committee shall be made in Korean currency.

3. Each Party waives all its claims against the other Party for injury or death suffered in Korea by a member or an employee of its armed forces, while such member or employee was engaged in the execution of his official duties in case where such injury or death was caused by a member of the armed forces, or an employee of the other Party acting in the execution of his official duties.

4. Claims (other than contractual claims and those to which paragraph 5 or 6 of this Article shall apply) arising out of acts or omissions of members of or employees of the United Nations forces or civilian component done in the execution of official duty, or out of any other act, omission or occurence for which the United Nations forces or civilian component is legally responsible, and causing damage in Korea to third Parties, shall be dealt with by Korea in accordance with the following provisions:

(a) Claims shall be filed, considered and settled or adjudicated in accordance with the laws and regulations of Korea with respect to claims arising from the activities of its own armed forces.

(b) Korea may settle any such claims, and payment of the amount agreed upon or determined by adjudication shall be made by Korea in its currency.

72

0039

0040

54-11-46

(c) Such payment, whether made pursuant to a settlement or to adjuciation of the case by a competent tribunal of Korea, or the final adjudication by such a tribunal denying payment, shall be binding and conclusive.

(d) The cost incurred in the course of settling or adjudicating claims pursuant to the preceeding subparagraph to be agreed by the two Parties shall be shared on terms.

(e) Every claim paid by Korea shall be communicated to the United Nations forces periodically, together with full particulars and request for reimbursement . Such reimbursement shall be made within the shortest possible time in the currency of Korea.

(f) A member of the United Nations forces or civilian component shall not be subject to any preceeding for the enforcement of any judgement given against him in Korea in a matter arising from the execution of his official duties.

5. Claims against members of the United Nations forces or civilian component arising out of tortious acts or omissions in Korea not done in the execution of official duty shall be dealt with in the following manner:

73

0041

0042

(a) The Korean authorities shall consider the claim and assess compensation to the claimant in a fair and just manner, taking into account all the circumstances of the case, including the conduct of the injured person, and shall prepare a report on the matter.

(b) The report shall be delivered to the United Nations forces authorities, who shall then decide without delay whether they will offer an <u>ex gratia</u> payment, and if so, of what amount.

(c) If an offer of <u>ex gratia</u> payment is made, and accepted by the claimant in full satisfaction of his claim, the United Nations forces authorities shall make the payment themselves and inform the Korean authorities of their decision and of the sum paid.

(d) Nothing in this paragraph shall affect the jurisdiction of the courts of Korea to entertain an action against a member of the United Nations forces or of a civilain component unless and until there has been payment in full satisfaction

0044

of the claim.

6. Claims arising out of the unauthorized use of any vehicle of the United Nations forces shall be dealt with in accordance with paragraph 5 of this Article , except in so far as the armed forces or civilian component is legally responsible.

7. Each Party shall have the primary right, in the execution of the foregoing paragraphs, to determine whether its personnel were engaged in the execution of official duty. Such determination shall be made as soon as possible after the arising of the claim concerned. When the other Party disagrees with the results of such determination, that Party may bring the matter before the Joint Committee for consultation under the provisions of Article XVI.

8. The Unified Command shall not claim immunity from the jurisdiction of the courts of Korea for members of its armed forces or civilian component in respect of the civil jurisdiction of the courts of Korea except to the extent provided in paragraph 4 (f) of this Article.

9. The authorities of Korea and the United Nations forces authorities shall cooperate in the procurement of evidence for a fair hearing and disposal of claims in regard to which the two Parties are concerned.

10. In case any private movable property, excluding that in use by the United Nations forces, which is

0046

'54. 11-43

subject to compulsory execution under Korean law, is within the facilities and areas in use by the United Nations forces, the United Nations forces authorities shall upon the request of Korean courts, possess and turn over such property to the Korean authorities.

ARTICLE VI

1. Members of the United Nations forces or civilian component and their dependents may purchase locally goods necessary for their own consumption, and such services as they need, under the same conditions as the nationals of Korea.

2. Goods and services which are required and can be procured from local sources for the subsistance of the United Nations forces or civilian component shall be procured, in conformation to the United Nations policy to aid Korean economy, in a manner most likely to help maintain Korean economical stability and least to adversely affect it, and in coordination with and, when desirable, through or with the assistance of the competent authorities of Korea.

3. Local civilian labor requirements of the United Nations forces or civilian component shall be satisfied with the assistance of the Korean authorities. Care should be constantly taken, however, not to unnecessarily strain Korean manpower so that eqally or more important

76 0047

0048

projects may not suffer from lack of hands.

4. Except as may otherwise mutually be agreed, the conditions of employment and work, such as those relating wages, supplementary payments, and conditions for the protection of workers, shall be those laid down by the legislation of Korea.

5. The United Nations forces shall refrain from employing foreign laborers in the territory of Korea as well as its territorial waters with a view to not compromising the employment of Korean laborers.

ARTICLE VII

1. The United Nations forces shall not be subject to taxes or similar charges on property held, used or transferred by such forces in Korea.

2. Members of the United Nations forces, the civilian component, and their dependents shall not be liable to pay any Korean taxes to the Korean Government or to any other taxing agency in Korea on income received as a result of their service with or employment by the United Nations forces, or by the organizations provided for in Article IX.

3. Nothing in this Article shall prevent taxation of members of the United Nations forces or civilian component or their dependents with respect to any income dereived from sources other than those provided for in

77

0049

0050

paragraph 2 of this Article.

4. Members of the United Nations forces, the civilian component and their dependents shall be exempt from taxation with respect to any movable property, the presence of which in Korea is due solely to their temporary presence in Korea, provided that such exemption shall not apply to property held for the purpose of investment or the conduct of business in Korea.

ARTICLE VIII

1. Save as provided to the contrary in this Agreement, members of the United Nations forces, the civilian component, and their dependents shall be subject to the laws and regulations administered by the customs authorities of Korea.

2. The United Nations forces or the organizations provided for in Article IX may import free of duty all materials, supplies and equipment, exclusively for the official use of the United Nations forces or for the use of the members of the United Nations forces, the civilian component, and their dependents. The duty free importation shall be verified by a certificate issued by the United Nations forces authorities in a form agreed between Korea and the United Nations forces.

3. Property consigned to and for the personal

005178

0052

54-11-40

use of members of the United Nations forces, the civilian component and their dependents, shall be subject to customs duties, except that no duties shall be paid with respect to:

(a) Furniture, household goods and other personal effects for their private use imported by the members of the United Nations forces, civilian component and their dependents at the time of their first arrival in Korea;

(b) Reasonable quantities of clothing and household/ goods of a type which would ordinarily be purchased in their home states for everyday use for the private use of members of the United Nations forc civilian component, and their dependents, which are mailed into Korea through the United Nations forces military post offices.

4. Official documents under official seal and mail in the United Nations forces postal channels shall not be subject to customs inspection.

5. Goods which have been imported duty-free under

79

0053

0054

paragraph 2 and 3 above:

(a) may be re-exported freely, provided that, in the case of goods imported under paragraph 2, a certificate is issued by the United Nations forces authorities in a form agreed between Korea and the United Nations forces;

(b) shall not normally be disposed of in Korea by way of either sale or gift. However, in particular cases such disposal may be authorized on conditions, agreed between the authorities of Korea and the United Nations forces.

6. Exportation and re-importation of goods purchased in Korea shall be subject to the regulations in force in Korea. Such goods shall be regarded exported when deposited in a warehouse and deemed imported when removed from the warehouse.

7. In paragraph 2, 3 and 5 of this Article, "duty" means customs duties and all other duties and taxes payable on importation or exportation, as the case may be, except dues and taxes which are no more than charges for services rendered.

8. (a) The customs authorities of Korea shall have the right, when desirable, in cooperation with the

80

0055

0056

authorities of the United Nations forces to search members of the United Nations forces or civilian component and their dependents and examine their luggage and vehicles, and to seize articles pursuant to the laws and regulations administered by the customs authorities of Korea.

(b) In order to prevent offences against customs and fiscal laws and regulations, the authorities of Korea and of the United Nations forces shall assist each other in the conduct of inquiries and the collection of evidence.

(c) The authorities of the United Nations forces shall render all assistance within their power to ensure that articles liable to seizure by, or on behalf of, the customs or fiscal authorities of Korea are handed to those authorities.

(d) The authorities of the United Nations forces shall render all assistance within their power to ensure the payment of duties, taxes and penalties payable by members of the United Nations forces or civilian component or their dependents.

ARTICLE IX

1. (a) Navy exchange, post exchange, messes, social clubs, thearters, newspapaers and other non-appropriated funds organizations authorized and rgulated by

81 0057

0058

the United Nations forces authorities may be established in the facilities and areas in use by the United Nations forces for the use of members of such forces, the civilian component and their dependents. Except as otherwise provided in this Agreement, such organizations shall no t be subject to Korean regulations, license, fees, taxes or similar controls.

(b) When a newspaper authorized and regulated by the United Nations forces authorities is sold to the general public, it shall be subject to Korean regulations, license, fees, taxes or similar controls so far as such circulation is concerned.

2. No Korean tax shall be imposed on sales of merchandise and services by such organizations, except as provided in paragraph 1 (b) of this Article, but purchases whthin Korea of merchandise and supplies by such organizations shall be subject to Korean taxes.

3. Except as such disposal may be authorized by the Korean and the United Nations forces authorities in accordance with mutually agreed conditions, goods which are sold by such organizations shall not be disposed of in Korea to persons not authorized to make purchases from such organizations.

4. The organizations referred to in this Article shall provide such information to the Korean authorities as is required by Korean legislations.

82

0059

0060

54-11-36

ARTICLE X

The Unified Command shall have the right to establish and operate, within the facilities and areas in use by the United Nations forces, the United Nations forces military post offices for the use of members of the United Nations forces, the civilian component and their dependents, for the transmission of mail between the United Nations forces military post offices in Korea and between such military post offices and their home states post offices.

ARTICLE XI

Korea shall accept as valid, without a driving test or fee, the driving permit or license or military driving permit issued by the States sending the United Nations forces under the Unified Command to a member of the United Nations forces, the civilian component, and their dependents.

ARTICLE XII

1. Members of the United Nations forces shall normally wear uniform. Subject to any arrangement to the contrary between the authorities of Korea and the United Nations forces, the wearing of civilian dress shall be on the same conditions as for members of the armed forces of Korea.

83

0061

0062

54-11-35

2. Official vehicles of the United Nations forces and the civilian component shall carry a distinctive nationality mark and individual markings which will readily identify them.

3. Privately owned vehicles of members of the United Nations forces, the civilian component, and their dependents shall carry Korean number plates to be acquired under the same conditions as those applicable to Korean nationals.

ARTICLE X III

1. Members of the United Nations forces or civilian component may possess and carry arms, on condition that they are authorized to do so by their orders. The authorities of the United Nations forces shall give sympathtic consideration to request from Korea concerning this matter.

2. Dependents of members of the United Nations forces or of civilian component and their dependents may possess and carry arms in accordance with the laws and regulations of Korea.

ARTICLE XIV

84

0063

64-11-34

0064

Members of the United Nations forces, the civilian component, and their dependents shall respect the law of Korea and abstain from any activities inconsistent with the spirit of this Agreement, and, in particular, shall not engage in any political activity in Korea.

ARTICLE XV

In the event of hostilities, or imminently threatened hostilities, in Korea, the Governments of Korea and the Unified Command shall immediately consult together with a view to agreeing on such modifications as they may consider desirable regarding the application of this Agreement.

ARTICLE XVI

1. A Joint Committee shall be established as the means for consultation between .rea and the Unified Command on all matters requiring mutual consultation regarding the implementation or interpretation of this Agreement.

2. The Joint Committee shall be composed of a representative of Korea and of the Unified Command, each of whom shall have one or more deputies and a staff. The Joint Committee shall determine its own procedures, and arrange for such military organs and adminstrative services as may be required. The Joint Committee shall be so organizaed that it may meet immediately at any time at the request of the resprentative of

0065 85

0066

54-11-33

either Korea or the Unified Command.

3. If the Joint Committee is unable to resolve any matter, it shall refer that matter to the Parties for further consideration through appropriate channe ls

ARTICLE XVII

This Agreement shall come inot force on the date of signature by the representatives of Korea and of the Unified Command.

ARTICLE XVIII

Either Party may at any time request the revision of any Article of this Agreement. The request shall be addressed to the Joint Committee.

ARTICLE XIX

This Agreement and agreed revisions thereof, shall remain in force while the United Nations forces stay in Korea.

This Agreement shall be suspended upon the withdrawal of the United Nations forces from Korea, and shall resume its force automatically whenever such forces return to Korea.

In witness whereof the representatives of the two Parties duly authorized for the purpose, have signed

0068

54-11-32

this Agreement.

Done in Seoul, in duplicate, in the Korean and English languages, both equally authentic, this ............ the day of ...........,1957.

For the Government of Republic of Korea:

For the Government of the United States of America acting as the Unified Command:

0070

54-11-31

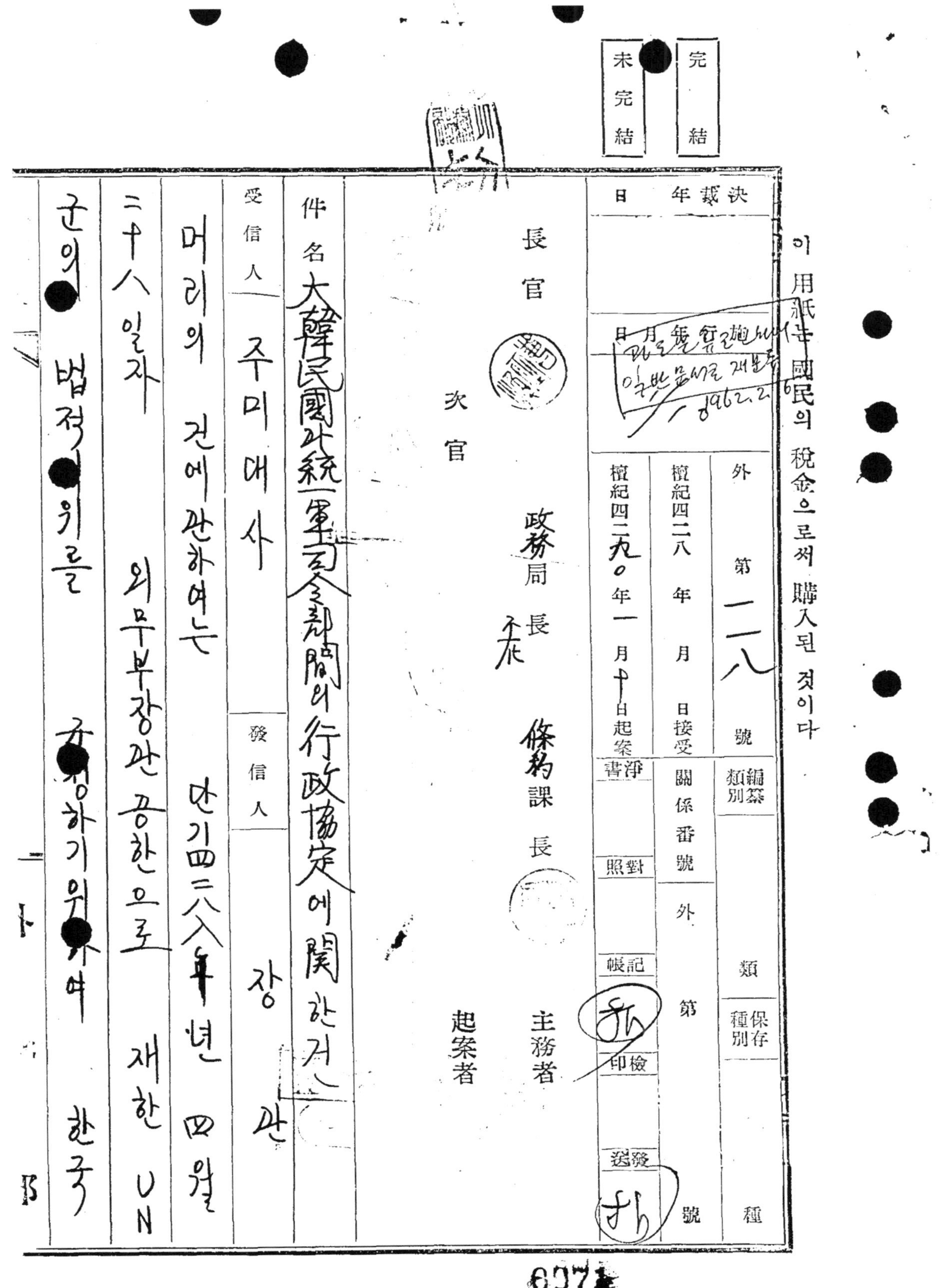

未完結 | 完結

決裁 年 月 日

長官

次官

政務局長

條約課長

主務者

起案者

外 第 一一八 號

檀紀四二八 年 月 日 接受

檀紀四二九〇年 一月 十日 起案

件名 大韓民國과 統一軍司令部間의 行政協定에 關한 件

受信人 주미대사

發信人 장관

머리의 건에 관하여는 단기四二八八년 四월 二十八일자 외무부장관 공한으로 재한 UN 군의 법적 지위를 규정하기 위하여 한국

이 用紙는 國民의 稅金으로써 購入된 것이다

0071

과 UN군 통일사령부간의 행정협정을 체
결할 것을 제안한 바 있었으나 미국정부로
부터 이에 대한 동의회답은 받지 못하
고 있었음을 금반 十월 二十일자 대통령
각하의 분부에 의하여 차 문제를 촉
진코저 하는바, 四二八년 七월 二十일자
총리로부터 레므니쳐 장군 앞 공한으로 본건 협
정의 체결을 위한 교섭이 곤란하다는
이유로서 두가지 점을 지적하였으나 동
二개 점은 현재로서는 벌서 문제
가 되지 않는다는 것을 밝히여 별첨
공한 사본과 여히 본건 협정의 체

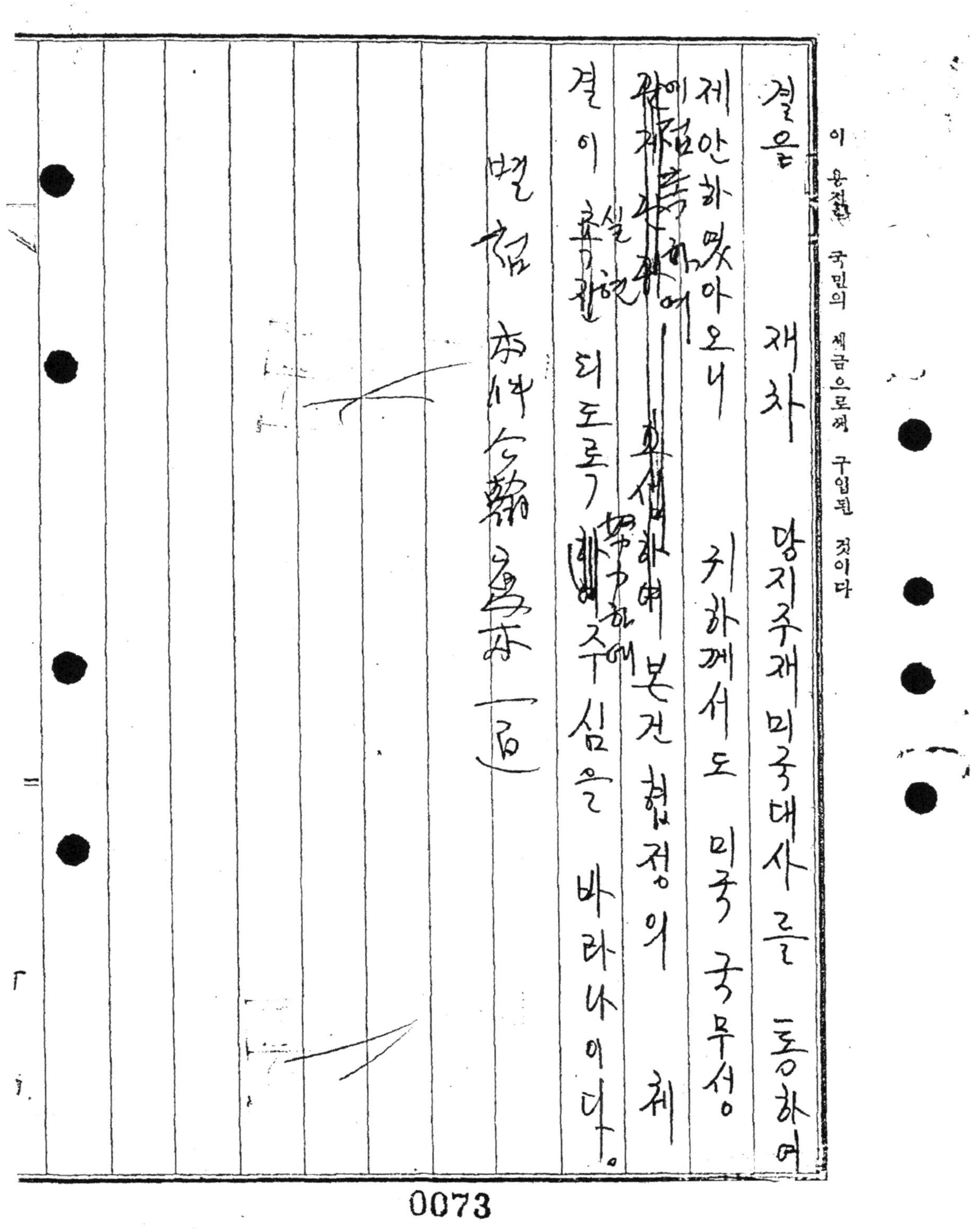

이 용지는 국민의 세금으로써 구입된 것이다

결을 재차 당지주재 미국대사를 통하여 제안하였아오니 귀하께서도 미국 국무성에 교섭하여 관계당국과 협의하여 본건 협정의 체결이 조속 실현되도록 하여 주심을 바라나이다.

별첨 本件 公翰 寫本 一通

0073

November

Excellency:

I have the honour to refer the Foreign Minister's note addressed to Mr. Carl W. Strom, Charge d'Affairs ad interim of the Embassy of the United States of America in Korea dated April 28, 1955 enclosing a draft of an Administrative Agreement between the Republic of Korea and the Unified Command for establishment of the Status of the United Nations Forces in Korea.

In the afore-said note, the Minister informed the Government of the United States of America of the desire of the Korean Government to commence negotiations with the United States Government for the said Status of Forces Agreement which will also define the former's customs functions as referred to in my letter of December 2, 1954.

To this proposal, however, no acceptance has been given as yet, although the American Charge d'Affairs notified in his replying note of May 9, 1955, that upon obtaining his Government's view on the said request, he would communicate with the Minister.

I hereby wish again to propose, on behalf of my Government, that negotiation be commenced at an earliest possible date between the representatives of the Korean Government and the United States Government. In connection with this re-proposal, I would like further to refer to the note of July 26, 1955 addressed to the Foreign Minister /by General

His Excellency

The right honourable

Walter C. Dowling

Ambassador

Republic

Seoul, Korea

과도분류로 인하여
Ⅲ급비밀로 재분류
1962. 2. 15

0074

by General Lemnitzer advising on this matter, a copy of which is enclosed herewith for information.

General Lemnitzer expressed ~~his~~ views on the possibility of negotiating the said agreement in the above note to the effect that the United States Government envisages difficulties in commencing immediately negotiations for a proposed agreement for the following two reasons:

The one reason was that it would be preferable to the American Government that negotiations for a proposed treaty of Friendship, Commerce and Navigation between the two countries as well as an agreement guaranteeing investment be completed before the initiation of negotiation for an agreement in question. The other was that the Unified Command cannot participate in negotiation of such agreement without the prior consent of Allies within the Unified Command and it is anticipated that the task of obtaining such consent will be difficult.

Attention, however, is paid to the fact that points indicated above constitute no longer difficulties about negotiating the said agreement under the present circumstances.

Negotiation for a proposed treaty of Friendship, Commerce and Navigation has been completed and the treaty is now waiting to be formally signed. As regards the agreement guaranteeing investments, discussions have been completed on provisions of its draft and now the work of finalizing it remains only. ~~On the other hand, since Allies within the Unified Command have been decreased in number into twelve states, and since the American forces form the predominant components of the~~ United Nations Forces, there exist no difficulties, it is believed, in securing consent of other allies as to the matter. And thus, in case such consent has not been obtained as yet, it is, therefore, proposed, that preliminary negotiations be started first between both representatives of the Korean Government and the United States Government, since it is considered that negotiations with other allies can be carried on seperately in accordance with terms agreed upon between the two countries above.

/Under the

0075

~~Under the circumstances~~ It is sincerely requested that the concurrence of the United States Government be given to the wish of the Korean Government ~~to~~ have negotiation for the agreement.

Please accept, Excellency, the renewed assurances of my highest consideration.

Chung W. Cho
Acting Minister
of Foreign Affairs

Enclosure: A copy of General Lemnitzer's Letter
dated July 26, 1955

관리번호 43

외정 호

단기 四二九○년 一월 十일

외무부 장관

주미대사 귀하

大韓民國과 統一軍司令部間의 行政協定에 관한 머리의 건에 관하여는 단기 四二八八년 二十八일 外務部長官 공한으로 재한 UN군의 법적지위를 규정하기 위하여 한국과 UN군 통일사령부 간의 행정협정을 체결할 것을 제안한바 있었으나 미국 정부로부터 이에 대한 동의회답은 받지 못하고 있으므로 금반 차문제를 촉진

기록문류 일반문서로 재분류 1962. 2. 6.

이 용지는 국민의 세금으로서 구입된 것이다

0077

코저 하는바 統一軍司令官 렘니쩐 장군으로부터 四二八년 七월 二十六일자 공한으로 본건 협정의 체결을 위한 교섭이 곤난하다는 이유로서 두가지 점을 지적하였으나 동 二개점은 현재로서는 별 문제가 되지 않는다는 것을 밝히여 별첨 공한 사본과 여히 본건 협정의 체결을 재차 당지 주재 미국대사를 통하여 제안 하였아오니 귀하께서도 미국 국무성에 접촉하여 본건 협정의 체결이 실현되도록 노력하여 주심을 바라나이다

별첨 본건 공한 사본 일통

0078

C
O
P
Y

January 5, 1957

Excellency:

I have the honour to refer to the Foreign Minister's note addressed to Mr. Carl W. Strom, Charge d'Affairs ad interim of the Embassy of the United States of America in Korea dated April 28, 1955 enclosing a draft of an Administrative Agreement between the Republic of Korea and the Unified Command for establishment of the Status of the United Nations Forces in Korea.

In the afore-said note, the Minister informed the Government of the United States of America of the desire of the Korean Government to commence negotiations with the United States Government for the said Status of Forces Agreement which will also define the former's customs functions as referred to in my letter of December 2, 1954.

To this proposal, however, no acceptance has been given as yet, although the American Charge d'Affairs notified in his replying note of May 9, 1955, that upon obtaining his Government's view on the said request, he would communicate with the Minister.

I hereby wish again to propose, on behalf of my Government, that negotiation be commenced at an earliest possible date between the representatives of the Korean Government and the United States Government. In connection with this re-proposal, I would like further to refer to the note of July 26, 1955 addressed to the Foreign Minister

/by General



His Excellency

The right honourable

Walter C. Dowling

Ambassador of the United States of

America to the Republic of Korea

Seoul, Korea

0079

by General Lemnitzer advising on this matter.

General Lemnitzer expressed his views on the possibility of negotiating the said agreement in the above note to the effect that the United States Government envisages difficulties in commencing immediately negotiations for a proposed agreement for the following two reasons:

The one reason was that it would be preferable to the American Government that negotiations for a proposed treaty of Friendship, Commerce and Navigation between the two countries as well as an agreement guaranteeing investments be completed before the initiation of negotiation for an agreement in question. The other was that the Unified Command cannot participate in negotiation of such agreement without the prior consent of allies within the Unified Command and it is anticipated that the task of obtaining such consent will be difficult.

Attention, however, is paid to the fact that the points indicated above constitute no longer difficulties about negotiating the said agreement under the present circumstances.

The Treaty of Friendship, Commerce and Navigation has been already signed and is now waiting to be formally ratified. As regards the agreement guaranteeing investments, discussions have been completed on provisions of its draft and now the work of finalizing it remains only. On the other hand, since allies within the Unified Command have been decreased in number into twelve nations and since the American forces form the predominant components of the United Nations Forces, there exist no difficulties, it is believed, in securing consent of other allies as to the matter.

And thus, even in case the consent of the other allies has not been obtained as yet, it is, therefore, proposed that

/negotiations

0080

negotiations be started first between both representatives of the Korean Government and the United States Government and that negotiations with other allies shall be carried on seperately in accordance with terms to be agreed upon between Korea and the United States of America. It is sincerely requested that the concurrence of the United States Government be given to the wish of the Korean Government to commence negotiations for the agreement proposed.

Please accept, Excellency, the renewed assurances of my highest consideration.

Chung W. Cho
Minister
of Foreign Affairs

0081

-copy-

American Embassy,
Seoul, Korea,
January 15, 1957.

Excellency:

I have the honor to acknowledge the receipt of your note of January 5, 1957, proposing that negotiations be commenced at the earliest possible date between the representatives of the Republic of Korea and of the United States of America, in respect to an Administrative Agreement between the Republic of Korea and the Unified Command for Establishment of the Status of the United Nations Forces in Korea as proposed by the Government of the Republic of Korea in a draft transmitted on April 28, 1955.

I have transmitted a copy of your note to my Government, and have requested its instructions. I shall look forward to further consultation with you as soon as these instructions have been received.

Please accept, Excellency, the renewed assurances of my highest consideration.

His Excellency
Cho Chung-Hwan,
Minister for Foreign Affairs,
Republic of Korea,
Seoul.

0082

February 4, 1957

MEMORANDUM TO: Minister Han

SUBJECT: Administrative Agreement

FROM: First Secretary Han

과도분류로 인하여 일반 문서로 재분류 1962. 2. 19.

과도분류로 인하여 III급 비밀로 재분류 1962. 2. 15

I had a conference this morning on the above subject with Mr. David Nes, Chief of Korea Desk of the State Department. As you know, our Government wants to commence negotiations on this subject and has instructed this Embassy to expedite the matter at this end.

Mr. Nes said that only a few days ago the State Department received a dispatch from its Embassy in Seoul enclosing the latest letter (dated January 5, 1957) from Foreign Minister Cho to Ambassador Dowling. He said that inasmuch as this problem involves the Defense Department and legal authorities, the State Department cannot decide alone what to do and will have to have inter-departmental conferences before a decision can be reached. He estimated that four to six weeks would be required for this purpose. He promised to work on it actively and said he will let us know as soon as his government decides what to do. At the same time, he said, a detailed reply will be sent to Foreign Minister Cho through the Embassy in Seoul.

Commenting on the difficulty of starting negotiations on this matter, Mr. Nes said that legally Korea is still in a state of war and that it would be difficult for the United States to negotiate an administrative agreement such as that exists with NATO countries or with Japan. He mentioned that in the Treaty with NATO countries, there is a provision that provides for instant termination of the Treaty in case of a war.

I said that this matter of Administrative Agreement was first taken up by our government in April, 1955, at which time we presented to the American Embassy in Seoul a draft of the Agreement for its study. I said that although there were several exchanges of communications with the Embassy in Seoul and also with Gen. Lemnitzer after that, no definite reply has yet been given by the U.S. government. I said that according to General Lemnitzer's letter to our Foreign Minister dated July 26, 1955, there were

0083

미문 PO-15121

0083 0020

0084

two reasons why negotiations could not be started. First, the U.S. government preferred to start negotiations after the Treaty of Friendship, Commerce and Navigation had been signed. Second, the United States had to get prior consent of the countries whose forces are in the United Nations Forces. The first reason, I said, no longer exists. As for the second reason, I said it should not be too difficult if our two governments started negotiations first and then arrived at a conclusion as to the draft of the Agreement, and then got the Allies concerned to agree to it or negotiate on it. Whatever we do, I said, something should be done to get the ball rolling.

Mr. Nes replied that although Gen. Lemnitzer gave those two reasons, he, or rather, the State Department does not think that they constituted the major difficulties. The State Department believes, he said, that the major difficulty lies in that Korea is still legally in a state of war. Anyway, he said, no definite answer could be given unless some conclusions were reached at inter-departmental conferences, after which both our Foreign Minister and this Embassy would be notified in detail as to what the American position is on the matter.

政美課에서 Action을 取한것임. (9/12)

COPY

June 29, 1957

파도분류로 인하여 일반문서로 재분류 1962.2.17.

My dear Mr. Ambassador:

I have the honor to remind your Government, as I have orally mentioned to you on several occasions, that the conclusion of an Administrative Agreement defining and setting forth in detail the status of United States troops stationed in Korea is still pending.

On April 28, 1955, our draft proposal of an Administrative Agreement between this Government and the Unified Command, to establish the status of United Nations forces in Korea, was addressed to your Embassy. On November 1, 1956, it was proposed that a separate agreement be negotiated between representatives of this Government and the United States Government, in case of difficulty in obtaining early consent of the other Allied Governments.

In the absense of such an administrative agreement, a temporary agreement was made through the exchange of Notes at Taejon, on July 12, 1950, concerning the exclusive jurisdiction by court-martial of the United States over members of the United States Military Establishment in Korea. This agreement, which is still in force, was improvised to meet an emergency situation and is not considered sufficient to meet effectively all the complex and complicated problems arising from the

/presence of

His Excellency
Ambassador Walter Dowling,
American Embassy,
Seoul.

~~파도분류로 인하여 Ⅲ급비밀로 재분류~~ 1962.2.15

0086

presence of United States troops in Korea.

This Government is strongly convinced that ~~the early~~ conclusion of a formal and ~~detailed~~ agreement on the status of United States troops in Korea would serve to strengthen cordial relations between our people and American military personnel, and would provide great satisfaction to the mutual cause and interest of both countries.

I wish to state again that this Government is most desirous of receiving the concurrence of the United States Government in order to commence negotiations for an administrative Agreement along the lines of the proposal of April, 1955. Your Government's earliest favorable consideration of this matter is most sincerely desired.

Accept, Excellency, renewed assurances of my highest consideration.

Chung W. Cho
Minister

일반문서로 재분류
(협정체결시)

0087

C O [illegible]

0083

American Embassy,
Seoul, Korea,
July 1, 1957.

My dear Mr. Minister:

I have the honor to acknowledge receipt of your letter of June 29, 1957, concerning the desire of your Government to negotiate an Administrative Agreement defining the status of United States troops stationed in Korea, and to inform you that the substance of the letter has been cabled to the Department of State.

In this connection I am glad to inform you that your Government's note of January 5, 1957 is currently being given careful consideration in Washington. I shall, of course, communicate with you again as soon as I receive pertinent information.

With renewed assurances of my highest consideration, I am

Faithfully yours,

11

His Excellency
Chung W. Cho,
Minister of Foreign Affairs,
Republic of Korea.

0088

57-3-8

5Ⅱ-3-5 (1)

미·문에-간

0088

0083

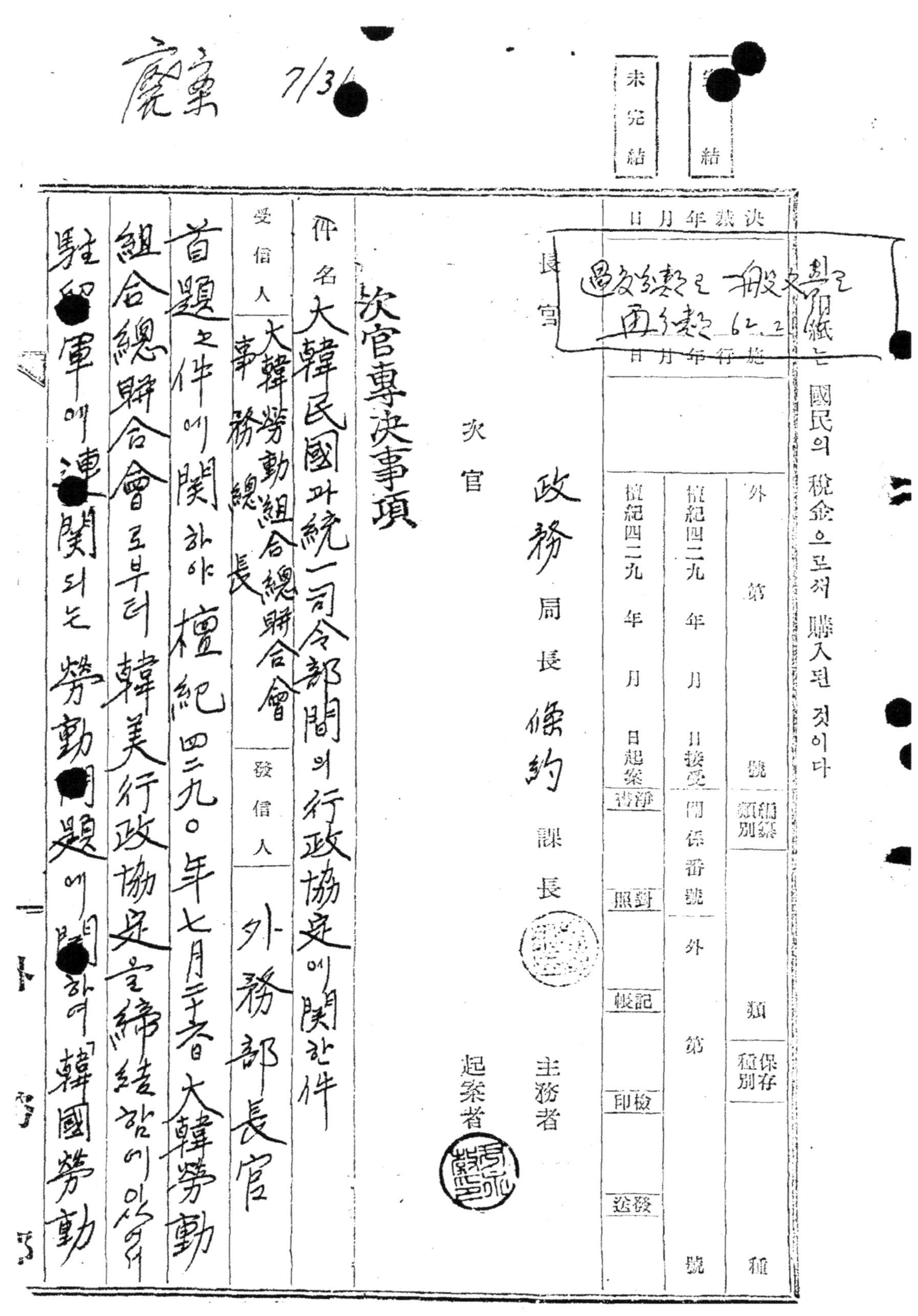

廢棄 7/31

未完結 | 完結

過去文書로 一般文書로 再分類 62.2

決裁年月日

長官

施行年月日

次官

政務局長 條約課長

外第　號

分類記號

檀紀四二九年　月　日接受

檀紀四二九年　月　日起案

保存種別

主務者

起案者

件名 大韓民國과統一司令部間의行政協定에關한件

受信人 大韓勞動組合總聯合會 事務總長

發信人 外務部長官

次官專決事項

首題之件에關하야 檀紀四二九○年七月二十一日 大韓勞動組合總聯合會로부터 韓美行政協定을締結함이있어야 駐留軍에連關되는 勞動問題에關하여 韓國勞動

이 用紙는 國民의 稅金으로서 購入된 것이다

0090

者의 勞動條件은 韓國法律에 順應하도록」하는 條項

의 挿入」을 要請한데 對하여 別紙와 如히 回答함이

어떠하오리까 高裁를 仰請하나이다.

案(二)

標記의 件 檀紀四二九○年七月二十六日 大韓勞動組合總聯合會事務總長으로부터 要請하여온 韓國勞動者의 勞動條件에 關하여는, 外務部에서 準備한 大韓民國 및 統一司令部間의 國際聯合軍의 地位에 關한 行政協定草案에는 左記와 如히 同趣旨가 挿入規定되어 있음을 通告하나이다.

記

「相互間에 別途로 合意되는 境遇를 除外하고는

0091

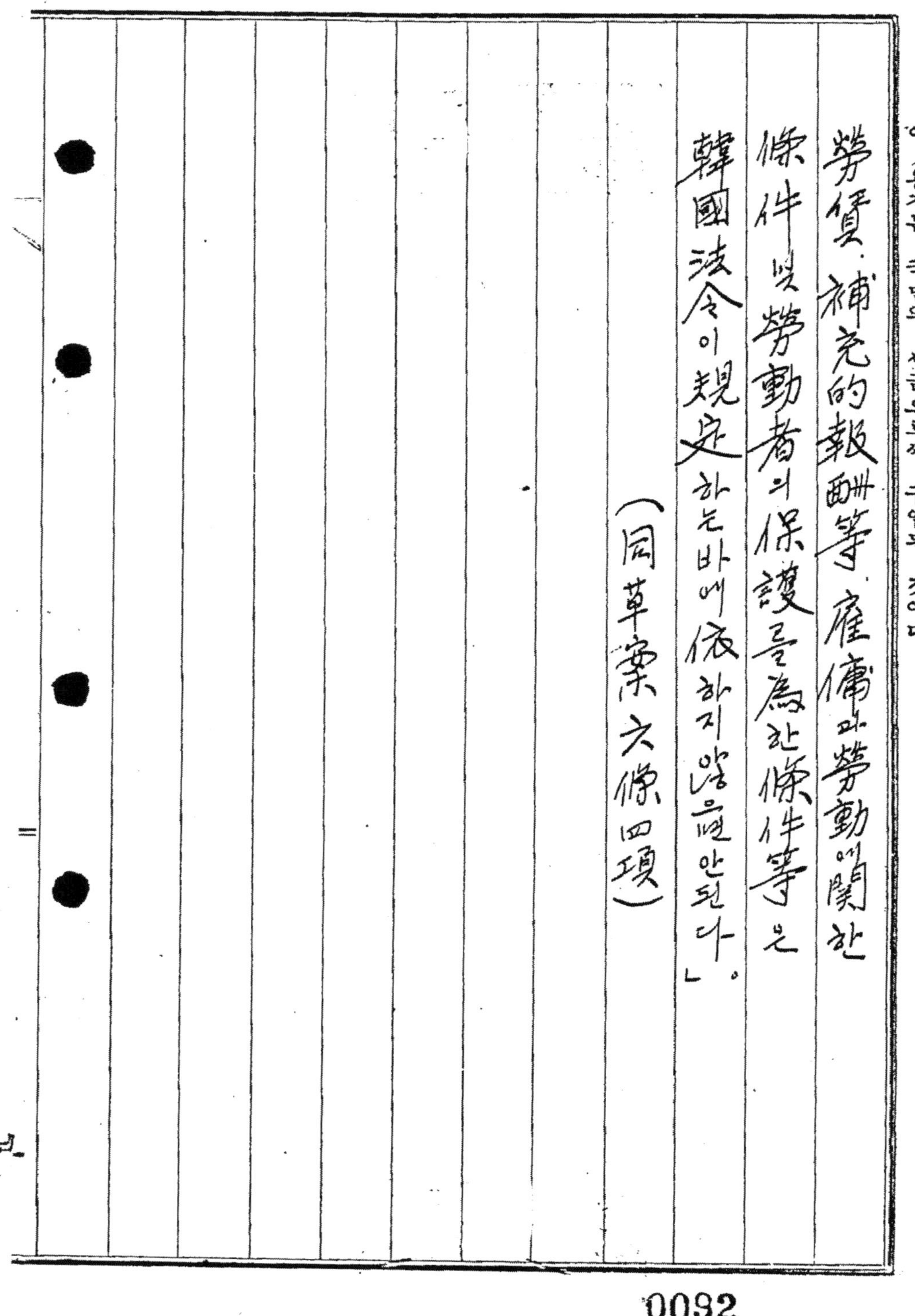



勞賃, 補充的報酬等, 雇傭과 勞動에 關한 條件 및 勞動者의 保護를 爲한 條件等은 韓國法令이 規定하는 바에 依하지 않으면 안된다.」

(同草案 六條四項)

0032

POLITICAL AFFAIRS BUREAU

Document No.__________ Date 7/31

MEMO

To: 條約課長 貴下

O For your file
O For your information
O For your action
O Urgent.
O Time Limit: By__________

本件은 文書로 하기 보다
關係者의 來訪을 要하여
口頭로 傳함이 可하다고
思料됨. 課長님으로
來訪을 要하시압

0093

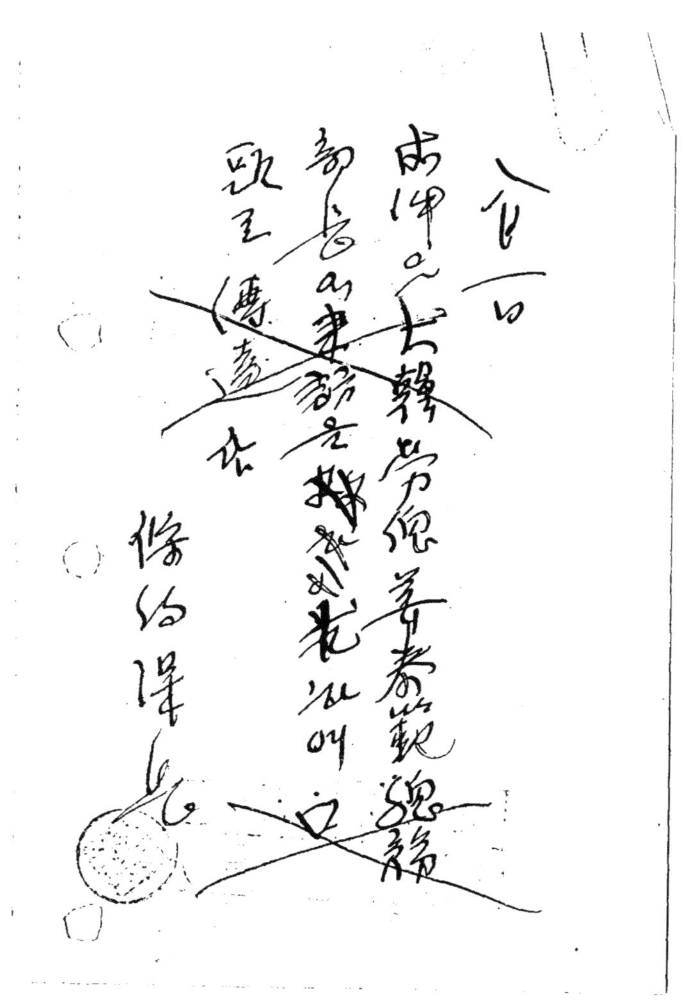

0094

COPY

검토필(1960.12.17.)

September 10, 1957

SUBJECT: Proposed Agreement on the Status of United Nations or United States Forces in Korea

The Government of the Republic of Korea, keenly desiring to conclude an agreement which would define the status of the United Nations armed forces in Korea, with the Government of the United States of America acting for the Unified Command in accordance with "The Resolution on the Settlement of the Unified Command" of the Security Council of the United Nations of July 7, 1950, initially proposed to the Government of the United States of America through the Foreign Minister's note of April 28, 1955, attached hereto as Annex A, that negotiations should be opened for that purpose.

It is also recalled that, as there was no positive reaction on the part of the United States Government on the said matter, the Korean Government again renewed its proposal to the United States through the Foreign Minister's notes of January 5, 1957 and June 29, 1957 respectively, copies of which are attached hereto as Annex B and Annex C. No definite reply stating the position of the United States Government in regard to these proposals has been received as yet.

Attention is invited to the note (Annex D hereto) of General Lemnitzer of July 26, 1955 addressed to the Foreign Minister, in which the former, in expressing his views on the possibility of negotiations on the said Agreement, stated that the United States Government envisages difficulties in commencing negotiations immediately for two reasons:

1) It would be preferred by the United States Government that the negotiations for the proposed treaty of Friendship, Commerce and Navigation between the two countries as well as

an agreement

0095

an agreement guaranteeing investments be completed before the initiation of negotiations for the agreement in question;

2) The Unified Command could not participate in negotiations of such an agreement without the prior consent of the allies within the Unified Command, and the task of obtaining such consent is time consuming.

As for the first reason mentioned above, the Korea-United States Treaty of Friendship, Commerce and Navigation has been already signed and is now only awaiting exchange of the instruments of ratification. As for the agreement guaranteeing investment, i.e. the so-called MSA Guarantee Agreement proposed by the United States Government, the Korean Government is preparing the final draft, and a definite agreement should be reached in the immediate future.

As for the second reason, the Government of the Republic of Korea is of the opinion that, as the United States forces in Korea actually constitute the preponderant components of the United Nations Forces under the Unified Command, the negotiations could be commenced first between the Korean Government and the United States Government regarding the status of the United States forces in Korea.

Apart from the above-mentioned two reasons, it is presumed that the reluctance on the part of the United States Government to commence negotiations on this subject is based on the fact that Korea is technically still in a state of war. Needless to say, however, active hostilities ceased in 1953, and the danger of a recurrence of hostilities is not considered imminent. It cannot be predicted how long the current situation will last.

Under these circumstances, it is not realistic to consider the current situation, which has lasted so long, a state of war in a

virtual sense.

0096

virtual sense. Therefore, the Korean Government does not consider that anything in the current situation in Korea prevents the Governments of the Republic of Korea and the United States of America from entering into the relations which would be established if the Agreement under reference be concluded. As for the anxiety concerning the possible recurrence of hostilities in Korea, there would be no reason why the parties to the proposed Agreement should not review the applicability of the provisions concerned in such case.

What the Korean Government desires to conclude with the United States is nothing but such agreements similar to those concluded by the latter with NATO powers in 1951 and with Japan in 1952 on the same subject.

In the absence of such an agreement between the Republic of Korea and the United States of America, and in view of the then-prevailing conditions of warfare and urgent necessity, a *modus vivendi*, which partly defined the status of the United States forces in Korea, came into being between the two governments through the exchange of notes at Taejon on July 12, 1950 concerning the exclusive jurisdiction by court-martial of the United States over its military personnel in Korea. In view of the changed conditions after the summer of 1953, the aforesaid provisional arrangement of 1950 is no longer appropriate in its nature nor sufficient to meet and solve adequately, under the circumstances, all of the complicated problems and matters arising daily because of the stationing and disposition of United States forces in Korea.

In this connection, it is with regret that numerous incidents must be mentioned which occurred between the United States army personnel and local civilians; in most cases, incidents caused by delinquency on the part of members of the United States forces in

0097 /Korea,

Korea, involving many casualties and much damage to valuable property. All of such incidents, according to the provisional arrangement of 1950, are exclusively within the jurisdiction of the United States. The Korean Government especially fears that such incidents, and the present way of application of justice, may injure the friendly relationship existing between the peoples of the two countries.

The Government of the Republic of Korea again requests the Government of the United States of America to give favorable consideration to the proposal of the Korean Government so that negotiations between the two governments may be commenced as early as possible. A prompt conclusion of the Agreement in question would undoubtedly serve to promote increased friendship between the peoples of the two countries.

0098

ANNEX A.

April 28, 1955

Dear Mr. Chargé d'Affaires:

I have the honour to initiate a proposal to conclude an Administrative Agreement between the Government of the Republic of Korea and the Government of the United States of America, and enclose herewith a draft of the Agreement. With regard to this proposal, I would like first to refer to my note dated December 2, 1954, concerning a conclusion of provisional Agreement regarding the functions of Korean customs authorities with respect to the United Nations forces in Korea. Particular reference was made in the note to the effect that such customs agreement will remain in force pending conclusion of a General Administrative Agreement which shall cover other subjects also.

Having in mind that the United Nations forces under the Unified Command are and will be disposed in and about the territory of the Republic of Korea until the objective of the United Nations in Korea will have been achieved pursuant to the resolutions of the United Nations Security Council of June 25, 1950, June 27, 1950 and July 7, 1950, it is the belief of the Korean Government that terms shall be provided, for the interests of both parties, to govern the disposition of and render convenience to the said forces in and about Korea, and that they shall be determined through mutual agreement between the Republic of Korea and the United States of America acting as the Unified Command in accordance with "The Resolution on the Settlement of the Unified Command" of the Security Council of the United Nations of July 7, 1950. A practical and effective Administrative Agreement to be concluded between the said two parties will help minimize misunderstanding and maximize cooperativeness between the Korean people and United Nations forces personnel in Korea.

In the belief that a conclusion of the Agreement is in the mutual interests, I wish to propose formally, on behalf of the Government of the Republic of Korea, that negotiation will be commenced between the representatives of Korean Government and the United States Government. Upon the receipt of your consent, we will proceed to decide the date and place of the conference, which will be mutually agreeable.

Accept, dear Mr. Chargé d'Affaires, the assurances of my highest consideration.

Enclosure: Draft of Administrative Agreement

Y. T. Pyun
Minister of Foreign Affairs

The Honourable Carl W. Strom,
Chargé d'Affaires,
Embassy of the United States of America
Seoul, Korea

0093

A N N E X B.

Excellency:

I have the honour to refer to the Foreign Minister's note addressed to Mr. Carl W. Strom, Charge d' Affairs ad interim of the Embassy of the United States of America in Korea dated April 28, 1955 enclosing a draft of an Administrative Agreement between the Republic of Korea and the Unified Command for establishment of the Status of the United Nations Forces in Korea.

In the afore-said note, the Minister informed the Government of the United States of America of the desire of the Korean Government to commence negotiations with the United States Government for the said Status of Forces Agreement which will also define the former's customs functions as referred to in my letter of December 2, 1954.

To this proposal, however, no acceptance has been given as yet, although the American Chargé d'Affairs notified in his replying note of May 9, 1955, that upon obtaining his Government's view on the said request, he would communicate with the Minister.

I hereby wish again to propose, on behalf of my Government, that negotiation be commenced at an earliest possible date between the representatives of the Korean Government and the United States Government. In connection with this re-proposal, I would like further to refer to the note of July 26, 1955 addressed to the Foreign Minister by General Lemnitzer advising on this matter.

/General Lemnitzer

His Excellency
The right honourable
Walter C. Dowling
Ambassador of the United States of America to the Republic of Korea
Seoul, Korea

0100

General Lemnitzer expressed his views on the possibility of negotiating the said agreement in the above note to the effect that the United States Government envisages difficulties in commencing immediately ~~negotiations for~~ a proposed agreement for the following two reasons:

The one reason was that it would be preferable to the American Government that negotiations for a proposed treaty of Friendship, Commerce and Navigation between the two countries as well as an agreement guaranteeing investments be completed before the initiation of negotiation for an agreement in question. The other was that the Unified Command cannot participate in negotiation of such agreement without the prior consent of allies within the Unified Command and it is anticipated that the task of obtaining such consent will be difficult.

Attention, however, is paid to the fact that the points indicated above constitute no longer difficulties about negotiating the said agreement under the present circumstances.

The Treaty of Friendship, Commerce and Navigation has been already signed and is now waiting to be formally ratified. As regards the agreement guaranteeing investments, discussions have been completed on provisions of its draft and now the work of finalising it remains only. On the other hand, since allies within the Unified Command have been decreased in number into twelve nations and since the American forces form the predominant components of the United Nations Forces, there exist no difficulties, it is believed, in securing consent of other allies as to the matter.

And thus, even in case the consent of the other allies has not been obtained as yet, it is, therefore, proposed that

/negotiations

negotiations be started first between both representatives of the Korean Government and the United States Government and that negotiations with ~~other allies~~ shall be carried on separately in accordance with terms to be agreed upon between Korea and the United States of America. It is sincerely requested that the concurrence of the United States Government be given to the wish of the Korean Government to commence negotiations for the agreement proposed.

Please accept, Excellency, the renewed assurances of my highest consideration.

Chung W. Cho
Minister of
Foreign Affairs

0102

ANNEX C.

June 29, 1957

My dear Mr. Ambassador:

I have the honor to ~~remind~~ your Government, as I have orally mentioned to you on several occasions, that the conclusion of an Administrative Agreement defining and setting forth in detail the status of United States troops stationed in Korea is still pending.

On April 28, 1955, our draft proposal of an Administrative Agreement between this Government and the Unified Command, to establish the status of United Nations forces in Korea, was addressed to your Embassy. On November 1, 1956, it was proposed that a separate agreement be negotiated between representatives of this Government and the United States Government, in case of difficulty in obtaining early consent of the other Allied Governments.

In the absence of such an administrative agreement, a temporary agreement was made through the exchange of Notes at Taejon, on July 12, 1950, concerning the exclusive jurisdiction by court-martial of the United States over members of the United States Military Establishment in Korea. This agreement, which is still in force, was improvised to meet an emergency situation and is not considered sufficient to meet effectively all the complex and complicated problems arising from the presence of United States troops in Korea

/This Government

His Excellency
Ambassador Walter C. Dowling
American Embassy,
Seoul.

0103

This Government is strongly convinced that the early conclusion of a formal and detailed agreement on the status of United States troops in Korea would serve to strengthen cordial relations between our people and American military personnel, and would provide great satisfaction to the mutual cause and interest of both countries.

I wish to state again that this Government is most desirous of receiving the concurrence of the United States Government in order to commence negotiations for an administrative agreement along the lines of the proposal of April, 1955. Your Government's earliest favorable consideration of this matter is most sincerely desired.

Accept, Excellency, renewed assurances of my highest consideration.

Chung W. Cho
Minister

0104

A N N E X  D.

26 July 1955

Dear Minister Pyun:

Thank you very much for your letter of 13 June 1955, in which you acknowledge receipt of General Taylor's letter of 14 May 1955, with the inclosures pertaining to customs functions of the Republic of Korea.

I have noted the desire of the Korean Government to commence negotiations with the Government of the United States for a Status of Forces Agreement between the Korean Government and the Unified Command. This matter is presently under study by the Departments of my government in Washington.

Current thinking on this matter is that it would be preferable that negotiations now in progress or pending be completed before the initiation of negotiations for an agreement of the type in question. Ambassador Lacy advises me that a proposed treaty of friendship, commerce and navigation between our respective governments is under consideration, as well as an agreement guaranteeing investments, and that he is anxious to complete these matters before taking up any other major negotiations.

I am sure you are also aware that the Unified Command cannot participate in a negotiation of any Status of Forces Agreement without the prior consent of our allies within the United Nations Command. It is anticipated that the task of obtaining this consent will be difficult and time consuming.

Sincerely,

/s/
L. L. LEMNITZER
General, United States Army
Commander-in-Chief

His Excellency Pyun Yung-Tai
Minister for Foreign Affairs of
The Republic of Korea

협정 체결시 일반문서로
재분류

0105

COPY

American Embassy,
Seoul, Korea,
July 1, 1957

My dear Mr. Minister:

I have the honor to acknowledge receipt of your letter of June 29, 1957, concerning the desire of your Government to negotiate an Administrative Agreement defining the status of United States troops stationed in Korea, and to inform you that the substance of the letter has been cabled to the Department of State.

In this connection I am glad to inform you that your Government's note of January 5, 1957 is currently being given careful consideration in Washington. I shall, of course, communicate with you again as soon as I receive pertinent information.

With renewed assurances of my highest consideration, I am

Faithfully yours,

/s/ Walter C. Dowling

His Excellency
Chung W. Cho
Minister of Foreign Affairs,
Republic of Korea.

과도분류로 인하여
일반문서로 재분류
1962.2.17

0106

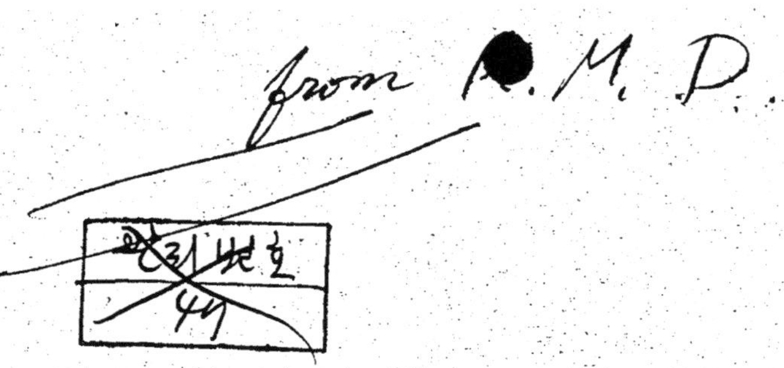


November , 1957

Dear Mr. Ambassador:

I have the honor to refer to my letter of November 13, 1957 regarding the agreement on the status of United States forces in Korea. In this letter I suggested we commence negotiations to conclude separate agreements on particular items such as taxation, customs duties, etc., instead of concluding a full-scale agreement.

In this connection, I have pleasure in forwarding a memorandum on the position of my Government on the separate agreemtns to be concluded between our two Government.

It would be greatly appreciated if you would give favourable attention to this memorandum.

With warmest personal regards, I remain

관리번호 3637

Sincerely yours,

과도분류로 인하여 III급비밀로 재분류 1962.2.15

Chung W. Cho
Minister

His Excellency
Walter C. Dowling
Ambassador,
American Embassy,
Seoul

0107

Position of the Korean Government on separate agreements regarding the status of United States forces in Korea.

Considering the present stalemate which exists between Korea and the United States regarding the commencement of negotiations for the conclusion of a full-scale administrative agreement to govern the entire status of United States forces in Korea, ~~it is recommended~~ that several agreements between the two Govern~~ments be separately~~ concluded so that the status of United States forces ~~in Korea~~ can be regulated as far as possible upon a mutually acceptable basis:

1) Agreement concerning Procurement, Taxation and Customs Duties of United States forces in Korea. (Ref. Art. 6, 7, 8, of Draft Administrative Agreement proposed by the Korean Government.)

2) Agreement concerning Settlement of Claims relative to the stationing of United States forces in Korea. (Ref. Art. 5)

3) Agreement concerning Facilities and Areas to be used by United States forces in Korea. (Ref.Art. 3, para. 10 of Art. 4, Art. 9, 10)

4) Agreement concerning Entry and Exit of United States forces in Korea. (Ref. Art. 2)

5) Agreement concerning Criminal Jurisdiction over Offences by United States forces in Korea. (Ref.Art. 4, 13, 14)

1. Agreement concerning Procurement, Taxation and Customs Duties of United States forces in Korea.

It is vital for the Republic of Korea Government to check the smuggling conducted through the supply routes of United States forces in Korea. This agreement is one of the most urgent to be concluded between the two countries. For the purpose of preventing and checking the aforesaid smuggling, the Korean Customs Officials wish to have access, for inspection purposes, to the wharves and military airports, which are now exclusively held and controlled

0108

by the United States military authorities.

As for procurements, goods and services which are required and can be obtained from local sources for the subsistance of United States forces should be procured in a manner most likely to help maintain Korean economic stability, and least probable of adversely affecting it, also in coordination with and, when desirable, through or with the assistance of competent authorities of Korea.

2. Agreement concerning Settlement of Claims relative to United States forces in Korea.

This agreement is to govern civil jurisdiction, particularly the settlement of claims arising out of injuries and damages. It is aimed to clarify the responsibility for injuries of and damages to Korean nationals and their properties caused by United States forces, and to facilitate settlement of the claims arising out of such injuries and damages. On the other hand, the Korean Government will undertake to make every effort to protect United States forces and their members from injuries to them and damage to their properties.

3. Agreement concerning Facilities and Areas to be used by United States forces in Korea.

While the Korean Government is willing to grant to United States forces the use of certain facilities and areas and certain rights, powers and authority necessary for carrying out their mission, this agreement is aimed to clarify the scope of exemption from the liabilities of compensation or restoration accruing from the use of such facilities and areas.

This agreement will also contain provisions in regard to military post office and non-appropriated fund organizations, and further, such provisions as will enable the Korean Government to make interim use of any of such facilities or areas of target ranges and maneuver grounds, which are temporarily not used by United States forces.

5. ~~Agreement concerning Entry and Exit of United States forces in Korea.~~

It is proposed to request the United States Government to amend the existing Taejon agreement of 1950 to suit the changed conditions caused by the cessation of actural hostilities. As for the amendment, efforts should be made to limit the jurisdiction of the United States court-martial over members of United States forces to such cases as have occurred in the course of execution of official duties, and further to make additional provisions for judicial cooperation, including joint search and investigation.

일반문서로 재분류
(협조정 체결서)

0110

2nd draft

November 13, 1957

Dear General Decker:

We appreciate your letter of October 10, 1957, expressing your profound concern over the unfortunate shooting incidents which have occured in recent weeks involving members of the U.S. Forces and Korean civilians.

The problems referred to in your letter are of grave concern to us, and we realize they can be effectively solved only with the concerted effort and full cooperation of authorities of our Government and the U.S. Forces.

According to our police records, there have been a total of 25 shooting incidents during the months from January to October of this year. As a result of these incidents, 12 Korean nationals were killed and 22 seriously wounded by members of the U.S. Forces. Though it is established that the majority of these incidents have involved U.S. military personnel on guard duty, this is no way justifies shootings which resulted in the death of Korean civilians.

Please believe that the Korean people will never forget the noble sacrifice of American soldiers who shed their blood in Korea to preserve our national independence and for our common defense against communist aggression, and they will never believe that the U.S. Forces will turn against them. None the less, it is difficult for our Government authorities to soothe public apprehension when it appears that human lives are valued lightly. Therefore I earnestly ask you again to urge the men under your Command to take every precaution in handling fire arms and to refrain from firing at Koreans except in the case of self-defense under imminent threat.

As to the problem of pilferage, I am as deeply concerned as you are over the loss of U.S. military supplies vital to the defense of our Country. Police records show that from January 1 to October 13, police authorities arrested the offenders involved in 64 cases out of the total 86 reported cases of pilferage of

0111

U.S. supplies. Records also show that since 7 ~~August, suspects~~ involved in 10 out of 19 cases of pilferage ~~were apprehended~~, including 3 out of 4 cases in the Yangju Gun area. Through such police actions, considerable quantities of stolen supplies were recovered; for example 1,340 gallon of fuel oil and 57,205 feet of wire.

Let me assure you, General Decker, this Ministry is accelerating its drive against pilferage of U.S. supplies and our National Police throughout Korea have been ordered to make every effort to apprehend and punish offenders. We are also taking preventive measures and we are gratified to learn that on the part of U.S. Forces preventive measures to reduce the number of cases where unnecessary force is used are being instituted.

In conclusion, I suggest that a basic arrangement between authorities of the United States Forces and the Korean National Police be concluded as soon as possible to meet problems which arise involving members of the U.S. Forces and Korean civilians. On our part we pledge our wholehearted cooperation as we work together to find immediate ways for dealing effectively with these matters.

Sincerely yours,

Kun Jik Lee,
Minister of Home Affairs

0112

## 韓美間 諸協定의 再檢討와 是正案

검토필(1962. 12. 29.)

(1) 마이어 協定 第3條 13項의 廢棄

가. 題目: 마이어 協定 3條 13項을 廢棄하고저 함

나. 現況: 本條項은 韓國 國民을 除外한 統合司令部의 個人 또는 機關에 對하여 只今까지 協定 또는 諒解事項에 依하여 賦與되었거나 또는 次後 當事國에 依하여 公式 또는 非公式으로 合議된 韓國內에서의 그들의 職務遂行에 必要한 特权 免除및 便宜를 提供한다고 規定하고 있는바 지난 2月 8日 새로이 韓美間의 締結発効한 経済技術援助 協定의 成立과함께 同 協定의 一部 條項은 廢棄 되었으나 條項은 繼続 効力을 存続 시키기로 合議하였음.

다. 討論: 이 條項은 原来 統一司令部가 對韓 援助事務를 担當하게 됨으로 統一司令部를 援助機関으로서 그 機関이나 그 職員에게 그 職務遂行에 支障이 없도록 諸般 特权과 便益을 附與하며는

검토필(1966. 12. 30.)

~1~

0113

미·문 70-13(6)

0114

趣旨에서 規定된 것이나 그 用語가 曖昧하여 解釋如何에 따라서는 適用範囲를 아주 廣範하게 統一司令部 麾下 全將兵으로 拡大시킬수도 있게되었음 이러한 協定上의 用語의 曖昧한 点을 利用하여 美國側은 実際에 있어서 이條項을 駐韓 美軍및軍屬에게까지 適用할것을 主張하고 있어 本條項 適用上 累次 美國側과 意見差異 내지 紛爭을 일으키고 있음

라. 結 論. 지난 2月8日 새로이 締結된 韓美間의 經濟技術援助協定에 依하여 우리나라에 駐在하는 美國援助機関및 그 職員에 對하여는 그 職務遂行에 必要한 程度의 特权과 免除는 充分히 附與하기로 規定하고 있으므로 아무 実益이 없는 本條項을 措置함으로써 美國側에게 濫用의 機会를 줄 必要는 없을 것으로 生覺함

마. 建 議: 이 條項을 全部 廃棄하여 駐韓 美國援助機関 및 그 職員의 特权과 免除의 限界를 明確히 規定하고 美軍 및 軍屬의 特权 및 免

~2~

0115

미·문 po-13

0116

除는 韓美 行政 協定에서 別途規定하여야 할 것이라고 生覺함

2. 1954年의 韓美合議議事錄 一部條項의 修正

가. 題 目: 1954年의 韓美 合議々事錄 韓國側 約定事項 第2項을 修正하고저함

나. 現 況: 本 條項은 國際联合軍司令部가 大韓民國의 防衛를 爲한 責任을 負担하는 동안 大韓民國軍을 國際联合軍司令部의 作戰指揮权下에 둔다 그러나 両國의 相互的 또는 個別的 利益이 変更에 依하여 가장 잘 成就될 것이라고 合議되는 境遇에는 이를 変更할수 있다 라고 規定하고 있고 韓國軍의 作戰指揮权 問題는 軍事革命 直後인 5月 26日의 韓美共同声明에 依하여 共産侵略으로 부터 韓國을 防衛하는 데만 使用하도록 合議한바 있음

다. 討 論: 現今의 國內外 情勢로 보아 韓國軍의 作戰 指揮权은 軍의 統率 其他 作戰上의 見地에서 볼때 繼續 國際联合軍司令官에게 歸

~3~

0117

미·문 70-13

0118

呈시키는 것이 無妨하다고 思覺되다 이 作戰指揮权은 어디 까지나 共産 侵略으로 부터 우리 나라를 防衛 하는데만 行使하도록 制限할 것이며 국가의 自主权이 毁損 된다던가 또는 必要以上의 유엔軍司令官의 干涉을 招來하는 일이 있어서는 안될 것이다

라. 結 論: 그러므로 國際联合軍司令官에게 韓國軍의 指揮权을 주되 그 行使에는 一定한 制限을 두도록 함이 좋을 것이다

마 建 議: 本 合議々事錄 韓國側 約定事項 第2項을 다음과 같이 改正하도록 한다 즉

國際联合軍 司令部가 大韓民國의 防衛를 爲한 責任을 負担하는 동안 大韓民國軍을 國際联合軍 司令部의 作戰指揮权下에 둔다. 國際联合軍司令官은 共産 侵略으로부터 韓國을 防衛하는 데만 이 作戰指揮权을 行使한다

미문PO-13
0120

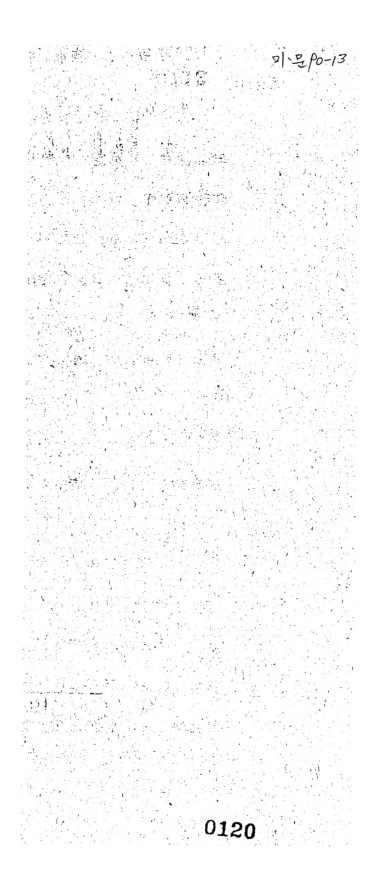

3. 在韓 美國軍隊의 管轄权에 關한 韓美協定의 件

가. 現況: 本協定은 在韓美國軍隊 構成員에 對하여 排他的인 裁判权을 行使할수 있다"는 것을 重要骨子로 하고 있으며 檀紀 4283年7月12日 外務部와 駐韓美國大使館사이에 兩國의 覺書交換으로 成立된 것임

이 協定으로 因하여 우리나라에 駐屯하고 있는 美國軍에 對한 裁判管轄权이 美軍當局에 依하여 行使되고 있음

나. 討論: 本協定은 6.25事变直後 當時 傀儡의 南侵으로 因하여 切迫된 事態에 鑑하여 締結된 關係로 國家主权이 平等의 原則에서 距離가 멀다고 할수 있으며 비록 共產傀儡의 再侵의 可能性이 있는 이때나마 休戰이 成立되지 8年이 經過하고 當時 事情과는 判異하게 되었으며 美國은 自由友邦國家와 上記 原則에 立脚하여 軍隊指揮에 關한 協定을 締結한 例가 許多함으로 本協定을 하루 速히 廢棄함이 우리나라

미·문 pol-13

0122

의 生权保護에 이바지하는 것이 되리라 思料함

다. 結論 : 故로 本協定을 廢棄하여야 할것임.

라. 建議 : 本協定을 廢棄하고 이에 關한 事項을 韓美兩國間의 軍隊指揮에 關한 協定(所謂 行政協定)에서 規律하여야 할 것임.

일반문서로 재분류
(1965. 2. 28)

0123

-62-

미문 PO-13(6)
0124

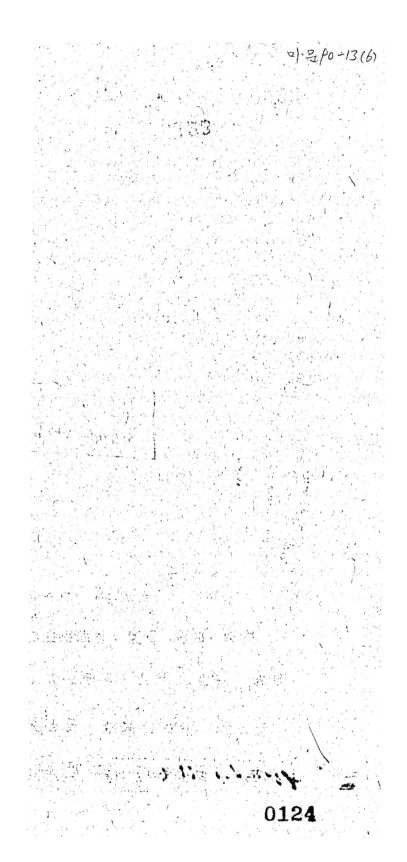

Recommendation on seperate agreements between Korea and the United States regarding the status of United States forces in Korea

歐美局長 一般文書로 再分類 62. 2. 16.

Considering the present deadlock between Korea and the United States regarding the commencement of negotiations for the conclusion of a full-scaled administrative agreement to govern entire status of United States forces in Korea, it is recommended to conclude between the two governments under-mentioned several agreements seperately so that the status of United States forces in Korea can be regulated as far as possible upon mutually acceptable basis:

1) Agreement concerning Procurement, Taxation and Custom Duties of United States forces in Korea (Ref. Art. 6, 7, 8, 9 of Draft Administrative Agreement proposed by the Korean Government.)

2) Agreement concerning Settlement of Claims relative to the stationing of United States forces in Korea (Ref. Art. 5)

3) Agreement concerning Entry and Exit of United States forces in Korea (Ref. Art. 2)

4) Agreement concerning Facilities and Areas to be used by United States forces in Korea (Ref. Art. 3, para. 10 of Art. 4)

5) Agreement concerning Criminal Jurisdiction over Offences by United States forces in Korea (Ref. Art. 4, 13, 14)

For the general provisions, each agreement will contain commonly such clauses as on Expression of Terms, Uniforms and Markings, Measures in the Events of Hostilities, Joint Committee, Coming into Force, Revision, and, Validity and Suspension. (Ref. Art. 1, 12, 15, 16, 17, 18, 19)

1. Agreement concerning Procurement, Taxation and Customs Duties of United States forces in Korea.

Significance:

It is vital for the Republic of Korea to prevent and crack down the sumuggling conducted through the supply route of United States forces in Korea. This agreement is one of the most urgent

0125

agreements to be concluded between the two countries. For the purpose of preventing and checking the aforesaid smuggling, the Korean Customs Officials should have opportunity to access to and supervise the wharves and military airports which are now exclusively held and controled by the United States military authorities.

As for procurements, due consideration should be made so that such procurements may bring about no adverse effect upon Korean economy.

Scope:

I) Procurement

1. General assurances of the Korean Government for the procurement of United States forces.
2. Considerations to the economic stabilization of Korea.
3. Provisions on the labor.

II) Taxation

1. Exemption from taxation of the property owned by United States forces.
2. Exemption from taxation of the income accruing from the particular income sources relative to United States forces.
3. Taxation of income accruing from other than sources described hereinbefore.
4. Exemption from taxation of movable property owned by United States forces members and their dependents.

III) Customs Duties

1. General provisions.
2. Exemption from Customs Duties of the reasonable amount of goods and commodities exclusively necessary for the use of United States forces.
3. Taxation of customs duties on the property consigned to and for the personal use of members of United States forces and their dependents exept some special cases.
4. Exemption from customs duties on official documents and the United States forces postal mails.

0126

5. Re-export and disposal of goods imported duty-free previously.
6. Export and re-import of goods procured by United States forces.
7. Definition of "duty" for the purpose of this agreement.
8. Provisions in respect with the rights of the Korean Customs Officials and mutual cooperation between the authorities of the two countries.

IV) Non-appropriated fund organizations.

1. Establishment ~~of the organizations~~ and exemption, to some extent, from the obligations for such organizations. Circulations of the army newspapers for the general public.
2. Exemption from taxation of procurements by the organizations.
3. Scope of disposal of goods to be sold by the organizations.
4. Delivery of information to the Korean authorities.

2. Agreement concerning Settlement of Claims relative to United States forces in Korea.

Significance:

This agreement is to govern the civil jurisdiction, particularly the settlement of claims arising out of injuries and damages. This agreement is aimed to clarify the responsibility of the injuries of and damages to the Korean national and their properties caused by United States forces, and to facilitate settlement of the claims arising out of such injuries and damages. On the other hand, the Korean Government will undertake to make efforts to protect the United States forces and their members from the injuries of and damages to their bodies and properties.

Scope:

1. Waiver of claims arising out of damages occurred under the special situation.

Claims for the maritime salvages.

0127

2. Claims arising out of damages occurred to the national property and payments for them.

3. Claims arising out of injuries of persons in the execution of official duties.

4. Settlements of claims arising out of damages to the third persons.

5. Settlements of claims arising out of damages to the third persons.in the other than execution of official duties.

6. Claims arising out of unauthorized use of vehicles.

7. Provisions on the driving permit or license (Ref. Art. 11)

8. Determination on whether or not in the execution of official duties.

9. Civil jurisdiction of the Korean courts over the members of United States forces.

10. Mutual cooperation.

11. Assistance for the compulsory execution over the private movable property within the facilities and areas used by United States forces.

12. Joint Committee.

3. Agreement concerning Entry and Exit of United States forces in Korea.

Significance:

This agreement will clarify the scope of exemption from Korean immigration laws and regulations for the members of United States forces including the civilian component and their dependents, thus minimizing smuggling or stowaway cases.

Scope:

1. Scope of exemption from Korean immigration laws and regulations.

2. Documents to be carried upon entry or exit.

3. Passports for the civilian components and dependents.

4. Measures to be taken in case of alteration on the status

0128

of persons entitled to the privileges described hereinbefore.

5. Entry or Departure of vessels and aircrafts operated for the official purposes

And provisions concerning cargo or passengers carried on such vessels and aircrafts.

4. Agreement concerning Facilities and Areas to be used by the United States forces in Korea

Significance:

While the Korean Government is willing to grant to United States forces the use of certain facilities and areas and some kinds of rights, power and authority necessary for carrying out their mission, this agreement is aimed to clarify the scope of exemption from the liabilities of compensation or restoration accruing from the use of such facilities and areas.

This agreement will also contain provisions regulating the military post office and non-appropriated fund organizations, and further such provisions as enabling the Korean Government to make interim use of such facilities or areas as target ranges or maneuver grounds which are temporarily not used by United States forces.

Scope:

1. Use and return of facilities and areas, and interim use by the Korean Government of such facilities and areas as target ranges and maneuver grounds.

2. Rights, power and authority of United States forces within the facilities and areas.

3. Restoration and compensation in respect with the facilities and areas.

4. Coordination on the systems relative to air traffic, navigation, communication, etc.

5. Use of public utilities and facilities.

0123

6. [illegible]

6. Mutual cooperation relating to the neteorological services.

7. Establishment of military post office (Ref. Art. 10)

8. Right to police the facilities and areas. (Ref. Para. 10 of Art. 4)

5. <u>Agreement concerning Criminal Jurisdiction over Offences by United States forces in Korea</u>

<u>Significante:</u>

Since it seems that the United States Government is very reluctant to conclude such an agreement, it is thought unwise to propose to the United States Government to commence negotiations for concluding an entirely new agreement in this regard despite the existance of the so-called Taejon Agreement concluded in 1950 by exchange of notes which provides for exclusive jurisdiction of the United States court-marshal over the members of United States forces. It is, therefore, recommended to suggest the United States Government to amend the aforesaid existing agreement so as to suit the conditions changed since the cessation of actual hostilities. As for the amendment, efforts should be made to limit the jurisdiction of the United States court-marshal over the members of the United States forces to such cases as occured in the course of execution of official duties, and further to make additional provisions for judicial cooperation including joint search and investigation.

<u>Scope:</u>

1. General provisions on the criminal jurisdiction.
2. Scope of exclusive jurisdiction.
   And definition of a security offense against a State.
3. Concurrence of rights to exercise jurisdiction.
4. Jurisdiction over the nationals of ordinarily resident in Korea.
5. Judicial cooperation - arrest, notification of arrest or

0130

custody.

6. Judicial cooperation -- investigation, collection of evidence, seizure, etc.

7. Execution of the sentenses including a death sentence.

8. Provisions on double jeopardy.

9. Rights to be enjoyed by the accused.

10. Right to police the facilities and areas.

11. Carrying of arms. (Ref. Art. 13)

12. Ban on political activities. (Ref. Art. 14)

0131

COPY



Recommendation on seperate agreements between Korea and the United States regarding the status of United States forces in Korea



Considering the present deadlock between Korea and the United States regarding the commencement of negotiations for the conclusion of a full-scaled administrative agreement to govern entire status of United States forces in Korea, it is recommended to conclude between the two governments under-mentioned several agreements seperately so that the status of United States forces in Korea can be regulated as far as possible upon mutually acceptable basis:



1) Agreement concerning Procurement, Taxation and Customs Duties of United States forces in Korea (Ref. Art. 6, 7, 8, 9 of Draft Administrative Agreement proposed by the Korean Government.)

2) Agreement concerning Settlement of Claims relative to the stationing of United States forces in Korea (Ref. Art. 5)

3) Agreement concerning Entry and Exit of United States forces in Korea (Ref. Art. 2)

4) Agreement concerning Facilities and Areas to be used by United States forces in Korea (Ref. Art. 3, para. 10 of Art. 4)

5) Agreement concerning Criminal Jurisdiction over Offences by United States forces in Korea (Ref. Art. 4, 13, 14)

For the general provisions, each agreement will contain commonly such clauses as on Expression of Terms, Uniforms and Markings, Measures in the Events of Hostilities, Joint Committee, Coming into Force, Revision, and, Validity and Suspension. (Ref. Art. 1, 12, 15, 16, 17, 18, 19)

1. Agreement concerning Procurement, Taxation and Customs Duties of United States forces in Korea

It is vital for the Republic of Korea to prevent and crack down the smuggling conducted through the supply route of United States forces in Korea. This agreement is one of the most urgent agreements to be concluded between the two countries. For the

0132

purpose of preventing and checking the aforesaid smuggling, the Korean Customs Officials should have opportunity to access to and supervise the wharves ~~and military~~ airports which are now exclusively held and controlled by the United States military authorities.

As for procurements, due consideration should be made so that such procurements may bring about no adverse effect upon Korean economy.

2. Agreement concerning Settlement of Claims relative to United States forces in Korea.

This agreement is to govern the civil jurisdiction, particularly the settlement of claims arising out of injuries and damages. This agreement is aimed to clarify the responsibility of the injuries of and damages to the Korean national and their properties caused by United States forces, and to facilitate settlement of the claims arising out of such injuries and damages. On the other hand, the Korean Government will undertake to make efforts to protect the United States forces and their members from the injuries of and damages to their bodies and properties.

3. Agreement concerning Entry and Exit of United States forces in Korea

This agreement will clarify the scope of exemption from Korean immigration laws and regulations for the members of United States forces including the civilian component and their dependents, thus minimizing smuggling or stowaway cases.

4. Agreement concerning Facilities and Areas to be used by the United States forces in Korea

While the Korean Government is willing to grant to United States forces the use of certain facilities and areas and some kind

0133

of rights, power and authority necessary for carrying out their mission, this agreement is aimed to clarify the scope of exemption from the liabilities of compensation or restoration accruing from the use of such facilities and areas.

This agreement will also contain provisions regulating the military post office and non-appropriated fund organizations, and further such provisions as enabling the Korean Government to make interim use of such facilities or areas as target ranges or maneuver grounds which are temporarily not used by United States forces.

5. <u>Agreement concerning Criminal Jurisdiction over Offences by United States forces in Korea.</u>

Since it seems that the United States Government is very reluctant to conclude such an agreement, it is thought unwise to propose to the United States Government to commence negotiations for concluding an entirely new agreement in this regard despite the existance of the so-called Taejon Agreement concluded in 1950 by exchange of notes which provides for exclusive jurisdiction of the United States court-martial over the members of United States forces. It is, therefore, recommended to suggest the United States Government to amend the aforesaid existing agreement so as to suit the conditions changed since the cessation of actual hostilities. As for the amendment, efforts should be made to limit the jurisdiction of the United States court-martial over the members of United States forces to such cases as occured in the course of execution of official duties, and further to make additional provisions for judicial cooperation including joint search and investigation.

Ⅲ급 비밀로 재분류 1962. 2. 9

0134

November 26, 1957

Dear Mr. Charge d'Affaires:

I refer to my letter of November 13, 1957, addressed to Ambassador Dowling, regarding the agreement on the status of United States forces in Korea. In this letter I suggested we commence negotiations to conclude separate agreements on particular items such as taxation, customs duties, etc., instead of concluding a full-scale agreement.

In this connection, I have pleasure in forwarding a memorandum on the position of my Government on the separate agreements to be concluded between our two Governments.

It would be greatly appreciated if you give favourable attention to this memorandum.

With warmest personal regards, I remain

Sincerely yours,

Chung W. Cho
Minister

Mr. T. Eliot Weil,
Charge d'Affaires, a.i.,
American Embassy,
Seoul

검토필 (1966. 12. 30)

관리번호 38

과도분류로 인하여 일반비밀로 재분류 1962.2.15

검토필 (1966. 12. 30)

검토필 (1962. 12. 17)

0135

M E M O R A D U M

Considering the present stalemate which exists between Korea and the United States regarding the commencement of negotiations for the conclusion of a full-scale administrative agreement to govern the entire status of United States forces in Korea, it is recommended that several agreements between the two Governments be separately concluded so that the status of United States forces in Korea can be regulated as far as possible upon a mutually acceptable basis:

1) Agreement concerning Procurement, Taxation and Customs Duties of United States forces in Korea. (Ref. Art. 6, 7, 8, of Draft Administrative Agreement proposed by the Korean Government.)

2) Agreement concerning Settlement of Claims relative to the stationing of United States forces in Korea. (Ref. Art. 5)

3) Agreement concerning Facilities and Areas to be used by United States forces in Korea. (Ref. Art. 3, para. 10 of Art. 4, Art. 9, 10)

4) Agreement concerning Entry and Exit of United States forces in Korea. (Ref. Art. 2)

5) Agreement concerning Criminal Jurisdiction over Offences by United States forces in Korea. (Ref. Art. 4, 13, 14)

1. Agreement concerning Procurement, Taxation and Customs Duties of United States forces in Korea.

It is vital for the Republic of Korea Government to check the smuggling conducted through the supply routes of United States forces in Korea. This agreement is one of the most urgent to be concluded between the two countries. For the purpose of preventing and checking the aforesaid smuggling, the Korean Customs Officials wish to have access, for inspection purposes, to the wharves and military airports, which are now exclusively held and controlled by the United States military authorities.

0136

As for procurements, goods and services which are required and can be obtained from local sources for the subsistance of United States forces should be procured in a manner most likely to help maintain Korean economic stability, and least probable of adversely affecting it. also in coordination with and, when desirable, through or with the assistance of competent authorities of Korea.

2. Agreement concerning Settlement of Claims relative to United States forces in Korea.

This agreement is to govern civil jurisdiction, particularly the settlement of claims arising out of injuries and damages. It is aimed to clarify the responsibility for injuries of and damages to Korean nationals and their properties caused by United States forces, and to facilitate settlement of the claims arising out of such injuries and damages. On the other hand, the Korean Government will undertake to make every effort to protect United States forces and their members from injuries to them and damage to their properties.

3. Agreement concerning Facilities and Areas to be used by United States forces in Korea.

While the Korean Government is willing to grant to United States forces the use of certain facilities and areas and certain rights, powers and authority necessary for carrying out their mission, this agreement is aimed to clarify the scope of exemption from the liabilities of compensation or restoration accruing from the use of such facilities and areas.

This agreement will also contain provisions in regard to military post office and non-appropriated fund organizations, and further, such provisions as will enable the Korean Government to make interim use of any of such facilities or areas of target ranges and maneuver grounds, which are temporarily not used by United States forces.

4. Agreement concerning Entry and Exit of United States forces in Korea.

This agreement will clarify the scope of exemption from Korean immigration laws and regulations for the members of United States forces, including civilian components and their dependents.

5. Agreement concerning Criminal Jurisdiction over Offences by United States forces in Korea.

It is to propose to the United States Government to amend the existing Taejon agreement of 1950 to suit the changed conditions caused by the cessation of actual hostilities. As for the amendment, efforts should be made to limit the jurisdiction of the United States court-martial over members of United States forces to such cases as have occurred in the course of execution of official duties, and further to make additional provisions for judicial cooperation, including joint search and investigation.

일반문서로 재분류
(협정체결시)

Ministry of Foreign Affairs
Seoul, Korea

November 26, 1957

0138

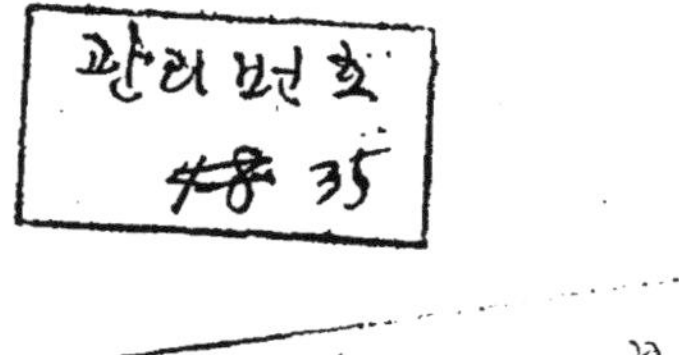

검토필(196.4.12.10)

American Embassy,
Seoul, Korea,
~~December 3~~, 1957.

관도분류로 인하여 분반된 (1962.2.17)

My dear Mr. Minister:

I have the honor to acknowledge receipt of your letter of November 26, 1957 with which was enclosed a memorandum concerning the position of your Government on the question of negotiating separate agreements on various subjects pertaining to the status of United States forces in Korea.

I have forwarded copies of your letter and enclosure to Washington for consideration by my Government.

I shall hope, in due course, to send you a further communication on the subject of your Government's memorandum.

With warmest personal regards, I am

검토필(1965.6.30.)

Sincerely yours,

T. Eliot Weil

T. Eliot Weil
Charge d'Affaires ad interim

His Excellency
Chung W. Cho,
Minister of Foreign Affairs,
Republic of Korea.-

0139

to K.M.D.

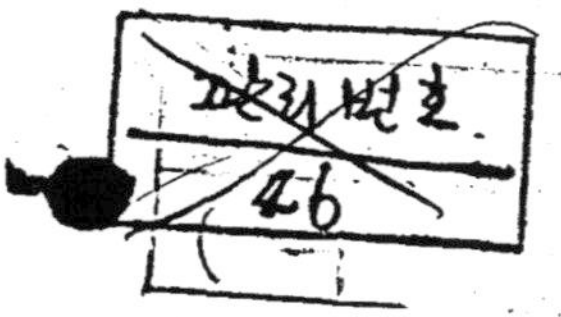

**Explanation on the Military Post Office and non-Appropriate Fund Organizations to be regulated by the Separate Agreement**

As for the military post office and non-appropriated fund organizations, the full-scale draft agreement ~~on the status of~~ United Nations forces between Korea and the ~~Unified Command~~ proposed by the Korean Government to the United ~~States Government~~ contains provisions regarding the military post office and non-appropriated fund organizations such as navy exchanges, post exchanges, messes, social clubs, theaters and newspapers. It is intended that the substance of the above-mentioned provisions, that is Articles 9 and 10 of the draft agreement, be included in the seperate agreement to be concluded between the two Governments. The provisions of Articles 9 and 10 of the draft agreement is attached hereto. Since the memorandum to be forwarded to the American Embassy is purported to indicate only essential points to be included in the separate agreements and since the position of the Korean Government on how to regulate the matters is already expressed in the draft agreement referred to in the above, it is considered appropriate to point out in the memorandum only the subjects to be regulated by the seperate agreement.

0140

Draft Administrative Agreement regarding
the Status of the United Nations Forces
proposed by the Korean Government to
the United States Government.

판단분류로 인하여
일반문서로 재분류
1962. 2. 17.

Article IX

1. (a) Navy exchanges, post exchanges, messes, social clubs, theaters, newspapers and other non-appropriated funds organizations authorized and regulated by the United Nations forces authorities may be established in the facilities and areas in use by the United Nations forces for the use of members of such forces, the civilian component, and their dependents. Except as otherwise provided in this Agreement, such organizations shall not be subject to Korean regulations, license, fees, taxes or similar controls.

(b) When a newspaper authorized and regulated by the United Nations forces authorities is sold to the general public, it shall be subject to Korean regulations, license, fees, taxes or similar controls so far as such circulation is concerned.

2. No Korean tax shall be imposed on sales of merchandise and services by such organizations, except as provided in paragraph 1 (b) of this Article, but purchases within Korea of merchandise and supplies by such organizations shall be subject to Korean taxes.

3. Except as such disposal may be authorized by the Korean and the United Nations forces authorities in accordance with mutually

0141

agreed conditions, goods which are sold by such organizations shall not be disposed of in Korea to persons not authorized to make purchases from such organizations.

4. The organizations referred to in this Article shall provide such information to the Korean authorities as is required by Korean legislations.

Article X

The United Command shall have the right to establish and operate, within the facilities and areas in use by the United Nations forces, the United Nations forces military post offices for the use of members of the United Nations forces, the civilian component and their dependents, for the transmission of mail between the United Nations forces military post offices in Korea and between such military post offices and their home states post offices.

일반문서로 재분류
(협정 체결시)

0142

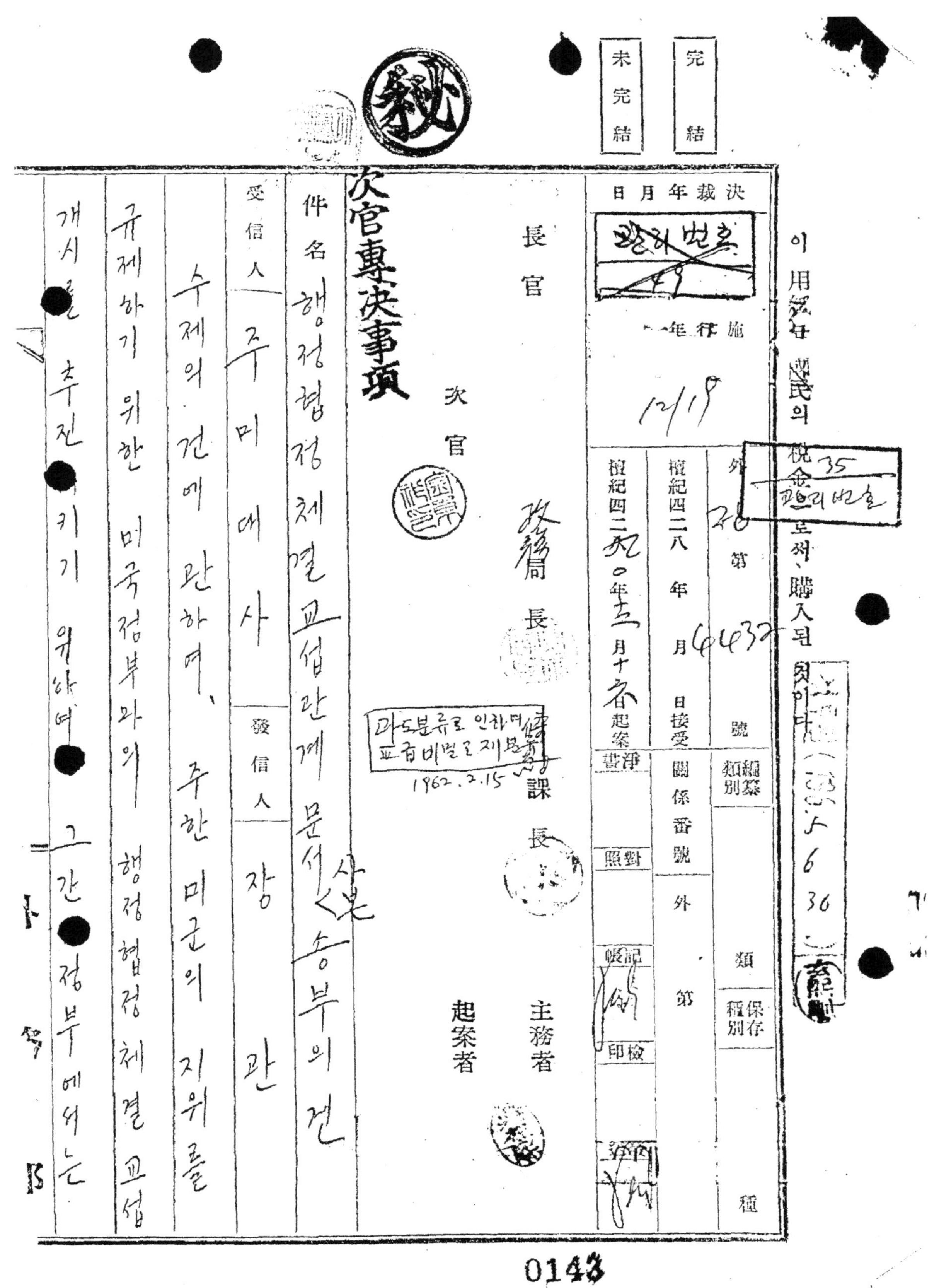

未完結 | 完結

次官專決事項

| 決裁年月日 | 관리번호 |
|---|---|
| 施行年月日 | 12/19 |
| 外 第 號 | |
| 檀紀四二八 年 月 日 接受 | |
| 檀紀四二九○年二月十六日 起案 | |

長官

次官

政務局長

課長

主務者

起案者

과도분류로 인하여 교섭비밀로 재분류 1962.2.15

件名: 행정협정체결교섭관계문서송부의 건

受信人: 주미대사

發信人: 장관

수제의 건에 관하여, 주한 미군의 지위를 규제하기 위한 미국정부와의 행정협정 체결교섭 개시를 추진하기 위하여 그간 정부에서는

이 用紙는 國民의 稅金으로써 購入된 것이다.

0143

수차에 걸쳐 우리측의 견해를 미국측에 전달하고, 특히 지난 九월 「허터」 국무차관의 래한을 계기로 이를 강력히 촉구한바 있으며, 최근에는 우리정부가 종래에 요청하여온 전면적인 행정협정 체결을 지양하고 주한 미군의 지위를 부분적으로 규제하는 몇가지 협정의 체결을 제안하였는바, 이에 그간 양국 정부간에 교환된 중요교섭문서(사본)을 송부

0144

하오니 참고하시기 바라오며、귀하께서도 앞으로 더욱 본건에 관하여 미국정부의 성의를 촉구하시고 그 결과를 수시로 보고하시기 바라나이다.

별첨 一、「허터」국무장관에게 수교한 한국정부의 견해 사본

별첨 二、부분적 협정 체결 제안에 관한 외무부장관 공한 사본

별첨 三、부분적 협정 체결에 관한 한국정부의 견

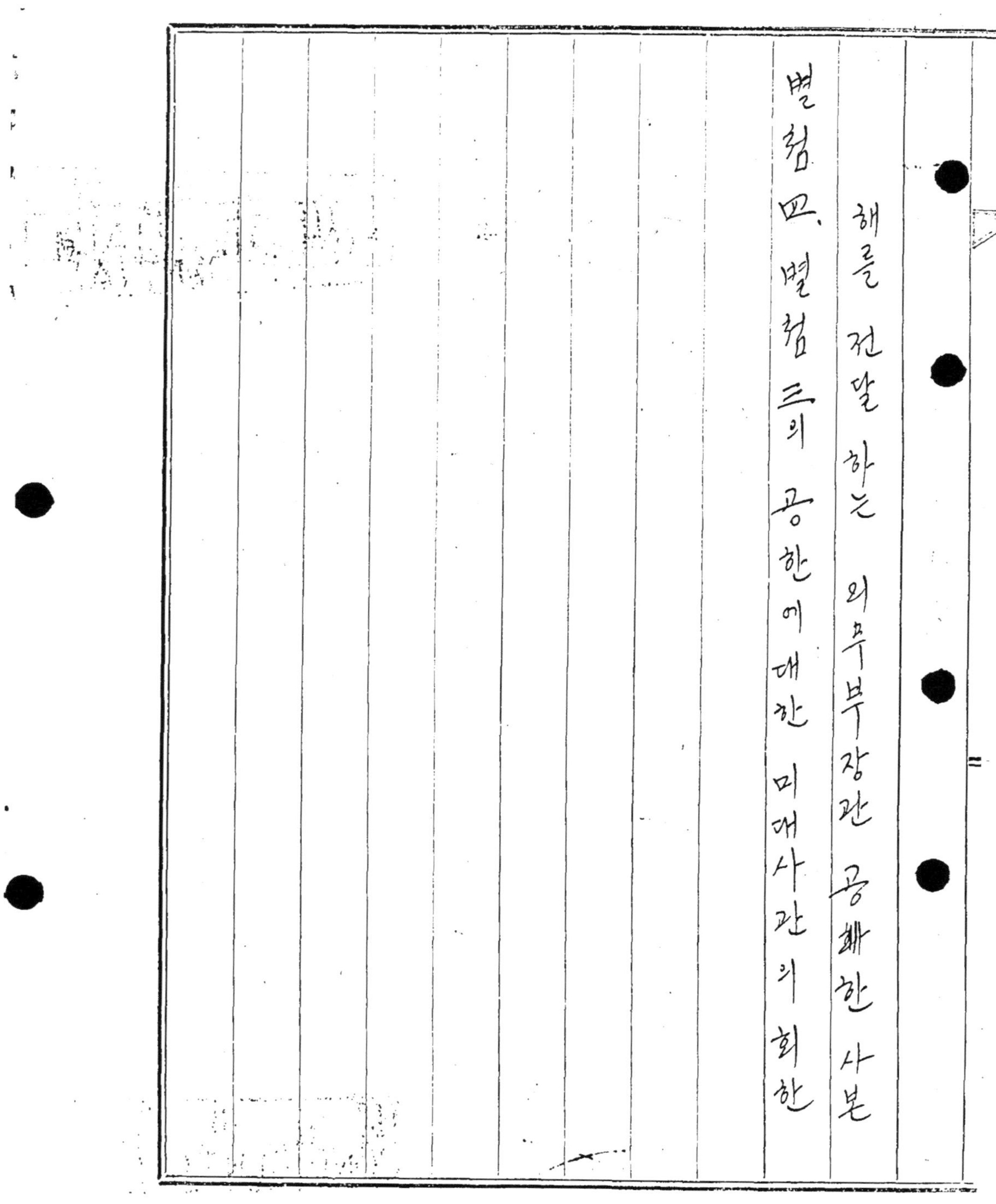

해를 전달하는 외무부장관 공翰한 사본

별첨四. 별첨三의 공한에 대한 미대사관의 회한

0146

별첨

예고문에 의하여 일반문서로 재분류 1962.12.15

검토필(1962.12.7.)

# COPY

~~ROK views transmitted to U.S. Under Secretary Herter~~

~~September~~ 10, 1957

SUBJECT: Proposed Agreement on the Status of United Nations or United States Forces in Korea

검토필(1965.6.30)

관리번호

The Government of the Republic of Korea, keenly desiring to conclude an agreement which would define the status of the United Nations armed forces in Korea, with the Government of the United States of America acting for the Unified Command in accordance with "The Resolution on the Settlement of the Unified Command" of the Security Council of the United Nations of July 7, 1950, initially proposed to the Government of the United States of America through the Foreign Minister's note of April 28, 1955, attached hereto as Annex A, that negotiations should be opened for that purpose.

검토필(1966.12.30.)

It is also recalled that, as there was no positive reaction on the part of the United States Government on the said matter, the Korean Government again renewed its proposal to the United States through the Foreign Minister's notes of January 5, 1957 and June 29, 1957 respectively, copies of which are attached hereto as Annex B and Annex C. No definite reply stating the position of the United States Government in regard to these proposals has been received as yet.

Attention is invited to the note (Annex D hereto) of General Lemnitzer of July 26, 1955 addressed to the Foreign Minister, in which the former, in expressing his views on the possibility of negotiations on the said Agreement, stated that the United States Government envisages difficulties in commencing negotiations immediately for two reasons:

1) It would be preferred by the United States Government that the negotiations for the proposed treaty of Friendship, Commerce and Navigation between the two countries as well as an agreement guaranteeing investments be

0147

investments be completed before the initiation of negotiations for the agreement in question;

2) The Unified Command could not participate in negotiations such an agreement without the prior consent of the allies within the Unified Command, and the task of obtaining such consent is time consuming.

As for the first reason mentioned above, the Korea-United States Treaty of Friendship, Commerce and Navigation has been already signed and is now only awaiting exchange of the instruments of ratification. As for the agreement guaranteeing investment, i.e. the so-called MSA Guarantee Agreement proposed by the United States Government, the Korean Government is preparing the final draft, and a definite agreement should be reached in the immediate future.

As for the second reason, the Government of the Republic of Korea is of the opinion that, as the United States forces in Korea actually constitute the preponderant components of the United Nations Forces under the Unified Command, the negotiations could be commenced first between the Korean Government and the United States Government regarding the status of the United States forces in Korea.

Apart from the above-mentioned two reasons, it is presumed that the reluctance on the part of the United States Government to commence negotiations on this subject is based on the fact that Korea is technically still in a state of war. Needless to say, however, active hostilities ceased in 1953, and the danger of a recurrence of hostilities is not considered imminent. It cannot be predicted how long the current situation will last.

Under these circumstances, it is not realistic to consider the current situation, which has lasted so long, a state of war in a virtual sense.

0148

virtual sense. Therefore, the Korean Government does not consider that anything in the current situation in Korea prevents the Governments of the Republic of Korea and the United States of America from entering into the relations which would be established if the Agreement under reference be concluded. As for the anxiety concerning the possible recurrence of hostilities in Korea, there would be no reason why ~~the~~ parties to the proposed Agreement should not review the applicability of the provisions concerned in such case.

What the Korean Government desires to conclude with the United States is nothing but such agreements similar to those concluded by the latter with NATO powers in 1951 and with Japan in 1952 on the same subject.

In the absence of such an agreement between the Republic of Korea and the United States of America, and in view of the then-prevailing conditions of warfare and urgent necessity, a <u>modus vivendi</u>, which partly defined the status of the United States forces in Korea, came into being between the two governments through the exchange of notes at Taejon on July 12, 1950 concerning the exclusive jurisdiction by court-martial of the United States over its military personnel in Korea. In view of the changed conditions after the summer of 1953, the aforesaid provisional arrangement of 1950 is no longer appropriate in its nature nor sufficient to meet and solve adequately, under the circumstances, all of the complicated problems and matters arising daily because of the stationing and disposition of United States forces in Korea.

In this connection, it is with regret that numerous incidents must be mentioned which occurred between the United States army personnel and local civilians, in most cases, incidents caused by delinquency on the part of members of the United States forces in

/Korea,

0149

Korea, involving many casualties and much damage to valuable property. All of such incidents, according to the provisional arrangement of 1950, are exclusively within the jurisdiction of the United States. The Korean Government especially fears that such incidents, and the present way of application of justice, may injure the friendly relationship existing between the peoples of the two countries.

The Government of the Republic of Korea again requests the Government of the United States of America to give favorable consideration to the proposal of the Korean Government so that negotiations between the two governments may be commenced as early as possible. A prompt conclusion of the Agreement in question would undoubtedly serve to promote increased friendship between the peoples of the two countries.

일반문서로 재분류
(협정체결시)

0150

ANNEX A.

April 28, 1955

Dear Mr. Charge d'Affaires:

I have the honour to initiate a proposal to conclude an Administrative Agreement between the Government of the Republic of Korea and the Government of the United States of America, and enclose herewith a draft of the Agreement. With regard to this proposal, I would like first to refer to my note dated December 2, 1954, concerning a conclusion of provisional Agreement regarding the functions of Korean customs authorities with respect to the United Nations forces in Korea. Particular reference was made in the note to the effect that such customs agreement will remain in force pending conclusion of a General Administrative Agreement which shall cover other subjects also.

Having in mind that the United Nations forces under the Unified Command are and will be disposed in and about the territory of the Republic of Korea until the objective of the United Nations in Korea will have been achieved pursuant to the resolutions of the United Nations Security Council of June 25, 1950, June 27, 1950 and July 7, 1950, it is the belief of the Korean Government that terms shall be provided, for the interests of both parties, to govern the disposition of and render convenience to the said forces in and about Korea, and that they shall be determined through mutual agreement between the Republic of Korea and the United States of America acting as the Unified Command in accordance with "The Resolution on the Settlement of the Unified Command" of the Security Council of the United Nations of July 7, 1950. A practical and effective Administrative Agreement to be concluded between the said two parties will help minimuze misunderstanding and maximize cooperativeness between the Korean people and United Nations forces personnel in Korea.

In the belief that a conclusion of the Agreement is in the mutual interests, I wish to propose formally, on behalf of the Government of the Republic of Korea, that negotiation will be commenced between the representatives of Korean Government and the United States Government. Upon the receipt of your consent, we will proceed to decide the date and place of the conference, which will be mutually agreeable.

Accept, dear Mr. Charge d'Affaires, the assurances of my highest consideration.

Enclosure: Draft of Administrative Agreement

Y. T. Pyun
Minister of Foreign Affairs

The Honourable Carl W. Strom,
Chargé d'Affaires,
Embassy of the United States of America
Seoul, Korea

0151

ANNEX B.

January 5, 1957

Excellency:

I have the honour ~~to refer~~ to the Foreign Minister's note addressed to Mr. Carl W. Strom, Chargé d'Affairs ad interim of the Embassy of the United States of America in Korea dated April 28, 1955 enclosing a draft of an Administrative Agreement between the Republic of Korea and the Unified Command for establishment of the Status of the United Nations Forces in Korea.

In the afore-said note, the Minister informed the Government of the United States of America of the desire of the Korean Government to commence negotiations with the United States Government for the said Status of Forces Agreement which will also define the former's customs functions as referred to in my letter of December 2, 1954.

To this proposal, however, no acceptance has been given as yet, although the American Chargé d'Affairs notified in his replying note of May 9, 1955, that upon obtaining his Government's view on the said request, he would communicate with the Minister.

I hereby wish again to propose, on behalf of my Government, that negotiation be commenced at an earliest possible date between the representatives of the Korean Government and the United States Government. In connection with this re-proposal, I would like further to refer to the note of July 26, 1955 addressed to the Foreign Minister by General Lemnitzer advising on this matter.

/General Lemnitzer

His Excellency
The right honourable
Walter C. Dowling
Ambassador ~~of the~~ United States of
America to the Republic of Korea
Seoul, Korea

0152

General Lemnitzer expressed his views on the possibility of negotiating the said agreement in the above note to the effect that the United States Government envisages difficulties in commencing immediately negotiations for a proposed agreement for the following two reasons:

The one reason was that it would be preferable to the American Government that negotiations for a proposed treaty of Friendship, Commerce and Navigation between the two countries as well as an agreement guaranteeing investments be completed before the initiation of negotiation for an agreement in question. The other was that the Unified Command cannot participate in negotiation of such agreement without the prior consent of allies within the Unified Command and it is anticipated that the task of obtaining such consent will be difficult.

Attention, however, is paid to the fact that the points indicated above constitute no longer difficulties about negotiating the said agreement under the present circumstances.

The Treaty of Friendship, Commerce and Navigation has been already signed and is now waiting to be formally ratified. As regards the agreement guaranteeing investments, discussions have been completed on provisions of its draft and now the work of finalising it remains only. On the other hand, since allies within the Unified Command have been decreased in number into twelve nations and since the American forces form the predominant components of the United Nations Forces, there exist no difficulties, it is believed, in securing consent of other allies as to the matter.

And thus, even in case the consent of the other allies has not been obtained as yet, it is, therefore, proposed that

/negotiations

0153

negotiations be started first between both representatives of the Korean Government and the United States Government and that negotiations with other allies shall be carried on separately in accordance with terms to be agreed upon between Korea and the United States of America. It is sincerely requested that the concurrence of the United States Government be given to the wish of the Korean Government to commence negotiations for the agreement proposed.

Please accept, Excellency, the renewed assurances of my highest consideration.

Chung W. Cho
Minister of
Foreign Affairs

일반문서로 재분류
(협정 체결시)

0154

ANNEX C.

My dear Mr. Ambassador:

I have the honor to remind your Government, as I have orally mentioned to you on several occasions, that the conclusion of an Administrative Agreement defining and setting forth in detail the status of United States troops stationed in Korea is still pending.

On April 28, 1955, our draft proposal of an Administrative Agreement between this Government and the Unified Command, to establish the status of United Nations forces in Korea, was addressed to your Embassy. On November 1, 1956, it was proposed that a separate agreement be negotiated between representatives of this Government and the United States Government, in case of difficulty in obtaining early consent of the other Allied Governments.

In the absence of such an administrative agreement, a temporary agreement was made through the exchange of Notes at Taejon, on July 12, 1950, concerning the exclusive jurisdiction by court-martial of the United States over members of the United States Military Establishment in Korea. This agreement, which is still in force, was improvised to meet an emergency situation and is not considered sufficient to meet effectively all the complex and complicated problems arising from the presence of United States troops in Korea.

/This Government

His Excellency
Ambassador Walter C. Dowling
American Embassy,
Seoul.

0155

This Government is strongly convinced that the early conclusion of a formal and detailed agreement on the status of United States troops in Korea would serve to strengthen cordial relations between our people and American military personnel, and would provide great satisfaction to the mutual cause and interest of both countries.

I wish to state again that this Government is most desirous of receiving the concurrence of the United States Government in order to commence negotiations for an administrative agreement along the lines of the proposal of April, 1955. Your Government's earliest favorable consideration of this matter is most sincerely desired.

Accept, Excellency, renewed assurances of my highest consideration.

Chung W. Cho
Minister

0156

A N N E X   D.

26 July 1955

Dear Minister Pyun:

Thank you very much for your letter of 13 June 1955, in which you acknowledge receipt of General Taylor's letter of 14 May 1955, with the inclosures pertaining to customs functions of the Republic of Korea.

I have noted the desire of the Korean Government to commence negotiations with the Government of the United States for a Status of Forces Agreement between the Korean Government and the Unified Command. This matter is presently under study by the Departments of my government in Washington.

Current thinking on this matter is that it would be preferable that negotiations now in progress or pending be completed before the initiation of negotiations for an agreement of the type in question. Ambassador Lacy advises me that a proposed treaty of friendship, commerce and navigation between our respective governments is under consideration, as well as an agreement guaranteeing investments,and that he is anxious to complete these matters before taking up any other major negotiations.

I am sure you are also aware that the Unified Command cannot participate in a negotiation of any Status of Forces Agreement without the prior consent of our allies within the United Nations Command. It is anticipated that the task of obtaining this consent will be difficult and time consuming.

Sincerely,

/s/
L. L. LEMNITZER
General, United States Army
Commander-in-Chief

His Excellency Pyun Yung-Tai
Minister for Foreign Affairs of
The Republic of Korea

0157

별첨 二

COPY

Minister of Home Affairs to the Commander-in-Chief of United Nations Command in Korea

Dear General Decker: November 13, 1957

We appreciate your letter of October 10, 1957, expressing your profound concern over the unfortunate shooting incidents which have occurred in recent weeks involving members of the U.S. Forces and Korean civilians.

The problems referred to in your letter are of grave concern to us, and we realize they can be effectively solved only with the concerted effort and full cooperation of authorities of our Government and the U.S. Forces.

According to our police records, there have been a total of 25 shooting incidents during the months from January to October of this year. As a result of these incidents, 12 Korean nationals were killed and 22 seriously wounded by members of the U.S. Forces. Though it is established that the majority of these incidents have involved U.S. military personnel on guard duty, this in no way justifies shootings which resulted in the death of Korean civilians.

Please believe that the Korean people will never forget the noble sacrifice of American soldiers who shed their blood in Korea to preserve our national independence and for our common defense against communist aggression, and they will never believe that the U.S. Forces will turn against them. None the less, it is difficult for our Government authorities to soothe public apprehension when it appears that human lives are valued lightly.

/Therefore

General George H. Decker,
Commander-in-Chief,
United Nations Command.

0158

Therefore I earnestly ask you again to urge the men under your Command to take every precaution in handling fire arms and to refain from firing at Koreans except in the case of self-defense under imminent threat.

As to the problem of pilferage, I am as deeply concerned as you are over the loss of U.S. military supplies vital to the defense of our Country. Police records show that from January 1 to October 13, police authorities arrested the offenders involved in 64 cases out of the total 86 reported cases of pilferage of U.S. supplies. Records also show that since 7 August, suspects involved in 10 out of 19 cases of pilferage were apprehended, including 3 out of 4 cases in the Yangju Gun area. Through such police actions, considerable quantities of stolen supplies were recovered; for example, 1,340 gallon of fuel oil and 57,205 feet of wire.

Let me assure you, General Decker, this Ministry is accelerating its drive against pilferage of U.S. supplies and our National Police throughout Korea have been ordered to make every effort to apprehend and punish offenders. We are also taking preventive measures and we are gratified to learn that on the part of U.S. Forces preventive measures to reduce the number of cases where unnecessary force is used are being instituted.

In conclusion, I suggest that a basic arrangement between authorities of the United States Forces and the Korean National Police be concluded as soon as possible to meet problems which arise involving members of the U.S. Forces and Korean civilians. On our part we pledge our wholehearted cooperation as we work together to find immediate ways for dealing effectively with these matters.

Sincerely yours,

Kun Jik Lee
Minister of Home Affairs

0159

0161

Foreign Minister to the United States Charge d'Affaires, a.i.

November 26, 1957

Dear Mr. Charge d'Affaires:

I refer to my letter of November 13, 1957, addressed to Ambassador Dowling, regarding the agreement on the status of United States forces in Korea. In this letter I suggested we commence negotiations to conclude separate agreements on particular items such as taxation, customs duties, etc., instead of concluding a full-scale agreement.

In this connection, I have pleasure in forwarding a memorandum on the position of my Government on the separate agreements to be concluded between our two Governments.

It would be greatly appreciated if you give favorable attention to this memorandum.

With warmest personal regards, I remain

Sincerely yours,

Chung W. Cho
Minister

Mr. T. Eliot Weil,
Charge d'Affaires, a.i.,
American Embassy,
Seoul.

0160

0161

# M E M O R A N D U M (57. 11. 26)

Considering the present stalemate which exists between Korea and the United States regarding the commencement of negotiations for the conclusion of a full-scale administrative agreement to govern the entire status of United States forces in Korea, it is recommended that several agreements between the two Governments be separately concluded so that the status of United States forces in Korea can be regulated as far as possible upon a mutually acceptable basis:

1) Agreement concerning Procurement, Taxation and Customs Duties of United States forces in Korea. (Ref. Art. 6, 7, 8, of Draft Administrative Agreement proposed by the Korean Government.)

2) Agreement concerning Settlement of Claims relative to the stationing of United States forces in Korea. (Ref. Art. 5)

3) Agreement concerning Facilities and Areas to be used by United States forces in Korea. (Ref. Art. 3, para. 10 of Art. 4, Art. 9, 10)

4) Agreement concerning Entry and Exit of United States forces in Korea. (Ref. Art. 2)

5) Agreement concerning Criminal Jurisdiction over Offences by United States forces in Korea. (Ref. Art. 4, 13, 14)

1. Agreement concerning Procurement, Taxation and Customs Duties of United States forces in Korea.

It is vital for the Republic of Korea Government to check the smuggling conducted through the supply routes of United States forces in Korea. This agreement

0162

50-3-24

57-3-8

미문 80-6

0163

is one of the most urgent to be concluded between the two countries. For the purpose of preventing and checking the aforesaid smuggling, the Korean Customs Officials wish to have access, for inspection purposes, to the wharves and military airports, which are now exclusively held and controlled by the United States military authorities.

As for procurements, goods and services which are required and can be obtained from local sources for the subsistance of United States forces should be procured in a manner most likely to help maintain Korean economic stability, and least probable of adversely affecting it, also in coordination with and, when desirable, through or with the assistance of competent authorities of Korea.

2. Agreement concerning Settlement of Claims relative to United States forces in Korea.

This agreement is to govern civil jurisdiction, particularly the settlement of claims arising out of injuries and damages. It is aimed to clarify the responsibility for injuries of and damages to Korean nationals and their properties caused by United States forces, and to facilitate settlement of the claims arising out of such injuries and damages. On the other hand, the Korean Government will undertake to make every effort to protect United States forces and their members from injuries to them and damage to their properties.

3. Agreement concerning Facilities and Areas to be used by United States forces in Korea.

0164

While the Korean Government is willing to grant to United States forces the use of certain facilities

57-3-25

해 -3-8

미문 10-6

0165

and areas and certain rights, powers and authority necessary for carrying out their mission, this agreement is aimed to clarify the scope of exemption from the liabilities of compensation or restoration accruing from the use of such facilities and areas.

This agreement ~~will~~ also contain provisions in regard to military ~~post office~~ and non-appropriated fund organizations, ~~and further~~, such provisions as will enable the Korean Government to make interim use of any of such facilities or areas of target ranges and maneuver grounds, which are temporarily not used by United States forces.

4. Agreement concerning Entry and Exit of United States forces in Korea.

This agreement will clarify the scope of exemption from Korean immigration laws and regulations for the members of United States forces, including civilian component and their dependents.

5. Agreement concerning Criminal Jurisdiction over Offences by United States forces in Korea.

It is to propose to the United States Government to amend the existing Taejon agreement of 1950 to suit the changed conditions caused by the cessation of actual hostilities. As for the amendment, efforts should be made to limit the jurisdiction of the United States court-martial over members of United States forces to such cases as have occurred in the course of execution of official duties, and further to make

0166

57-3-26

57-3-8 아문80-6

0167

0183

additional provisions for judicial cooperation, including joint search and investigation.

Ministry of Foreign Affairs
Seoul, Korea
November 26, 1957

0168

57-3-27

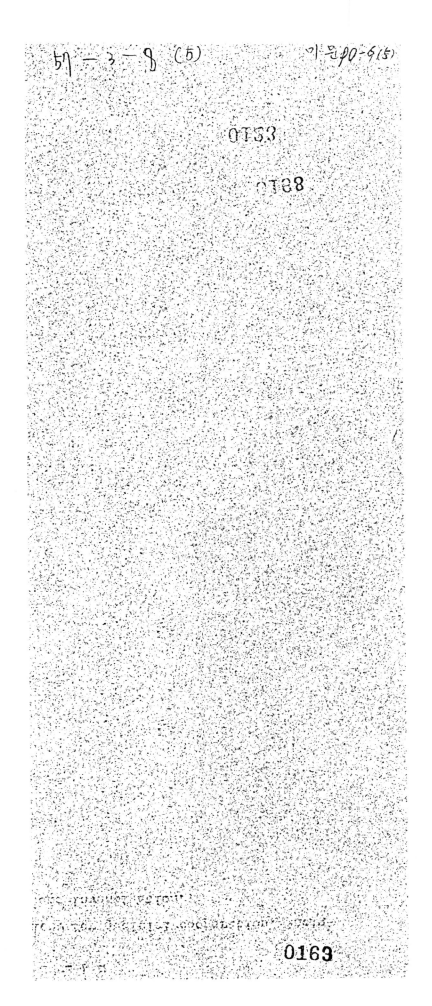

별첨 四

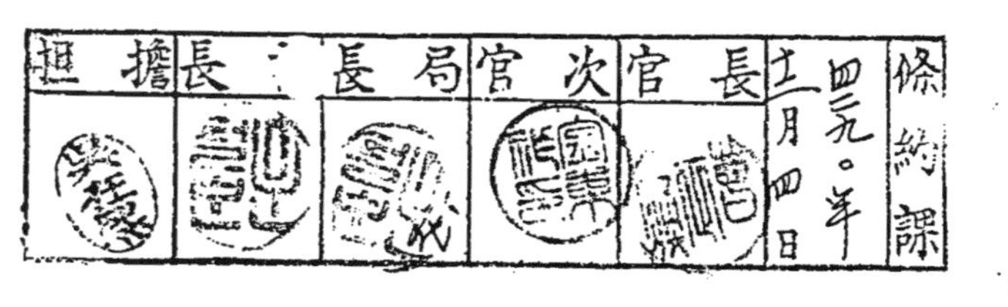

공람

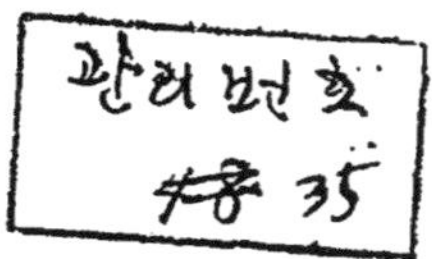

American Embassy,
Seoul, Korea,
~~December 3, 1957~~

My dear Mr. Minister:

I have the honor to acknowledge receipt of your letter of November 26, 1957 with which was enclosed a memorandum concerning the position of your Government on the question of negotiating separate agreements on various subjects pertaining to the status of United States forces in Korea.

I have forwarded copies of your letter and enclosure to Washington for consideration by my Government.

I shall hope, in due course, to send you a further communication on the subject of your Government's memorandum.

With warmest personal regards, I am

Sincerely yours,

T. Eliot Weil

T. Eliot Weil
Charge d'Affaires ad interim

His Excellency
Chung W. Cho,
Minister of Foreign Affairs,
Republic of Korea.

0170

to K.M.D.

Explanation on the Military Post Office
and non-Appropriate Fund Organizations
to be regulated by the Separate Agreement

관도문류로 인사에
올바른 기로 재분류
1962.2.16.

As for ~~the~~ military post office and non-appropriated fund organizations, the full-scale draft agreement ~~on the status of United Nations forces~~ between Korea and the ~~Unified Command~~ proposed by the Korean Government to the Uni~~ted States Government~~ contains provisions regarding the military post office and non-appropriated fund organizations such as navy exchanges, post exchanges, messes, social clubs, theaters and newspapers. It is intended that the substance of the above-mentioned provisions, that is Articles 9 and 10 of the draft agreement, be included in the seperate agreement to be concluded between the two Governments. The provisions of Articles 9 and 10 of the draft agreement is attached hereto. Since the memorandum to be forwarded to the American Embassy is purported to indicate only essential points to be included in the separate agreements and since the position of the Korean Government on how to regulate the matters is already expressed in the draft agreement referred to in the above, it is considered appropriate to point out in the memorandum only the subjects to be regulated by the separate agreement.

0171

Draft Administrative Agreement regarding the Status of the United Nations Forces proposed by the Korean Government to the United States Government.

과도분류로 인하여 일반문서로 재분류 1962. 2. 17.

Article IX

1. (a) Navy exchanges, post exchanges, messes, social clubs, theaters, newspapers and other non-appropriated funds organizations authorized and regulated by the United Nations forces authorities may be established in the facilities and areas in use by the United Nations forces for the use of members of such forces, the civilian component, and their dependents. Except as otherwise provided in this Agreement, such organizations shall not be subject to Korean regulations, license, fees, taxes or similar controls.

(b) When a newspaper authorized and regulated by the United Nations forces authorities is sold to the general public, it shall be subject to Korean regulations, license, fees, taxes or similar controls so far as such circulation is concerned.

2. No Korean tax shall be imposed on sales of merchandise and services by such organizations, except as provided in paragraph 1 (b) of this Article, but purchases within Korea of merchandise and supplies by such organizations shall be subject to Korean taxes.

3. Except as such disposal may be authorized by the Korean and the United Nations forces authorities in accordance with mutually

0172

agreed conditions, goods which are sold by such organizations shall not be disposed of in Korea to persons not authorized to make purchases from such organizations.

4. The organizations referred to in this Article shall provide such information to the Korean authorities as is required by Korean legislations.

Article X

The United Command shall have the right to establish and operate, within the facilities and areas in use by the United Nations forces, the United Nations forces military post offices for the use of members of the United Nations forces, the civilian component and their dependents, for the transmission of mail between the United Nations forces military post offices in Korea and between such military post offices and their home states post offices.

일반문서로 재분류
(협정체결시)

0173

# 대 통 령 비 서 실

대비제 호

단기 4291년 3월 19일

외 무 부 장 관
국 방 부 장 관 각 하
상 공 부 장관

별첨 의명 송부하오니 사수 하시고 우리나라에서도 피엑스(P.X.) 나 콤밋사리(Commissary)의 사용을 제한하는 방도를 연구하여 지급 실천에 옮기도록하고 보고하라 하시오니 의명 전달 하나이다.

이 상

대통령비서관 박 찬 일

0174

4

EXCERPT FROM
THE PHILIPPINE NEWSLETTER

March 7, 1958

U.S. CURBS PX PRIVILEGES

MANILA: Exchange and commissary privileges previously extended by the U.S. Armed Forces in the Philippines to exchange employees and to dependents of active-duty U.S. military personnel not attached to any activity in the Philippines have been curtailed effective Feb. 28. The move stemmed from the desire of the U.S. Armed Forces in the Philippines to cooperate with the Philippine government's austerity program and to stop the flow of tax-free PX goods into the local market.

More curtailment of PX privileges is scheduled to become effective April 15, 1958, which will apply to U.S. Federal employees who are residents of the Philippines and the reserve personnel of the U.S. Armed Forces, except when on active duty for two weeks or longer.

0175

未完結

完結

| 決裁年月日 | |
|---|---|
| 施行年月日 | 4/2 |

| 外 第 1225 號 | 檀紀四二九一年 月 日接受 | 檀紀四二九一年 三月 二八日起案 |
|---|---|---|
| 編纂類別 | 關係番號 外 第 號 | 淨書 |
| 類 | | 照對 |
| 保存種別 | | 記帳 |
| 種 | | 檢印 |
| | | 發送 |

長官

次官

정무 局長

구미 課長

主務者

起案者

件名 비율빈에서의 미군 P.X나 Commissary의 사용에 관한 조치에 관한 문의의 건

受信 주비율빈대사 귀하

장관

머리의 건에 관하여 별첨 상공부장관

이 用紙는 國民의 稅金으로써 購入된 것이다

0176

공한으로 전달하오니 사수하시와 본건에 관한
상세한 정보와 자료를 시급히 본부로 송부
하여 주시기 바라나이다

별첨

一. 본건 상공부장관 서한 一통

0177

(사본)

상역제 九五〇호

단기 四二九一년 三월 二十四일

상공부장관 김일환

외무부 경유

주 비율빈 대사 귀하

비율빈에서의 미군 P.X. 일반인 사용 금지 조치에 관한 조회의 건

二월 二十六일자 (PACIFIC. STARS AND STRIPES) 신문에 전재된 마니라 발 UP 통신에 의하면. 비율빈 정부가 내핍생활

0178

정책에 따라 당지 미군당국은 PX 및 구매
처의 사용에 있어 군관계 이외의 일반인
사용을 제한 하였다는 것이바 우리정부
로서도 방책을 강구 코저 하오니 이에
관한 상세한 자료를 조사 회보하여 주십
을 경망 하나이다.

0179

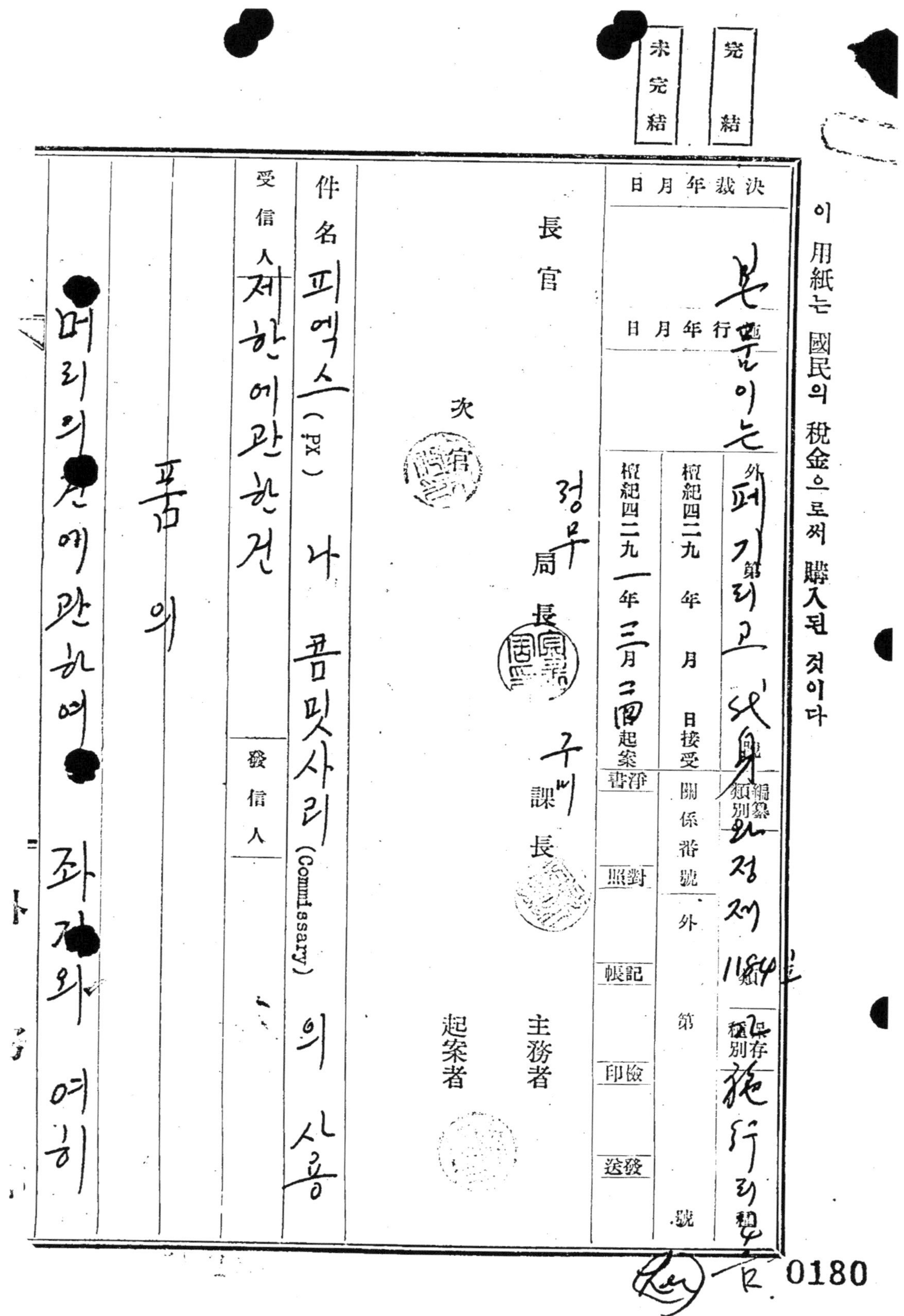

未完結 | 完結

이 用紙는 國民의 稅金으로써 購入된 것이다

| | |
|---|---|
| 決裁年月日 | |
| 施行年月日 | |
| 分類記號 文書番號 | 外 외정제 1184 |
| 保存種別 | |
| 起案 | 檀紀四二九一年 三月 二四日 |
| 接受 | 檀紀四二九 年 月 日 |
| 關係番號 | 外 第 號 |
| 淨書 / 照對 / 記帳 / 檢印 / 發送 | |

長官

次官

정무局長

구미課長

主務者

起案者

受信人

發信人

件名 피엑스(PX)나 콤밋사리(Commissary)의 사용 제한에 관한 건

품의

머리의 건에 관하여 좌기와 여히

0180

경무대에 회시함이 어떠할지 고재를
앙청하나이다

기

외무부장관

대통령비서실 박찬일 비서관 귀하

동건 (대비기밀 九一번 三월 十九일자 공한)

머리의 건 대호 공한으로 지시하신 표기
건에 관하여 당부로서 검토하여 본 결과 주
한 미군에 소속되고 있는 피엑스(PX) 나 콤멧사
리 (Commissary) 는 미군 산하의 정식 군기관

0181

임으로 주한미군이 국제법상 가지고있는
특권을 향유하고있음에 비추어 당부

단기四二九○년 十월 七일자 Recommendation on seperate
Agreements between Korea and the United States regarding the Status of United States Forces
in Korea
에서 언급된 Agreement concerning Procurement, Taxation and Custom Duties
of the United States Forces in Korea 등을 체결하여 그

속에 피엑스 ( PX ) 나 콤밋사리 (Commissary) 의
활동제한을 규정하기전에는 별를상

0182

이의 제한을 요구할 수는 없는 것으로 사료
되오나 다만 현재에 있어서 당부로서 본
건에 관한 조처를 취한다면는 별첨안과
같은 피·엑스(PX)나 콤밋사리(Commissary)의
대상인의 사용제한과 물품의 횡류방지 에 협력하여 달라는 요지의
서한을 주한 미대사관에 발송할 수 있을
정도라고 사료되옵기 동서한안 사본 일통
을 이에 상달하나이다 어떠하오리까

본건 안 별첨 일통

0183

상역제 九九 호

단기四二九一년三월二十八일

상공부장관 김 일 환

외무부장관 귀하

피엑스(P.X.) 및 콤멧사리(Commissary) 사용

에 관한 협의회 개최의 건

표제건 외신보도에 의하면 비율빈국에서는 정부정책에 따라 당지 미군당국은 피엑스 및 콤팻사리의 일반인 사용을 제한하였다는 것이 전하여 진바있고 우리나라에서도 이에 대한 시급한 대책강구가 요청되는바 금반 상부로부터의 지시도 유하옵기 좌기와 같이 협의회를 개최코자 하오니 참석하심을 경망하나이다

0184

가

一 일 시 四二九一년 三월 三十一일 상오 十시 三〇분

一 장 소 상공부 제二회의실

一 참석자 상공부 상역국장

외무부 정무국장

내무부 치안국장

재무부 세관국장

법무부 검찰국장

국방부 관리국장

13

0185

/DRAFT/

~~March 24~~ April 8, 1958

I have the honor to refer to the Post Exchange and the Commissary which are operated and maintained by the United States Armed Forces in Korea.

It is understood that the commodities on sale at the Post Exchange or Commissary are presently free of customs duties and taxation solely for the benefit of the military personnel of the U.S. Armed Forces in Korea and their dependents. Frequently, however, the goods originated from the Post Exchange and the Commissary flow into the market in Korea causing an adverse influence on the stabilization and the reconstruction of Korean economy.

It would be greatly appreciated if you would advise, with the spirit of cooperation, the military authorities concerned to take appropriate actions to restrict the possible abuses of the PX privileges with a view to preventing illegal flow of goods into the local market to the detriment of the Korean economy.

With my highest personel regards,

Sincerely yours,

His Excellency
Walter C. Dowling, Ambassador
American Embassy
S e o u l

0186

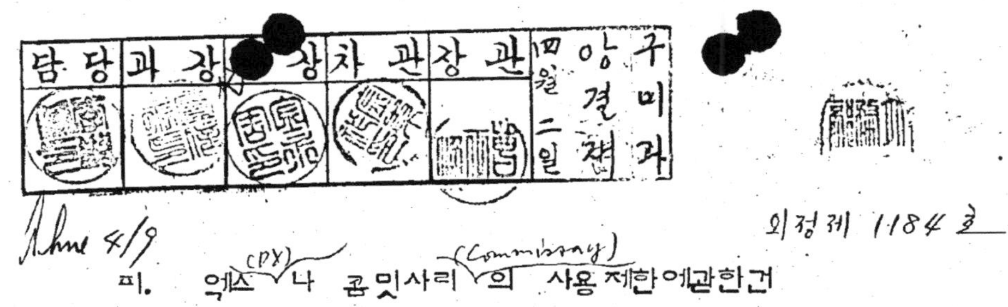

외정제 1184호

피. 엑스(PX)나 콤밋사리(Commissary)의 사용제한에관한건

품 의

머리의건에 관하여 하기와 여히 경무대에 회시함이 어떠하올지 고재를 앙청 하나이다.

기

대통령 비서실 박 찬일 비서관 귀하

외 무 부 장 관

동건 ( 대 단기 4291년 3월 19일자 공한 )

머리의 건 대호공한으로 지시하신 표기건에 관하여 단기 4291년 3월 31일 상공부 제 2회의실에서 외무, 내무, 재무, 국방, 법무 및 상공의 육부 관계관이 모인 가운데 본건에 대한 토의를 한 결과

1 ) 일반 민중 으로하여금 피. 엑스 나 콤밋사리를 통하여 유출 되는 물품의 매매는 관세법에 위반되는 범법행위임을 인식토록 계몽하되 동 계몽 사업에는 상공 및 국방 양부가 주동이 되고

2 ) 여사한 범법행위의 방지를 위하여 법무, 내무, 재무의 삼부가 주동이 되어 단속행위를 하고 중요 대한 사건에 대하여는 외무부를 통하여 미국측에 통고 할것과

3 ) 미국측과의 전면적인 교섭에 있어서는 주한 미군의 지위에 관한 협정이 체결되어 있지 않으므로 법률상 피. 엑스 나 콤밋사리의 제한을 요구 강제 할수는 없고 다만 추상적으로 미국측에 협조를 의뢰 하며 또는 단속행위중 발견된 중요한 사건을 통보하는 이외에는 별다른 조치를 취할수 없다

는데 대체적인 의견의 일치를 보았던바 당부로는 현재로서 본건에 관하여 별첨 안과 같이 피. 엑스 나 콤밋사리의 사용제한과 물품의 횡류방지에 협력 하여 달라는 요지의 서한을 주한 미대사관에 발송 할수 있을정도 라고 사료 되옵기 동서한안 사본 일통을 이에 상담 하오며 이와같이 시행함이 어떠 하오리까?

별 첨

1. 본건 안 1통.

0187

D R A F T

April 8, 1958

I have the honor to refer to the Post Exchange and the Commissary which are operated and maintained by the United States Armed Forces in Korea.

It is understood that the commodities on sale at the Post Exchange or Commissary are presently free of customs duties and taxation solely for the benefit of the military personnel of the U.S. Armed Forces in Korea and their dependents. Frequently, however, the goods originated from the Post Exchange and the Commissary flow into the market in Korea causing an adverse influence on the stabilization and the reconstruction of Korean economy.

It would be greatly appreciated if you would kindly advise, ~~with the spirit of coöperation,~~ the military authorities concerned to take appropriate actions to restrict ~~the~~ possible abuses of the P.X. privileges ~~with a view~~ to prevent~~ing~~ the illegal flow of goods into the local market ~~to the detriment of the Korean economy.~~ with a spirit of cooperation in order to help the healthy development of Korean economy.

~~With my highest personal regards,~~

Sincerely yours,

His Excellency
Walter C. Dowling, Ambassador
Ambarican Embassy
S e o u l

0188

외정제 1184 호

단기 4291년 4월 8일

외 무 부 장 관

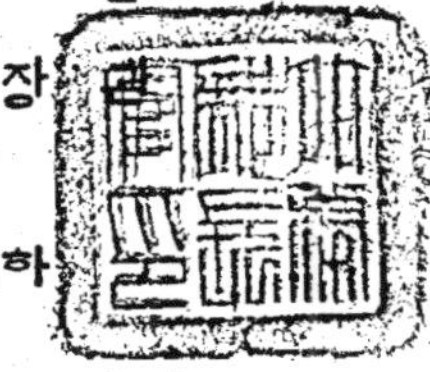

대통령 비서실
박 찬일 비서관 귀하

건 명 . . . 피. 엑스(P. X)나 콤밋사리(Commissary)의 사용 제한에 관한 건 (대 단기 4291년 3월 19일자 공한)

머리의건 대호 공한으로 지시 하신 표기건에 관하여 단기 4291년 3월 31일 상공부 제2회의실 에서 외무, 내무 재무, 국방, 법무 및 상공의 육부 관계관이 모인 가운데 본건에 대한 토의를 한 결과,

1) 일반 민중 으로 하여금 피. 엑스 나 콤밋사리를 통 하여 유출 되는 물품의 매매는 관세법에 위반되는 범법 행위임을 인식토록 계몽 하되 동 계몽 사업에는 상공 및 국방 양부가 주동이 되고

2) 여사한 범법행위의 방지를 위하여 법무, 내무, 재무의 삼부가 주동이 되어 단속행위를 하고 중대한 사건에 대 하여는 외무부를 통하여 미국측에 통고할것과,

3) 미국측 과의 전면적인 교섭에 있어서는 주한 미군의 지위에 관한 협정이 체결 되어 있지 않으므로 법률상 피. 엑스(P. X)나 콤밋사리(Commissary)의 제한을 요구 강제 할수 없고 다만 우상적으로 미국측의 협조를 의뢰 하며 또 는 단속행위중 발견된 중요한 사건을 통보 하는 이외에는 별다른 조치를 취할수 없다는데 대체적인 의견의 일치를 보았던바 당부로는 현재로써 본건에 관하여 별첨 안과 같이 피. 엑스( P. X )나 콤밋사리(Commissary)의 사용제한과 물 품의 횡류 방지에 협력 하여 달라는 요지의 서한을 주한 미 대사관에 발송 할수 있을 정도 라고 사료 되옵기 동 서한안 사본 일통을 이에 상달 하오며 이와같이 시행함이 어떠 하오리까?

별 첨

1. 본건안 1통.

0189

returned from KMD for reconsideration

외정제 호

단기 4291년 4월 8일

외 무 부 장 관

대통령 비서실
박 찬일 비서관 귀하

건 명 . . . 피. 엑스( P.X )나 콤밋사리(Commissary )의 사용 제한에 관한 건 ( 대 단기 4291년 3월 19일자 공한)

머리의건 대호 공한으로 지시 하신 표기건에 관하여 단기 4291년 3월 31일 상공부 제2회의실 에서 외무, 내무 재무, 국방, 법무 및 상공의 육부 관계관이 모인 가운데 본건에 대한 토의를 한 결과,

1 ) 일반 민중 으로 하여금 피. 엑스 나 콤밋사리를 통 하여 유출 되는 물품의 매매는 관세법에 위반되는 범법 행위임을 인식토록 계몽 하되 동 계몽 사업에는 상공 및 국방 양부가 주동이 되고

2) 여사한 범법행위의 방지를 위하여 법무, 내무, 재무의 삼부가 주동이 되어 단속행위를 하고 중대한 사건에 대하여는 외무부를 통하여 미국측에 통고할것과,

3 ) 미국측 과의 전면적인 교섭에 있어서는 주한 미군의 지위에 관한 협정이 체결 되어 있지 않으므로 법률상 피. 엑스(P. X )나 콤밋사리(Commissary)의 제한을 요구 강제 할수 없고 다만 우선적으로 미국측의 협조를 의뢰 하며 또는 단속행위중 발견된 중요한 사건을 통보 하는 이외에는 별다른 조치를 취할수 없다는데 대체적인 의견의 일치를 보았던바 당부로는 현재로써 본건에 관하여 별첨 안과 같이 피. 엑스( P. X )나 콤밋사리(Commissary)의 사용제한과 물품의 횡류 방지에 협력 하여 달라는 요지의 서한을 주한 미 대사관에 발송 할수 있을 정도 라고 사료 되옵기 동 서한안 사본 일통을 이에 상달 하오며 이와같이 시행함이 어떠 하오리까?

별 첨

1. 본건안 1통.

0190

<u>DRAFT</u>

April 8, 1958

I have the honor to refer to the Post Exchange and the Commissary which are operated and maintained by the United States Armed Forces in Korea.

It is understood that the commodities on sale at the Post Exchange or Commissary are presently free of customs duties and taxation solely for the benefit of the military personnel of the U.S. Armed Forces in Korea and their dependents. Frequently, however, the goods originated from the Post Exchange and the Commissary flow into the market in Korea causing an adverse influence on the stabilization and the reconstruction of Korean economy.

It would be greatly appreciated if you would advise, with the spirit of cooperation, the military authorities concerned to take appropriate actions to restrict the possible abuses of the P.X. privileges with a view to preventing illegal flow of goods into the local market to the detriment of the Korean economy.

With my highest personel regards,

Sincerely yours,

His Excellency
Walter C. Dowling, Ambassador
American Embassy
S e o u l

returned from KMD

0191 APR 10 1958

Lim.

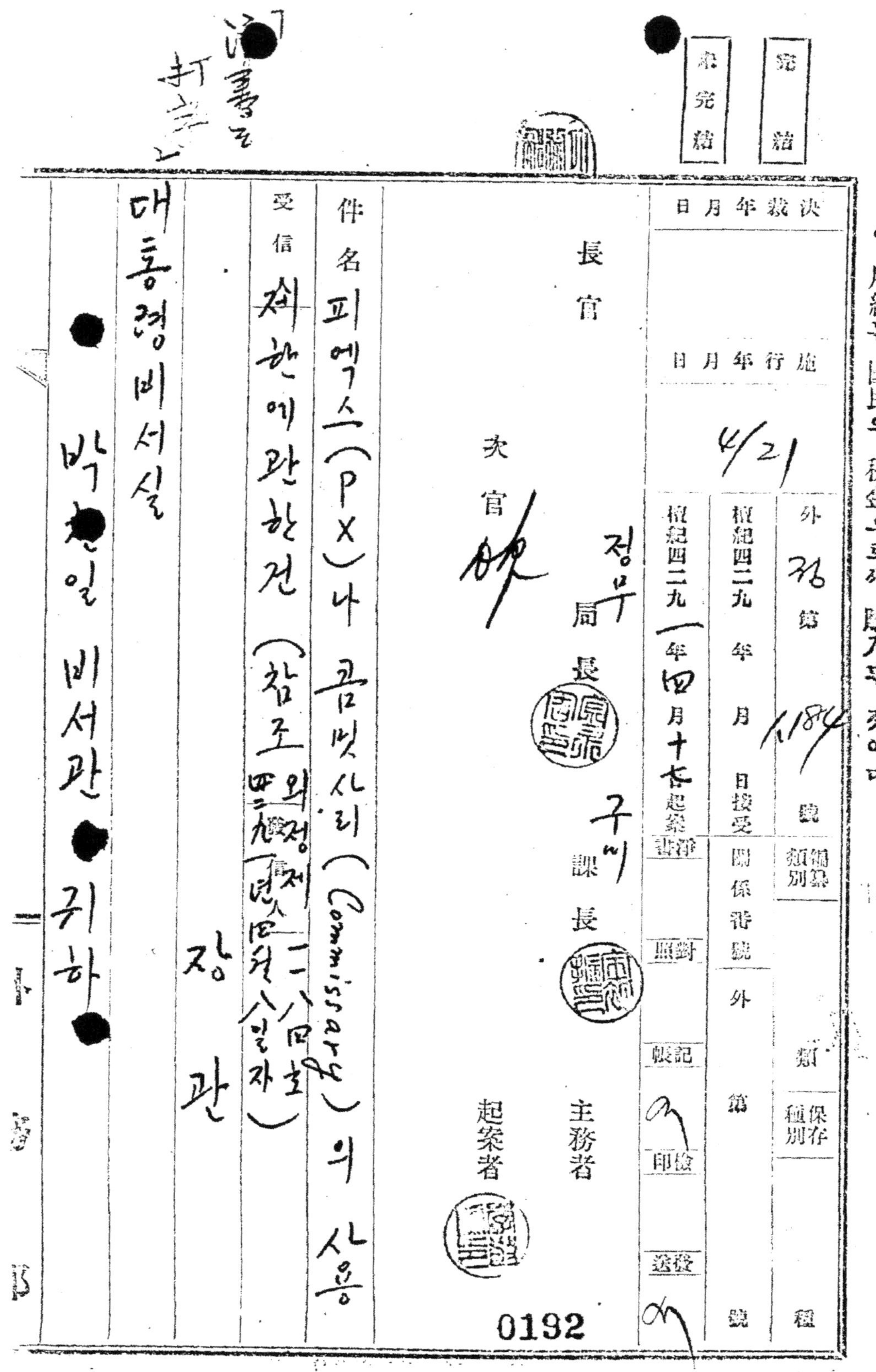

未完結 完結

決裁年月日

施行年月日 4/21

外정 第 1184 號

檀紀四二九一年四月十一日起案

檀紀四二九 年 月 日接受

長官

次官

정무局長

구미課長

主務者

起案者

件名 피엑스(PX)나 콤밋사리(Commissary)의 사용에 관한 건

受信 대통령비서실 박찬일 비서관 귀하

(참조 : 외정 제 2814호 (1958. 4. 8 시행))

장관

이 用紙는 國民의 稅金으로써 購入된 것이다

0192

어리의 건에 관하여는 이미 표기 참조 공한
으로 보고한바 있아오나 본건에 관련하여
주비율빈대사관에게 비율빈에서의 미군 PX
의 사용제한 조치에 관한 상세한 정보를
문의하였든바 별첨사본과 같은 회한이
내도하였기 동 회한 사본 一통을 이에 상달
하나이다.

별첨

一. 본건 주비율빈대사 공한 사본 一통

0193

외정제 호

단기 4291년 4월 19일

외 무 부 장 관

대통령 비서실

박찬일 비서관 귀하

피엑스( PX )나 콤밋사리( Commissary )의
사용 제한에 관한 건 ( 참조. 외정제 1184,
단기 4291년 4월 8일)

머리의건에 관하여는 이미 표기 참조 공한으로 보고 한바 있아오나 본건에 관련 하여 주 비율빈 대사관 에게 비율빈 에서의 미군 PX 의 사용 제한 조치 에 관한 상세한 정보를 문의 하였던바 별첨 사본과 같은 회한이 내도 하였기 동 회한 사본 1통을 이에 상답 하나이다.

별 첨

1. 본건 주 비율빈 대사 공한 사본 1통.

0194

이 용지는 국민의 세금으로써 구입된 것이다

| 광 | 대 | 상 | 과장 | 국장 | 관 | 차관 | 장 |
|---|---|---|---|---|---|---|---|
| | | | | 代 | | | MAR 31 1958 |

# 復命書

大使館 二等書記官 盧信永

外務部政務局長 貴下

피엑스 (P.X.) 및 콤미사리 (Commissary) 사용에 관한 협의회에 참석하고 그 결과를 좌기와 같이 보고하나이다.

記

一. 日時 檀紀四二九一年 三月 三十日 上前 十時 三十分

一. 場所 商工部 (第二 會議室)

一. 參席部署

1. 外務部 政務局
2. 內務部 治安局
3. 財務部 稅關局
4. 國防部 管理局
5. 法務部 檢察局
6. 商工部 商易局

一. 討議內容

商工部 商易局長 司會로 開催된 本會議에서는 P.X. 및 Commissary 를 通하여 市場에 流出되는 物品의 統制 및 管理方案을 協議하고 大略 다음과 같은 세가지 方法에 合議를 보는 同時에 앞으로도 如斯한 協議會를 자주 갖도록 함이

0196

이 용지는 국민의 세금으로써 구입된 것이다

有益할 것이라는데 意見의 一致를 보았음.

1. 啓蒙事業.

一般民衆으로 하여금 P.X 또는 Commissary 를 通하여 流出된 物品의 賣買는 關稅法에 違反되는 犯法行爲임을 認識할수 있도록, 百貨店, 其他 要所에 標語를 揭示하고 其他 必要한 啓蒙事業을 하되, 民間에 對하여는 商工部가, 軍部에 對하여는 國防部가 各各 主動이 됨.

2. 團束行爲.

法務部 및 內務部와 財務部가 主動이 되어 行하고. 其中. 重大한 事件에 對하여는 外務部를 通하여 美國側에 通告함.

0197

3. 美國側과의 交涉

駐屯軍의 地位에 關한 協定이 締結되어 있지 않고 또한 U.S.에서 賣買되는 物品의 種類와 數量에 對하여 아무런 情報도 갖고 있지않을 뿐만 아니라. 이에 對하여 干涉할 權限을 갖고 있지 못하는 우리 나라의 現狀態로서는, 外務部가 本件을 美國側과 直接協議하여 얻을 수 있는 效果라는 것은 極히 稀少함을 指摘하고. 다만 抽象的으로 美國側에 協調를 依賴하며, 또는 關係行爲가 發生한 個々의 重要事件의 通報를 行하는 以外에는 別다른 措置를 取할 수 없음을 力說하였음.

其他

0198

이 용지는 국민의 세금으로써 구입된 것이다

協議를 끝마치자. 商工部에서는 本件 事務는 아직은 行政協定締結問題도 있고, 또한 美國側과의 交涉이도 있는 것이니, 外務部가 主動이 되어 行함이 可할 것이라는 意見을 提出하였으나, 前記한 바와 같이, 本件은 美國側과의 交涉으로 解決될 문제가 아님이고, 오히려 取締機関의 行動과 商工部의 啓蒙事業만이 効果를 期待할 수 있는 方法이므로, 財務部 稅関局, 內務部 治安局, 이 積極活動을 하고, 商工部와 法務部 그리고 國防部와 外務部는 이에 助力하는 것이 妥當하리라는 小官의 意見陳述로, 前記提案을 撤回하였음.

0193

다음에도 如斯한 協議會를 자주 갖는 것이

有益하리라는 点에는 意見의 一致를 보았으나,

그 時日과 場所等 具体的인 方法에 對하여서는

合議를 본바없이 午后 散會하였음.

以上.

0200

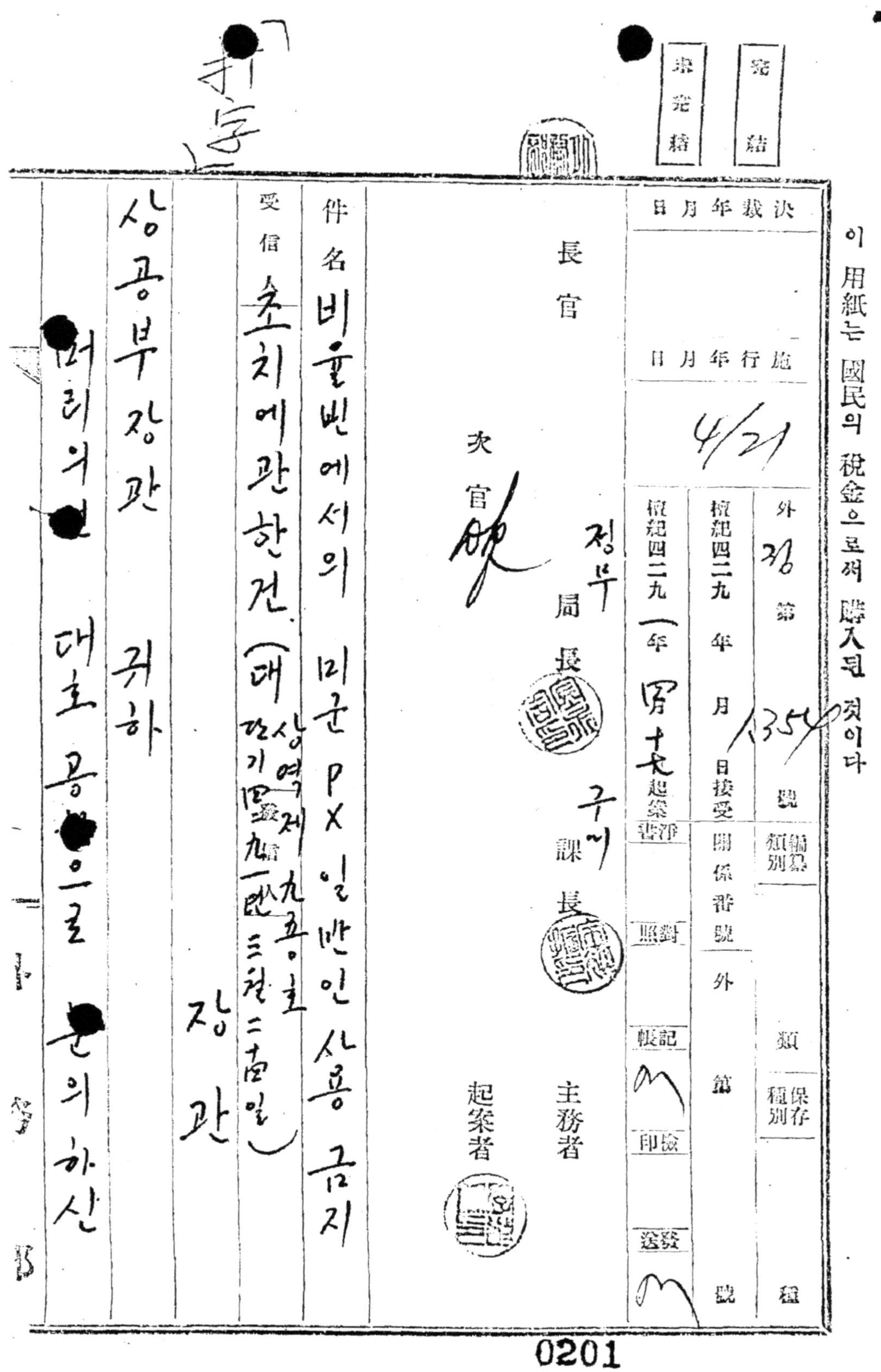

이 用紙는 國民의 稅金으로서 購入된 것이다

| 決裁年月日 | |
|---|---|
| 施行年月日 | 4/21 |

外정 第 1354 號

檀紀四二九一年 四月十七日 起案

檀紀四二九 年 月 日 接受

長官

次官

정무 局長

구미 課長

主務者

起案者

件名: 비율빈에서의 미군 PX 일반인 사용 금지 조치에 관한 건 (대 상역제 九五공호 단기 四二九一년 三월 二十一일)

受信: 상공부장관 귀하

장 관

머리의 대호 공문으로 문의 하신

0201

표기건에 관하여 주비율빈대사관으로부터 별첨과 같은 회시가 내조하였기 이를 전달하나이다.

별첨.

一. 본건 주비대사 공한 一통

0202

외정제 호

단기 4291년 4월 19일

외 무 부 장 관

상 공 부 장 관 귀 하

비율빈 에서의 미군 PX 일반인 사용금지 조치에 관한 건 (대 상역제 950호, 4291년 3월 24일)

머리의건 대호 공한 으로 문의 하신 표기건에 대하여 주 비율빈 대사관 으로부터 별첨과 같은 회시가 래도 하였기 이를 전달 하나이다.

별 첨

1. 본건 주비대사 공한 1통.

0203

# EMBASSY OF THE REPUBLIC OF KOREA
MANILA

주비대 제 91/101 호　　　　　　　　　　단기 4291년 4월 9일

외무부장관 각하
경유
상공부장관 각하

주비대사

비율빈에서의 미군 PX 일반인 사용
금지 조치에 관한 건

대력의건에 관하여 PX 급 구매처는 미국해외주재군인 및 동가족을 위하여 설치 된 것이오며 응급하신 2월 26일부 기사 Pacific Stars and Stripes 로서 미국정부 의 내핍생활 정책 에 따라 일반사용 을 제한 하였다고 하오나 그와같은 정부 는 볼수없아오며 당지 미국 PX 및 구매처는 미국군인 및 동가족 과 각국무관 외에는 현재까지 사용 불가능 이오며 심지어는 각국주비대사, 공사에게도 동 사용자격 이 부여되어있지 않은 을 보고 하나이다.

추

자유중국에서는 미국대사관으로부터 각국공관장 과 차석 에 대해서 PX 사용 의 특권 을 부여하고 일반 외교관에는 미국대사관에서 경영 하는 소위 American Embassy Shop 사용권 이 부여되어 있음을 을 부언 하나이다.

0204

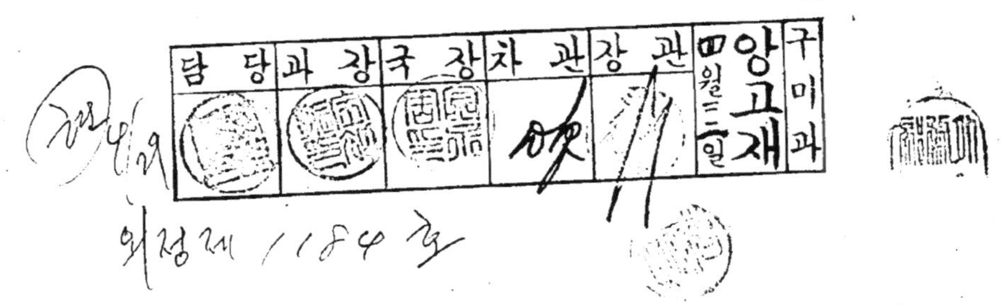

피. 엑스 ( PX ) 나 콤밋사리 ( Commissary ) 의
사용 제한에 관한건

품 의

머리의 건에 관하여 하기와여히 경무대에 회시함이 어떠하올지 고재를 앙청하나이다.

기

외 무 부 장 관

대통령 비서실
박찬일 비서관 귀하

동 건

머리의 건에 관하여는 단기 4291년 3월 19일자 공한으로 지시를 받고 외정제 1.184호 ( 4291.4.8 ) 로서 회시하였든바 재검토의 지시를 받았기 이에 다시 보고 하나이다.

1. 본건에 관하여 단기 4291년 3월 31일 상공부에서 외무, 내무, 재무, 국방, 법무 및 상공의 6부 관계관이 회합하여 토의한바

(가) 일반 민중으로 하여금 피. 엑스 나 콤밋사리를 통하여 유출되는 물품의 매매는 관세법에 위반 되는 범법행위 임을 인식토록 계몽하되 동 계몽사업에는 상공, 및 국방 양부가 주동이 되고

(나) 여사한 범법행위의 방지를 위하여 법무, 내무, 재무의 3부가 주동이되어 단속행위를 하고 중대한사건에 대하여는 외무부를 통하여 미국측에 통고할것과

(다) 미국측과의 전면적인 교섭에 있어서는 주한 미군의 지위에관한 협정이 체결되어 있지않으므로 법률상 피. 엑스 나 콤밋사리의 제한을 요구 강제 할수없고 다만 추상적으로 미국측의 협조를 의뢰하며 또는 단속행위중 발견된

0205

중요한 사건을 통보하는 이외에는 별다른 조치를 취할수 없다는데 대체적인 의견의 일치를 보았음.

2. 또한 본건에 관하여는 이미 외정제 1.184호 (4291년 4월 19일자)로서 상달한 비율빈 에서의 미군 피. 엑스의 사용제한조치에 관한 주비율빈대사의 보고서 사본에서 보는바와같이 비율빈에서의 미군 피. 엑스의 사용은 종전에 있어서의 사용과 같다는 요지임.

상술한 점으로보아 당부로는 현재로서 본건에 관하여 별첨 안과같이 피. 엑스 나 곰밋사리의 사용제한과 물품의 횡류 방지에 협력하여달라는 요지의 서한을 주한 미대사관에 발송할수있을 정도라고 사료되옵기 동서한안 사본 1통을 이에 상달하오며 이와같이 시행함이 어떠하오리까.

별 첨

1. 본건안 1통

0206

D R A F T

April 22, 1958

Dear Mr. Ambassador:

I have the honor to refer to the Post Exchange and the Commissary which are operated and maintained by the United States Armed Forces in Korea.

It is understood that the commodities on sale at the Post Exchange or Commissary are presently free of customs duties and taxation solely for the benefit of the military personnel of the U.S. Armed Forces in Korea and their dependents. Frequently, however, the goods originated from the Post Exchange and the Commissary flow into the markets in Korea causing an adverse influence on the stabilization and the reconstruction of Korean economy.

It would be greatly appreciated if you would kindly advise the military authorities concerned to take appropriate actions to restrict possible abuses of the P.X. privileges to prevent the illegal flow of goods into the local markets with a spirit of cooperation in order to help the healthy development of Korean economy.

Sincerely yours,

His Excellency
Walter C. Dowling, Ambassador
American Embassy
Seoul

0207

Mr. K. Lee

歐

상역제九九三호

단기四二九一년五월一일

상공부장관 김일환

외무부장관 귀하

피엑스(P.X)및콤밋사리(Commissary)
사용에관한협의회개최의건

표제건 지난三월二十一일 상역국장실에서 상오 十시三十분관계자참석하에 협의회를 개최한바 있으며 각부소관 대책을 작성하여 종합안작성을위해 재차회합하도록 합의한바 있음으로 금번재차협의회를 좌기와 같이개최하고자하오니 참석하심을 경망



0208

하나이다

기

一、일시 四二九一년 五월 三일 상오 十시

一、장소 상공부 제二회의실

一、참석자

상공부 상역국장

외무부 정무국장

내무부 치안국장

재무부 세관국장

법무부 검찰국장

국방부 관리국장

추기. 대책을 지참하시기 바람

이상

0203

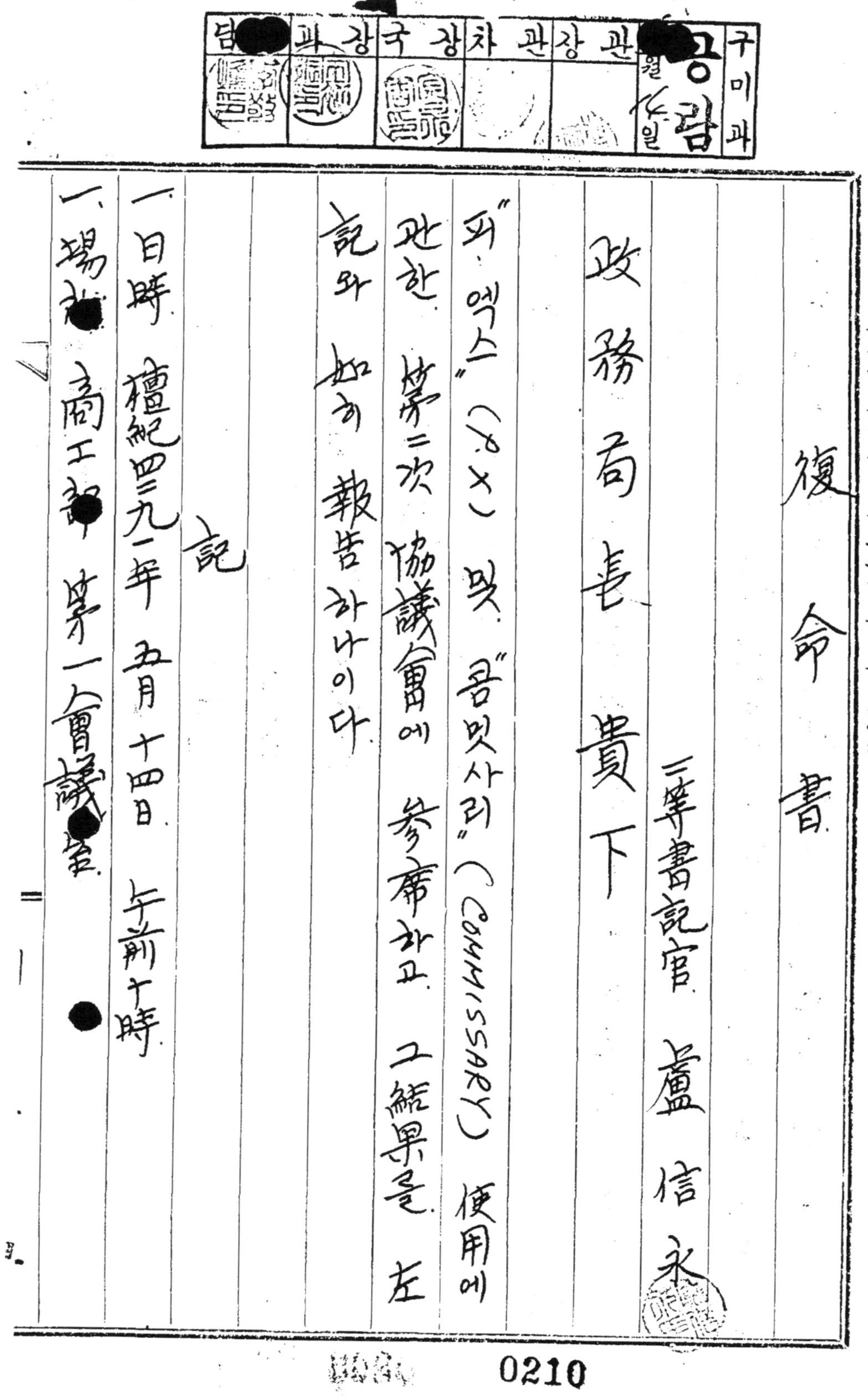
담당 | 과장 | 국장 | 차관 | 장관 | 공람 | 구미과

# 復命書

二等書記官 盧信永

政務局長 貴下

"피·엑스"(P.X) 및 "콤밋사리"(COMMISSARY) 使用에 관한 第二次 協議會에 參席하고 그 結果를 左記와 如히 報告하나이다.

記

一. 日時 檀紀四二九一年 五月 十四日 午前十時

一. 場所 商工部 第一會議室

이 용지는 국민의 세금으로써 구입된 것이다

0210

一. 參席機關

1. 外務部 政務局

2. 內務部 治安局

3. 財務部 稅關局

4. 國防部 管理局

5. 法務部 檢察局

6. 商工部 商易局

一. 討議內容

商工部 商易局長 司會로 開催된 第二次

本會議之

1. "피.엑스" 를 通하여 市場에 流出된다고 推測되는

主要商品, 特히 "洋담배" "時計" "寫眞機" "래디오" 等의

0211

出處와 流出經緯의 調査問題 및 그 數量과 額數의 算定問題 와

2. 如斯한 物品의 市場化를 造成하는 媒介手段인 美軍票의 暗去來 團束問題 및

3. 우리나라에 居住하다가 本国으로 歸国하는 外国人들이 販賣하는 免稅物品의 市場化防止問題 및

4. 本件 取扱의 円滿한 解決과 協力을 爲한 韓美間의 專門委員會構成問題 等에 관하여 長時間 討議한 結果

駐屯軍의 地位에 관한 協定이 아직 締結되어 있지 않는 現在의 우리나라 事情으로서는 P.X 에서 賣買되는 商品의 數量과 額數와 表面的이고 正確한 總体的 數

0212

字로 把握할 수가 있으며 또한 軍票의 暗去来를
積極的으로 團束하고 이미 市場에 流出된 모든 脫稅
商品의 出處를 甚하게 追窮함과 같은 行爲는
오히려 從前의 陽性的인 商去来를 陰性化할뿐 別로
效果가 없을 것이고 또한 外務部에서 抽象的인 內容의
公翰으로 P.X. 利用에 관한 美國側의 協力만을 要求한다
고 해야. 그러한 效果는 期待할수 없으리라는데 大体的인
意見의 一致를 보았으므로 基本協定이 締結되어
本件에 관한 全面的인 解決을 볼때 까지에는 우선

1. 財務, 商工, 內務의 關係各部에서 國産品愛
用에 관한 國民啓蒙運動을 展開함과 아울러
P.X로 부터 流出된 脫稅物品의 賣買,

收受는 犯罪行爲임을 認識시켜, 国民들의
自発的 協助를 要求하도록 努力하고, 併行하여
財務部에서는 如斯한 脫稅商品에 对한 課稅
問題를 硏究하고
2. 関係捜査機関에서는 市井에 큰 波紋을 이르
키지 않도록 操心하면서 如斯한 物品의 流出을
継續 团束하고
3. 团束行爲中 確証을 얻은 美国人의 犯法行爲는
이를 外務部에 通告함으로서 外務部로 하여금
美国側에 証據를 提示하고 抗議할수 있게 한다
는 結論에 到達하였고
本會議의 結果는 商工部에서 一括하여 이를 景武台에



0214

報告하기로 한後, 散會하였음.

0215

외 무 부

NOT ADOPTED

년 월 일

SEP 19 1958

This Memorandum was orally presented by Vice-Foreign Minister Dong Jo Kim to His Excellency the President on September 19, 1958 at Kyung Mu Dai. His Excellency disapproved the "Points of View contained in the said Memorandum. ~~His Excellency~~ stated that we should request an agreement on 'jurisdiction'.

0216

MEMORANDUM KPO/101

관리 번호
6

REPUBLIC OF KOREA

MINISTRY OF FOREIGN AFFAIRS

September 18, 1958

MEMORANDUM FOR THE OFFICE OF THE PRESIDENT

1. U.S. Ambassador Walter C. Dowling called on Vice-Foreign Minister Dong Jo Kim at the latter's office at 5:00 p.m., September 18, 1958 to convey the view of the Department of State on the issue of the proposed Agreement on Status of U.S. Forces in Korea, which has been pending since these four years between the two Governments.

2. Before entering discussion on the main subject, Mr. Dowling wanted to exchange views on prospect of the Korea-Japan talks though he expressed nothing new. Then, he stated that U.S. Secretary of State Dulles, in his speech made at the U.N. forum today, delivered U.S. viewpoints straight out particularly on the problems of admission of the Republic of Korea into the United Nations, Formosa straits situation, etc.

3. Turning to the main subject, Ambassador Dowling delivered the following points of view from Washington:

A) Though there is no actual shooting now in Korea, the current situation is rather deemed as a state of cessation of hostilities, complete state of peace being yet to be resumed. Under this situation, time has not yet come when the two Governments have talks to define status of forces under the United Nations

/Command, accordingly

0217

Command, accordingly, what is related to jurisdiction of the said Command.

B) However, this is not to prevent the two Governments from exploring the possibility of reaching agreements on such problems as of purely administrative nature, unless it touches upon the problem of the 'jurisdiction of the Command' [by the term, 'jurisdiction' he had in mind 'criminal jurisdiction' ]; such problems may include enforcement of customs regulations, taxation, entry and exit of personnel, etc.

C) After an exploratory talks for defining the scope of terms, agreements may be reached in the form of Memorandum of Understanding, Exchange of Notes and so on, and such agreements would surely serve further promotion of friendly relations existing between the two nations.

D) But, the U.S. side is suggesting the above on condition that the Korean side will not further propose negotiation for an agreement on jurisdiction of the Command, as next step. so long as the present circumstances in Koreancontinue to prevail; therefore, if the negotiation is to be commenced, the U.S. desires that the two Governments issue a Joint Statement to put in record a clear-cut understanding to that effect.

E) He (Ambassador Dowling) is now authorized to start talks with the Korean side for this purpose; if the Korean side concurs with U.S., negotiation can be

/commenced after

0218

commenced after his return from trip to Japan which will be made from 21 to 25 September 1958.

4. Vice-Minister Kim told Mr. Dowling that he would study the U.S. suggestion.

POINTS OF VIEW NOT ADOPTED

1. It has been our anxious desire to expedite the conclusion of Agreement on Status of U.S. Forces in Korea since we first proposed it to the United States in 1954. From the beginning, the proposal was not favorably reacted. But it has been also our policy to settle even partially the problems which arise from the stationing of foreign armed forces in Korea.

2. Therefore, the U.S. suggestion conveyed by Ambassador Dowling on September 18, 1958 marked a step forward in the direction of the settlement of the problem long-pending between the two Governments. There is no reason why we should not respond to the U.S. suggestion.

3. However, it is not advisable for our Government to join the U.S. in issuing a statement to the effect that we will never enter talks for conclusion of agreement on criminal jurisdiction of U.S. military personnel, because it may bring a great disappointment to our people while such statement is tantamount to perpetuating legally the validity of Korea-U.S. Agreement on Criminal Jurisdiction of U.S. Military Personnel which was signed at Taejon in July, 1950.

4. In view of the above, ~~it~~ would be advisable for us to commence ~~talks~~ by ~~assuring~~ orally what the U.S. wishes to be assured instead of issuing a Joint Statement.

0213

MEMORANDUM
for
the Office of the President

(Recent development of the problem of the proposed Agreement on Status of U.S. Forces in Korea)

1. It has been our anxious desire to expedite the conclusion of an Agreement on Status of U.S. Forces in Korea since we first proposed it to the United States in 1954. From the beginning, the proposal was not favorably reacted.

2. It was on October 10, 1957 that the U.S. Government, through Ambassador Dowling's conversation with Foreign Minister Cho, conveyed its view to us that "there might be room for reaching a sepearte agreement on particular items as was done in the utilities problems." In response to this suggestion, Foreign Minister, in his letter to Ambassador Dowling dated November 13, 1957, said that he would be "very happy to proceed with negotiations for separate agreements with the U.S. Government on particular items; for instance, taxation, customs duty, and criminal jurisdiction." In his letter of November 26, 1957, Foreign Minister Cho paraphrased his letter of November 13, 1957 enclosing a memorandum which clarified the Korean position on the issue.

3. Foreign Minister Cho's letter of November 26, 1957 was acknowledged by Mr. T. Eliot Weil, Charge d'Affaires a.i. of the American Embassy in Seoul

/though he

0220

though he reserved comments at that time pending consideration by the Washington authorities.

4. It was on September 18, 1958 that Ambassador Dowling called on Foreign Minister Cho, and orally delivered the view from Washington on the possibility of negotiation for conclusion of separate agreement. The points were:

A) Though there is no actual shooting now in Korea, the current situation is rather deemed as a state of cessation of hostilities, complete state of peace being yet to be resumed. Under this situation, time has not yet come when the two Governments have talks to define status of forces under the United Nations Command, accordingly, what is related to jurisdiction of the said Command.

B) However, this is not to prevent the two Governments from exploring the possibility of reaching agreements on such problems as of purely administrative nature, unless it touches upon the problem of the 'jurisdiction of the Command' /by the term, 'jurisdiction' he had in mind 'criminal jurisdiction'/; such problems may include enforcement of customs regulations, taxation, entry and exit of personnel, etc.

C) After an exploratory talks for defining the scope of terms agreements may be reached in the form of Memorandum of Understanding,

Exchange of

0221

Exchange of Notes and so on, and such agreements would surely serve further promotion of friendly relations existing between the two nations.

D) But, the U.S. side is suggesting the above if it is mutually understood that the Korean side will not further propose negotiation for an agreement on jurisdiction of the Command, as next step, so long as the present circumstances in Korea continue to prevail.

E) He (Ambassador Dowling) is now authorized to start talks with the Korean side for this purpose; if the Korean side concurs with the U.S., negotiation can be commenced after his return from trip to Japan which will be made from 21 to 25 September 1958.

5. On the same day (September 18, 1958), Ambassador Dowling, in his meeting with Vice-Minister Dong Jo Kim at the latter's office, repeated what he delivered to Foreign Minister Cho.

6. On September 19, 1958, the contents of the above-mentioned U.S. representation were orally reported to His Excellency the President at Kyung Mu Dai. Upon receipt of this report, His Excellency expressed a great deal of dissatisfaction over the U.S. view, particularly over the point that the U.S. was trying to exclude the possibility of concluding eventually an agreement on criminal jurisdiction of U.S. forces in Korea thus claiming 'extraterritorial right'. His Excellency also wondered why the U.S. was so reluctant to conclude a full agreement on status of force while it has already entered such relations with other nations.

0222

/7. U.S.

7. The U.S. suggestion of September 18, 1958 is informal in its form, but is a reply to our position of November 26, 1957. The suggestion partly meets our position but is still unsatisfactory as it urges us to give up the possibility of concluding an agreement on criminal jurisdiction of military personnel. If the understanding is reached between the two Governments as the U.S. urges, it would be tantamount to perpetuating legally the validity of the Korea-U.S. modus vivendi on criminal jurisdiction of U.S. military personnel which was signed at Taejon in July, 1950.

일반문서로 재분류
(협정 체결시)

0223

## 주한 미 주둔군의 지위에 관한 한미간의 협정 체결을 위한 교섭 경위

<1958.9.>

1. 협정의 목적

국제연합 안전보장이사회의 1950년 6월 25일, 6월 27일 및 7월 7일자 결의에 의거하여 통합사령부하에 국제연합군이 한국에 주둔하고 있으나, 1953년 7월27일자로 휴전협정이 체결되어 한국에서의 실제 전투는 중지되고 군사작전에 수반되는 긴박상태가 완화되었음으로 국제연합군의 한국내 배치에 수반되는 제문제에 관하여 아국 국민과 국제연합군 인원간의 오해를 최소한으로 감소하고, 협조성을 최고로 증진시키기 위하여 아국정부와 통합사령부로서 행동하는 미합중국간에 주한 미주둔군의 지위에 관한 한미간의 협정을 체결하기 위한 교섭이 개시되었다.

2. 협정 체결을 위한 교섭 경위

1) 4286년 8월 7일자 이대통령과 덜레스 국무장관의 공동성명에서 "....... 우리 양국정부는 한미상호 방위조약이 발효케 된 이후 미국이 한국에 주둔하게 될 군대의 지위 그리고 또한 우리들의 공동사업을 수행하는데 필요한 한국측 시설과 인원의 사용에 관한 협약을 즉시 상의하고저 한다. 그동안 한편으로 한국은 계속 국제연합군 사령부와 협력할 것이며 한국에 있는 국제연합군의 지위와 그들에 대한 한국측 시설 및 인원의 사용은 현재대로 계속 될 것이다..." 고 천명하여 주둔군의 지위에 관한 한미간의 협정 체결의 기

0224

58 - 21 - 2 (6)

미문 00-4(6)

0225

운이 공표되었다.

2) 4287년 12월 2일 조 외무부장관은 주한 미국대사 앞으로의 공한에서 "국제연합군의 한국 주둔에 관한 한미간의 협정 체결"을 제의하였다.

3) 4288년 1월 27일 주한 미국대사는 외무부장관 앞으로의 공한에서, 전기 제의를 접수한 당시 이미 국제연합 통합사령부에서는 이 문제에 관한 자발적인 검토를 하고 있다고 말하였음.

4) 4288년 4월 28일 조 외무부장관은 주한 미국 대리대사 앞으로의 공한에서 재한 미 주둔군의 지위에 관하여 한미간의 협정을 체결하고 국제연합군의 지위에 관한 여러가지 문제를 해결할 것을 제의하였다.

5) 동년 5월 9일자로 미국대사는 전기 한국정부의 제안을 본국정부에 전달 하였다는 것을 회보하여 왔음.

6) 그후 오랫동안 기다렸으나 아무런 반응을 보이지 않음으로 4290년 1월 5일자로 외무부장관은 미국대사 앞으로 공한을 보내어 교섭개시를 독촉하는 동시에 국제연합군 전 가맹국과의 교섭이 시간을 요한다면 대한민국과 미합중국간의 단독협정으로 체결할 것을 제의하였음.

7) 이에 대하여 동년 1월 15일자로 미국대사는 공한을 보내와 본국정부의 훈령이 없어 아직 대기중이라고 하였음.

8) 동년 6월 29일자로 외무부장관은 미국대사앞으로의 공한에서 이 문제의 해결을 위한 교섭개시를 재차 독촉하였음.

9) 이에 대하여 동년 7월 1일자로 미국대사는 외무부

0226

58 — 21 — 2

미·문 90-4

0227

장관 앞으로의 회한에서 본국정부로 부터 검토중이라는 훈령을 받았음을 통고하여 왔음.

10) 이와같이 미국측의 반응이 미온적임에 우리정부는 때마침 우리나라를 방문한 "허 터 " 국무차관에게 제차 이문제를 강력히 촉구하였음. (4290년 9월 10일)

11) 동년 11월 13일자로 외무부장관은 주한 미국대사에게 공한을 발송하여 " 4290년 10월 10일 외무부장관실에서 미국대사가 청구권문제와 같이 부분적협정으로 하고, 전면적협정을 지양하는 것이 오히려 편리할 것이라고 말한것을, 환영하는 바이며 따라서 우리나라 정부는 과세, 관세, 형사재판 관활권문제 등으로 구분하여 협정체결을 하기를 원한다는" 뜻을 표명하였다.

12) 동년 11월 26일에는 외무부장관이 다시 미국 대리대사에게 각서를 통하여, "구매, 과세, 관세에 관한 협정, 주둔군에 관련되는 청구권 청산협정, 주둔군에 의하여 사용되는 시설 및 지역에 관한 협정, 출입국에 관한 협정, 형사재판 관활권에 관한 협정" 으로 분리하여 협정을 체결할 것을 제의하였음.

13) 4290년 12월 3일자로 미국대사는 전기 각서를 본국정부에 송달하였다는 회한을 보내왔음.

14) 최근의 진전상황

위에서 말한 바와 같이 미국측의 반응이 미미하다가 금년(4291년) 9월 18일 미국대사가 외무부장관을 방문하고 미국정부의 의견을 구두로 개진하였는 바 그 내용은

가) 전후상태는 중지되었으나 이것은 전투상태의 중지에 불과한 것이고 완전한 평화상태는 아니며, 따라서 아직 양국정부간에서

0228

58-21-10

58 - 21 -2

미운 PO-4

0229

주둔군의 지위에 관한 협정을 위한 교섭시기가 되지 않았다고 본다는 것,

나) 재판관할권 이외의 것에 관한 것, 즉 순전히 행정적인 문제에 관한 것만 띄어서 협정을 체결한다면, 응할 용이가 있다는 것,

다) 이러한 순전히 행정적인 문제에관한 것이라고 하드라도 협정이라는 형식을 취하지 아니하고 양해각서, 교환각서의 형식으로 하자는 것,

라) 단 순전히 행정적인 문제에 관한 해결을 지은 다음에는 관할권에 관한 것은 일단 재언급 하지 말것을 조건으로 양해하여 달라는 것,

마) 위의 여러가지 조건에 우리정부가 동의 한다면, 곧 교섭을 개시할 용이가 있다는 것,

등을 제의하여 왔으나 이는 주둔군의 지위에 관한 문제 중 가장 중요한 형사재판 관할권 문제를 제외하려는 점으로 인하여 우리측에서는 지극히 불만족적인 것이라고 하지 않을 수 없다. 따라서 의일 위의 교섭경위를 대통령 각하에게 구두로 진언하였든 바 대통령께서도 이에 대하여 불만을 표시하였다.

그러면, 미국은 왜 우리나라와의 재판관할권 문제에 관하여 고집을 세우며, 다른나라와는 관할권 문제에 관하여 어떠한 관계에 있는 가를 고찰하여 보려고 한다. 0230

3. 미국의 입장의 근거 및 타국과의 관계 협정체결 현황

1) 미국이 이러한 입장을 취하는 근거

18-21-11

58 - 21-2

0231

미국의 일부 입법인사는 미국군대가 세계의 어떤곳에 가든지 항상 미국국기와 미국헌법의 보호를 받으며, 더욱이 국제법상 주둔군은 피주둔국의 형사재판관할권으로 부터 면제된다는 원칙이 있다고 생각하고 있다. 이러한 생각은 NATO 협정에 대하여 상원이 비준동의를 할때에도, 이협정을 선례로 하지 않겠다는 것등 네가지에 걸친 양해사항이 있었다는 점에서 보아도 현저한 것이다. 그 후에도 미국의 하원에서는 매년 "대통령은 외국법정에 의한 미국군대의 재판권을 인정하는 현행협정을 개정 또는 폐기하여야 한다"는 내용의 문제가 외교위원회에서 논의되든중 작년 6월27일에는 하원외교위원회에서 18대 8로 이 문제에 대한 결의안을 채택하여 결국 본회의에 까지 상정하였던 것이다. 본회의에서는 비록 134대 134로 부결되기는 하였으나 아직 이 문제는 완전히 해결되었다고 볼수없고 더욱이 우리나라와 같이 주둔군의 지위에 관한 협정을 체결할 단계에 있는 입장에서는 예단을 불허하는 바 있다.

2. 협사재판권에 관한 규정을 가진 협정의 현황

1) 미국이 체결 또는 가입한 협정중 주둔군의 지위에 관한 규정을 두고 있는 것은 다음과 같다. (도표 1참조)

2) 협정의 운영상황(도표 2 참조)

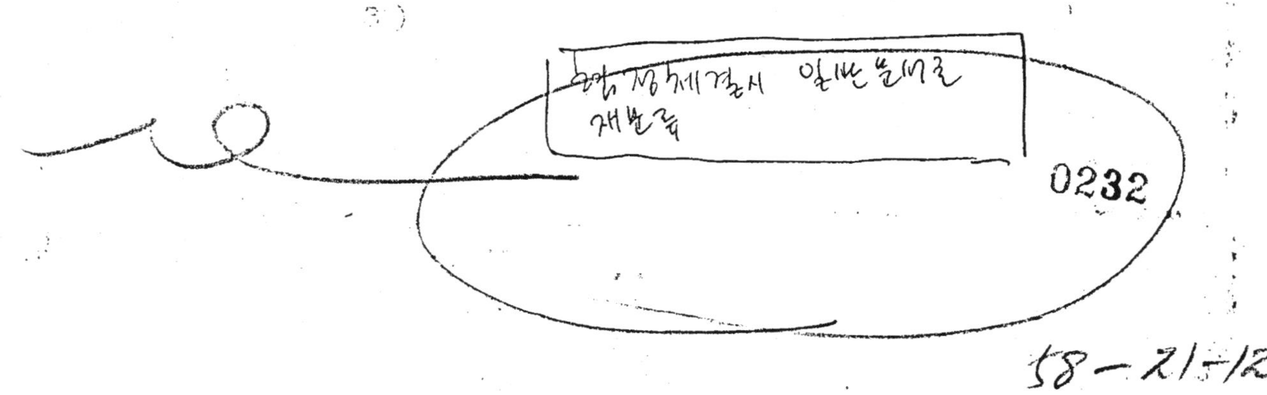


0232

58-21-12

58 - 21 - 2

미관 90-4

0233

도표 1

1. 피주둔국과 주둔군이 경합 재판권을 가지는 협정 당사국

가) NAAOT O 행정협정 당사국( Belgium, Canada, Denmark, France, Great Britain, Greece, Italy, Luxembourg, Netherlands, Norway, Portugal, Turkey,

나) 일본

합계 13개국

2. 주둔군의 전속 재판권을 인정한 협정 당사국

가) 주둔군과의 개별협정에서 전속 재판권이 인정된 당사국
Ethiopia, Iceland, Korea, Libya, Saudi Arabia.

나) 군사고문단의 설치와 군사고문단에 대한 전속 재판권을 인정한 당사국

0234 Bolivia, Brazil, Burma, Chile, China, Colombia, Costa Rica, Cuba, Ecuador, El Salvador, Guatemala, Haiti, Honduras, Vietnam, Indonesia, Iran, Iraq, Liberia, Nicaragua, Pakistan, Panama, Paraguay, Peru, Spain, Thailand, Urguay, Venezuela, Yugoslavia,

이하 제외

합계 33개국

83—[illegible] [illegible] (1019)

日本及びNATO協定発効国に駐留する合衆国軍隊に対する刑事裁判権行使状況一覧表

(本一覧表は，合衆国陸軍法務当局の資料に基くものである。なお各年度とも一月ないし一二月の合計であるが，一九五六年度のみは，一月ないし六月の合計である)

| 国名及び協定発効日 | 駐留国の裁判権に属する事件 | | | | | 駐留国による裁判 | | | | | 懲役または禁錮刑の判決のあったもの | | | | | 懲役または禁錮刑で執行猶予とならなかったもの | | | | |
|---|---|---|---|---|---|---|---|---|---|---|---|---|---|---|---|---|---|---|---|---|
| | 1953 | 1954 | 1955 | 1956 | 計 | 1953 | 1954 | 1955 | 1956 | 計 | 1953 | 1954 | 1955 | 1956 | 計 | 1953 | 1954 | 1955 | 1956 | 計 |
| ベルギー (1953年8月23日) | 1 | 20 | 7 | 9 | 37 | 1 | 0 | 2 | 1 | 4 | 1 | 0 | 1 | 0 | 2 | 0 | 0 | 0 | 0 | 0 |
| カナダ (1953年9月27日) | 2 | 312 | 505 | 242 | 1,061 | 0 | 249 | 426 | 159 | 834 | 0 | 6 | 0 | 0 | 6 | 0 | 6 | 0 | 0 | 6 |
| デンマーク (1955年6月27日) | … | 0 | 0 | 0 | 0 | … | … | 0 | 0 | 0 | … | … | 0 | 0 | 0 | … | … | 0 | 0 | [illegible] |
| フランス (1953年8月23日) | 267 | 2,600 | 3,172 | 1,902 | 7,941 | 21 | 283 | 439 | 251 | 994 | 17 | 75 | 92 | 49 | 233 | 15 | 31 | 28 | 17 | 91 |
| ギリシア (1955年7月26日) | … | 0 | 0 | 0 | 0 | … | 0 | 0 | 0 | 0 | … | 0 | 0 | 0 | 0 | … | 0 | 0 | 0 | 0 |
| イタリー (1956年1月21日) | … | … | … | 25 | 25 | … | … | … | 16 | 16 | … | … | … | 6 | 6 | … | … | … | 0 | 0 |
| ルクセンブルグ (1954年7月23日) | … | 0 | 27 | 22 | 49 | … | 0 | 6 | 8 | 14 | … | 0 | 0 | 1 | 1 | … | 0 | 0 | 0 | 1 |
| オランダ (1953年8月23日) | 2 | 5 | 11 | 20 | 38 | 0 | 1 | 0 | 1 | 2 | 0 | 1 | 0 | 0 | 1 | 0 | 1 | 0 | 0 | 0 |
| ノルウェー (1953年8月23日) | 0 | 1 | 2 | 5 | 8 | 0 | 0 | 1 | 1 | 2 | 0 | 0 | 0 | 0 | 0 | 0 | 0 | 0 | 0 | [illegible] |
| ポルトガル (1955年11月22日) | … | … | … | 0 | 0 | … | … | … | 0 | 0 | … | … | … | 0 | 0 | [illegible] | [illegible] | [illegible] | 0 | [illegible] |
| トルコ (1954年6月17日) | … | 12 | 18 | 15 | 45 | … | 8 | 12 | 9 | 29 | … | 2 | 3 | [illegible] | 9 | [illegible] | 0 | 1 | 1 | 2 |
| イギリス (1954年1月13日) | … | 492 | 1,235 | 1,065 | 2,792 | … | 271 | 1,225 | 900 | 2,396 | … | 6 | 32 | 18 | 56 | … | 6 | 37 | 13 | 56 |
| 日本 (1953年10月28日) | 0 | 3,056 | 3,937 | 2,675 | 9,712 | 0 | 107 | 178 | 44 | 329 | 0 | 64 | 100 | 16 | 176 | 0 | 25 | 47 | 4 | 76 |
| 合計 | [illegible] | 6,492 | 8,964 | [illegible] | 21,708 | 22 | 919 | [illegible] | [illegible] | [illegible] | 18 | 156 | [illegible] | 91 | 490 | 15 | 69 | 107 | [illegible] | 226 |

58-21-13

58-21-2 (6) 미문 PO-4 (6)

0235

주한 미 주둔군의 지위에 관한 한미간의
협정 체결을 위한 교섭 경위

1. 협정의 목적

국제연합 안전보장이사회의 1950년 6월 25일, 6월 27일 및 7월 7일자 결의에 의거하여 통합사령부하에 국제연합군이 한국에 주둔하고 있으나, 1953년 7월27일자로 휴전협정이 체결되어 한국에서의 실제 전투는 중지되고 군사작전에 수반되는 긴박상태가 완화되었음으로 국제연합군의 한국내 배치에 수반되는 제문제에 관하여 아국 국민과 국제연합군 인원간의 오해를 최소한으로 감소하고, 협조성을 최고로 증진시키기 위하여 아국정부와 통합사령부로서 행동하는 미합중국간에 주한 미주둔군의 지위에 관한 한미간의 협정을 체결하기 위한 교섭이 개시되었다.

2. 협정 체결을 위한 교섭 경위

1) 4286년 8월 7일자 이대통령과 덜레스 국무장관의 공동성명에서 "....... 우리 양국정부는 한미상호 방위조약 위조약이 발효케 된 이후 미국이 한국에 주둔하게 될 군대의 지위 그리고 또한 우리들의 공동사업을 수행하는데 필요한 한국측 시설과 인원의 사용에 관한 협약을 즉시 상의하고저 한다. 그동안 한편으로 한국은 계속 국제연합군 사령부와 협력할 것이며 한국에 있는 국제연합군의 지위와 그들에 대한 한국측 시설 및 인원의 사용은 현재대로 계속 될 것이다..." 고 천명하여 주둔군의 지위에 관한 한미간의 협정 체결의 기

0236

윤이 공포되었다.

2) 4287년 12월 8일 조 외무부장관은 주한 미국대사 앞으로의 공한에서 "국제연합군의 한국 세관업무에 관한 한미간의 협정 체결"을 제의하였다.

3) 4288년 1월 27일 주한 미국대사는 외무부 장관 앞으로의 공한에서 전기 제의를 접수한 당시 이미 국제연합 통합사령부에서는 이 문제에 관한 자발적인 검토를 하고 있다고 말하였음.

4) 4288년 4월 2°일 조 외무부장관은 주한 미국 대리대사 앞으로의 공한에서 재한 미 주둔군의 지위에 관하여 한미간의 협정을 체결하고 국제연합군의 지위에 관한 여러가지 문제를 해결할 것을 제의하였다.

5) 동년 65월 9일자로 미국대사는 전기 한국정부의 제안을 본국정부에 전달 하였다는 것을 회보하여 왔음.

6) 그후 오랫동안 기다렸으나 아무런 반응을 보이지 않음으로 4290년 1월 5일자로 외무부장관은 미국대사 앞으로 공한을 보내어 교섭개시를 독촉하는 동시에 국제연합군 전 가맹국과의 교섭이 시간을 요한다면 대한민국과 미합중국간의 단독협정으로 체결할 것을 제의하였음.

7) 이에 대하여 동년 1월 15일자로 미국대사는 공한을 보내와 본국정부의 훈령이 없어 아직 대기중이라고 하였음.

8) 동년 6월 29일자로 외무부장관은 미국대사앞으로의 공한에서 이 문제의 해결을 위한 교섭개시를 재차 독촉하였음. 0237

9) 이에 대하여 동년 7월 1일자로 미국대사는 외무부

장관 앞으로의 회한에서 ~~본국정부로 부터 지호중이라는~~ 훈령을 받았음을 통고하여 왔음.

10) 이와같이 미국측의 반응이 미온적임에 우리정부는 때마짐 우리나라를 방문한 "허 터 " 국무차관에게 제차 이문제를 강력히 촉구하였음. (4290년 9월 10일)

11) 동년 11월 13일자로 외무부장관은 주한 미국대사에게 공한을 발송하여 " 4290년 10월 10일 외무부장관실에서 미국대사가 청구권문제와 같이 부분적협정으로 하고 전면적협정을 지양하는 것이 오히려 편리할 것이라고 말한것을 환영하는 바이며 따라서 우리나라 정부는 과세, 관세, 형사재판 관할권문제 등으로 구분하여 협정체결을 하기를 원한다는" 뜻을 표명하였다.

12) 동년 11월 26일에는 외무부장관이 다시 미국 대리대사에게 각서를 송하여, "구매, 과세, 관세에 관한 협정, 주둔군에 관련되는 청구권 청산협정, 주둔군에 의하여 사용되는 시설 및 지역에 관한 협정, 출입국에 관한 협정, 형사재판 관할권에 관한 협정" 으로 분리하여 협정을 체결할 것을 제의하였음.

13) 4290년 12월 3일자로 미국대사는 전기 각서를 본국정부에 송달하였다는 회한을 보내왔음.

14) 최근의 진전상황

위에서 말한 바와 같이 미국측의 반응이 미더하다가 금년(4291년) 9월 18일 미국대사가 외무부장관을 방문하고 미국정부의 의견을 구두로 개진하였는 바 그 내용은

가) 전후상태는 ~~종지되었으나~~ 이것은 전후상태의 중지에 불과한 것이고 완전한 평화상태는 아니며 ~~따라서~~ (아직) 양국정부간에서

0238

주둔군의 지위에 관한 협정을 위한 교섭시기까지 [도래히] [완왔]다고 본다는 것,

나) 재판관할권 이외의 것에 관한 것, 즉 순전히 행정적인 문제에 관한 것만 띄어서 협정을 체결한다면, 응할 용이가 있다는 것,

다) 이러한 순전히 행정적인 문제에관한 것이라고 하드라도 협정이라는 형식을 취하지 아니하고 양해각서, 교환각서의 형식으로 하자는 것,

라) 단 순전히 행정적인 문제에 관한 해결을 지운다음에는 관할권에 관한 것은 일단 재언급 하지 말것을 조건으로 양해하여 달라는 것,

마) 위의 여러가지 조건에 우리정부가 동의 한다면, 곧 교섭을 개시할 용이가 있다는 것,

등을 제의하여 왔으나 이는 주둔군의 지위에 관한 문제중 가장 중요한 형사재판 관할권 문제를 제외하려는 점으로 인하여 우리측에서는 지극히 불만족적인 것이라고 하지 않을 수 없다. 따라서 익일 위의 교섭경위를 대통령 각하에게 구두로 진언하였든 바 대통령께서도 이에 대하여 불만을 표시하였다.

그러면, 미국은 왜 우리나라와의 재판관할권 문제에 관하여 고집을 세우며, 다른나라와는 관할권 문제에 관하여 어떠한 관계에 있는 가를 고찰하여 보려고 한다.

3. 미국의 입장의 근거 및 미국의 관계 협정체결 현황

1) 미국이 이러한 입장을 취하는 근거

0239

미국에서는 해외에 파견된 군대에 대하여 피주둔국의 형사재판 관할권을 인정하면, 주둔군 인원은 미국의 헌법상의 보장을 못받게 되는 것이 아니냐, 둘째로 그러한 협정자체가 무효라고 하는 것인 바 이와같은 협정 폐기론 및 무효론은 미국 국회에서 문제화되어 작년 6월 27일자로 미국 하원의 외교위원회는 "대통령은 외국법정에 의한 미국군대의 재판권을 인정한 주둔군의 지위에 관한 협정이 개정 또는 폐기를 도모하여야 한다"는 결의안을 18대 8로 가결하여 행정부에 대하여 압력을 가하고 있는 바이며, 이 이전에 행정협정에 대하여 비준동의 할 때에도 형사재판권조항은 이후의 선례로 하지 않을 것, 피주둔군의 법령을 검토할것, 가능한 한 피주둔군의 재판권 포기를 요청할 것, 미국정부의 대표는 언제나 그러한 재판에 입회할 것, 등을 조건으로 한 점에서 보아도 미국이 자국군대의 전속재판권을 얼마나 강력하게 주장하고 있는 가를 알수있다.

2) 미국이 행정협정을 체결하고 있는 나라

현재 미국은 자유진영 49개국과 주둔군의 지위에 관한 협정을 체결하고 있는 바 그 내용을 보면 다음과 같다. (도표 1 참조)

0240

허버드 로우 리뷰에 나타난 미국과 피주둔국과의 사이에 체결한 협정의 운용상황 통계(도표2 참조)에 의하면, 해외에 주둔하는 미국군대의 범행으로서 피주둔국의 재판관할권에 속하는 것 [illegible] 건중 당해국가가 재판권을 행사한 것은 4,620으로서 불과 20%에 불과한 형편으로 미국의 태도는 이 통계만 보아도 분명히 알수 있다.

도표 1 미국군대의 지위에 관한 협정 체결 현황

| | |
|---|---|
| 군대의 지위에 관한 NATO 당사국간의 協定 | 白耳義, 佛蘭西, 諾威, 加奈陀, 丁抹, 룩셈불그, 和蘭, 英伊, 土耳其, 希臘, (10個國) |
| 美日行政協定 | 日本. (1個國) |
| 其他 美駐屯軍에 對하여 專屬裁判權을 認定하는 協定을 締結한 國家 | 韓國, 볼리비아, 브라질, 버-마, 치리, 中國, 코롬비아, 코스타리카, 큐-바, 에쿠아돌, 엘사바돌, 에치오피아, 希臘, 과테마라, 하이티, 혼쥬라스, 아이스랜드, 印度, 이란, 이락, 伊, 리베리아, 리비아, 멕시코, 니카라과, 파키스탄, 파나마, 파라과이, 페루, 比, 포도갈, 사우디 아라비아, 스페인, 泰, 우루과이, 베네주에라, 유-고스라비아, 越南, (38個國). |

日本及びNATO協定[illegible]国に駐留する[illegible]

(本一覧表は、[illegible]いし一二月の合計であるが、一九五六年[illegible]のみは、一月ないし[illegible])

| 国名 | 協定発効日 | 駐留国の裁判権に属する事件 | | | | | 駐留国による裁判 | | | | | 懲役または禁錮刑の判決のあったもの | | | | | [illegible] | | | |
|---|---|---|---|---|---|---|---|---|---|---|---|---|---|---|---|---|---|---|---|---|
| | | 1953 | 1954 | 1955 | 1956 | 計 | 1953 | 1954 | 1955 | 1956 | 計 | 1953 | 1954 | 1955 | 1956 | 計 | 1953 | 1954 | 1955 | 1956 |
| ベルギー | (1953 8月23日) | 1 | 20 | 7 | 9 | 37 | 1 | 0 | 2 | 1 | 4 | 1 | 0 | 1 | 0 | 2 | [illegible] | 0 | 0 | [illegible] |
| カナダ | (1953 9月27日) | 2 | 312 | 505 | 242 | 1,061 | 0 | 249 | 426 | 159 | 834 | 0 | 6 | 0 | 0 | 6 | 0 | 6 | 0 | 0 |
| デンマーク | (1955 6月27日) | … | 0 | 0 | 0 | 0 | … | … | 0 | 0 | 0 | … | … | 0 | 0 | 0 | … | … | 0 | 0 |
| フランス | (1953 8月23日) | 267 | 2,606 | 3,172 | 1,962 | 7,941 | 21 | 283 | 439 | 251 | 994 | 17 | 73 | 92 | 47 | 233 | 15 | 31 | 28 | [illegible] |
| ギリシア | (1956 7月26日) | … | 0 | 0 | 0 | 0 | … | 0 | 0 | 0 | 0 | … | 0 | 0 | 0 | 0 | … | 0 | 0 | 0 |
| イタリー | (1956 1月21日) | … | … | … | 25 | 25 | … | … | … | 16 | 16 | … | … | … | 6 | 6 | … | … | … | 0 |
| ルクセンブルグ | (1954 7月23日) | … | 0 | 27 | 22 | 49 | … | 0 | 6 | 8 | 14 | … | 0 | 0 | 1 | 1 | … | 1 | 0 | 0 |
| オランダ | (1953 8月23日) | 2 | 5 | 11 | 20 | 38 | 0 | 1 | 0 | 1 | 2 | 0 | 1 | 0 | 0 | 1 | 0 | 1 | 1 | 0 |
| ノルウェー | (1953 8月23日) | 0 | 1 | 2 | 5 | 8 | 0 | 0 | 1 | 1 | 2 | 0 | 0 | 0 | 0 | 0 | 0 | 0 | 0 | 0 |
| ポルトガル | (1955 12月22日) | … | … | … | 0 | 0 | … | … | … | 0 | 0 | … | … | … | 0 | 0 | … | … | … | [illegible] |
| トルコ | (1954 6月17日) | … | 12 | 18 | 15 | 45 | … | 8 | 12 | 9 | 29 | … | 2 | 3 | [illegible] | [illegible] | … | 0 | [illegible] | [illegible] |
| イギリス | (1954 1月13日) | … | 492 | 1,235 | 1,065 | 2,792 | … | 271 | 1,225 | [illegible] | 2,396 | … | 6 | 32 | [illegible] | 53 | … | 6 | 51 | [illegible] |
| 日本 | (1953 10月28日) | 0 | 3,030 | 3,987 | 2,675 | 9,712 | 0 | 107 | 178 | 44 | 329 | 0 | [illegible] | 160 | [illegible] | [illegible] | [illegible] | [illegible] | 47 | [illegible] |
| 計 | | 27[illegible] | 6,4[illegible] | [illegible] | 5,9[illegible] | [illegible] | 22 | 91[illegible] | [illegible] | [illegible] | [illegible] | [illegible] | [illegible] | [illegible] | [illegible] | [illegible] | [illegible] | [illegible] | [illegible] | [illegible] |

1958. 9. 末日

MEMORANDUM
for
the Office of the President

(Recent development of the problem of the proposed Agreement on Status of U.S. Forces in Korea)

미군지위협정 2차 보고 1962. 2. 1

I. It has been our anxious desire to expedite the conclusion of an Agreement on Status of U. S. Forces in Korea since we first proposed it to the United States in 1954. From the beginning, the proposal was not favorably reacted.

2. It was on October 10, 1957 that U. S. Govenmnt, through Ambassxador Dowlings conversation wit Foreign Minister Cho, conveyed its view to us that " there might be room for reaching a separate ageeement on particlu lar items as was done in the utilities problems." In response to this suggestion, Foreign Minister, in his letter to Ambassador Dowling dated November 13, 1957, said that he wouod be "very happy to proceed with negotiations separtate agreements with the US Govenment on particluar itemsl for instance, taxation, custpms duty, and criminal jurisdiction." In his letter of Nov. 26, 1957, Foreign Minister Cho paraphrased his letter of Vevember 13, 1957, enclosing a memorandum which claraified the Korean position on the issue.

3. Foreign Minister Cho's letter of Novemeber 26, 1957 was acknowledged by Mr. T. Eliot Weil, Charge d'Affaires a. i. of the American Embassy in Seoul though he reserved comments at htat time pending consideration by the Washington authroties.

4. It was on September 18, 1958 that Ambassador Dowling called on Foreign Minister Cho, and orally delivered the view form Washington on the possibility of negoviation for conclusion of separate agreement.

0242

The points were;

A) Though tere is no actual shooting now in Korea, the

currentsituation is rather deemed as s state of cessation of hostilities, complete state of peace being yet to be resumed. Under this situation, time has not yet come when the two Governements have talks to define status of forces under the United Nations Command, accordingly, what is related to jursidiction of the said Command.

B) Howefer, this is not to prevent the two Governments from exploring the possibility of reaching agreements on such problems as of purely administrative nature, unless it touches upon the probl em of 'jurisdiction of the Comamand' [by the term, 'jurisdiction' he had in mind 'criminal jurisdiction']; such problems may include enforcement of cusmtoms regulations, taxation, enty and exit of personnel, etc.

C) After an exploratory talks for defining the scope of terms, Agreemens may be reached in the form of Memorandum of Understanding, Exchange of Notes and so on, and such afreements would surely serve further promotion of friendly relations existing between the two nationas.

D) But, the U. S, side is suggesting the above if of it is mutually understood that the Korean side will not furthere propose negotiation for an agreement on jurisdiction of the Commamand, as next step, so long as the present circumstances in Korea constinue to prevail.

E) He (Ambassador Dowling) is now authorized to start talks with the Korean side for this purpose; if the Korean side concurs with the U. S., negotiation can be commenced after his reurne from trip

0243

to Japan which will be made ~~from 21 to 25 September 1958~~

5. On the same day (September 18, 1958), Ambassador ~~Dowling, in his~~ meeting with Vice-Minister Dong Jo Kim at the latter's Office, ~~repeated~~ what he delivered to Foreign Minister Cho.

6. On September 19, 1958, the contents of the above-mentioned U.S. representation were orally reproted to His Excellency the President at Kyung Mu Dai. Upon receipt of this reprot, His Excellency expressed a great deal of dissatisfaction over the U.S. view, particlularly over the point that the U.S. was trying to exclude the possiblity of concluding U.S. eventually an agreement on criminal jurisdiction of U. S, forces in Korea thus claiming 'extraterritorial right'. His Excellency also wondered why the U.S. was so reluctant to conclude a full agreement on status of force while it has already entered sucj relations with other nations.

7. The U.S. suggestion of September 18, 1958 is informal in its form, but is a reply to our posisition of November 26, 1957. The suggestion partly meets our position but is still unsatisfaqotry as it urges us to give up the possibliity of concluding a n agreement on criinal jursidiction of military personnel. If the underbtanding is reached between the two Governements as the U. S. urges, it would be tantamount to perpetuating legally the validity of the Korea-US modus vivendi on criminal jurisdiction of U.S. military personnel which was sig ed at Taegon in July, 1950.

0244

주미대사관 →로부터 전달된 것임

Text of Press Release for Saturday, May 30

The Department of Defense announced today that settlement of tort claims of Korea citizens against the military services of the United States would be resumed June 1 under authority granted in the U. S. Foreign Claims Act.

通文書로 一般文書로 再分類 62.2.16.

Prior to the communist invasion of the Republic of Korea in 1950, claims against U. S. Forces in Korea were settled under authority of the Foreign Claims Act. However, following the invasion and during military operations, claims were not paid by the United States Forces for several reasons, primarily because most claims arose from combat operations. These claims are not compensable. In addition, rapid troop movements precluded consideration of claims and it was virtually impossible to place responsibility for non-combat reported claims.

Alleged incidents which have occurred during the past 12 months and resulted in property damage, personal injury or death and for which no claim has been made may be reported to the nearest United States Military installation. However, the report must be made within one year after the date of the alleged incident. Claims against military personnel of other United Nations Forces, of course, cannot be considered.

Future incidents also may be reported to the nearest U. S. military installation and advice and assistance will be given claiments in preparing and presenting claims. Such reports must be made within one year after the incident allegedly occurs in order to be considered.

Persons who already have received written acknowledgment of receipt of their claims do not need to take further action at this time.

0245

MAY 28 1959

외고문서 비밀해제: 주한미군지위협정(SOFA) 1

# 주한미군지위협정(SOFA) 서명 및 발효 1

초판인쇄 2024년 03월 15일
초판발행 2024년 03월 15일

지은이 한국학술정보(주)
펴낸이 채종준
펴낸곳 한국학술정보(주)
주 소 경기도 파주시 회동길 230(문발동)
전 화 031-908-3181(대표)
팩 스 031-908-3189
홈페이지 http://ebook.kstudy.com
E-mail 출판사업부 publish@kstudy.com
등 록 제일산-115호(2000. 6. 19)

ISBN 979-11-7217-012-7 94340
979-11-7217-011-0 94340 (set)


책에 대한 더 나은 생각, 끊임없는 고민, 독자를 생각하는 마음으로 보다 좋은 책을 만들어갑니다.